Withdrawn Stock
Dorset Libraries

DOUBLE
DOWN

D1392303

400 143 267 R

ALSO BY MARK HALPERIN AND JOHN HEILEMANN

*Game Change: Obama and the Clintons,
McCain and Palin, and the Race of a Lifetime*

(published in the UK as *Race of a Lifetime*)

DOUBLE DOWN

THE DRAMATIC INSIDE ACCOUNT
OF THE 2012 PRESIDENTIAL ELECTION

MARK HALPERIN ★ JOHN HEILEMANN

2 4 6 8 10 9 7 5 3 1

First published in the United States in 2013 by The Penguin Press

First published in the United Kingdom in 2013 by WH Allen

This edition published in 2014 by
WH Allen, an imprint of Ebury Publishing

A Random House Group Company

Copyright © Mark Halperin and John Heilemann 2013

Mark Halperin and John Heilemann have asserted their right under
the Copyright, Designs and Patents Act 1988 to be identified as
the authors of this work.

Every reasonable effort has been made to contact copyright holders
of material reproduced in this book. If any have inadvertently been
overlooked, the publishers would be glad to hear from them and
make good in future editions any errors or omissions brought
to their attention.

All rights reserved. No part of this publication may be reproduced,
stored in a retrieval system, or transmitted in any form or by any
means, electronic, mechanical, photocopying, recording or
otherwise, without the prior permission of the copyright owner.

Addresses for companies within The Random House Group Limited
can be found at www.randomhouse.co.uk/offices.htm

The Random House Group Limited Reg. No. 954009

A CIP catalogue record for this book is
available from the British Library

The Random House Group Limited supports the Forest
Stewardship Council® (FSC®), the leading international forest-
certification organisation. Our books carrying the FSC label are
printed on FSC®-certified paper. FSC is the only forest-certification
scheme supported by the leading environmental organisations,
including Greenpeace. Our paper procurement policy can be found at:
www.randomhouse.co.uk/environment

All photos © Christopher Anderson/Magnum Photos

Printed and bound by CPI Group (UK) Ltd, Croydon, CR0 4YY

ISBN: 9780753555576

To buy books by your favourite authors and register for offers, visit:
www.randomhouse.co.uk

For Karen and my family

—MEH

For Diana and my dad

—JAH

Dorset County Library	
Askews & Holts	2014
324.973093	£9.99

CONTENTS

PART THREE

DOUBLE DOWN

PROLOGUE

THE DEBATE WAS ONLY a few minutes old, and Barack Obama was already tanking. His opponent on this warm autumn night, a Massachusetts patrician with an impressive résumé, a chiseled jaw, and a staunch helmet of burnished hair, was an inferior political specimen by any conceivable measure. But with surprising fluency, verve, and even humor, Obama's rival was putting points on the board. The president was not. Passive and passionless, he seemed barely present.

It was Sunday, October 14, 2012, and Obama was bunkered two levels below the lobby of the Kingsmill Resort, in Williamsburg, Virginia. In a blue blazer, khaki pants, and an open-necked shirt, he was squaring off in a mock debate against Massachusetts senator John Kerry, who was standing in for the Republican nominee, Mitt Romney. The two men were in Williamsburg, along with the president's team, to prepare Obama for his second televised confrontation with Romney, forty-eight hours away, at Hofstra University, in Hempstead, New York. It was an event to which few had given much thought. Until the debacle in Denver, that is.

The debate in the Mile High City eleven days earlier jolted a race that for many months had been hard-fought but remarkably stable. From the moment in May that Romney emerged victorious from the most volatile and unpredictable Republican nomination contest in many moons, Obama held a narrow yet consistent lead. But after Romney mauled the president in Denver, the wind and weather of the campaign shifted dramatically in something like a heartbeat. The challenger was surging. The polls were tightening. Republicans were pulsating with renewed hope. Democrats were rending their garments and collapsing on their fainting couches.

Obama was nowhere in the vicinity of panic. "You ever known me to lose two in a row?" he said to friends to calm their nerves.

The president's advisers were barely more rattled. Yes, Denver had been atrocious. Yes, it had been unnerving. But Obama was still ahead of Romney, the sky hadn't fallen, and they would fix what went wrong in time for the town hall debate at Hofstra. Their message to the nervous nellies in their party was: Keep calm and carry on.

Williamsburg was where the repair job was supposed to take place. The Obamans had arrived at the resort, ready to work, on Saturday the 13th. The first day had gone well. The president seemed to be finding his form. He and Kerry had been doing mock debates since August, and the session on Saturday night was Obama's best yet. Everyone exhaled.

But now, in Sunday night's run-through, the president seemed to be relapsing: the disengaged and pedantic Obama of Denver was back. In the staff room, his two closest advisers, David Axelrod and David Plouffe, watched on video monitors with a mounting sense of unease—when, all of a sudden, a practice round that had started out looking merely desultory turned into the Mock from Hell.

The moment it happened could be pinpointed with precision: at the 39:35 mark on the clock. A question about home foreclosures had been put to POTUS; under the rules, he had two minutes to respond. Before the mock, Kerry had been instructed by one of the debate coaches to interrupt Obama at some juncture to see how he reacted. Striding across the bright red carpet of the set that the president's team had constructed as a precise replica of the Hofstra town hall stage, Kerry invaded the president's space and barged in during Obama's answer.

The president's eyes flashed with annoyance.

"Don't interrupt me," he snapped.

When Kerry persisted, Obama shot a death stare at the moderator—his adviser Anita Dunn, standing in for CNN's Candy Crowley—and pleaded for an intercession.

The president's coaches had persistently worried about the appearance of Nasty Obama on the debate stage: the variant who infamously, imperiously dismissed his main Democratic rival in 2008 with the withering phrase "You're likable enough, Hillary." His advisers saw glimpses of that side of him in their preparations for Denver—a manifestation of a personal antipathy for Romney that had grown visceral and intense. Now they were seeing it again, and worse. The admixture of Nasty Obama and Denver Obama was not a pretty picture.

Challenged by Kerry with multipronged attacks, the president rebutted them point by point, exhaustively and exhaustingly. Instead of driving a sharp message, he was explanatory and meandering. Instead of casting an eye to the future, he litigated the past. Instead of warmly establishing connections with the town hall questioners, he pontificated airily, as if he were conducting a particularly tedious press conference. While Kerry was answering a query about immigration, Obama retaliated for the earlier interruption by abruptly cutting him off.

In the staff room, Axelrod and Plouffe were aghast. Sitting with them, Obama's lead pollster, Joel Benenson muttered, "This is *unbelievable*."

Watching from the set, the renowned Democratic style coach Michael Sheehan scribbled furiously on a legal pad, each notation more alarmed than the last. Reflecting on Obama's interplay with the questioners, Sheehan summed up his demeanor with a single word: "Creepy."

After ninety excruciating minutes, the Mock from Hell was over. As Obama made his way for the door, he was intercepted by Axelrod, Plouffe, Benenson, and the lead debate coach, Ron Klain. Little was said. Little needed to be said. The ashen looks on the faces of the president's men told the tale.

Obama left the building and returned to his sprawling quarters on the banks of the James River with his best friend from Chicago, Marty Nesbitt, to watch football and play cards. His advisers retreated to the president's debate-prep holding room to have a collective coronary.

That the presidential debates were proving problematic for Obama came as no real surprise to the members of his team. Many of them—Axelrod, the mustachioed message maven and guardian of the Obama brand; Plouffe, the spindly senior White House adviser and enforcer of strategic rigor; Dunn, the media-savvy mother superior and former White House communications director; Benenson, the bearded and nudgy former Mario Cuomo hand; Jon Favreau, the dashing young speechwriter—had been with Obama from the start of his meteoric ascent. They knew that he detested televised debates. That he disdained political theater in every guise. That, on some level, he distrusted political performance itself, with its attendant emotional manipulations.

The paradox, of course, was that Obama had risen to prominence and power to a large extent on the basis of his preternatural performance skills— and his ability to summon them whenever the game was on the line. In late 2007, when he was trailing Hillary Clinton in the Democratic nomination fight by thirty points. In the fall of 2008, when the global financial crisis hit during the crucial last weeks of the general election. In early 2010, when his signature health care reform proposal seemed destined for defeat. In every instance, under ungodly pressure, Obama had set his feet, pulled up, and drained a three-pointer at the buzzer.

The faith of the president's people that he would do the same at Hofstra was what sustained them in the wake of Denver. For a year, the Obamans had fretted over everything under the sun: gas prices, unemployment, the European financial crisis, Iran, the Koch brothers, the lack of enthusiasm from the Democratic base, Hispanic turnout in the Orlando metroplex. The one thing they had never worried about was Barack Obama.

But given the spectacle they had just witnessed at Kingsmill, the Obamans were more than worried. After spending ten days pooh-poohing the widespread hysteria in their party about Denver, Obama's debate team was now the most wigged-out collection of Democrats in the country, huddling in a hotel cubby that had become their secret panic room. Three hours had passed since the mock ended; it was almost 2:00 a.m. Obama's team was still clustered in the work space, reading transcripts and waxing apocalyptic.

"Guys, what are we going to do?" Plouffe asked quietly, over and over. "That was a disaster."

Among the Obamans, there was nobody more unflappable than Plouffe— and nobody less shaken by Denver. The campaign's research showed that there was a deep well of sympathy for Obama among voters; in focus groups after the first debate, people offered excuse after excuse for his horrific presentation. In Florida, one woman said, almost protectively, "I just bet you he wasn't feeling well."

But what the research also told Plouffe was that Obama was "on probation" after Denver. The public might brush off a single bad debate showing; two in a row would not be so readily ignored. With Hofstra less than forty-eight hours away, the Obamans essentially had a day to diagnose the malady afflicting their boss—the sudden sickness that had robbed their great communicator of his ability to communicate under pressure—and find a remedy. What was wrong? What *would* they do? No one had a clue.

All Plouffe knew was that, if Obama turned in a performance at Hofstra like the one they had seen that night, the consequences could be dire.

"If we don't fix this," Plouffe said emphatically, "we could lose the whole fucking election."

THE MOST HELLISH DAYS of 2012 for Obama were heaven on earth for Mitt Romney. Before his turn on the debate stage in Denver, Romney had never achieved a moment in the campaign that was politically triumphal and, to his mind, revealing of who he was. His performance as a candidate was unartful, and in exactly the ways that both the Obamans and the GOP establishment had predicted at the start of the race. His greatest credential for the Oval Office—his enormous success in the private sector—was savagely turned against him. His public image from his first national run, in 2008, had been that of a flip-flopping Mormon; in 2012, he was rendered a hybrid of Gordon Gekko and Mr. Magoo. But at that first debate, the Romney in whom his advisers, friends, family, and supporters believed made a powerful appearance: a good and decent man with a formidable intellect, economic expertise, problem-solving know-how, and patriotic zeal. In an instant, the former Massachusetts governor looked like a plausible president. It was a conquest that propelled Romney toward the finish line with new fervor, and one he would savor long after the votes were counted.

With the benefit of hindsight, innumerable analysts would declare that the result of the election was foreordained: that Obama always had it in the bag. But the president and his people spent all of 2011 and most of 2012 believing nothing of the sort. The economic headwinds that Obama faced were ferocious and unrelenting. His approval ratings during his first term rarely edged above 50 percent. The opposition inspired by his presidency was intense and at times rabid, from the populist ire of the Tea Party to the legislative recalcitrance of the congressional wing of the GOP to the wailing and gnashing of the anti-Obama caucus in the business world and on Wall Street especially. The country was split almost cleanly down the middle, and more polarized than ever.

The two sides had few beliefs in common, but one of them was this: the outcome of the election mattered, and not a little. The ideological contrast between the parties had rarely been starker. In terms of specific policies, the size and role of government and the fundamental priorities of the nation, the practical implications of which man won were vast.

With so much at stake, the 2012 election had the feel of a big casino, as the players took on the complexion of compulsive gamblers, pushing more and more chips into the center of the table. On the right, a phalanx of millionaires and billionaires doubled down on Romney even after his flaws were all too clear, pouring gargantuan sums into his campaign and conservative super PACs. The Republican nominee, in turn, not only doubled down on the orthodoxies of the right but on his own controversial statements and positions. On the left, the Obamans were engaged in their own doubling down: on the coalition that had elected their man in 2008; on their pioneering use of new technology; on their grassroots get-out-the-vote machine. But no doubt the biggest wager they placed was on Obama.

On that mid-October night in Williamsburg, with the election three weeks away, it remained unclear who would leave the casino flush and who would exit with picked-clean pockets. In the end, the answer would lie in the hands of the president of the United States—who, at that hour, far from the cameras, was more imperiled than anyone imagined, his greatest gift having deserted him at the worst possible time. After four years of economic hardship, nagging uncertainty, and disappointment that change had come so slowly when it came at all, Obama would have to rise to a different kind of challenge—a challenge from within himself—before the country would double down on him.

PART ONE

★ 1 ★

MISSIONS ACCOMPLISHED

ARACK OBAMA WAS BACK in Chicago and back on the campaign trail, two realms from which he had been absent for a while but which always felt like home. It was April 14, 2011, and Obama had returned to the Windy City to launch his reelection effort with a trio of fund-raisers. Ten days earlier, his people had filed the papers making his candidacy official and opened up the campaign headquarters there. Five hundred and seventy-two days later, the voters would render their judgment. To Obama, Election Day seemed eons away—and just around the corner.

Working his way from two small events for high-dollar donors at fancy restaurants to a crowd of two thousand at Navy Pier, the incumbent served up the old Obama fire. He invoked the memory of the last election night in Grant Park, "the excitement in the streets, the sense of hope, the sense of possibility." He touted his achievements as "the change we still believe in." He ended the evening with a "Yes, we can!"

But again and again, Obama cited the burdens of his station. Although he'd always known that as president his plate would be full, the fullness was staggering—from the economic crisis to the swine flu pandemic, the BP oil spill, and the hijacking of an American cargo ship by Somali pirates. ("Who thought we were going to have to deal with pirates?") He acknowledged the frustrations of many Democrats at the fitfulness of the progress he'd brought about, the compromises with Republicans. He apologized for the fact that his head wasn't fully in the reelection game. "Over the next three months, six months, nine months, I'm going to be a little preoccupied," Obama said. "I've got this day job that I've got to handle."

The president's preoccupations at that moment were many and varied, trivial and profound. In public, he was battling with the GOP over the budget and preparing for a face-off over the federal debt ceiling. In secret, he was deliberating over an overseas special-ops raid aimed at a shadowy target who possibly, maybe, hopefully was Osama bin Laden. But the most persistent distraction Obama was facing was personified by Donald Trump, the real estate billionaire and reality show ringmaster who was flirting with making a presidential run under the banner of birtherism—the crackpot conspiracy theory claiming that Obama was born in Kenya and thus was constitutionally ineligible to preside as commander in chief.

Obama had contended with birtherism since the previous campaign, when rumors surfaced that there was no record of his birth in Hawaii. The fringe theorists had grown distractingly shrill and increasingly insistent; after he won the nomination in June 2008, his team deemed it necessary to post his short-form birth certificate on the Web. The charge was lunacy, Obama thought. Simply mental. But it wouldn't go away. A recent *New York Times* poll had found that 45 percent of Republicans and 25 percent of voters overall believed he was foreign born. And with Trump serving as a human bullhorn, the faux controversy had escaped the confines of Fox News and conservative talk radio, reverberating in the mainstream media. Just that morning, before Obama departed for Chicago, ABC News's George Stephanopoulos had asked him about it in an interview, specifically citing Trump—twice.

As Obama made his fund-raising rounds that night, he avoided mentioning Trump, yet the issue remained much on his mind. What confounded him about the problem, beyond its absurdity, was that there was no ready solution. Although Trump was braying for his original long-form birth certificate, officials in Obama's home state were legally prohibited from releasing it on their own, and the president had no earthly idea where his family's copy was. All he could do was joke about the topic, as he did at his final event of the night: "I grew up here in Chicago," Obama told the crowd at Navy Pier, then added awkwardly, "I wasn't born here—just want to be clear. I was born in Hawaii."

Obama was looking forward to spending the night at his house in Kenwood, on the city's South Side—the redbrick Georgian Revival pile that he and Michelle and their daughters left behind when they took up residence in the White House. He arrived fairly late, after 10:00 p.m., but then stayed up even later, intrigued by some old boxes that had belonged to his late mother, Ann Dunham.

Dunham had died seven years earlier, but Obama hadn't sorted through all her things. Now, alone in his old house for just the third night since he'd become president, he started rummaging through the boxes, digging, digging, until suddenly he found it: a small, four-paneled paper booklet the world had never seen before. On the front was an ink drawing of Kapi'olani Maternity and Gynecological Hospital, in Honolulu. On the back was a picture of a Hawaiian queen. On one inside page were his name, his mother's name, and his date of birth; on the other were his infant footprints.

The next morning, Marty Nesbitt came over to have breakfast with Obama. The CEO of an airport parking-lot company, Nesbitt was part of a tiny circle of Chicago friends on whom the president relied to keep him anchored in a reality outside the Washington funhouse. The two men had bonded playing pickup basketball two decades earlier; their relationship was still firmly rooted in sports, talking smack, and all around regular-guyness. After chatting for a while at the kitchen table, Obama went upstairs and came back down, wearing a cat-who-ate-a-whole-flock-of-canaries grin, waving the booklet in the air, and then placing it in front of Nesbitt.

"Now, that's some funny shit," Nesbitt said, and burst out laughing.

Clambering into his heavily armored SUV, Obama headed back north to the InterContinental hotel, where he had an interview scheduled with the Associated Press. He pulled aside his senior adviser David Plouffe and press secretary Jay Carney, and eagerly showed them his discovery.

Plouffe studied the thing, befuddled and wary: *Is that the birth certificate?* he thought.

Carney was bewildered, too, but excited: *This is the birth certificate? Awesome.*

Obama didn't know what to think, but he flew back to Washington hoping that maybe, just maybe, he now had a stake to drive through the heart of birtherism, killing it once and for all—and slaying Trump in the bargain. Striding into a meeting with his senior advisers in the Oval Office the next Monday morning, he reached into his suit pocket and whipped out the booklet, infinitely pleased with himself.

"Hey," Obama announced, "look what I found when I was out there!"

N O INCUMBENT PRESIDENT EVER travels a road to reelection paved with peonies and primrose. But Obama's plunge into the fever swamp of birtherism was just the latest detour on what had already been a long, strange trip—with many miles still to go.

From the outset of his improbable and dazzling journey to the presidency, Obama had been endowed with an almost superhuman confidence and self-possession. His ascension had taken place with astonishing speed, leaving both his public image and his private self-conception unblemished by the hyper-partisan freak show of American politics. On the eve of his decision to run for president, Obama pledged to his wife and team, "I'm going to be Barack Obama and not some parody—I'm going to emerge intact." And, amazingly, he had. By the end of the campaign, he had proven almost entirely impervious to the right-wing hit machine. On Election Day, he carried a majority of independent voters and nearly 10 percent of Republicans. He sailed into the White House as a transformational figure, an avatar of a new era of post-partisanship, a leader capable of mitigating the ruinous divisiveness that had bedeviled Washington for two decades.

Now, at forty-nine and on the brink of his bid for a second term, Obama confronted a different political reality. Rather than bringing the country together, he had become an even more polarizing presence than Bill Clinton or George W. Bush. When he glimpsed his own image in the media, it was no longer one he recognized; instead he saw a cartoon. His reelection campaign would be waged in the teeth of a feral opposition and an economy that had improved on his watch but remained god-awful, plagued by slow growth and high unemployment. He was vulnerable, beatable, perhaps even the underdog.

That he had been dealt a horrific hand upon assuming office was beyond reasonable dispute: an epochal economic meltdown, a worldwide financial crisis, a collapsing auto industry, an imploding housing market, and two costly, unpopular wars in need of denouement. That he had taken dramatic action was also inarguable. He had signed the $787 billion American Recovery and Reinvestment Act, the largest fiscal stimulus in U.S. history. He had rescued the financial sector and also reregulated it with the Dodd-Frank Wall Street reform law. He had tossed a lifeline to Detroit and was moving to end the conflicts in Iraq (rapidly) and Afghanistan (slowly). He had achieved a long-held Democratic dream with the passage of near-universal health care coverage through the Affordable Care Act.

Obama had no regrets about any of this. He had done the right things, the difficult things, the necessary things—of this he was certain. But he knew that the political price he would pay was steep. On the night of the passage of health care reform, in late March of 2010, Obama celebrated with his staff on the Truman Balcony of the White House. Holding a champagne flute, the president approached his political director, Patrick Gaspard, a wiry Haitian-born operative who earned his political stripes in New York's ruthless union backrooms. Tipping his glass and cocking an eyebrow, Obama said, "You know, they're gonna kick our asses over this."

Truth be told, the tuchus kicking had been going on from the start. Congressional Republicans assailed Obama at every turn, painting him as a profligate, reflexive liberal, opposing his legislative agenda loudly and in lockstep. In the business world, he was widely regarded as either clueless about or hostile to the private sector. On the far right, he was denounced as an amalgam of Hitler, Chairman Mao, and Huey Newton—even as the left was disappointed to discover that he wasn't a combination of Ted Kennedy, Norman Thomas, and John Lewis. In the middle of the electorate, the stimulus, the bailouts, and health care reform proved unpopular; independent voters abandoned him in droves. From a high of 69 percent on Inauguration Day, his approval ratings had slid to the mid-forties by summer 2010.

With the congressional midterm elections looming in November of that year, Obama and his people saw the writing on the wall. After a season they had christened "Recovery Summer," the economy was growing at just 2 percent, the unemployment rate was 9.5, and the Tea Party was on the rise.

Obama had watched this new force take shape from a remove, but with gathering alarm. The incendiary town hall meetings the previous year. The reports of vandalism at Democratic congressional district offices. The roiling populist outrage on display that reminded him of the jagged outbursts at McCain-Palin rallies at the end of the 2008 campaign. And the more Obama learned about the Tea Party candidates poised to win in November, the greater his incredulity—and disgust.

"If people vote for *this*," he said to one of his aides, "they deserve it."

But vote for it they did, on Election Day 2010, delivering to the president and his party what Obama aptly termed a "shellacking." Democrats were stripped of eleven governorships, including those in the battleground states of Iowa, Michigan, Ohio, Pennsylvania, and Wisconsin. In the Senate, they ceded six seats, while in the House they were massacred, suffering the largest midterm loss since 1938—sixty-three seats, many to be filled by Tea Party freshmen.

In the wake of the midterms, Obama was besieged by the Democratic establishment with calls for a midcourse correction. He should steal a page from the playbook employed by Bill Clinton when he endured a similar drubbing in 1994, Obama was told. Reach out to Republicans. Mend fences with business. Move to the middle.

Obama believed that he was already there. His lament on the topic was all too familiar to his advisers.

I didn't push for a single-payer health care law, he would say, pointing out that the individual mandate at the heart of his plan was a Republican idea, concocted at the Heritage Foundation and implemented by Mitt Romney as governor of Massachusetts. My climate change policy—cap-and-trade—was Bush 41's, Obama would complain. My auto rescue was more market-minded than the one proposed by Bush 43. I didn't nationalize the banks when everyone, even Alan Greenspan, said I should. And my critics call me a socialist? Please.

What the president did want to reboot was his political team, which throughout his career had been a tight and static crew. In the 2008 campaign, there were only five people he trusted on big decisions and with whom he actively conferred: his chief strategist, David Axelrod; his communications director, Robert Gibbs; his close friend Valerie Jarrett, from

Chicago, also an intimate of Michelle's; his campaign manager, Plouffe; and his Senate chief of staff, Pete Rouse. He carried four of them into the White House—Axelrod, Jarrett, and Rouse as senior advisers, Gibbs as press secretary—with Plouffe taking what he called a "two-year sabbatical" to write a book and hit the lecture circuit.

This cadre had been the essential cogs of a well-oiled campaign machine: disciplined, devoted, and light on drama. But inside the White House, with the core Obamans working alongside a claque of high-wattage Clintonites—notably chief of staff Rahm Emanuel and National Economic Council director Larry Summers—the dynamic was wildly, dysfunctionally different. The political and policy shops were often in conflict, arguing and rearguing issues in front of the president. Tactics frequently trumped strategy. On-the-fly decision making was more the rule than the exception. There was infighting and leaking, backchanneling and backbiting, much of it revolving around Jarrett, whose relationship to the first couple inspired envy and enmity. It was a noisy, tumultuous scene.

Michelle was unhappy with her husband's team, and she made no bones about it. The president was unhappy, too. He wanted the noise to stop.

Obama placed much of the blame on the brilliant, abrasive, frenetic Emanuel—but Rahm was already out the door, having departed the White House in October to run for mayor of Chicago after Richard M. Daley announced he would not seek reelection. As Emanuel's replacement, Obama chose Daley's youngest brother, Bill, who brought to the job a formidable résumé: commerce secretary under Clinton, chairman of Al Gore's 2000 presidential campaign, and, most recently, a top executive at JPMorgan Chase. Daley also had deep ties to Obamaworld, if not to Obama; he had known Axelrod for thirty years, served as Joe Biden's political director on his 1988 presidential bid, and was one of Emanuel's biggest boosters in Chicago. He was sixty-two years old, with a shiny bald head, a brawler's build, and no tolerance for bullshit—a word he employed as a noun, verb, adjective, adverb, and definite article.

The addition of Daley to Obama's White House team was coupled with a pair of even more significant subtractions: Axelrod and Gibbs. The fifty-five-year-old Axelrod, with his slouchy stance and sauce-splattered ties, had been Obama's "keeper of the message" since his start in national politics;

Gibbs had been with him since his Senate race in 2004. But Obama believed his communications operation was a mess. He was overexposed. The thread had been misplaced. *The reason I'm here,* Obama thought, *was that I told the American people a story—and somehow we lost track of that.*

Axelrod seemed burned out to Obama. Axelrod *was* burned out. He had planned to return home to Chicago in the spring to help guide the campaign. Obama told him no—he should go even sooner, after the State of the Union address in January.

As for Gibbs, Obama was convinced that the White House's relations with the media were needlessly contentious, thanks in part to his press secretary's combative briefing style. Gibbs had also recently become embroiled in a string of distracting flaps: annoying House speaker Nancy Pelosi in July by conceding on TV that Democrats could lose majority control of the lower chamber in the midterms; inflaming progressives by dismissing liberal activists as the "professional left"; and contributing to the White House's internal friction through his rocky relations with Michelle and Jarrett. The president wanted Gibbs off the podium. This was fine with the press secretary—he expected to step up into a broader West Wing role with a grander title—but Obama made it clear that he preferred to have Gibbs trumpet his message from outside the building. I need my own James Carville out there on cable, arguing my case, Obama told him. You'll make money, get to see your family more.

Axelrod and Gibbs were more than advisers or even friends to Obama; they were closer to kin. But the president betrayed little emotion as he ushered them out the door. "It's good," he said coolly to one intimate about the departures.

Obama's approach to his White House overhaul was shot through with such clinicality, and sharply focused on two challenges: coping with the newly Republicanized legislative landscape and gearing up for his reelection battle. Axelrod and Gibbs were household names, ubiquitous presences on TV, widely perceived as shameless partisans—so off to the campaign side they went. By contrast, Obama saw Daley as the solution to a multitude of problems. He would help repair the rift with business, be a potent economic spokesman and a bridge to Republicans on Capitol Hill, and, as a quasi outsider to Obamaworld, answer the accusation that the White House was suf-focatingly insular.

Significant as these changes were, Obama wasn't cleaning house entirely. Though Jarrett had become a lightning rod for criticism beyond the build-ing as well as within it, Obama left her role untouched. Rouse, who had been serving as acting chief of staff since Emanuel's exit, remained as influential as ever. (So influential that Obama told him that he wouldn't hand the job over to Daley if Rouse wanted to keep it.)

Most critically, Obama summoned Plouffe back to the fold. Data-driven and pretense-free, relentlessly cool and collected, Plouffe, forty-three, was in many respects the antithesis of both the disorderly Axelrod, his former con-sulting partner, and the volatile Emanuel. His remit was, in effect, to func-tion as the chief strategist for both the White House and the campaign.

While Obama reshuffled the personnel deck in the last days of 2010, he was dealing simultaneously with the lame-duck session of Congress. And to this he brought a similar sort of reelection-driven calculation. The message of the midterms, Obama believed, was that voters were exhausted by the partisan warfare of the previous two years. *They want to see Democrats and Republicans agreeing on . . . anything,* he thought.

The lame duck presented a golden opportunity, and Obama seized it. He abandoned his opposition to renewing the Bush-era income tax cuts for the wealthy, in return for $238 billion in new fiscal stimulus (an extension of unemployment insurance, a payroll tax holiday, and more). Then, in quick succession, he pocketed an array of additional victories with bipartisan support: the repeal of the military's "don't ask, don't tell" policy prohibiting gays from serving openly; ratification of the New START treaty on nuclear arms; a $4.2 billion compensation package for 9/11 first responders; and a child nutrition bill beloved by Michelle.

The left was livid with Obama for folding on the Bush tax cuts for the rich, which had been a campaign cornerstone for Democrats in the midterms. Obama didn't give a fig. The flagging economy needed juice, the deal would provide it, and the idea of letting the tax cuts expire for everyone in the hope that a better compromise could be brokered down the road—after Republi-cans had taken control of the House—was ludicrous on its face. Case closed.

Looking ahead, Obama had no doubt about the correct approach to the congressional Republicans: cooperate when possible, confront when necessary, exploit conservative overreaching. But Obama's reelection would depend on his ability to undertake a broader project. To occupy a higher plane than he had in his first two years, elevating himself above the posturing, petulance, and bile spewing of the linthead extremes in both parties. To play the role of presiding adult in a town full of adolescents. In other words, to be Barack Obama again.

For a moment, it looked as though he would have the chance. On the back of his legislative victories, his moving speech at the Tucson memorial after the shooting of Arizona congresswoman Gabrielle Giffords and eighteen others in a supermarket parking lot, and his State of the Union address, the president's approval ratings in the early weeks of 2011 edged up above 50 percent for the first time in more than a year.

As he rolled into reelection season, Obama's plan was to spend the months ahead talking incessantly about jobs, infrastructure, and the economy. But the world had other ideas—presenting the president with a series of distractions. Some were of global significance: the fall of Hosni Mubarak, the Libyan civil war, and myriad events of the Arab Spring. Others were time-honored Washington pseudo-crises: the threat in early April of a government shutdown, necessitating a down-to-the-wire negotiation with the new House speaker, John Boehner.

Obama had known that much of his job would be scrambling to cope with the unexpected. "Any president can only affirmatively effect 20 percent of his agenda—all the rest is reaction," he told his 2008 campaign team. His time in office had hammered that truth home. Distractions, high and low, were among the burdens that every incumbent faced and could do little about.

But if the distraction happened to be named Trump, that was a different story.

WHITE HOUSE COUNSEL BOB BAUER took one look at the booklet in Obama's hand and knew it wasn't the birth certificate. It was just a commemorative keepsake, the kind of thing hospitals give to parents as a token of the blessed day. But that Monday morning, April 18, in the Oval Office, the booklet proved to be something more: a spur to the Obamans to revisit a question they had debated many times before—whether to make a run at obtaining the actual long-form certificate from Hawaii.

Bauer had been Obama's chief legal adviser since his days in the Senate and was among the most preeminent campaign attorneys in the Beltway bar. He was against the idea, as he always had been, and for a straightforward reason. Under Hawaiian state law, Bauer pointed out, the short-form "certification of live birth" that the campaign had posted online three years earlier *was* Obama's birth certificate, and putting out the long form might be treated by some as tantamount to admitting that all along the short form had been insufficient.

Plouffe had a different objection. Listen, having this issue out there isn't the worst thing in the world for us, he said. Most voters think that the president was born in Hawaii, and most voters think the birthers are nuts. The more oxygen Donald Trump gets, the better off we are long term.

Nevertheless, Plouffe saw another side to the coin. The White House was starting to take incoming from the liberal punditocracy—MSNBC's Chris Matthews had been on a tear—for not putting the issue to rest. There were also implications for governing. If half of the Republican electorate believed that Obama was an illegitimate president, Plouffe observed, that only made it harder for their representatives on the Hill to do business with the White House.

Obama's views were more nuanced—and more personal. He and Michelle were both avid consumers of political commentary. Her habit was cable, and especially *Morning Joe*. (She watched the show religiously while working out, then fired off agitated e-mails to Jarrett about what this or that talking head had said.) The president indulged in a greater degree of channel flipping than he admitted, but was more immersed in the blogosphere, and not just its leftward precincts. On his iPad, to which he was so attached it seemed like an appendage, he monitored the hard-right realms of the online echo chamber, surprising friends with his familiarity with the work of ultra-con tyro Michelle Malkin. As for Fox News, he believed the network's relentless hostility toward him shaved five points off his approval ratings.

For two years, the conservative quadrants of the freak show had labored to delegitimize Obama, often in race-freighted fashion—from the suggestions that he was a closet Muslim to the idea, floated by writer Dinesh D'Souza and latched on to by Newt Gingrich, that he could be grasped only through the prism of "Kenyan anti-colonial behavior." The president rarely complained about the racial overtones of such commentary. "We all know what that's about," he would say, sloughing off the subject. But the birther charge was a provocation too far, especially as *real* topics were being ignored.

"This is everything that's wrong with our politics," Obama said that Monday in the Oval Office meeting after his Chicago trip. I understand that politically this is probably good for us, since it makes their party look crazy. But let's pop the balloon and shut down this foolishness once and for all.

Bauer was tasked with approaching the Hawaii department of health and requesting a waiver that would allow the release of the original long-form certificate. Nine days later, on April 27, the document was in hand in the West Wing and a press conference scheduled. There was never any doubt that the president would unveil it himself, delighting in the opportunity to shame the press and cuff the freak show. As he walked into the prep session before the presser, he spied Bauer and his lead wordsmith, Jon Favreau.

"We've got the lawyer and the speechwriter here, so this must be a big deal," Obama cracked.

By coincidence, Trump, as part of his dalliance with a presidential bid, was traveling to New Hampshire that day. As if to affirm Obama's belief that the media required a slap upside the head, a number of TV networks carried the two events—the Donald touching down in his branded helicopter in Portsmouth, the POTUS taking the podium at the White House—using a split screen.

"Normally I would not comment on something like this, because obviously there's a lot of stuff swirling in the press at any given day and I've got other things to do," Obama said. He noted that, in a week in which he and House Republicans put out competing budgets, "the dominant news story wasn't about these huge, monumental choices that we're going to have to make as a nation. It was about my birth certificate. And that was true on most of the news outlets that were represented here." Then Obama delivered the Trump de grâce: "We're not going to be able to solve our problems if we get distracted by sideshows and carnival barkers . . . We do not have time for this kind of silliness."

THE BARKER IN QUESTION, up in the Granite State, gave no indication that he realized the joke had been on him. "Today, I'm very proud of myself," Trump declared. "I've accomplished something that nobody else has been able to accomplish . . . I am really honored, frankly, to have played such a big role in hopefully, *hopefully* getting rid of this issue."

Favreau had no intention of allowing Trump to miss the point the next time—and oh, yes, there would be a next time, just four days later, when The Donald attended the annual White House Correspondents' Association Dinner, at which Obama would, by custom, deliver a presidential stand-up routine.

The morning of the dinner, Axelrod, Favreau, and another speechwriter, Jon Lovett, tromped into the Oval Office to run through the president's script with him. Favreau and Lovett wanted to do more than torment Trump; they wanted to torpedo his putative White House run. They recruited Hollywood comedy kingpin Judd Apatow, of *Bridesmaids* and *Knocked Up* fame, to help out with Obama's script. And Apatow, riffing over the phone, had contributed a cutting gibe that referred to an episode of Trump's reality TV show, *Celebrity Apprentice*.

Axelrod, Daley, and Plouffe all wondered whether Obama would find the Apatow joke too barbed. But the president pronounced it one of his favorite set pieces in the script. There was only one joke, in fact, to which Obama objected, and it didn't involve Trump. It was about another GOP presidential prospect, the former governor of Minnesota, Tim Pawlenty. "He *seems* all-American," the script said, "but have you heard his real middle name? Tim *Osama bin* Pawlenty."

"Osama is the middle name? I think we could do something a little more original than that," Obama said.

Favreau was perplexed. "What about Hosni?" he asked.

"That's great," said Obama. "Let's just go with Hosni."

That night, Obama took to the stage in the basement ballroom of the

Washington Hilton, in front of twenty-five hundred bejeweled women and black-tied men—celebrities, congresspeople, presidential wannabes, even some reporters. With impeccable comic timing, the president lit into Trump: "No one is happier, no one is prouder, to put this birth certificate matter to rest than the Donald. And that's because he can finally get back to focusing on the issues that matter. Like, did we fake the moon landing? What really happened in Roswell? And where are Biggie and Tupac?" The crowd roared with delight.

They howled again when Obama unloaded Apatow's *Apprentice* take-down: "The men's cooking team did not impress the judges from Omaha Steaks, and there was a lot of blame to go around. But you, Mr. Trump, recognized that the real problem was a lack of leadership. And so, ultimately, you didn't blame Lil Jon or Meat Loaf. You fired Gary Busey. And these are the kinds of decisions that would keep me up at night. Well handled, sir. Well handled."

Trump, meanwhile, sat rocking in his chair, simmering, simmering, his face turning burnt umber.

Only one of Obama's jokes fell flat: Tim *Hosni* Pawlenty. Favreau, in the audience, was rueful in the knowledge that it could have been so much funnier.

The next night, Favreau learned the reason for Obama's edit, when the president took to the airwaves to announce that halfway around the world in Pakistan, a team of U.S. Navy SEALs had killed bin Laden. No member of Obama's political team except Daley had been aware of the secret special-ops mission during its months of planning. The Obamans were stunned, overjoyed, and awestruck at their boss's composure the night before—his pitch-perfect comic performance just hours after giving the fateful order, as its outcome hung in the balance. Little did we know, Axelrod said to Favreau, we were just a bunch of Seinfelds in a Tom Clancy novel.

For Obama, the decision to launch the raid had entailed gargantuan risks. On the president's national security team, there was no consensus. Joe Biden and defense secretary Robert Gates counseled him to wait for more intel. Biden told an aide he believed that Obama had wagered his presidency on the move; had the mission gone awry and turned into another Desert One, the political consequences would have been catastrophic. When one of the helicopters crash-landed during the raid, two words appeared like a bill-board in Obama's mind: *Jimmy Carter.*

After Obama finished his brief and sober speech to the nation from the East Room, some of his advisers wanted to celebrate. *How about a fucking beer?* thought Daley. Out in Lafayette Park, in front of the White House, a frenzied, flag-waving crowd was chanting, "Obama got Osama! Obama got Osama!" But there would be no triumphalism inside the gates, at least not that night. The president walked silently to the elevator that would carry him up to the residence and to bed.

In the days ahead, Obama reveled plenty. True, there were tough fights with Republicans on the horizon, especially about raising the federal government's $14.7 trillion debt ceiling, over which the GOP was threatening a showdown, and about the budget. Republican House Budget Committee chairman Paul Ryan of Wisconsin had recently released a plan to cut the deficit by $4.4 trillion, which Obama attacked as draconian, putting forth his own $4 trillion alternative.

But there was no denying the glory and gratification of taking out bin Laden and taking down Trump in the space of twenty-four hours. The pursuit of OBL had bedeviled Bush for years. Now its completion had earned Obama the *ne plus ultra* national security credential heading into 2012 and sent his approval ratings skyward. And although beating back the birthers might have seemed more trivial, it lifted a weight from Obama's shoulders. A few weeks later, on a trip to Ireland, he jubilated in the discovery that—after all the right-wing insinuations that he was exotic, not a real American—his genetic roots stretched back to a small town on the Emerald Isle.

"My name is Barack Obama of the Moneygall O'Bamas," he proclaimed at Trinity College in Dublin. "And I've come home to find the apostrophe that we lost somewhere along the way."

THE WEAKNESS MEME

T HE FOURSOME HIT THE LINKS at Andrews Air Force Base, outside Washington, on Saturday morning, June 18: Obama, Biden, and a pair of Republicans from Ohio, John Boehner and the state's new governor, John Kasich—all four clad in polo shirts, Biden and Boehner wearing shorts.

Since the midterms, Obama had been encouraged by an assortment of establishment grandees to socialize with Boehner, get to know him, establish a human connection. Invite him up to Camp David, Obama was told, or to the White House to watch a movie. You and Boehner both smoke; bring him over, then break out the butts and a bottle of nice merlot, counseled one Beltway wise man.

Daley was a big proponent of this approach. It was Politics 101. But Obama and his people had come a long way practicing Politics 2.0. That winter, when the new chief of staff had floated the Camp David plan— a weekend getaway for the congressional leadership and their spouses— Michelle's East Wing staff shot it down: who wanted to be cooped up on a cold day in the woods with Mitch McConnell? The smoking summit was a nonstarter, too, since Obama apparently had finally quit although Daley marveled at how much Nicorette his boss chomped through every day. (*It's embarrassing,* Daley thought, restraining himself from chastising Obama. *Hey! Enough with the fucking gum!*)

The idea of a shared golf round was more promising. At first, Obama brushed off the idea, saying, "Nah, Boehner's too good." But now, with the deadline on lifting the debt limit looming, Republicans seeking $2 trillion in spending cuts for raising the ceiling, and Biden leading bipartisan negotiations with the Hill that were stuck in quicksand, Obama decided the time was ripe to hit the fairway. The famously competitive president wasn't about to lose to the speaker, though. When the Ohioans arrived at Andrews, their expectations of teaming up against the Democrats were dashed by an executive switcheroo.

"Hey, Boehner," Obama announced, "you and I, we're gonna take these two on."

Obama-Boehner edged Biden-Kasich on the final green. (Boehner described the narrow victory as a whipping, while Biden moaned about his swing and Kasich informed the VP that shorts were not a good look for him.) When the group repaired to the nineteenth hole, the conversation turned to the debt ceiling. Boehner pointed out that, despite the difficulties of the Biden talks, all sides—the White House, the Republicans, and Obama's Simpson-Bowles deficit commission—agreed in principle on the $4 trillion deficit-reduction goal. And Boehner said he still believed such a "big deal" was possible. Obama concurred and proposed that the two of them chat in more detail, one on one.

Four days later, Boehner arrived at the White House and huddled with Obama on the Truman Balcony. Achieving a big deal, the speaker said, would require entitlement reform, meaning significant cuts to Medicare and Social Security, programs that Democrats were loath to touch.

I'm open to that, Obama said. But Republicans would have to accept new tax revenues, which they'd been adamantly opposing.

We're not raising rates, Boehner countered, but we can do broad tax reform. "If we lower all the rates, clean out the garbage in the code, you know, there could be some revenues," he said.

Obama and Boehner circled each other warily, but with a dawning sense that they might be able to do business—that the big deal, a "grand bargain," was worth pursuing. They agreed to keep talking and have their staffs start consultations, all in strictest confidence.

After the meeting, Obama briefed his senior advisers. On a personal level, he liked Boehner, saw him as an old-fashioned Republican—a Kiwanis Club guy, a Rotarian. A conservative, sure, but not a nuthouse conservative, and certainly no Tea Partier. And therein lay the problem. Unlike Gingrich, who led the insurgency that seized the House in 1994, Boehner had played little part in fomenting the latest GOP revolution. Now he was coping with a caucus filled with raucous freshmen, over whom his sway was modest.

Like his boss, Plouffe was skeptical about whether Boehner could deliver. But from his place at the president's side, with one eye trained on governing and the other on reelection, the potential benefits of a big deal were simply too great not to chase. It would be another, far more powerful, demonstration of the president's ability to forge bipartisan consensus, as he had in the lame-duck session. And, in particular, it would help remediate the president's weakness with independent voters, who saw him as an insuppressible spender. Just as bin Laden's killing would make it hard for Republicans to attack Obama on national security, a grand bargain would neutralize them on the deficit. Heading into 2012, he would be clothed in a doubly dense suit of chain mail.

Not everyone in the White House was convinced that Obama would need such thick armor. In the afterglow of the OBL triumph, some had lost sight of just how dicey his reelection prospects were. Plouffe had not. In mid-June, Daley had arranged a senior staff retreat at Fort McNair, a leafy Washington Army base on the peninsula at the confluence of the Potomac and Anacostia rivers, but it was Plouffe who dominated the proceedings. In a detailed presentation, he ran through several swing states, showing how dips of only a few percentage points from 2008—in Obama's support among independents, in turnout among young voters or African Americans— could spell defeat in 2012.

"Guys, we have no margin for error here," Plouffe told his colleagues. What he was thinking was more pointed: *I need to scare the shit out of these people.*

Obama wasn't especially scared or even mindful of the electoral details that kept Plouffe awake at night. His focus was on the macro picture, not the micro-politics. His main objective was to avoid a default on America's debt, which would wreak financial havoc—and, for all its perils, a grand bargain that spread the pain around equally might actually be easier to pull off than a smaller one. It would boost business confidence, bolstering the economy. And it would put America's fiscal house in order for a decade or more.

But while the country's finances were his top priority, he wasn't ignoring his campaign's, or the epic clash of cash that the race ahead would bring. In the wake of the Supreme Court's landmark 2010 decision in the *Citizens United* case, which allowed unlimited spending by outside groups, a raft of conservative tycoons were lining up to shell out hundreds of millions of dollars to smite him down. Obama hoped that a grand bargain might reduce their ardor, along with that of their amen corner in the broader business world. Watching the Republican presidential field take shape, he and his people saw Mitt Romney as the likeliest nominee. They took him seriously as a candidate, yet he did not make them sweat. The money, however, was another story—in more ways than one.

TWENTY-SIX HOURS AFTER Obama hosted Boehner on the Truman Balcony, the president's motorcade deposited him at a venue that was a mite less exclusive but nearly as ornate: the restaurant Daniel, on East Sixty-fifth Street in Manhattan. Unlike the House speaker, the people in the dining room were supporters of Obama's, the kind willing to part with $35,800— the maximum annual contribution to a presidential candidate and his party—to share his company for an hour. Yet Obama brought a certain trepidation to the fund-raiser, for the crowd mostly hailed from Wall Street, a community with whom his relationship was, to put it gently, suboptimal.

At Obama's side was Jim Messina, his campaign manager. Messina was forty-one years old, pale-skinned, rapid-talking, and profane. As Plouffe's deputy on the 2008 campaign, Emanuel's in the White House, and chief of staff to Montana senator Max Baucus before those gigs, he had earned a reputation as a genially ruthless fixer—a very nice guy who would merrily club you with a truncheon if you crossed him. In 2002, while running Baucus's reelection effort, Messina okayed a notorious ad insinuating that his boss's opponent was gay; in 2010, he served as Obama's point man on the repeal of "don't ask, don't tell." Messina saw no conflict between these episodes. He was all about winning.

Dispatched to Chicago in February, Messina was busy building Obama's reelection operation into a colossus, as innovative as Google and as juggernautish as Exxon Mobil. For its headquarters he rented the sixth floor of One Prudential Plaza, a towering high-rise overlooking Lake Michigan, filling it with 160 staffers by late June. To reenlist Obama's grassroots army from 2008, he had already opened sixty field offices in thirty-nine states and was upgrading the campaign's high-tech tools and infrastructure for the age of Twitter, Tumblr, and Pinterest.

What Messina was doing most urgently was meeting with donors—all the time, all over the place. North of $750 million would be required to repel the coming Republican onslaught, he told anyone who would listen, although in truth his goal was more like $1 billion. (After all, Obama had rustled up $748 million the last time around.) To hit that target, Obama would need to work the circuit tirelessly for eighteen months. He would need to tap Hollywood, Silicon Valley, trial lawyers, and labor. But most of all, he would need to milk Wall Street for millions—because, to borrow from Willie Sutton, the Street was where the money was.

In 2008, Obama had done precisely that. Though the importance of the Web and small donors to the money machine that the Obamans built was often and rightly noted, the role of Gotham's financial elite was impossible to overstate. By Election Day, three of the top seven institutions bundling donations to him were New York megabanks: Goldman Sachs, Citigroup, and JPMorgan Chase, with UBS AG and Morgan Stanley further down in the top twenty.

In the course of collecting the bankers' checks, Obama began consulting several of them as informal advisers, notably JPMorgan CEO Jamie Dimon and UBS Americas CEO Robert Wolf. He nursed a network of hedge-fund and private-equity admirers, such as Boston Provident's Orin Kramer, Avenue Capital's Marc Lasry, and Third Point's Daniel Loeb. When the lords of finance gazed at Obama, they saw a version of themselves: a product of the meritocratic elite, a self-made Ivy Leaguer, a hyper-rational sophisticate transcending the hoary dogmas and histrionics of conventional party politics. Dimon was so smitten that he spent three days in Washington with his family during the inauguration. It all smacked of puppy love.

But once Obama took office, the romance went south fast. Like many other businessfolk, the Wall Streeters disparaged Obama's team for lacking anyone with a meaningful background in the private sector. When Jarrett would huff, "Well, I have one," they rolled their eyes; they considered her a political hack, ineffectual and entitled. Axelrod they saw as a combination of Trotsky and Rasputin, spouting class warfare on TV. Larry Summers and Tim Geithner they derided as gormless eggheads. "They're smart," remarked one hedge-fund hotshot, "but you'd never, like, let them run a business for you."

Even more than they disdained Obama's people, the Wall Streeters hated his policies. And not so much the Dodd-Frank reregulation as his proposals to raise taxes on "carried interest" (the main source of income for private-equity pooh-bahs) and on the sale of hedge funds. But above all, they despised what they perceived as Obama's hostile tone: his attacks on the financiers who resisted the terms of the administration's plan to rescue Chrysler as a "small group of speculators . . . who held out when everybody else is making sacrifices," his inveighing on 60 Minutes against "fat-cat bankers," his lecturing them piously that he was "the only thing between you and the pitchforks."

By the middle of 2010, many of Obama's Wall Street friends were heaping scorn on him behind his back and to his face. In a letter to his investors that August, Loeb, who had raised $200,000 for Obama in 2008, accused the administration of attempting to "fracture the populace by pulling capital and power from the hands of some and putting it in the hands of others." (A few months later, around the holidays, Loeb sent an e-mail to several other Obama bundlers that started "Dear Friends/battered wives" and suggested that the book He's Just Not That Into You would make an apt stocking stuffer.) At a private White House lunch, Dimon pulled a prepared speech from his pocket and admonished Obama for undermining business confidence. Goldman Sachs CEO Lloyd Blankfein was even starchier, telling friends, "These people are like the Chicago mob."

The Wall Streeters still loyal to Obama were concerned that all the bellowing would affect his ability to raise money among their peers. One night in New York, after listening to Blankfein and some other bankers trashing the president, Orin Kramer ran into Obama's lead pollster, Joel Benenson. Kramer was a storied bundler, having raised millions for Bill Clinton, Al Gore, John Kerry, and Obama. He knew the score.

"I was just with some people who have been supportive, financial types, and they sound kinda negative," Kramer said. "Should I care?"

"No," Benenson replied. "Money is never going to be a problem for Obama."

Obama's own attitude toward fund-raising struck his Wall Street supporters as equally blithe. When he wasn't bashing them in the nose, he was giving them the back of his hand. The stories of his aloofness and inattentiveness to his donors were legion. Of the first White House Christmas party, in 2009, when Obama declined to take photos with them and their families. ("Big deal," he said to Rouse. "They've all got pictures with me before.") Of the $30,000-a-plate dinner at the Four Seasons in 2010, at which Obama, after devoting a brisk seven minutes to each table, retreated to a private room to sup with Jarrett and his body man, Reggie Love—a tale that traveled so widely it became a sort of urban legend.

What made Obama's behavior come across all the shabbier was the unavoidable comparison with Bill Clinton, who intuitively grasped the neediness of the deep-pocketed—and fed it, massaged it, manipulated it. He listened (or pretended to). He made them feel esteemed. Anyone hosting a fund-raiser for 42 would get a personal thank-you call, a handwritten letter, a signed picture. For the eight years of Clinton, Wall Street Democrats had been solicited, served, and serviced by the master of donor maintenance. For the first two years of Obama's reign, they got . . . squat.

Obama's reaction to Wall Street's displeasure was acute indifference tinged with exasperation. On substance, he hadn't an ounce of sympathy for the plaints of the bankers. Not only had he resisted the calls to nationalize the banks, but his White House had helped thwart the proposals of some in his party to break them up. He had left the bankers' bonuses alone, incurring the wrath of the left. Sure, he had tossed brickbats at the fat cats. So what? You folks are too sensitive, you need to get over yourselves, he told his Wall Street friends. "I can take a punch," Obama said. "Why can't you guys take a punch?"

When it came to the whining about the lack of stroking and schmooz-ing, he shrugged. Obama had never courted donors. He had worked his tail off at fund-raising in 2008, but he hadn't toadied—and the money cascaded in. There was something inside him that made him recoil from even the faintest hint of political or personal indebtedness. If the Wall Streeters wanted to punish him for his policies, so be it. If they wanted him to kiss their behinds, to hell with that.

Obama was unwilling or unable to change his ways even when he needed to hook the most titanic financial fish—George Soros. Soros, of course, was a billionaire hedge-fund operator and philanthropist whose avid liberal leanings had led him to spend lavishly in campaigns past, including $27.5 million through an outside group in 2004. In the 2008 campaign, Obama's introduction to Wall Street took place in Soros's Manhattan office. But when Soros sought a meeting in the White House, he was repeatedly re-buffed for more than a year. Soros wasn't trying to have legislation tweaked or a regulatory rule revised. All he wanted, he insisted, was to discuss the economy.

Finally, in September 2010, a secret summit was set up at the Waldorf Astoria in New York by Patrick Gaspard, in the hope that Soros could be induced into serious check-writing on behalf of the Democrats ahead of the midterms. Soros held forth for forty-five minutes, lecturing Obama not about the economy but about how the president should *talk about* the economy—the financial savant as self-appointed message guru. In the room, Obama was annoyed and bored. Afterwards, he fumed, "If we don't get any-thing out of him, I'm never fucking sitting with that guy again."

Soros apparently felt no better about the meeting: no big checks were forthcoming. And the Democrats could have used them. In the first election cycle of the post–*Citizens United* era, Republican outside groups poured nearly $200 million into House and Senate races, more than double the total on the Democratic side. The flashiest new players were American Cross-roads and Crossroads GPS, both set up by Bush ur-strategist Karl Rove, and Americans for Prosperity, backed by right-wing billionaire brothers Charles and David Koch. But equally dramatic was the shift in Wall Street's contri-butions: from 70 percent to Democrats in 2008 to 68 percent to Republicans in 2010.

In a way, the spending figures were more of wake-up call for Obama than the midterm results; they signaled that the ground was shifting ominously beneath his feet. In 2008, the magical elixir of hope, change, Clinton fatigue, and Bush ennui had carried Obama a long way toward victory, but the fact that he had outspent John McCain by more than two to one hadn't exactly hurt. Now Obama faced the likelihood of spending parity or worse— a bracing reality brought home in early 2011, when Rove announced that Crossroads planned to raise $120 million for 2012, followed quickly by the Koch brothers pledging to kick in another $88 million.

Obama was hardly confronting a hanging at dawn, but the threat of a barrage of negative TV ads even before the GOP nominee was chosen did concentrate his mind. As Messina prepared to decamp from Washington for Chicago, Obama pulled him into the Oval Office. Plouffe had suggested the president might refrain from fund-raising until the summer so he could focus on governing. The president disagreed. We need to get going, get this money together, he told Messina. I don't want to wait.

In a political meeting before the midterms, Obama had observed that he saw no need to curry favor with business and finance then, because if Democrats lost the House, "we're gonna have to kiss their asses anyway." The appointment of Daley was, in effect, a big smooch on the backside of Wall Street. His presidential puckering up continued in March, when Obama invited two dozen bankers, hedgies, and private equitizers who had supported him in the past—Lasry, Kramer, Wolf, et al—for a meeting in the Blue Room of the White House.

"I know you guys take a lot of flak in your community for supporting me," the president said. Teasingly, he referred to some of their colleagues as "babies." Solicitously, he asked, "How do you think we're doing?" Then Obama questioned them about how he could do better. Some were cynical about the outreach: He's only doing this because he's worried. Others were heartened: Hey, at least he's trying.

Obama let the Wall Streeters know he planned to be in New York a lot in the months ahead. And by the time he turned up at the Daniel dinner, it was, in fact, his seventh event in the city in three months. The condensed stump speech he delivered amid the clink of crystal stemware was crisp and free of either pandering or apologies; he mentioned Wall Street only once.

But he deftly and charmingly acknowledged that he knew the bloom was off the rose.

"I hope you will be as enthusiastic as many of you were back in 2008," Obama said. "I've got to tell you that, partly because of the gray hair, I know that it's not going to be exactly the same as when I was young and vibrant and new. And there were posters everywhere: HOPE. The logo was really fresh. And let's face it, it was cool to support me back then. At cocktail parties you could sort of say, 'Yeah, this Obama guy, you haven't heard of him? Let me tell you about him.'"

Most of the Wall Streeters who had been in the Blue Room were at Daniel, too. They sat there smiling, chuckling, nodding—and wondering if it was all for naught. Lasry, a billionaire and close pal of Clinton's who often lent the former president his jet, was an admirer of Obama's. But he was well aware that this made him an outlier in his circle. The antipathy for Obama had become an emotional thing on Wall Street. Over at Goldman, Lasry had heard, an edict had come down that there would be no giving to the president. And when Lasry asked around among his friends who had raised money for Obama in 2008, three-quarters said they wouldn't vote for him again, let alone bundle or donate.

When Obama finished his Daniel remarks, he made a loop around the room, stopping at each table, asking the same question he'd posed in the Blue Room: How do you think we're doing?

Three months earlier, Lasry had sugarcoated his reply, offered some suggestions. This time he thought, *What the hell, tell the truth.* He said, It's not going well. Nobody here trusts you.

Obama flew back to Washington more convinced than ever that he needed to make the grand bargain work. It was the only plausible way, he thought, to reduce the dyspepsia of the plutocrats. On the surface, his fundraising looked healthy. In the three months since the reelect got up and running, he had raked in $86 million. But Obama sensed the fragility undergirding that big number. He knew it had required him to crank through thirty-one events, a pace he couldn't hope to maintain. And, indeed, as June turned to July and Obama became engrossed on a daily basis in negotiating with Boehner, he found himself having to cancel fund-raisers left and right.

That was the bad news. The good news was that he and Boehner seemed to be making progress. Oh, and another thing: in the president's absence from the fund-raising trail, his campaign had discovered a new star to take his place, one who happened also to be named Obama.

FOR ANYONE FAMILIAR WITH the first lady, her emergence as a top-drawer buck-raker would have once seemed as likely as Biden moonlighting as a mime. Michelle had long cast a jaundiced eye on politics, and, in truth, she still did. In her husband's first presidential campaign, she was initially a conscientious objector, then a reluctant conscript plagued by missteps that fed a caricature of her as an unpatriotic, aggrieved, and resentful black woman. But after her knockout speech at the 2008 Democratic National Convention and two years in the White House radiating warmth, humanity, and devotion to her daughters, her public image was pure platinum. Working mothers saw her as one of them, but with a bit more glamour. Independents loved her efforts to help military families and combat childhood obesity. Her approval ratings were in the high sixties, well above her husband's.

She enjoyed her celestial popularity and did much to protect and enhance it. She also enjoyed the perks of the White House, much as the admission pained her. But she chafed at the constraints of the bubble and the glare of nonstop scrutiny—"I have to put my makeup on to walk my dog in the backyard," she complained—and at times made it sound as if she considered being first lady a burden. She never wanted this position, never asked for this position, and it irritated her when people couldn't grasp the sacrifices she was making—any semblance of a normal life, for instance. When she planned to take Sasha and Malia on a swanky trip to Spain in the summer of 2010, she was warned it would cause a royal ruckus, as it did. ("A modern-day Marie Antoinette," scolded the New York *Daily News*.) But didn't she have a right to take her girls on holiday? Didn't they have a right to see the world? *Forget it,* she thought. *We're going.*

There were tensions, too, with the West Wing staff—with Rahm, Gibbs, Axe, and even Jarrett now and then. Michelle was exacting, lawyerly, precise; she thought them sloppy, disorganized, and presumptuous. (Mostly they were scared to death of her.) In the run-up to the midterms, they had begged her to campaign actively for Democratic candidates. She resisted for months, then demanded to see a detailed plan. At a meeting in the Oval Office in mid-September, they laid it all out for her, complete with reams of data and even a PowerPoint. Michelle said she was impressed with the level of preparation—but agreed to do only eight events, a sliver of what her husband's political team wanted. But here was another good-news/bad-news story: at the events she did, she sparkled.

In truth, Michelle didn't care about congresspeople. Her opinion of them was even lower than the president's. What she cared about was Barack. She worried that campaigning in a partisan way in the midterms would erode the pile of political capital she'd painstakingly amassed. *My husband's going to need every bit of it,* she thought. *That's what I want to use it for—I want to campaign for MY GUY.*

Messina prayed those sentiments applied equally to fund-raising. In March, he sat down with Michelle in her East Wing office to make his pitch. Like his colleagues in September, he put together a granular presentation. Her events would entail her stump speech only, no questions. She would just do day trips that yielded at least $1 million. (Biden's floor was $250,000.) She would never be away from the girls when her husband was traveling. She would lend her signature to e-mail and direct-mail solicitations, which she hadn't done in 2010. Messina expected her to push back at least on some elements of the plan—this was Michelle. Instead she changed nothing, approved it all without hesitation.

And then she killed, pulling in $10 million in that first fund-raising quarter. As the summer rolled on, her mail and online pleas for money outperformed her husband's. And while she couldn't say she was having a ball, she was surprisingly game. When Messina sat down with her again to discuss her schedule for the fall, Michelle studied his cautiously culled requests and said, "That's all?"

From the moment the first couple arrived in the White House, Michelle had confided to friends that she could live with her husband being a one-term president. But the accumulation of the attacks from the right, the repudiation embodied by the midterms, and what she saw as the know-nothing ingratitude of the middle—"Look at all these great things he's doing, and nobody knows," she would say to Jarrett—had changed her tune. She was "absolutely determined," she said, that her husband be reelected, for that was the only source of vindication for what he—and they—had accomplished.

"We're in it to win—we're *gonna* win," Michelle told one donor. "We're gonna show everyone."

HAD OBAMA'S DEALMAKING BEEN going as well as FLOTUS's rainmaking, the summer of 2011 might have been a day at the beach. Instead, it was a season of misery.

On July 22, after weeks of dark nights and false dawns, the president's talks with the speaker faded to black. Looking wan in a televised press briefing, Obama grouched that, for a while, he "couldn't get a phone call returned" by Boehner and that he'd been "left at the altar." With the debt-ceiling deadline fast approaching, Geithner briefed Obama on the consequences of default. "Catastrophic," the treasury secretary said; it might trigger a cataclysm worse than the Great Depression. Obama's longest-serving advisers were concerned about their chief: never had they seen him more strained, more fretful, more weighed down by the burdens of his office.

And then, voilà, a breakthrough. On Sunday night, July 31, Obama again went before the cameras and announced that an agreement had been reached: $1.2 trillion in spending cuts over ten years, with a special committee of Congress tasked with finding another $1.2 trillion. "Is this the deal I would have preferred? No," Obama said, in an epic understatement.

What the president had done was avert Armageddon, which wasn't nothing, and he had managed to protect certain categories of safety-net spending, along with a deferral of the next debt-ceiling vote until after the election. But having beaten the drum all summer long for a "balanced approach" of cuts and new revenue, he secured none of the latter. The Republicans had taken America's full faith and credit hostage, and Obama had paid them ransom.

From every corner, the deal was greeted by a deafening Bronx cheer. The stock market, jittery for weeks over the prospect of default, shed twelve hundred points in the days after it was forestalled. Meanwhile, every Democrat to the left of Obama castigated the pact. Emanuel Cleaver, the chair of the Congressional Black Caucus (CBC), dubbed it a "sugar-coated Satan sandwich," which Nancy Pelosi helpfully expanded to include "Satan fries on the side." In *The New York Times,* Paul Krugman wrote that the deal would "take America a long way down the road to banana-republic status."

That Wednesday afternoon, August 3, Obama flew to Chicago for a fund-raiser. Backstage in a holding room, he had a quick dinner with Messina, who informed him that the campaign had been testing ads with four different messages to try to put the best face on the deal. But all fell flat. Voters think you're the adult in the room, Messina told Obama. They don't think you're the prick. They think you're trying to fix the mess, but also they think you're failing.

So which ad are we gonna run? Obama asked.

"We're not gonna run anything," Messina replied. They were stymied.

The next day, Obama turned fifty. Michelle staged a lovely party for him, starting on the South Lawn and ending in the East Room. Obama drew up the guest list himself—a mixture of old friends and celebrities such as Jay-Z and Tom Hanks—using the task to distract himself during spare moments in the debt negotiations. The first lady, determined to lift her husband's sagging spirits, moved through the crowd, pulling folks aside, imploring them to stay late. She delivered the evening's one toast to her man, and it was moving, funny, and frank, acknowledging that she had been hard on him sometimes, but he had been a trouper. Obama had a ball, dancing with his wife to Stevie Wonder, who performed live. His capacity for compartmentalization was otherworldly but not total, as he spent part of the evening lobbying Geithner's wife, Carole, to persuade Tim to stay on at Treasury through 2012. (Obama then handed her over to Hanks for the same purpose; spying Carole and Tom talking in the Rose Garden, Daley turned to Geithner and said, "You're fucked—it's over, okay?")

The next morning, though, the gloom engulfed Obama again. Throughout the summer, the credit-rating agencies had been threatening to downgrade the United States' debt. Now, despite the deal, Standard & Poor's notified the Treasury that it would do so after the market closed. Geithner met with Obama and informed him that the S&P's analysis contained a basic mathematical error, causing it to overstate the federal debt by $2 trillion—and yet the agency was going ahead anyway. Geithner, usually impassive, was angry and agitated. America's credit rating was about to be downgraded for the first time in history, a black mark on his boss's legacy, as a result of pure hackwork.

Obama was almost always impassive about events over which he had no control. The administration would push back against S&P as best it could, but there was nothing more to be done. That afternoon, he boarded Marine One for Camp David, where he and Michelle would be spending the weekend with friends from Chicago. But the bedlam followed him there, too. The next day, a NATO helicopter was shot down in eastern Afghanistan, killing thirty Americans, including twenty-two Navy SEALs, most of them from Team 6—the same unit that had taken out bin Laden.

On the phone with one of his national security aides, Ben Rhodes, a shaken Obama learned that none of the servicemen from that fabled mission had died, but that provided no comfort. It was the largest loss of American life in a single incident in the Afghan war—and, Obama would later tell Rhodes, the most wrenching moment of his time in office.

He returned to Washington in a foul mood that would quickly turn rancid as the criticism being heaped upon him intensified. Obama had sought a big deal with Boehner because he believed it was the correct thing to do, but also to get right with the monarchs of high capitalism. He had cut the small deal to avert an economic conflagration. Here he was that Monday, August 8, facing the cameras in the State Dining Room, addressing the downgrade, citing Warren Buffett, articulating an obvious truth: "No matter what some agency may say, we've always been and always will be a triple-A country." And still the stock market kept on falling—635 points that day, 200 *while he was speaking*.

Then there was the ululating of the left, now aimed less at the deal than directly at Obama. On the op-ed page of *The New York Times* the Sunday he was at Camp David, liberal psychology professor Drew Westen gutted him in a jeremiad that was burning up the blogosphere: "Like most Americans, at this point, I have no idea what Barack Obama . . . believes on virtually any issue." California congresswoman Maxine Waters and the rest of the CBC were shelling him mercilessly. The African American TV talk show host

Tavis Smiley and Princeton professor Cornel West, on a sixteen-city poverty tour, were doing the same. "Too often [Obama] compromises, too often he capitulates," West told ABC News. "I think the Republicans know that. I think they laugh when he's not around."

Obama had little patience for the "professional left," and vanishingly close to zero for what one of his senior African American aides, Michael Strautmanis, referred to as "professional blacks" (as opposed to black professionals). Apart from Georgia congressman John Lewis and Jim Clyburn of South Carolina, Obama had nearly as much contempt for the CBC as he did for the Tea Party Caucus. New York's Charlie Rangel he derided as a hack; Jesse Jackson Sr. was effectively banned from the White House. Obama remembered all too well a conversation with West in 2009, in which the professor used the precious time to complain about his seating at the inauguration.

Still, Obama never fully shrugged off criticism from those quarters. In a meeting with civil rights leaders in 2010, he had answered a question about black unemployment by saying "a rising tide lifts all boats," and since then the reply had been thrown back in his face frequently to question his commitment to his race—and his racial authenticity, he thought. One day in the spring of 2011, as he sat with some staffers preparing for a speech to Al Sharpton's National Action Network, Obama rattled off a list of his policies. Cracking down on predatory lending. Education reform. Student loan reform. Most important, health care reform. All with an outsize impact on African Americans. All achieved at a time when half of the GOP believed he'd been born in Kenya. Obama threw up his hands. After all that, he said, "am I still not black enough?"

Jarrett, in charge of constituency politics at the White House, always kept close, if wary, tabs on the president's standing with the professional black community—while arguing that it had no bearing on his popularity with black voters. But in the wake of the debt-ceiling debacle, she began to wring her hands, provoking scoffs from the rest of his political team, which saw no evidence in the polling that Obama was suffering with his base, African American or Caucasian. "If we're in trouble with the black community, fuck it," Daley told Jarrett. "Let's just wrap it up and go home."

For Obama, however, polling data was beside the point. Across the ideological spectrum, he was being derided and belittled. On Wall Street and on CNBC, he was flayed for his lack of leadership, for not bringing the grand bargain home. In the CBC and on MSNBC, he was flogged for caving to the GOP, for being coreless, rudderless, at sea. Inside the Beltway, he was lashed for his maladroit handling of the levers of power, for being unable to work his will on Congress. (And this showed up in his campaign's focus groups, where a startling number of people would cite Lyndon Johnson's ability to twist arms and get his way and ask why Obama couldn't do the same.) The critiques were different in important ways but shared a central theme, which had now become a meme: Obama was weak.

He was scheduled to take off on August 15 for a three-day midwestern bus tour, and then for a ten-day holiday on Martha's Vineyard. But before he left, he convened a meeting of his senior advisers in the Roosevelt Room. The president rarely railed on his people, and many of them turned up expecting a pep talk and not what they received: a reaming.

Look, Obama said, this has been hard. We all need a vacation. But we can't continue like this. Things need to improve, we need to improve. *You* need to improve. We didn't execute the way we needed to execute. This can't ever happen again. I know everybody's been working hard. We need to work harder. This has been a tough summer, but I don't want to hear any whining. We were the ones that pulled the country back from the brink of a default that would have devastated the economy, and somehow we're the ones getting our asses kicked over it. It doesn't make any sense. We need to do better at explaining what it is that we did, why we did it, and why this is good for the American people.

The communications piece of the puzzle gnawed at Obama. A year had passed since he made the decision to retool his message team; Axelrod and Gibbs had been gone for seven months. And yet somehow he and his operation still hadn't figured out how to speak with the clarity of purpose people remembered from the last campaign. "The deal was better than we're getting credit for," Obama told his communications director, Dan Pfeiffer, regarding the compromise that avoided the default. "It feels to me like we're not doing enough to shape the overall narrative here."

Pfeiffer was thirty-six years old, droll, acerbic, faintly cynical, and whip smart. He had been with Obama for four years—and in every one of them, without fail, he found himself on the receiving end of this gripe from his boss. So Pfeiffer did what he always did: pounded out a memo with various suggestions. More off-the-record briefings for Daley and Plouffe with reporters. More outreach to liberal columnists, bloggers, and the talking heads at MSNBC. Blah, blah, blah.

"We could do all those things, but part of this is about strategic choices," Pfeiffer told Obama. "We made a strategic choice that we were gonna portray you, because you are, as reasonable. But in today's media environment, there is no caucus for reasonableness, with the possible exception of David Brooks. And there is no communications strategy that will make David Brooks and Paul Krugman like the same thing. So you're gonna have to choose."

Pfeiffer walked out of the Oval Office thinking that Obama grokked his argument. But the truth was, Pfeiffer himself was plagued by a different possibility. What if they had reached the same kind of turning point that George Bush had in the summer of 2005? What if they simply could not come back?

What if people are saying we're just tired of listening to you? Pfeiffer thought.

OBAMA WAS TOO CONFIDENT in the power of his voice to harbor such bleak thoughts, but as he set off for the Vineyard he was as low, frustrated, and exhausted as he had ever been. The bus tour through Illinois, Iowa, and Minnesota had been a decidedly mixed bag: a blessed escape from confinement in the White House, yet filled with variations on the weakness meme—as voters, his voters, asked him over and over, Why did you negotiate with those guys? Why'd you let that happen? The stock market continued to quake and quiver. Gas prices were sky-high. Unemployment was still stuck at 9 percent. And Gallup now had his approval rating at an all-time low of 38.

But the Vineyard always bucked Obama up, gave him time to think. Four years earlier, he had come there in a similar state of discombobulation over his faltering White House bid; after eight days of pondering, long walks, and long talks, he returned to the mainland and changed the game.

There were some in the White House now who suggested he forgo this vacation or at least go someplace else, someplace less chichi. But the girls loved
the Vineyard, and that was that concerning venue. As for bailing entirely,
Plouffe shut down that idea quick. This would be Obama's last chance to get
away before the campaign began in earnest. Without it, his performance on
the trail might suffer.

For the next ten days, the Obamas lolled about on a twenty-nine-acre
farm turned fortified compound in Chilmark—the humbler digs in Oak
Bluffs where they'd once stayed were a distant memory. Obama managed
to squeeze in a scooch of politicking, masked as socializing: a reception
at the home of an old Harvard Law School professor of his, Charles Ogle-
tree, which included prominent African American progressives, such as
Spike Lee; another at the estate of Comcast CEO Brian Roberts, where the
crowd was lousy with corporate chieftains. (It'll be good for you to have
Brian embrace you publicly, Jarrett told him.)

Obama returned to the White House raring to go, ready to turn his public focus to jobs, the topic that had eluded him for so long. Before decamping
for the Vineyard, he had asked Gene Sperling, head of the National Economic Council, to put together a jobs bill for introduction to Congress in
September. The economy had gained 117,000 jobs in July. The consensus
forecast for August was a measly 68,000, though Obama was hoping, as he
did every month, that the jobs report would surprise him.

The latest tabulation arrived on Thursday, September 1, in the hands of
Sperling, who walked into the Oval Office bearing a copy for Obama. The
president was standing in front of his desk, Plouffe hovering nearby.

Obama could see from Sperling's expression that he was not bearing
glad tidings.

What's the number? Obama asked.

"Zero," Sperling said.

"What do you mean, zero?"

"Zero," Sperling repeated.

"You mean *exactly* zero?"

"Yes."

"You mean if I take that piece of paper from you, there will actually be a zero on it?" Obama pressed. In a $16 trillion economy with more than 130 million jobs, it seemed impossible.

"Zero."

"Has that ever happened before?" Obama asked.

"I have never seen anything like it," Sperling said.

No one could believe it. Even a negative number would have been better in a way—more explicable, less hauntingly symbolic. The Obama economy: a big fat goose egg. *You couldn't make it up*, thought Plouffe.

Obama took the paper from Sperling and stared at it a good long time, focusing and refocusing his eyes, gazing at it from various angles.

"I'm looking at this all kinds of different ways, but it's zero," Obama said. "How can it be zero?"

OBAMA'S LIST

FOUR HUNDRED AND FIFTY BILLION was the much larger figure Obama faced four days later. Once again, the setting was the Oval Office. Once again, the number was presented by Sperling, this time as the proposed price tag on the jobs bill Obama would introduce later that week. The legislation and the speech to launch it were important to the president. They would likely be his last chance to accomplish anything substantial before electioneering began in earnest, and thus his last opportunity to boost the economy. They would also represent a shift to a new posture. For the past three months, as he dickered endlessly with congressional leaders, Obama often felt as though he was "wrestling with pigs," as he put it to one aide. Now he wanted to soar above the trough. But gaining altitude would prove much harder than he could possibly have imagined.

The measure, dubbed the American Jobs Act, was a Sperling special. Enamored of his work in the way that James Bond enjoyed martinis, Sperling had lived at the nexus of budget policy and politics most of his adult life, including eight full years in the Clinton White House. All summer, he had been cobbling together proposals to shrink the jobless rate, presenting some at the Fort McNair conclave, back in June. But after the debt-ceiling imbroglio concluded, Obama threw Sperling into his favorite mode: overdrive. Tell me what you think is the best economic policy, the president instructed him. Don't self-edit based on political feasibility. Be big, brash, and bold. And get it done in a hurry.

Working around the clock, Sperling and his team drew up a long, expensive wish list. Extending the payroll tax cut: $175 billion. Investing in transportation infrastructure: $50 billion. Rehiring teachers and first responders: $35 billion. And so on. Sperling's goal was a package that, if implemented, would create 1.5 million jobs and push GDP growth up by two points. He had thought $375 billion would do the trick—until the August employment report delivered that awful aught, leading many economists to predict that a double-dip recession was in the offing. So now Sperling stood before Obama and informed him that an even larger payload was required: $447 billion, to be precise. Obama signed off without blinking.

Three nights later, September 8, the president stood in the well of the House and declaimed, "I am sending this Congress a plan that you should pass right away." Fifteen more times, he made a nearly identical plea: "pass this bill," "pass this jobs bill," "pass this jobs bill right away." Leaning in on the payroll tax cut extension, Obama said, with a pinch of sarcasm, "I know some of you have sworn oaths never to raise any taxes on anyone for as long as you live. Now is not the time to carve out an exception and raise middle-class taxes."

There was nothing eloquent about the speech, but eloquence wasn't his aim. Since the midterms, Obama had played the inside game, spending countless hours in quiet rooms, laboring to find a middle ground where none existed. Just as the Beltway panjandrums advised, he had courted Boehner the old-fashioned way—with golf, wine, and cigarettes, away from the cameras. And it got him worse than nowhere. He had positioned himself as the capital's reasonable grown-up. But reasonableness in the face of reckless unreasonableness looked a lot like impotence. From now on, there would be no more pointless reaching out, no more parleys in hushed compartments. Instead he would take his case to the country, galvanize public opinion. If it compelled the Republicans to act, fantastic; if not, the contrast would be clear. And though people would say he was being political, campaigning rather than governing, at least no one would call him a doormat.

And, indeed, they didn't. From the hog pen on the Hill, Boehner and

House majority leader Eric Cantor emitted conciliatory squeaks, while congressional Democrats oinked approval. The liberal blogosphere and cable-verse squealed with delight, and even Krugman was pleased. The next day, Obama hit the trail to sell the plan in the swing state of Virginia (in Cantor's district, no less). A few days after that, he was in Ohio (not far from Boehner's domain). The campaign to rehabilitate Obama's public image was under way, but it would be no easy thing. His approval rating didn't budge, and would flatline for months to come. The weakness meme was like a virus: nasty, infectious, and hard to shake. And it would keep on cropping up in new quarters all the time, including the most quaint. In the era of the infinite elastic news cycle, of Twitter and blog posts, Obama's nemesis was the book—several books, in fact—that threatened the White House's no-drama image.

"THIS IS LARGELY A PIECE of fiction," Obama griped to Plouffe, referring to a new book by journalist Ron Suskind. *Confidence Men* chronicled the travails of Obama and his economic team in their first two years, painting a withering portrait of the president: as a clever, well-meaning neophyte, a feckless, passive ditherer undermined and overridden by his bumptious advisers at every turn. "I went through that whole book," Obama said. "I don't recognize myself."

Endowed with acute writerly sensibilities and sensitivities, Obama could be prickly when it came to books about him. And that September, the West Wing was awash in authors. Among the scribes were A-listers such as David Maraniss, the Pulitzer Prize–winning Clinton biographer who had spent two years digging deep into Obama's personal history, and Bob Woodward, who had already published one Obama book and was eyeing another. Political books sometimes seemed the vestigial tails of mass media, but when their authors were credible, they retained a distinct power: to create headlines, drive news coverage, influence elite perceptions. Thus far, the president's treatment by mainstream authors had been (at best) beatifying or (at worst) benign.

Confidence Men broke that string of good luck. Beyond its judgments about the president, the book was teeming with tittle-tattle. Summers was quoted as telling former Office of Management and Budget (OMB) director Peter Orszag, "We're really home alone . . . There's no adult in charge." Obama's communications adviser Anita Dunn was quoted as saying that his White House "fit all of the classic legal requirements for a genuinely hostile workplace to women." Making matters worse was the degree of access granted Suskind. Everyone had talked to him, including the president, who sat with the author for forty minutes in the Oval Office.

Obama's participation in the book did little to mitigate his anger about it. Like every president before him, he complained ceaselessly about leaks and gum-flapping to the press. His impulse to keep a tight lid on information—from national-security secrets to White House scuttlebutt— was intense and omnidirectional. Breaches of confidentiality, airing of soiled linen, and settling of scores: all were present in Suskind's pages, and all of it drove Obama crazy.

Particularly irritating were Dunn's remarks about sexism in the White House. "I just don't understand why someone would say something like that," Obama sputtered. When he was told that Suskind had truncated Dunn's quote in a way that made it more damaging, he snapped, "Why is she even talking about this?"

To Dunn, now serving as an outside consultant to the White House, and to the rest of the communications team, *Confidence Men* demonstrated that they had lost control of the process by which they handled book authors. The access given to Suskind enhanced his credibility. But before the book's publication, no one knew precisely to whom he had talked, what they told him, or what he had in his pocket—so they were all blindsided.

And the same thing was about to happen again, with a book on the first couple by Jodi Kantor of *The New York Times,* due to hit shelves in January. Kantor had covered the Obamas since 2007, conducting a rare joint interview with the couple about their marriage in 2009, which led to a magazine article that in turn led to her book contract. It was anyone's guess how much time Kantor had logged with Jarrett and other officials, especially in the East Wing, and with folks in Chicago. Really, the Obamans only knew one thing: Kantor had nailed down a specific anecdote they had labored to suppress for more than a year.

The story involved Jarrett, Gibbs, and, indirectly, Mrs. Obama. It took place in September 2010, in the aftermath of a claim in yet another book—one published in France, in which the French first lady, Carla Bruni-Sarkozy, allegedly said that Michelle had told her that living in the White House was "hell." When the story hit the wires, Gibbs scrambled, eliciting an official denial from the Élysée Palace by 11:00 a.m. But in a meeting of senior advisers the next morning, Jarrett contended that Michelle thought his efforts had been insufficiently vigilant. Gibbs, whose relationship with Jarrett was poisonous by then and who suspected she was representing her own views rather than Michelle's, blew a gasket.

"You don't know what the fuck you're talking about!" he screamed. When Jarrett replied tartly that the first lady would disapprove of his language, Gibbs exclaimed, "Then fuck her, too!" and stalked out of the room.

The rest of the senior staff sat in silence, many sharing the same thought: that Gibbs, whose hold on his job was already tenuous, had just sealed his doom.

Emanuel said softly, Robert's our friend. He lost his temper. This should never leave this room.

And yet it slipped out. Kantor had the story, in all its gory detail, from multiple sources. Worse still, when she got Gibbs on the phone, he fulminated even further, calling Jarrett a liar and trashing her violently, all of it on the record. Jarrett got wind of what he'd told Kantor and went ballistic, demanding that Gibbs, now serving as a consultant to the reelection campaign, somehow retract what he had said. Axelrod and Rouse, desperate to save their friend from being consigned to purdah, urged him to try to walk back his comments. But Gibbs was a prideful man—no dice.

Obamaworld feared the Kantor book would lay bare the breadth and depth of the White House's dysfunction; reveal the contentiousness around Jarrett, the touchiest of Obama's top advisers; and even scuff up the shimmering veneer on Michelle's public image—which the West Wing was astonished hadn't happened already, even as the East Wing scurried to safeguard it.

For all her popularity with the public, FLOTUS had received mixed reviews in official Washington. On Capitol Hill, she was seen as standoffish, raising hackles among congressional better halves. She rarely invited them, even the Democrats, to the White House, and when she did, she treated the occasions as perfunctory. Attending the annual Congressional Club spouses' luncheon, where she was the guest of honor, she spoke briefly and then split, inspiring unfavorable comparisons with Laura Bush, who had always brightly worked the tables. Michelle's upmarket tastes and fashionista tendencies sparked concerns in the White House, too. A few stories about her designer clothes had turned up in the press, but delivered only glancing blows. What if Kantor had a trove of tales?

Around that time, Michelle made a surprise visit to a local Target, where an AP photographer got some apparently candid snaps of her dressed down and pushing her own shopping cart. The official line was that the pictures were happenstance, but more than a few of Obama's West Wing advisers wondered if the East Wing was trying to get ahead of any negative stories on the horizon. Daley considered making inquiries but then decided to let it go. *The less you know about this, the better off you are,* he thought.

Obama didn't know much, either. Not about the Kantor book, not yet. But the Suskind experience had him steaming. Even after the post-midterm reshuffle, his White House staff remained fractious, replete with infighting and prone to smack-talking in the press. Since January, Daley had been telling Obama that another shakeup was in order, exhorting him before he took off for Martha's Vineyard, "You have one last shot to make changes if you want" before the campaign season kicked in. On returning from vacation, Obama had given his answer: "The team is what it is."

But now, in the wake of a pair of Democratic losses in congressional special elections in New York and Nevada on Tuesday, September 13, both widely attributed to Obama's unpopularity, James Carville was singing from the Daley hymnal. "Fire somebody. No—fire a lot of people," Carville wrote in an op-ed on CNN.com. "For God's sake, why are we still looking at the same political and economic advisers that got us into this mess?"

Obama wasn't inclined to heed Carville's advice, but if he was going to stand behind his people, they needed to pull together and start acting with a unity of purpose. On Saturday, his extended political squadron would be gathering in Washington for the first of a series of meetings to discuss campaign strategy. They would talk about the Republican nomination fight, which was heating up. They would talk about coordination between the White House and Chicago, which had been patchy. But most of all they would talk about Obama: what he had to do to win reelection, the kind of president he had been—and the kind he actually wanted to be.

OBAMA WALKED INTO THE State Dining Room that morning and there they were, two dozen aides and operatives crowded around a long oaken table under the famous George Peter Alexander Healy oil painting of a hand-on-chin Abraham Lincoln. From the West Wing: Daley, Plouffe, Jarrett, Rouse, Pfeiffer, Carney, deputy senior adviser Stephanie Cutter, deputy chief of staff Alyssa Mastromonaco, and Jarrett's deputy, Michael Strautmanis. From the East Wing: Michelle's chief of staff, Tina Tchen. From Biden's office: the VP, his chief of staff, and his counselor. From Chicago: Axelrod, Messina, and media guru Larry Grisolano. From the DNC: Gaspard, who had become the committee's executive director. From the far-flung universe of outside adjutants: lead pollster Benenson, focus-group maestro David Binder, ad maker Jim Margolis, Gibbs, Dunn (raising eyebrows), and Bauer, no longer the White House counsel but instead the campaign's lawyer.

Plouffe looked at the humongous assemblage and thought it was insane. Any meeting resembling a scene from a David O. Selznick movie was a meeting not worth convening. Whenever you have more than ten people, you have problems, he'd told Obama beforehand. Pick a setting, it doesn't matter: family, campaign, church. It's less about the people than it is about the math—the law of averages. Stuff is gonna leak.

But Obama insisted on the big group, and as he opened the meeting he explained why.

Carville says that I should fire you all, but I'm not gonna fire you, Obama said. Everyone around this table is here because I want you here. This is the team I believe in. You're my people, I trust you, we gotta trust each other. I have to be able to walk in here, say whatever I need to say, and know it's gonna stay in this room.

Now, we've come through a rough period, Obama continued, and a lot of what I read about myself in the press these days bears no resemblance to who I am. That I'm not strong. That I don't stand for anything. I'm not sure how we got here, but we have to fix it. This is gonna be a tough campaign, tougher than 2008. The economy is weak, and it's not likely to get much better. We're not going to get a grand bargain out of this Congress, or much of anything else that would help. So from now on, we're going to pick clear fights and pocket victories where we can. The stakes for the country were high last time, but they're even higher now. "And if I go down in this," Obama said, "I'm not gonna go down being punk'd."

Benenson took the floor and presented his polling data. The numbers showed that the debt-ceiling imbroglio had inflicted significant damage to Obama. He had suffered setbacks with three crucial swing constituencies—young voters, independent women, and low-income whites—and with portions of his base. Whereas in 2008 Obama claimed 96 percent of black voters and 67 percent of Hispanics, he now stood at 89 and 55. At the same time, the GOP had also taken on tremendous water. Undecided voters were horrified by the Tea Party and suspicious of Republican policies on taxing and spending, which they saw as strongly tilted toward the rich. Benenson's conclusion was crystalline: We need to make this election into a choice about economic values.

This would be no slam dunk, Benenson went on. Though the Republican field was crowded with entrants, the Obamans continued to believe that Romney would almost certainly be the party's standard-bearer. Head to head with the former Massachusetts governor, Obama had 45 percent of the vote and a one- or two-point lead. But his base of strong support was both smaller and softer than Romney's.

Many around the table looked at the data and took comfort: After everything we've been through, we're still in this thing. Plouffe's view remained: *No margin for error, but I'd rather be us than them.* Daley thought: *It'll go down to the wire, and he'll either win by a few or lose by a lot.* But Obama's reaction was more visceral and stark: *Man, I'm in deep shit.*

Axelrod followed Benenson with a video presentation: a clip from Obama's iconic keynote at the 2004 Democratic National Convention, some ads from 2008, and footage from the summer of 2011. When the first snippet came on, Axelrod poked at the president, "I didn't know you had a younger brother!" But in truth the contrasts were sobering—the Obama of yesteryear fiery and soaring, the Obama of today pallid and sluggish, spouting bromidic Washingtonese. *(Oh, God, he sounds like Harry Reid,* thought Gaspard.) Pointing to the earlier clips, Axelrod declared, "That's the guy they elected president, and that's the guy they want to be president."

After eight months outside the White House, Axe had regained his equilibrium. And while his message was ostensibly for the entire group, he was really hurling it like a dart at an audience of one. "You were seen as someone who would run through the wall for the middle class," Axelrod said. "We need to get back to that."

Obama bristled slightly. I've been talking about the middle class for almost three years, he said.

Maybe, Axelrod replied, but we've also sent mixed messages. We talk all the time about accountability and responsibility, but what voters see is Wall Street paying no price for having crashed the economy. We talk about tax fairness, but what voters see is Jeff Immelt in the presidential box at the jobs speech. (Immelt was the CEO of General Electric, which had made headlines for earning $14 billion in profits in 2010 but paying not a dime in taxes.)

Axelrod wasn't alone in these views. Most of Obama's outside advisers shared them, and so did Biden. Middle-class people, they don't think we've done anything for them, the VP said. I hear it all the time when I'm on the road. They think the wealthy are going gangbusters. They think health care reform will help the poor and illegal immigrants. But, man, they think nobody's doing squat for *them.*

On and on it went like this, for four and a half hours. Obama sat there, taking in the critiques—and maybe it was all true. Maybe he'd lost sight of the middle class. Maybe he'd been bridled by the Beltway. But there was one thing the president knew: under any of these Republicans running to replace him, everything would be so much worse.

We can't turn this thing over to them, Obama said. We can't turn the country over to them. We can't let them take us straight back to the Bush years. We've made a bunch of hard decisions and taken a lot of fire. We've made progress—not enough, but some. Eventually the economy's going to turn the corner, and when it does, I don't want it to be President Mitt Romney who gets the credit for the work we've done.

"I'm a competitive guy," Obama said defiantly, in conclusion. "There's nothing that I hate more than losing—and I do not intend on losing this election to *that guy*."

THE NEXT MONDAY MORNING, September 19, Obama delivered a major address from the Rose Garden. The so-called supercommittee created by the debt-ceiling deal to find $1.2 trillion in cuts and/or revenues to reduce the deficit was holding hearings as it worked toward a Thanksgiving deadline. In his speech, Obama returned to his framework from the summer, proposing a $3.6 trillion mix of spending cuts and tax increases. But he also etched a line in the sand: "I will veto any bill that changes benefits for those who rely on Medicare but does not raise serious revenues by asking the wealthiest Americans or biggest corporations to pay their fair share."

The veto threat had been a subject of debate within Obamaworld. Daley and a number of White House advisers were against it, fearing the president would be blamed for messing with the supercommittee. Chicago and the rest of the external gang disagreed. Their worry was that, for all the bravado about playing an outside game and picking fights, Obama was in danger of being sucked into the morass of haggling with Capitol Hill again. We need to take a stand and stick to it, Axelrod said. "We really can't afford another 'Obama caves' moment."

Obama didn't plan on caving. He was spoiling for a scrap. But his political instincts were muddier now than they had ever been. In his charmed electoral career, Obama was almost entirely unacquainted with loss, let alone humiliation. In 2000, after three years in the state senate, he had challenged Bobby Rush, the incumbent congressman from Illinois's first district, and been trounced by a two-to-one margin. But taking on Rush was a suicide mission—one that everybody from Michelle and Jarrett to Richie Daley warned him against—and after a brief period of mortification he was back in the saddle, running for the U.S. Senate. He'd been beaten by Hillary Clinton in various primaries in 2008, yet ultimately won the war. The midterms had been a historic drubbing for his party, but despite all the commentary (and common sense) to the contrary, deep down he never saw that election as a referendum on himself.

The debt ceiling was different: a high-stakes contest in which he'd in-

vested himself personally, followed his gut on strategy and tactics, fought
to the bitter end—and got creamed. Still reeling, Obama ruminated on his
first term, how he had conducted himself throughout, and on the constraints of his office and politics itself. All too often, Obama had felt as if he
were driving with his foot on the brake. The causes for this were multitudi-
nous: relentless Republican obstructionism, Democratic sclerosis, the nonstop crisis management, the sometimes conflicting advice of his advisers.
Now his campaign team was telling him to be more aggressive, unshackle
his 2008 self. But on many issues the complications were ever present and
confounding.

At the next strategy meeting, the following Saturday, Obama brought up
one example: climate change. In the 2008 campaign, he had singled out the
transition to green energy as the most urgent issue facing the country. But
the White House's push for cap-and-trade had been halfhearted at best—
"Look, the dolphins will be okay for another year" was what Emanuel said
about it privately—and, even in the aftermath of the BP spill in the summer
of 2010, the bill had stalled in the Senate. Obama knew that raising the climate change banner with unemployment sky-high would pose electoral
risks in places like Ohio and Michigan. But it might rouse young voters,
and, more important, he cared about the issue, wished he'd done more,
wished he'd said more.

Axelrod keeps talking to me about authenticity, Obama said. Maybe I
should just come out and say what I really feel about this. Maybe I should
just go out and say what I think about *everything*.

Flipping through a pile of color-coded maps showing how narrow
Obama's path to 270 electoral votes might be, Gibbs looked up and said,
"Well, Mr. President, I don't really see a *Bulworth* scenario in here."

Everyone in the room cracked up, but Obama was at least partly serious.
There was a range of issues that he might want to start talking differently
about than he had been. Maybe he ought to jot them down. Maybe he should
draw up a list.

Yes, yes, Axelrod said. That could be a useful exercise.

Obama was an inveterate list maker. He loved sitting down with a yellow
legal pad and filling up pages with his thoughts. It helped him to quiet his
mind. At important meetings during the 2008 campaign, he often showed

up with a list. He did the same in the White House when he was working with Favreau on a big speech. Upstairs in the residence late at night, he would retreat to his personal office—the Treaty Room, which, unlike the Oval, he'd outfitted with a computer, a printer, and a TV for monitoring ESPN—and station himself behind his cluttered desk, scratch-scratch-scratching away.

The Obamans met again on September 30, a Friday afternoon. An hour beforehand, the president was on the phone with talk radio host Michael Smerconish, savoring the major news of the day: a Predator drone strike, ordered by Obama, had killed Anwar al-Awlaki, an American-born firebrand Islamist preacher who had become a senior Al Qaeda leader in Yemen. Al-Awlaki had been connected to the failed efforts of at least two would-be terrorists—the "underwear bomber," in December 2009, and the Times Square bomber, in May 2010—imperiling American lives during Obama's tenure. "We are very pleased," the president told Smerconish, "that Mr. al-Awlaki is no longer going to be in a position to directly threaten the United States homeland."

A few minutes later, Obama strode into the Roosevelt Room, just across the hall from the Oval, to which the meetings had been relocated with a slightly (but only slightly) slimmed-down cast. In his hand the president held a stack of yellow legal pages—nine or ten of them—filled with his neat, compact southpaw handwriting.

Last time, I told you guys I wanted to spend time thinking about some issues, he began. Now, we have a three-year track record that I feel good about. We've delivered on many of the promises I made when I ran for this office. We've faced incredible challenges, foreign and domestic, and done a good job meeting them, by and large.

Obama didn't need to run through this preamble. Everyone knew the litany of his achievements. Foremost on that day, with the fresh news about al-Awlaki, it seemed the president was pondering the drone program that he had expanded so dramatically and with such lethal results, as well as the death of bin Laden, which was still resonating worldwide months later. "Turns out I'm really good at killing people," Obama said quietly. "Didn't know that was gonna be a strong suit of mine."

Around the room, everyone was transfixed by the pile of pages Obama had placed on the table in front of him. Most of his advisers had expected him to bring a list—but an index card, not *War and Peace*. They were even more surprised by what the president was saying now: that as much as he had been faithful to his beliefs, there were places where his efforts had been insufficient. Where he'd trimmed his sails or been inhibited by the exigencies of the politics of the moment. Where he'd been less than honest about where he stood.

For the next half hour, Obama, speaking evenly, made his way through the items on his list—as his advisers sat mute and motionless, their smartphones for once idle.

Obama talked about energy and climate change. He understood why cap-and-trade had failed, why they hadn't sought to further elevate the debate. But the issue remained vital, and they would need to return to it. "We're never gonna outdrill the other guys," Obama said. "We gotta take some risks on this issue."

He talked about immigration reform. We made a calculated decision not to push hard for it, Obama said, because although it's popular with Hispanics, it's less popular with the rest of the country, especially in an economic downturn. But he had been pounded for being pusillanimous by his Latino allies, and they weren't wrong, he said. It was a moral matter as well as an economic one, and the campaign would give him another chance to push on it. "This election could be the thing that picks the lock," Obama said.

He talked about poverty among African Americans, Hispanics, Native Americans, and poor whites in places like Appalachia. We need to do more, we need to reaffirm that we haven't abandoned that concern as a country, Obama said.

He talked about Israel and Palestine. We all know that Bibi Netanyahu is a pain in the ass, Obama said. But the president blamed himself for accepting the distorted political prism through which every effort to achieve a settlement in the region was mediated.

He talked about Guantánamo Bay. Obama's vow to close the prison there had been one of his most deeply felt promises from 2008. Yes, he had tried. Yes, Congress had thwarted him. But he hadn't pushed hard enough, he said, and he wanted to take up the cause again. "No one is gonna persuade me that we should run a penal colony in perpetuity in America," Obama said.

And he talked about gay marriage. Obama's public posture on the issue had been all over the map. In 1996, in a questionnaire supplied by a gay newspaper in Chicago, he said that he favored marriage rights for same-sex couples. Two years later, he answered "undecided" on the publication's questionnaire, and by 2008 he was officially against it. In the White House, he remained opposed but said that his position was "evolving"—even as he fought for the repeal of "don't ask, don't tell" and deemed the Defense of Marriage Act unconstitutional, ordering his attorney general to stop defending it in court.

But now Obama uncloseted his unvarnished convictions. Look, he said, everybody here probably knows that I've long since evolved on this issue. I haven't been comfortable for some time with where I am publicly. I don't want to keep ducking it. Gay marriage is now legal in New York, and a bunch of other states are heading in the same direction. Things are moving fast. It's only a matter of time before someone is going to ask me the question the right way: If you were still a state senator in Springfield and this came up, how would you vote? And if I get the question that way, I'm going to answer it honestly: I would vote in favor.

Among the advisers around the table, most believed that Obama had been for gay marriage all along. Gibbs had heard him say so as far back as 2004. In debate prep in 2008, Obama had seemed uncomfortable with his public opposition. Two years later, after seeing a screening of the movie *The Kids Are All Right*, he remarked to a handful of aides, You know, at some point, we're gonna have to give up the ghost on this. And indeed, he had been talking for months in 2011 with a group of confidants—Axelrod, Daley, Jarrett, Plouffe—about the question of when and how he would switch his stance. But this was the first time he had been candid with a wider group.

Taken in sum, Obama's list was a revealing document. Throughout his time in public life, and most markedly in his presidency, there had always been a tension in Obama's governing philosophy between its moderate, reformist threads and its more traditionally liberal strands. The best working definition of Obamaism was "pragmatic progressivism," with all the inherent strain that suggested. With his list, Obama was saying he believed that over the past three years his progressive impulses had too often been trumped by the demands of pragmatism. That he had trimmed his sails in just the way his critics on the left had charged. That Obama the president hadn't always lived up to the Obama brand of politics.

To those in the Roosevelt Room, there were few things on the list that were surprising. These were his people. They knew him well. And yet most were amazed by what they were witnessing: a sitting president reviewing the regrets of his time in office, at times reflectively, at times defensively, at times self-reproachfully. Regret wasn't the only element, however. There was also resolve—Obama talking about his unfinished business, laying out in a rudimentary way what his second-term agenda might look like.

Obama was not a man given to self-critique. Or acts of public intimacy. Or displays of vulnerability. Some around the table regarded his reading of the list as brave or moving, others as simply tough-minded. Still others mused about the fate of those yellow pages. *They'll end up in his presidential records,* thought Dunn.

But Daley had a different thought.

Holy shit, we have a bunch of leakers here. I hope to God this doesn't get out.

THE PRESIDENTIAL OFFICES OF Bill Clinton occupied the top floor of a fourteen-story brick-and-glass building on West 125th Street in Harlem, two blocks from the Apollo Theater. On November 9, six weeks after hearing Obama's list, a four-man traveling party—Axelrod, Benenson, Gaspard, and Messina—set off to that destination on a goodwill mission: to draw the former president further into the orbit of the current one and, in particular, to enlist his assistance in getting Obama reelected.

The last time an Obamaworld contingent had made the pilgrimage to Harlem was in September of 2008, under sharply different circumstances. Obama himself was there for the first tête-à-tête between him and Clinton since the sour Democratic nomination fight. Eager to avoid any awkwardness, Obama kept the conversation focused on governance rather than politics. But as they were wrapping up, Clinton dutifully offered to hit the trail with the nominee. Obama assented, although his people were ambivalent about the prospect. They didn't believe that Clinton would move many votes, and were interested in having the two men appear together only to quiet media speculation about the relationship. The joint rally finally took place six days before the election, and was flat and lifeless. The Obamans didn't care. As one of them put it afterwards, "We were all just so far past the Clintons."

But, of course, they weren't—not when Obama was already thinking of making Hillary his secretary of state. From the moment they'd met, in 2004, he liked her, respected her, admired her. And for all of the rancor of 2008, he emerged wanting her on his team.

He was less enamored of her husband. Obama had long thought Bill Clinton's style of politics was cynical, self-serving, ignoble. Clinton's behavior during the nomination tussle only darkened that view: the railing against Obama's Iraq War record as a "fairy tale"; the rope-line explosion in South Carolina; the comparison of Obama's victory there to Jesse Jackson's in 1988. In Obama's 2006 book, *The Audacity of Hope,* he had postulated that the partisan wars of the nineties were an outgrowth of baby boomer "psychodrama." Watching WJC in 2008, BHO thought, *QED.*

His appointment of Hillary sparked a hint of détente. At first, she hadn't wanted the job, she required persuasion, and both Obama and her husband pressured her hard. That Obama not only made the overture but pursued her so aggressively meant a lot to Bill. Once his wife was ensconced in Foggy Bottom, he returned his attention to his philanthropic labors. He spent scant time licking his wounds. Instead Clinton did what he always did: got back to work.

Which isn't to say Clinton was shy about critiquing Obama's performance in office. On policy, there was little daylight between them. Clinton was for the stimulus and Dodd-Frank, and was mightily impressed by Obama's ability to get a health initiative passed, as he himself had been unable to do. At the same time, he was baffled by Obama's failures at the basic blocking and tackling of politics, his insularity, his alienation of business. Obama got all the hard stuff right, Clinton believed, but didn't do the easy stuff at all.

Clinton had plenty of advice in mind and was desperate to impart it. But for the first two years of Obama's term, the calls that Clinton kept expecting from his successor rarely came. The cold shoulder had little to do with

Obama not liking Clinton; 44 rarely called anyone for advice, so why would it be different with 42? Obama didn't think he *needed* Clinton.

But then came the midterm shellacking—and Clinton's phone began to ring. On December 10, 2010, in the midst of the lame duck, Obama invited him to meet in the Oval Office. The current president had just negotiated the compromise on the Bush tax cuts and was facing the insurrection on the left. After talking for more than an hour, their longest conversation since Obama had taken office, they decided to stage an impromptu press conference, walking out of the Oval with Obama chirping, "Let's go have some fun!"

Their sudden and unscheduled joint appearance in the White House briefing room sent a jolt through the press corps and cable-news control-room producers everywhere. At the podium, Obama explained that he and Clinton had "just had a terrific meeting" and he thought "it might be useful" to "bring the other guy in" to "speak very briefly" about the deal while he went off to attend a Christmas party (Michelle was waiting).

"I feel awkward being here, and now you're going to leave me all by myself," Clinton said, smiling sheepishly—then proceeded to field questions alone for twenty-three minutes after Obama bailed.

Clinton's intercession marked the beginning of the end of the liberal rebellion over tax cuts. But the next day there were stories and cable chatter chiding Obama for abdicating the big stage to the Big Dog. *Classic Washington,* Obama thought. *One minute they tell me to be more like Clinton, the next they trash me for embracing him.*

Obama's people had always harbored more anti-Bill venom than their boss. But after the August inferno, they realized they could no longer let old scores stand in the way of survival. Clinton's name was synonymous with a period of broad prosperity, his capacity to raise money was considerable, and he had special traction with the white working-class and suburban voters (and Jewish ones in Florida) that Obama found hard to reach. With the election on the horizon looking more daunting every day, it was clear that having 42 on board would be less a luxury than a necessity.

The early phases of the reconciliation were riddled with mutual ambivalence. As reticent as the Obamans were about Clinton, they were leerier of Doug Band, his longtime aide-de-camp, who had a reputation as a tenacious (and self-serving) gatekeeper. Drawing the short straw, Gaspard was as-signed to deal with Band, who had a number of ideas about how to break the presidential ice.

Clinton has noticed how frequently the president golfs, Band said, and he's never been asked—even though Obama found time to play a round with New York City mayor Mike Bloomberg. And at some point, you guys need to come up here and sit down and walk Clinton through the race. His mind's not on politics, so you gotta get him to exercise that muscle. Once he does, he's gonna want more.

Obama and Clinton convened on the first tee at Andrews on September 24. Two more different types of duffer would be difficult to imagine: Obama intent on playing the game, getting up and down; Clinton cracking jokes and yakking, taking mulligan after mulligan. Even though ample time had been set aside, they didn't finish eighteen holes. When Obama came off the course, he was asked by an aide how it went.

Obama grimaced and replied, "I like him . . . in doses."

Clinton wasn't swept away either. A week later, at a Little Rock reunion of his campaign troops from 1992, Clinton spent much of the time button-holing people about Obama's deficiencies. You've gotta explain your accom-plishments, boil them down to a card that fits in voters' pockets, Clinton said. Obama doesn't do it. I don't know why. It's not that hard!

In mid-October, Daley invited a passel of former Clinton staffers to a meeting at the White House to offer political advice. When word got around, the push-back from the Obamans was immediate. Invite some non-Clinton people, Daley was told. (*You want a bunch of Carter people? Really?* Daley thought.) Plouffe begged off. Rouse left early. Pfeiffer looked as if he would have rather been receiving a root canal. Obama poked his head in, said hello, and exited at once—though he heard later from Jarrett that the meet-ing had gone well. Daley told Obama, "We should do it again, you should sit in, and tell your staff to stay out."

The Harlem meeting started off more propitiously. Aware of Clinton's voracious appetite for data, the Obamans brought a ton of it: polling, elec-toral scenarios, the works. Sitting across the table from Clinton, Benen-son began putting slides up on a monitor. Soon enough, 42 was on his feet, moving closer to the screen, peppering the Obamans with detailed questions, spouting aperçus and opinions. Drilling down on low-income white voters, he argued that Obama's deficiencies with them could be overcome—especially if their opponent was Romney, with his personal wealth and regressive economic policies. But Obama would have to work it.

These people have been through a rough time, Clinton said. They're going to be looking to blame someone, so you gotta make sure they know you're on the right side on taxes and all that.

Clinton had been watching the Republican debates and was impressed with Romney's skills, but he saw soft spots in his performances. He's good on the first question, bad on the second, Clinton said. You're gonna want to make sure in your debate negotiations to get follow-ups and lots of back-and-forth.

Clinton also offered a blunt warning: "Do not underestimate how much money he's gonna raise." Every bank, every hedge fund in this town will finance his campaign—they hate you guys. But working stiffs would wind up feeling the same way about Romney. "In the end," Clinton said, "they're going to figure out who he is."

Flattery goes a long way in life, and even further with Clinton. And, to a large extent, flattery was what the Harlem sojourn was about. After ninety minutes, Clinton was cheerfully sated—yet unable to resist a parting shot. One thing you fellas should keep in mind, he said, is that running as an incumbent won't be like it was for you last time. Incumbents don't have the media in their hip pocket. This time you'll get to see what a real election is like.

The Obamans bit their lips and held their tongues. Beyond general-purpose ingratiation, they had a specific request to make: that Clinton appear in a long-form video being crafted for the campaign by the Academy Award–winning documentarian Davis Guggenheim. Band had told them repeatedly that Clinton would not agree. He doesn't do videos anymore, Band said. "Don't ask."

The Obamans thanked Clinton profusely for giving them so much time. We're happy to do another briefing whenever you like, they said. Finally, as they packed up their things and headed for the door, Axelrod and Messina, disregarding Band's admonitions, popped the question.

There's one more thing, Mr. President. We're really trying to get this video done. We know you're busy, incredibly busy, but we'd really appreciate it if you'd give us a little bit of time and we could get some footage of you.

"Absolutely," Clinton said. "Love to."

The Obamans would soon come to understand that an easy yes from Clinton always had strings attached. But for now they were triumphant. From LaGuardia, they headed back to Washington for another strategy meeting with Obama the next day. None expected the fury that would face them in the morning.

O ABMA EXHALED HEAVILY WHEN he learned the news. He was stunned, then angry, then disappointed, then hurt. "I can't believe this," Obama said. "This is exactly what I said couldn't happen."

Obama was in the Oval Office early that Thursday, November 10—and being told that his list had leaked. The details came from Plouffe and Messina, who had learned that two authors writing a book on the 2012 campaign knew all about the extraordinary session six weeks earlier; they had the whole roster of Obama's regrets in copious detail.

"How could someone do this to me?" Obama asked. "If I can't be honest with you people, how can we keep having these meetings?"

"Well, that's the issue," Plouffe replied, reminding Obama of the warning he'd been given at the outset. "I think we obviously can't."

The immediate problem was that the next session was scheduled to start in a few minutes, at 10:00 a.m. The group was assembling in the Roosevelt Room, while Obama was doing a slow burn across the hall. Maybe they should just cancel the thing, shut it down? No, Obama said. I want to go in there and say my piece.

He walked into the room looking stern, asked Messina to explain to every one what had occurred—and then laid into his team.

When we started having these meetings, Obama said, I told you that I trusted everyone in this room. But now somebody has betrayed that trust. The fact is, I can't trust anybody here anymore. I was cautioned about there being too many people in the meetings. But I thought we were all in the trenches together and that all of you should be included on every part of this journey. I've found these meetings helpful and productive, because everybody here has been able to speak openly. But I no longer feel I can do that. So unless and until the person who did this comes to me, tells me they did this, and apologizes, these meetings are over. I'm gonna be in the Oval Office. When somebody is ready to come forward and own up to this, you know where to find me.

With that, Obama stood up and walked out the door, leaving a crashing silence behind him.

Everyone in the room had seen the president upset before. The Mr. Cool caricature was largely accurate, but Obama had a temper. No one had experienced anything like this, though—the combination of bone-chilling iciness and simmering fury, the sense that he felt wounded, even violated, by his own people. For what seemed an eternity, they stared at their shoes. And then the voice of Biden broke the hush.

That guy is the most amazing guy, the VP said, with evident emotion. It's been a privilege for me to serve under him. I would throw myself in front of a bus for him if he asked me to do it. This guy sticks up for everybody in this room. You make mistakes, he sticks up for you. He doesn't always tell you to your face, but when he's out talking to other people, he's incredibly proud of you. He's always got our back. And we have to have his back. To violate his trust this way is a serious, serious blow. It's unconscionable—just unconscionable.

Obama had spoken for maybe four minutes. Biden's soliloquy lasted twice that long. When he ran out of steam, he pushed back from the table and stomped out of the room, too.

For the next two hours, the remaining Obamans sat there shell-shocked, sorting through the rubble of the POTUS-VPOTUS double walkout. A discussion ensued about what had now become an even more pressing topic than before: how to subdue the plague of books and authors. Gibbs, himself mired in controversy over the story about him in the upcoming Kantor tome, let fly with a red-faced tirade in which the operative word was "fucking." ("This is fucking unprecedented" . . . "It's fucking bullshit" . . . "He fucking doesn't deserve this" . . . "We can't fucking win this election if we can't fucking trust each other, and we're letting him fucking down.") Others angrily insisted that the question of books was a side issue. Someone stuck a knife in the president's back; he wanted the perpetrator to come forward. And we're talking about these process questions? Say what?

Obama, meanwhile, returned to the Oval to wait for a confessor to arrive—a wait that would turn out to be interminable. Surely Plouffe was right that the strategy meetings would need to be shrunken down, but that was merely falling action. Obama had just come through the worst political stretch he had ever suffered. Now he was hurtling into the campaign, the greatest challenge of his life. He needed help, he needed focus, he needed the team to right the ship, set their course, and sail into 2012. Instead he felt like he was splashing around in a sea of drama, with no land in sight.

Obama had no time to brood; his schedule was always packed. From the tsuris of the Roosevelt Room, he would move on to a White House tour for "wounded warriors," then to lunch with his cabinet secretaries—and then to an indignity so fitting and ironic it made his head spin. At 2:55 p.m. he had a meeting in the Oval Office. The meeting was with David Maraniss. For a fucking book interview.

4

THE UNCLE JOE PROBLEM

DALEY DIDN'T FOLLOW BIDEN out the door that day, but in spirit he was right there with him. The chief of staff and the vice president were a pair of plump green peas in a pod: both Irish Catholic sexagenarians with old-school tastes, old-school tendencies, and old-school values. In the hypermodern Obama White House, they often seemed the odd men out—which in the late fall of 2011 was creating yet another set of headaches for Obama.

Biden and Daley talked all the time about their alienation from their colleagues. They didn't use the term "alienation," though—that was a ten-cent word. The COS's office was across the hall from the VP's, and Daley would often go in there and close the door and the two of them would let loose. Plouffe they considered as sharp as a scalpel but just as sterile, a guy incapable of glad-hand bullshitting, which was Joe and Bill's avocation. They cackled about the fact that Emanuel referred to Jarrett and Rouse as Uday and Qusay, after Saddam Hussein's power-mad sons, and over the nickname others had bestowed on Jarrett: the Night Stalker, for the way she would visit the Obamas in the residence after hours and eviscerate her rivals. They admired the president, but marveled at his lack of bonhomie. ("He doesn't even know how to swear right," Biden complained.) They were like the gray-haired hecklers in the balcony on *The Muppet Show,* the Statler and Waldorf of the White House.

What set Biden and Daley apart was about more than personalities, however. It was also about their approach to politics, which centered around the New Deal coalition and its attendant geography: blue-collar voters, Catholics, ethnic whites, and senior citizens in places like Ohio, Pennsylvania, and Wisconsin. The Obamans cared about those people and places but were more intently focused on the coalition that had elected their man: African Americans, Latinos, college-educated whites (especially single women), and young voters in new swing states such as Colorado and Virginia. The tension between these views bubbled beneath the surface throughout Obama's term, with implications for the reelect. And in November, the conflict reached a boil over a potentially scalding issue: contraception.

The source of the controversy, as with so many others, was the Affordable Care Act. Under the law, insurers were compelled to offer "preventive health services" to women for free, but Congress had left it to the Department of Health and Human Services to determine which benefits to include. In August 2011, HHS secretary Kathleen Sebelius—with the backing of Jarrett, Michelle's chief of staff, and several other female White House aides—issued interim rules saying that contraceptives would be covered. While the agency provided an exemption for "religious employers," it was so narrow that it largely left out Catholic hospitals, universities, and other church-affiliated institutions.

Dozens of Catholic groups cried foul. Father John Jenkins, the president of Notre Dame, who had invited Obama to give the commencement address at the school in 2009 over the objections of many Catholic bishops, wrote the president a letter contending that the rule would violate religious freedom. As the initial uproar made its way into the press, some of the administration's prominent Catholics began to fret. "Now we're fighting the Catholics?" defense secretary Leon Panetta complained to Daley by phone. "What's going on here?"

Biden and Daley objected to the policy, thinking the religious exemption should be broadened. And they worried about the political fallout from getting crosswise with Catholic voters and the church hierarchy, already up in arms over the administration's decision to no longer support the Defense of Marriage Act—which Archbishop Timothy Dolan of New York declared could "precipitate a national conflict between church and state of enormous proportions and to the detriment of both institutions."

Dolan was a towering figure in the church, chair of the U.S. Conference of Catholic Bishops, and a cagey political operator. Biden knew him well. In early November, with Dolan planning to be in town ahead of the conference's annual plenary, the VP slipped the archbishop's name onto Obama's schedule—without alerting the White House staff.

Obama walked into the meeting with little preparation, believing it would be about a range of issues—then found himself cornered on contraception. He hadn't analyzed the arguments surrounding the exemption in detail, let alone reached a conclusion. On top of that, he was sympathetic to the church's position. Now on the spot, feeling ambushed, Obama edged out over the tips of his skis, telling Dolan he would seek a solution agreeable to both sides.

That was all the pink-cheeked prelate needed to box Obama in. On November 14, Dolan told reporters at the plenary about the meeting, describing it as "extraordinarily friendly" and adding that Obama had been "very sensitive" to church concerns over the contraceptive mandate. "He was very ardent in his desire to assure me that this is something he will look long and hard at. And I left there feeling a bit more at peace about this issue than when I entered."

The signal that the White House was considering widening the exemption touched off a tizzy. With Obama having left on a trip to Asia, congressional Democrats burned up the phone lines on conference calls with Rouse and Jarrett, telling them it was crazy for a pro-choice president to be wavering this way. In a tense meeting with Daley, Planned Parenthood president Cecile Richards threatened that the group would run ads against Obama if he abandoned Sebelius's original plan.

When the president returned from abroad just before Thanksgiving, he found the issue front and center, and temperatures running hot. The women's caucus, led by Jarrett, accused Biden and Daley of sandbagging Obama with the Dolan meeting, and argued that women's health should be the only priority regarding the exemption. Daley, Biden, and Biden's staff pushed back hard. We'll lose Ohio, Pennsylvania, the Catholic vote, and the election, they blustered. Axelrod, Messina, and Plouffe thought that the old-timers were out of their minds. Biden and Daley had no data to back up the scare talk—just instinct, pure gut. And in their obsession with the Catholic vote, they were ignoring the constituency that really mattered to Obama's prospects: unmarried women, of whom the vast majority, including Catholics, favored the idea of contraceptives being included in health care plans.

Obama was comprehensively pissed off about being put in a no-win position. If he broadened the exemption now, the women's groups would accuse him of caving to the bishops, providing fresh fuel for the weakness meme. If he stuck with the narrow exemption, Catholic leaders would believe, with justification, that he misled Dolan—and there were few things the president liked less than having his veracity challenged. Obama pressed his people to find a middle path, something like the rule in effect in Hawaii, where the cost of contraceptives was shifted to insurance companies. But Sebelius and HHS maintained that the federal government didn't have the authority to impose an Aloha State–style compromise.

Biden didn't like where this was headed. Daley, who insisted he'd had nothing to do with the Dolan meeting, liked it even less. The long knives were out for the chief of staff, and he knew it.

In almost every way, Daley's tenure had been a bust. When he took the job, Obama had informed him that his hiring and firing authority would be limited. ("Oh, you're fucked," Panetta assured Daley.) One of Daley's main roles was supposed to have been that of economic spokesman on the Sunday shows. But after he did a couple, Plouffe and Pfeiffer halted his bookings. (He tested poorly with their focus groups.) When Daley reduced the size of meetings with Obama and limited their access, the staff circumvented his roadblocks. Behind his back, they derided him as an officious dinosaur, mocking him for wanting to be called "chief." In late October, his frustrations swelling, Daley gave a cringe-inducing interview to Politico, in which he referred to Obama's time in office as "ungodly" and said that the president couldn't fathom why his approval ratings were as high as 44 percent. Not long after that, he was effectively demoted, with Rouse taking over day-to-day management of the White House and Daley left to handle . . . what?

We need to be more streamlined, Obama explained. You'll be the chairman and Pete will be the chief operating officer.

Fine, Daley thought. *You're the boss. Do what you want.*

From the day that Daley took the chief of staff job, one fear ran through his mind: *What if the wedding cake is already baked, and I'm just the little plastic groom being put on top?* Now, nearly a year later, there was no avoiding the fact that he was knee-deep in icing.

Biden had warned Daley from the outset about the ferocious insularity of Obamaworld. He felt sorry for his pal Bill. "You're either on the way up or you're on the way down" was a favorite Biden adage, and Daley was clearly not ascendant. But the truth was, the VP had his own status anxieties in the autumn of 2011—not least that he too was little more than an ornament on a fancy piece of pastry.

O NE WEEKDAY THAT NOVEMBER, Biden summoned his inner circle to his Washington residence at the U.S. Naval Observatory, on Massachusetts Avenue. The Biden Strategy Group, as it was dubbed by one of its members, consisted of a handful of outside advisers who'd been with Joe forever, a few folks from his vice-presidential staff, his sons, Beau and Hunter, and his sister, Valerie. The group had convened sporadically over the past three years, neither exactly in secret nor entirely in the open. But never before had they gathered to discuss what was on today's agenda: the campaign that lay ahead—and the one that might come after that.

There were coffee and rolls on the dining room table and a lot on Biden's mind. The stories in the press about the possibility of his being replaced on the ticket by Hillary Clinton were heating up again, making Joe slightly mental. But what was eating at him even more was the way he was being neglected by the Obamans. The new year was just around the corner, and no one had bothered to lay out his campaign role and responsibilities. Biden was raring to hit the hustings, rile up the base, hassle the Republicans. He knew that the president would be the star of the reelect, but he wanted it to be a joint production: Obama-Biden 2012. The way things were shaping up, however, Biden worried that it was going to be a solo act: The Barack Obama Show.

That was how it had been four years earlier, as Biden well remembered. By historical standards, he had been selected as Obama's running mate very late, at the end of August. With his working-class appeal, foreign policy credentials, and thirty-six years in the Senate, Biden was a smart pick for Obama. But the truth was that the Davids would have preferred their boss not to have an understudy at all. On a glide path to history, they quailed at having to introduce an unpredictable variable. For the next two months, Biden and Obama rarely stumped together and barely spoke by phone, with the former shut out of Chicago's nightly conference calls with the latter. Apart from his debate with Sarah Palin, Biden's part in the 2008 fall campaign was less that of a supporting actor than of a lowly extra.

All this had an effect on Biden as he stepped into the vice presidency. Unlike Gore, who had joined the 1992 Democratic ticket when Clinton was in third place and spent much of the summer bus-touring and bonding with his new buddy, Biden felt little political complicity in Obama's victory or human connection between them. He had nurtured plenty of doubts about accepting the number-two slot, and they had not abated by Inauguration Day. "This is what I should be doing," he told his chief of staff, Ron Klain. "But I'm not sure I'm going to be as happy as vice president as I was in the Senate."

Things were rocky between him and Obama right out of the chute. During the campaign, the nominee had been frustrated by his running mate's routine gaffes. ("How many times is Biden going to say something stupid," Obama growled.) The day after the inauguration, when Biden ribbed Chief Justice John Roberts for botching the oath of office, Obama threw a sharp STFU look at the VP. At a House Democratic Caucus retreat that February, Biden remarked about the implementation of the stimulus, "If we do everything right . . . there's still a 30 percent chance we're gonna get it wrong." Asked about the comment later by a reporter, Obama replied snidely, "I don't remember exactly what Joe was referring to. Not surprisingly."

The crack upset Biden more than he let on. Joe was perfectly aware of the widespread caricature of him as a clownish gasbag. He understood that the image was largely self-inflicted but hated it all the same, and he was intensely concerned that being vice president would only exacerbate the problem. Biden even had a name for the trap that he was determined to avoid:

the Uncle Joe Syndrome, which would leave him looking not only buffoon-
ish but irrelevant.

Days later, at one of the first of what would be their weekly private
lunches, Biden dove right in and raised the issue with his boss. Mr. President, I've got your back and you gotta have my back, he said. I'm in this with
you. And it doesn't do you any good for the world to be laughing at me. I can
get a lot of work done for you. But people have to know that you have confidence in me.

Obama apologized, told Biden that what he'd said had come out wrong,
that there would be no mistaking his degree of faith in Joe—considering the
heaping pile of responsibilities he was about to put on the vice-presidential
plate.

The substantive portfolio mattered a great deal to Biden; it was another
way of warding off Uncle Joe. In signing on with Obama, Biden had insisted
on an agreement that he would be the last person with the president's ear on
every major policy decision. Not only did Obama honor that, but he offered
Biden carte blanche to attend any Oval Office meeting and assigned him
two crucial pieces of business in that first year: the stimulus and the draw-
down of American forces in Iraq.

Obama valued Biden's advice, especially on foreign policy, and his dealmaking savvy on the Hill. And Biden was blown away by Obama's brain-
power and backbone. Before they took office, Biden had considered himself
more qualified to be president than Obama. Soon he no longer did. After
one economic conference call led by the president, a flabbergasted Biden
told an aide, "The kind of decisions he made, the way he absorbed this
stuff—I couldn't have done that."

Biden wasn't surprised about the mutual professional esteem. What he
hadn't anticipated was the personal chemistry that flowered between them.
Biden liked to tell the story of how, on election night, after he and Obama
climbed down from the stage in Grant Park, they had shared a moment with
Biden's ninety-one-year-old mother, Jean. Taking Obama's hand, Jean
cooed, "Honey, come here, it's going to be okay," and then grabbed her son's
and offered him reassurance, too: "Joey, he's going to be your friend." Biden
smiled—*Love you, Mom*—but wasn't remotely sure she was right. Stylisti-

cally and temperamentally, after all, he and Obama were chalk and Camembert.

It was the family thing that made the flavors rhyme. Family meant the world to Joe, and also to Barack. Their wives hit it off, with Jill Biden teaming up with Michelle on her military-families work. Sasha Obama went to school at Sidwell Friends with Biden's granddaughter Maisy, where they both played basketball—and the president delighted in coaching them and hanging out with his VP at their games. And then there was Beau's stroke, which drew Biden and Obama closer than before.

When Biden learned that his eldest son, the forty-one-year-old attorney general of Delaware, had been rushed to the hospital in the spring of 2010, he was panicked and disconsolate. Since the death of his first wife and infant daughter in a 1972 car crash, Biden had maintained a close bond with his two sons, who survived the accident, and always lived in fear of the next mortal phone call. The stroke was publicly described as minor, but in fact was life-threatening. There were initial questions about how full his recovery would be. When the shaken vice president returned to the White House once Beau was out of the woods, Obama came sprinting down the hall to embrace him. Biden would tell this story to anyone who would listen, always stressing the same takeaway: "People say this guy Obama is lacking in emotion—don't buy it."

The truth was, Biden discerned a lot of Beau in Obama. *They're cool, they're cerebral, they keep their passions in check—they're the modern politician,* he thought. And while Biden père was none of those things, he did see one similarity between himself and the president: *He doesn't pretend to be what he's not, and I don't pretend to be what I'm not.*

Obama prized Biden's lack of phoniness, for sure. But he was even more impressed by Biden's loyalty—the fact that, as promised, he always had Obama's back. During the lame-duck session, when Joe was on the Hill selling the tax-cut deal to a roomful of House Democrats, New York congressman Anthony Weiner took a shot at Obama. The VP upbraided him so forcefully and profanely that he earned a standing ovation. A few months later, Biden did something similar in the White House to Netanyahu. The stories always got back to Obama, who relished them.

Not that Obama ever stopped cringing at Biden's persistent indiscipline or sporadic outright blunders. But he came to accept them as part and parcel of Joe being Joe. When Biden would rabbit on for too long in a meeting, Obama no longer got agitated the way he used to—and instead would just reach over and put his hand on Biden's shoulder. Obama even found himself adopting some of Joe's (countless) folksy aphorisms. During the debt-ceiling brouhaha, Obama said that his guiding principle was a Biden mantra: "Don't die on a small cross."

Obama was as gobsmacked as Biden was at the way their comradeship had blossomed. At one of their weekly lunches in 2011, Obama announced, "You know, I'm surprised—we've become friends."

To which Biden cheekily replied: "*You're* fucking surprised?!"

A ND YET FOR ALL the personal peachiness between them, Biden's insecurities about 2012 continued to fester. In Joe's mind, it shouldn't have been so. For him, the personal and the political were inextricably entwined—but for Obama they were at once separable and separate. And in the political arena, the president was guided by the members of his brain trust, who liked Biden fine but still viewed him as a sideshow.

For the first two years, the situation was manageable. Axelrod and Emanuel had soft spots for Biden. Klain, who had solid West Wing relationships, served as an easement for Biden into Obamaworld and an emollient when his feelings were bruised. But even then, Biden often felt ignored when it came to the White House's political strategy and tactics.

Biden fancied himself a natural politician, on the order of Bill Clinton and Ronald Reagan, with a fingertip feel for voters and what swayed them. In the run-up to the midterms, Biden argued that it was foolish to try to frame the election as anything but what it plainly was: a referendum on the administration's performance. What was needed, therefore, was a full-throated defense of Obama's record—of the stimulus, the Detroit bailout, and even health care.

What Biden wanted was to draft a pamphlet (yes, a pamphlet) laying out the case, print up millions (yes, millions) of copies, and have them sent to targeted voters across the country. In this cause, he enlisted a potent ally:

Bill Clinton. Soon enough, the two of them were talking daily by phone, faxing drafts back and forth, refining the argument, marshaling the data. Here's the latest version from Clinton, Biden would tell Klain. You think it's good? I think it's good. Well, maybe one more tweak.

When Biden was finally satisfied, he raised the concept with Obama, who told him, "Work with Axe." But Axelrod's affection for Biden did not extend to this cockamamie plan. (*A brochure is gonna change the election?* he thought. *Right.*) But Biden wouldn't desist, pressing the matter until Axelrod snapped, "We're not printing a couple million of *anything* and dropping it at people's houses—*okay*?"

The fall of 2010 also brought the first flotation of the rumor that Hillary might take Biden's job, with him assuming hers at Foggy Bottom in the bargain. Giving the gossip a dash of credibility and a hefty dose of buzz was that it was first conveyed by Bob Woodward, who declared flatly on CNN that the idea was "on the table."

The White House immediately denied that any such notion was on any table (or any bench, bureau, or buffet). And Biden didn't credit the speculation for a minute. But as the JRB-HRC swap rumor popped up again and again all through 2011, it preyed on him nonetheless. Biden and his people all believed that the hearsay was emanating from Hillary's orbit—not from her personally, but from her staff, outside advisers, or the denizens of Greater Clintonia. It was clearly designed to undermine the president (Obama is failing), undercut Biden (he isn't helping), and elevate Hillary (only she can save the day). But Biden also found the White House's reaction annoying. Sure, they denied the story, but they never took the extra step and explained that no swap was needed because the vice president was, well, so awesome. And by not doing so, Biden believed, they were feeding the Uncle Joe Syndrome.

By then, Axelrod, Emanuel, and Klain had all left the White House. And while Axe was still a big player in Chicago, Biden increasingly was left to the less tender mercies of Plouffe and Messina, who cast a gimlet eye and imposed a heavy hand on his maneuvers.

Midway through the year, Biden decided he wanted to hire a new counselor to be his de facto campaign chief of staff. His choice for the job was Kevin Sheekey, a raffish New York operative who had helped turn Mike

Bloomberg into a political force—and had been the maestro orchestrating the mayor's 2008 dabblings with an independent presidential bid. Though Biden had run for president twice, in 1988 and 2008, the first effort had ended with a plagiarism scandal before any ballots were cast and the second after he claimed just 1 percent of the vote in Iowa. Biden's only experience with a national campaign were those two months as Obama's running mate, when he basically did what he was told and nothing more. The challenge in 2012 would be greater, and with Sheekey on board, Biden believed, he would be prepared to meet it.

The Obamans objected strongly to Sheekey, however. They considered him a leaker, a self-promoter, not a team player. Which is to say they were threatened by his mojo and the prospect that he would vivify Biden's shop. When the vice president told Obama what he was planning to do, the president shut him down. I've heard some things that make me think that Kevin is not the right fit, he said—and that ended the matter.

Thus did Biden find himself in limbo that November morning when his outside strategy group assembled at NAVOBS around his dining table. The primary goal, of course, was to help Obama win reelection. But Biden also wanted to think about how, in that context, he could enhance his own political standing.

The question of 2016 hovered over the discussion. When Biden became Obama's number two, the premise had been that he was a pick in the mold of Dick Cheney: he would serve Obama free of ulterior motives or longer-range ambitions. Biden was then already sixty-six years old, seven years older than Cheney had been when he signed on with Bush. But almost as soon as he assumed office, his people put out the word that "we're not ruling anything in or out" about 2016, as Jay Carney, then Biden's flack, told *The New York Times*. And from that moment forward, Bidenland had kept on subtly stoking the embers.

In part, the 2016 whispers were merely an attempt to maintain Biden's currency and leverage—a home cure for the Uncle Joe Syndrome. But Biden also genuinely wanted to keep the option open, he told the strategy group. I haven't made any decision, he said. Who knows how I'll feel four years from now? But right now I feel great. In better shape than ever. People want me to say I'm not gonna run. I'm not gonna say that—and maybe I *will* run.

Behind Biden's bravado, there was massive insecurity. He had been a national figure for four decades: Joseph Robinette Biden Jr., former chairman of the Senate Foreign Relations Committee and the Senate Judiciary Committee. But, at bottom, he remained a parochial politician: Regular Joe, Amtrak Joe, Delaware Joe. He had no political organization. He had no fund-raising operation. Hailing from a puny state and having presided over two Senate committees with no taxing or spending authority (and thus lacking lobbyists or corporations swarming around them and currying his favor), he had no donor base. Standing in the shadow of the most prodigious political and fund-raising apparatus the Democratic Party had ever seen, he felt like a stranger to it, as if he'd walked into an opulent wedding where he knew no one.

Biden wanted to expand his network. Needed to, really. While he was campaigning for Obama, he thought he should meet some new people, stroke some donors, strike up some fresh relationships. Biden had a trip scheduled in January out to San Francisco and Los Angeles, where he would be talking about policy with some executives and raising money for Obama. Maybe they ought to tack on a meal or two with Silicon Valley and Hollywood bigwigs so Biden could broaden his horizons. He'd be out there anyway. It was, in a phrase Biden often used, a "collision of conscience and convenience."

But Plouffe and Messina had ears everywhere, and when they heard about the strategy-group meeting and the California plan, they hit the ceiling. To them, there was only one relevant question about any political activity: Did it benefit Barack Obama? And the answers regarding Biden scheming around 2016 and holding separate meetings with donors were both emphatically no.

Plouffe went to Biden and applied a polite but forceful dressing-down. "If you want to have meetings about your stump speech and how to help the president, great," Plouffe told him. But you can't be out there talking about some future election. And you can't be running bootleg meetings with donors. "We can't have side deals," he said.

Biden, chastened, apologized to Plouffe, then got all defensive with Daley.

What are they upset about? Biden wailed. This is crazy! I'm doing everything they ask. I'm with the program. I've been loyal—I've been *the most* loyal. Jesus Christ!

Daley tried to calm Joe down. He hated to see him all worked up, which was why he didn't tell Biden about the other things. In the aftermath of the leaking of list and the refusal of the leaker (or leakers) to come forward, Obama had decided to go along with Plouffe's recommendation that they shrink the reelection strategy meetings down to a handful of people—and Biden wasn't one of them.

But that was the least of what Daley was keeping from Biden. The more explosive details—nuclear, actually—were that the top echelon of Obama-world had in fact been discussing the wisdom of replacing Biden with Hill-ary; that, more than discussing it, they had been exploring it, furtively and obliquely, in the campaign's polling and focus groups; and that Daley him-self had been the most vocal exponent of looking into the merits of the idea.

Daley had no innate desire to see his friend dumped from the ticket, nor did the Davids and Messina—the tiny coterie of Obamans involved in the discussions. And all of them suspected that even the notion of a swap might be a nonstarter with Obama. But the president's political difficulties were severe, and plenty of sensible Democrats were arguing that switching in Hillary could be a game changer. To not perform due diligence on the op-tion, the Obamans believed, would be a dereliction of duty. They polled and focus-grouped every topic under the sun. Testing this one might have seemed hard-hearted, but refusing to do so out of affection for Joe would have been soft-headed—which in Obamaworld was the far more grievous crime.

When the research came back near the end of the year, it suggested that adding Clinton to the ticket wouldn't materially improve Obama's odds. Biden had dodged a bullet he never saw coming—and never would know anything about, if the Obamans could keep a secret.

What Biden could see, though, was that the campaign was turning his way in one respect, at least. From the start of the administration, the VP had advocated that the White House adopt a more populist stance on the economy. And he believed it even more strongly now, with Occupy Wall Street raging in Lower Manhattan and hundreds of other places around the country. Populism had never been a language in which Obama was fluent—but all of a sudden, the president was speaking in tongues.

OSAWATOMIE, KANSAS, was a dust-speck town sixty-one miles southwest of Kansas City. It had a population of 4,477 and a rich but slight political history as a Jayhawker stronghold in the Civil War. In 1910, Teddy Roosevelt went there for the dedication of a park to abolitionist John Brown, delivering a storied speech in favor of a progressive platform that he called the "New Nationalism." A hundred and one years later, Obama arrived to give an oration, less stirringly titled "Remarks by the President on the Economy in Osawatomie, Kansas."

Like Biden, Obama had taken note of the Occupy movement when it sprang up in September and pushed the topic of income inequality front and center. Obama decided he wanted to give a speech about that. The subject was important, he told his team, and he had things to say. Some of his advisers were less than overjoyed. They worried he would have no solutions to offer for the problem he was raising. They feared he'd get too close to the Occupy fire and come back with his eyebrows singed. But Obama was insistent: I'm giving this speech.

Axelrod argued that the address could be made bigger and broader, incorporating themes they had talked about in the first strategy meeting in the State Dining Room: the contest of economic values, the fight for the middle class. Obama agreed. Over his career he had given two economic speeches that he considered touchstones, the first at Knox College in 2005, on the disruptions caused by globalization, the second at the Nasdaq, in New York, in 2007, on the perils of Wall Street run amok. He told Favreau he was aiming for something like that again.

I want to frame what the election is going to be about, Obama said. A choice between a belief that there are things we can do as a country to combat the forces that have left a lot of workers dislocated and struggling—and a belief on the other side that we should let everybody fend for themselves and play by their own rules.

It was Favreau's assistant who came up with Osawatomie. Between the

Roosevelt connection and the fact that Obama's mother was from Kansas, she thought it might be a choice venue. When Favreau brought the suggestion to the president, he lit up. "Great, I love the Nationalism speech," he said. "It's pretty far out there—the most radical speech Teddy Roosevelt ever gave."

Obama's address wasn't as piping as TR's, but it had plenty of Tabasco in it. Onstage in the Osawatomie High School gym, the president homed in on the issue of inequality that had so animated him initially. Noting that the average income of the top 1 percent—the marker made totemic by Occupy—had risen 250 percent over the years, to $1.2 million, while everyone else treaded water, he argued that "for most Americans, the basic bargain that made this country great has eroded." Obama pounded on the "breathtaking greed" of Wall Street, on "insurance companies that jacked up people's premiums with impunity and denied care to patients who were sick, [and] mortgage lenders that tricked families into buying homes they couldn't afford." Contrasting Republican "you're-on-your-own economics" with his philosophy, which was aimed at creating an "economy that's built to last," Obama said, "This is not just another political debate. This is the defining issue of our time. This is a make-or-break moment for the middle class." And: "This isn't about class warfare. This is about the nation's welfare."

The Osawatomie address received only modest attention from the press, but Obama believed he had scored. Though his people had worried about turning out a crowd in a tiny town in a scarlet-red state, the atmosphere in the gym was electric. And while Obama, in an hour-long speech of more than six thousand words, never once uttered Mitt Romney's name, the themes he laid out were tailor-made for a campaign against him—a man whose calling card was having banked hundreds of millions of dollars at a private equity firm that could be painted as epitomizing much of what Obama decried in Kansas.

To the extent that Obama's trip garnered coverage, it was portrayed as part of his ongoing crusade to win the payroll tax cut extension—which he did indeed mention in the speech. ("If we don't do that, 160 million Americans, including most of the people here, will see their taxes go up by an average of $1,000 starting in January, and it would badly weaken our recovery.") The president had now been bludgeoning Republicans on the issue for three solid months. Boehner and McConnell were tied in knots, squabbling with their own caucuses, trying to figure out what kinds of budgetary offsets they should demand in return.

This was a trap that Sperling had set a year earlier, during the lame duck. Rather than push for a two-year extension then, he had argued for rolling the dollars from both years into one. That way, the economy would receive a bigger immediate boost—and a year later, especially if growth was still slow, Republicans would find it politically difficult not to vote in favor of another extension. Some on Obama's political team were hoping that they would do just that, giving the president the upper hand on a tax issue for the campaign. But Sperling was adamant that it was worth trading almost anything to get a deal. With the congressional supercommittee having failed to strike a deficit compromise by its Thanksgiving deadline, business confidence was as shaky as ever. And the payroll tax cut extension would be the last chance to significantly goose the economy again before Election Day.

Back in Washington, Obama affirmed to his staff privately what he had said publicly: he would demand that Congress stay in town until the issue was resolved—through Christmas, if need be. As the holiday approached, the Senate passed a two-month extension, but the House was in disarray. On Sunday morning, December 18, Boehner appeared on *Meet the Press* and said, "Well, it's pretty clear that I and our members oppose the Senate bill—it's only for two months. How can you do tax policy for two months?"

The Obamans were over the moon at the sight of the most powerful Republican in the country announcing his opposition to a tax cut. *The Wall Street Journal* noted the insanity of the speaker's stance in an editorial headlined THE GOP'S PAYROLL TAX FIASCO, which pummeled the party's leaders for having "somehow managed the remarkable feat of being blamed for opposing a one-year extension of a tax holiday that they are surely going to pass."

Boehner called Obama to try and negotiate. Obama was having none of it. Like the *Journal,* he was confident not only that Boehner would cave now but that, after the new year, the politics of tax cutting would make it all but inevitable that the White House would ultimately get the full-year extension through.

The next day, December 23, the House gave the president his victory. A year earlier, Obama had prevailed in the lame duck by forging bipartisan compromise. Now he had won through partisan confrontation, as his new posture of playing the outside game bore its first fruit. In the White House briefing room, Obama told reporters, "This is some good news, just in the nick of time for the holidays." Michelle and the girls were already over in Hawaii. He was eager to get there, too. Cocking a slight smile, he brought the political year to a close with a crisp "Aloha."

OBAMA GLANCED AT HIS schedule and was puzzled by an item on it: a 2:30 p.m. meeting with Dunn, Carney, Daley, Pfeiffer, and Plouffe to talk about some book. It was Tuesday, January 3, 2012, and the president was just off the plane back from Honolulu.

"What is this book?" Obama asked Pfeiffer. "What is this meeting?"

The book was Jodi Kantor's *The Obamas,* due to be published the following Tuesday, and the meeting was to brief Obama on the press shop's response strategy. The White House had obtained an early copy through sub-rosa channels and combed through it looking for items that were embarrassing, controversial, newsworthy, or all three. Happily for them, there wasn't much there—except for the "Then fuck her, too" anecdote involving Robert, Michelle, and Valerie.

It had long been a mystery in the West Wing as to whether either Obama knew about the incident. Some believed that Jarrett had tripped over herself to tell one or both of the first couple; others thought she had held her tongue. In any case, it now fell to Dunn, who had been brought in to deal with the Kantor book because of her strong relationship with Michelle, to fill in the Obamas—and see how the cookie crumbled.

Obama didn't seem especially perturbed when Dunn told him the Gibbs story. It was no secret to him that Robert had scratchy relationships with his wife and Valerie. "I guess that's going to be interesting to the press" was pretty much all Obama said. (Not long after, the former press secretary arranged a meeting with the president and apologized for cursing out his wife, though not for labeling Jarrett a scheming liar.)

A different tidbit in the book grated on the president more, however—a story about his and Michelle's vacation to Martha's Vineyard in the summer of 2010. They had been sitting on a deserted beach with two old friends, Allison and Susan Davis, when Allison reached over to fold some towels. Obama told her that his staff would handle that. "When I leave office, there are only two things I want," he said, according to Kantor's account. "I want a plane and I want a valet."

Obama, still rankled about Dunn's quotes about the White House's boys' club mentality in *Confidence Men,* stared at Anita. "Why do people who claim to care about me say really stupid things to book authors?" he asked pointedly.

Michelle, briefed separately by Dunn, seemed even less ruffled by the Gibbs story than her husband. "Oh, you know Robert, he says things," she said.

But Michelle was irritated with Kantor, who the White House felt had conveyed the impression that she had a closer relationship with the first lady than was the case. The day after *The Obamas* was published, Michelle did an interview with Gayle King of CBS News, in which she uncorked the kind of spiky comments that her aides believed were a thing of her distant past. "Who can write about how I feel? Who? What third person can tell me how I feel?" she said of Kantor. She then addressed the picture of herself in the book as a source of White House friction. "That's been an image people have tried to paint of me since, you know, the day Barack announced, that I'm some angry black woman."

Under normal circumstances, Daley would have grimaced; the first lady dredging up a racially loaded stereotype for no apparent reason was bound to kick up dust (and, self-defeatingly, generate publicity for the book). But none of this was Daley's problem anymore. On January 5, he had tendered his resignation. The final straw for him was an internal flap over the selection of a new domestic-policy adviser. Daley wanted an A-list name: former *Time* managing editor and Steve Jobs biographer Walter Isaacson or former Gates Foundation chief Patty Stonesifer. But he was overruled peremptorily by Jarrett and Rouse. And with that, Daley had had enough.

So had Obama. Within three months of Daley's appointment, the president could tell that it wasn't working, that he hadn't found the silver bullet. By the fall, Plouffe, reflecting a consensus in the building, was urging Obama to let Daley go. "It's your call, but you can't make a change six months from now." The populist shift in the president's posture—from kissing business's ass to kicking it in the teeth—only made Daley's continued presence more untenable. And the chief of staff had done nothing to improve relations with Congress. His replacement would be OMB head and policy maven Jack Lew, who would focus on governing and have almost nothing to do with the reelect, thus enhancing Plouffe's already estimable degree of power.

With Daley on his way out the door, Obama turned to deal with Biden. At one of their weekly lunches in January, Joe addressed the internal uproar over his strategy-group meeting, the California trip, and his alleged designs on 2016—all of which Obama had heard about in detail from the Davids.

This has all been a big misunderstanding, Biden said. I'd never do anything—anything—to jeopardize our chances of being reelected. Secondly, I'm not holding secret meetings. Any meeting I ever have on any topic, Axe and Plouffe are more than welcome. But here's the thing. In 2008, when I joined the campaign, I was an invited guest at your party. This time it's different. I'm the vice president. I've been working shoulder to shoulder with you for three years, living it every day. This isn't your campaign anymore, Mr. President. This has to be *our* campaign. I need to be more involved. I want to be your partner—the junior partner, but your partner.

Look, Joe, Obama replied. It's important people not think you have a separate agenda. People need to see us as one team. That's good for me, it's good for you. I accept that you didn't mean to do anything behind the campaign's back. But when it comes to 2016, the best thing for you is if we win. If we lose, it's not gonna matter anyway. And if we win, you'll be in a position to do whatever you need to do. So let's win.

Biden left the lunch satisfied, as did Obama: they seemed to have had a meeting of the minds. On the issue of contraception, however, they remained in different places. In mid-January, after weeks of internal deliberations, Obama was preparing to make a final decision on the religious exemption; he was sticking with the narrow rule Sebelius had put forward.

Biden still thought it a terrible mistake, and told Obama so. The president had avoided culture wars in 2008, much to his advantage. Now he was on the brink of engulfing himself in one, not just due to the ruling itself but by going back on his word to Dolan. Biden knew the archbishop well enough to predict that it would not be pretty.

On January 20, Obama phoned Dolan to let him know his decision. Within hours a video was on the bishops conference website, in which Dolan condemned the administration. "Never before," he said, "has the federal government forced individuals and organizations to go out into the market-place and buy a product that violates their conscience." Across the country, hundreds of bishops said much the same. And even many liberals were in-censed. Under a headline accusing Obama of a "breach of faith," *Washington Post* columnist and reliable White House defender E. J. Dionne blistered the president for "utterly botch[ing]" the decision and hit him squarely in the solar plexus of his political vanity. "This might not be so surprising if Obama had presented himself as a conventional secular liberal," Dionne wrote. "But he has always held himself to a more inclusive standard."

Obama wore a mask of misery. He had returned to Washington from Hawaii hoping to put 2011 behind him. It had been the worst year of his presidency—of his political life. With the Kansas speech and the payroll tax victory, he thought perhaps he had turned a corner. But now, just three weeks into 2012, the landscape was cruelly familiar. He had been compelled to choose a third chief of staff in as many years in office. His vice president was on the warpath, and his wife was out there making the wrong kinds of headlines. Conservative multimillionaires and billionaires were delivering checks hand over fist to Karl Rove, as were some of the president's former Wall Street supporters. His approval ratings remained stubbornly mired in the mid-forties. The economy was still dreadful. And more than two-thirds of voters believed the country was on the wrong track—which, if history was any guide, meant that he was hosed.

There was a silver lining in this cloud, however, and it was a sparkly thing to behold. In the other America, the red America, the Republican nomination contest was under way.

PART TWO

5

PRESERVING THE OPTION

T OM RATH DROVE DOWN from New Hampshire to Lexington, Massachusetts, cruising past the old Raytheon building just off Route 2 and into the parking lot of the low-slung brick structure at 80 Hayden Avenue. It was November 18, 2008, and Rath had come to the offices of Free and Strong America PAC for lunch with Mitt Romney, the man Rath believed should have been elected president that year—and who he dearly hoped would try again in 2012.

Romney's campaign for the 2008 GOP nomination had been an expensive and embarrassing flameout, but he'd decided to put off any postmortems until after Election Day. Now, with the eyes of the world trained on President-elect Obama and the all-enveloping financial crisis, Romney was reaching out to key supporters such as Rath to divine the lessons of his loss.

A former New Hampshire attorney general turned lawyer-lobbyist, strategist, and sherpa, Rath was a fixture in Granite State politics. Every four years, presidential hopefuls solicited his services in navigating the first-in-the-nation primary. Starting in 1980, he had advised the campaigns of Howard Baker, Bob Dole, Lamar Alexander, George W. Bush, and, finally, Romney. Gnomic and twinkle-eyed at sixty-three, with the waist of his khakis hiked up over his belly, Rath was a classic moderate New

England Republican, ideologically squishy but strategically and tactically shrewd.

They sat down over sandwiches from a local deli. Rath, an irrepressible kibitzer, could have spent half an hour bantering about the Patriots or the Red Sox. Romney's only aptitude for small talk revolved around his family, and after dispensing with such chitchat, he came to the point.

"What do you think we did wrong?" Romney asked.

"We told the wrong story," Rath replied.

The story Rath had wanted Romney to tell arose naturally from the candidate's résumé: former CEO of Bain and Company and founder of Bain Capital; savior of the beleaguered 2002 Salt Lake City Olympics; pragmatic one-term Bay State governor. It was the story of a man who accomplished extraordinary things in the private sector, then turned to public service. A candidate with a million-dollar head of hair and a multi-million-dollar net worth who could be cast as the ultimate Mr. Fix-It, offering managerial and economic perspicacity at a time when even Republicans acknowledged that Bush's detachment and incuriosity had created a hot mess.

But Romney's other advisers had proposed a different path. He and Rath recalled a fateful meeting two years earlier in Boston, at which Romney's pollster, brandishing a wad of survey data, argued that the Mr. Fix-It lane was occupied by former New York mayor Rudolph Giuliani—and that Romney should present himself as a more conservative alternative. With some reluctance, Romney acquiesced. He spent much of 2007 lunging to the right on social issues, emphasizing positions on everything from abortion to immigration that were at variance with his past. His plan was to steal the Iowa caucuses, where grassroots evangelicals ruled, then take New Hampshire, where his status as a former neighboring governor and his ownership of a spread on Lake Winnipesaukee made him a quasi hometown boy.

Instead, Romney's rightward swerve let his rivals and the media tattoo the lethal "flip-flopper" label on his forehead. He also demonstrated an unfortunate capacity for stumbling into cringe-making headlines: about how his gardeners were illegal immigrants; about his "lifelong" devotion to hunting when in fact he'd done it twice; about the time he and his family went on vacation and put their dog, Seamus, in a crate strapped to the roof of the car for a twelve-hour drive.

The quick knockout he envisioned administering to his rivals was inflicted on him instead. In Iowa, the evangelicals rejected him soundly, fueling a nine-point thumping by former Arkansas governor Mike Huckabee. Limping into New Hampshire, where he had led in the polls throughout 2007, Romney was beaten by John McCain—and that was pretty much all she wrote.

A month later, on February 7, 2008, Romney left the race, announcing his withdrawal at the annual Conservative Political Action Conference (CPAC) in Washington. Afterwards, sitting around a U-shaped table with an array of the conservative movement's leaders, he listened as they expressed dismay at the impending nomination of McCain, whom they had never trusted, and declared Mitt the future of the party. Thank you for accepting me, Romney said. On the causes and ideas you stand for, I still stand with you. "You haven't heard the last of me," he added.

Rath was determined to make sure of that. Romney had started the race as an unknown commodity to Republicans nationally. At a cost of $110 million, including $45 million of his own money, he established a profile and name recognition, but there was more work to do. "You've got to make friends," Rath told him in February. "You've created an asset. You need to tend the asset."

Rath codified his plan for tending the asset in a three-page memo. For the duration of 2008, Rath wrote, "we need to be the proverbial good soldier." Romney should support McCain vigorously, raising money and campaigning for him and for GOP congressional candidates, doing whatever he was asked to do—"the more the better." He should form a PAC to dole out dollars to down-ticket Republicans. He should have an organized presence at the party's convention. He should be on TV regularly. He should write a book. "Some of this may seem elementary, but I wanted to lay it out," Rath wrote. "Were the Democrats to win in November, the 2012 cycle begins that night."

Romney did everything Rath suggested. He did so much for McCain that by the eve of the GOP convention in St. Paul, Minnesota, the rumor mill was churning up talk that he might receive the VP nod. Romney had taken some nasty shots at McCain during the nomination fight, but his solid soldiering seemed to have brought a thaw in their relationship. He submitted to being vetted, turning over years of income tax returns—a Mount Kili-manjaro of paper—to McCain's people. Romney's finance chair, Spencer Zwick, kept hearing from donors in Arizona that Mitt's selection was a done deal.

On the late-August morning when McCain revealed his vice-presidential pick, Romney and Zwick woke up in Los Angeles planning to catch a flight back to Boston—or straight to join McCain, if the call came. They were on a shuttle bus from the airport Marriott to LAX when Zwick's cell phone rang, with McCain on the line for Romney. After several mute seconds, Romney thanked McCain for calling and said, "I don't know Governor Palin very well, but best of luck with everything," while Zwick tapped Sarah Palin's name into Google on his smartphone to try to figure out who she was.

For the week of the convention, Romney's team rented out space on the bottom floor of the Saint Paul Hotel to host receptions for donors and sup-porters, but everyone could see that he was blue. Apart from the pain of being passed over for the ticket, Romney was downcast about playing the courtier at a shindig that should have been his coronation. His speech in the hall was ignored, credentials for his people were hard to come by, the whole thing was just . . . difficult.

Mitt's wife, Ann, was even more upset—and it was all about Palin. The Romneys had been married for thirty-nine years. Ann thought her husband hung the moon. She could barely comprehend McCain choosing anyone but Mitt, but this moose-hunting woman from Wasilla, Alaska? Really?

The night of Palin's speech, the Romneys expected to watch from the convention hall. They tried to get into a VIP suite, but their entourage was turned away at the door. Let's get out of here, they said, and hightailed it back to the hotel, where a private room was waiting. There they could watch the speech without the eyes of the media upon them—and Mitt's team could freely hoot at the woman who took the slot their man deserved. Even as Palin lit up the stage, Romney's crew chorused, You woulda crushed it, Guv, this is ridiculous. But Mitt's reaction was more subdued.

"I can't believe this, I can't believe it," he said. "Wow."

For the next two months, Romney continued to suck it up. After the collapse of Lehman Brothers and AIG, he emerged as one of McCain's most visible and energetic surrogates. During the nomination contest, the Arizona senator had routinely referred to Romney as a "fucking phony," and neither he nor his advisers ever seriously considered putting Mitt on the ticket. But McCain nevertheless came to have a grudging respect for him that fall. "I know the guy isn't holding his breath hoping I win," McCain told his team. "But, hey, give him credit—he's been terrific."

Romney's performance during the financial crisis only heightened his sense of what a missed opportunity 2008 had been. In the heat of battle, he and Ann had ascribed his problems to factors beyond his control: his Mormonism, his money, his roots in liberal Massachusetts—the three Ms. But now, in Lexington, two weeks after Election Day, Romney was starting to think he had been foolish to turn himself into a candidate of ideology rather than competence. "If I had listened to you," he told Rath, "I might have won."

As the talk turned to the future, Rath suggested some additional ideas for how Romney could stay in the mix. Though the afterglow of Obama's victory was still burning bright, "there's going to be another election," Rath said, "and you've got something."

But 2012 seemed a long way off to Romney. He was tentative, noncommittal. "I'm going to play it out, do some of the things you tell me to do," he said. "I'm going to preserve the option."

In fact, Romney told Rath, he'd written an op-ed that would appear the very next day in *The New York Times*. Its subject was the auto industry, a topic close to Romney's heart; his late father, George, had been chairman of American Motors and governor of Michigan in the fifties and sixties. Almost as much as the banking sector, Detroit was in free fall, and Romney had a plan to save it. The scheme, which was bold but contrary to what the industry wanted, might raise eyebrows.

"It's going to seem strange coming from me," Romney said.

H E WROTE THE OP-ED on his BlackBerry on the beach in front of his newest home, in La Jolla, California. A Spanish-style sanctuary on Dunemere Drive, it was called Fin de la Senda—the End of the Road. He and Ann had bought the place earlier that year for $12 million. Mitt loved that you could hear the waves crashing outside the window. And there was no better place than the sand down below to tap out big thoughts on the Lilliputian keyboard of his handheld device.

The argument in his op-ed was straightforward. The auto industry's leaders were clamoring for a bailout; a bill was being debated on Capitol Hill to divert to the Big Three $25 billion from the $700 billion bank-rescue fund. Romney thought such a move would doom Detroit by letting it evade the root-and-branch restructuring he regarded as necessary: new labor agreements to wring out the costs crippling the industry; new management that would work better with the unions; a renewed focus on investment and innovation. What the industry needed was "a managed bankruptcy," Romney wrote, which "would propel newly competitive and viable automakers, rather than seal their fate with a bailout check."

Romney's chief media adviser, Eric Fehrnstrom, a former journalist with a combative edge who had worked for Mitt since his statehouse days, took the op-ed first to *The Wall Street Journal,* which had published pieces by the governor before but passed this time. His second pitch was to the *Times,* where Fehrnstrom had tried to place op-eds repeatedly, to no avail. David Shipley, the paper's op-ed editor, quickly e-mailed back: Send it along, I'll take a look.

Shipley enjoyed featuring Republican voices on the op-ed page, and liked it even more when they were at variance with the official positions of the *Times*'s editorial board. Romney's biography made the piece extra appealing—not just his Detroit heritage but his Bain pedigree, too. *It's a no-brainer,* Shipley thought, assuming the op-ed was any good.

And, lo and behold, it was: tightly argued, highly prescriptive though not wildly controversial, what with the public outrage over bailouts generally and the auto unions in particular. Shipley made it a rule never to publish anything without receiving a final sign-off from the author. When Mary Duenwald, the editor assigned to handle the piece, called Fehrnstrom to suggest several tweaks, the flack said, "You need to talk to Mitt." A few seconds later, Romney was on the line, accepting the changes uncomplainingly or proposing his own. *What a nice guy,* Duenwald thought.

The headline—LET DETROIT GO BANKRUPT—was the only thing, per long-standing *Times* tradition, that the author didn't see beforehand. Shipley's view was that it captured the essence of Romney's argument and fit the space. The Timesman understood that a structured bankruptcy was a specific thing; even so, he thought, *A bankruptcy is a bankruptcy.* No one at the op-ed page considered the title unfair or raised a red flag. Nor did anyone from Romneyland protest when the piece was posted to the Web on the night of November 18, when Shipley still had time to alter the headline before it appeared in the paper.

The next morning, the reactions were all over the map. In the Bush White House, the president's counselor and former GOP chair Ed Gillespie glimpsed the headline and thought, *That's pretty stark,* figuring Romney was already angling for 2012 by taking an anti-bailout line that would resonate with the Republican base. Matt Rhoades, Romney's 2008 communications director, thought the opposite: *Kinda seems like the Guv's having a Bulworth moment; maybe he's not gonna run again.* Romney's supporters and donors from Michigan called Zwick and others, shocked by the headline. Romney's people were freaked about it, and piqued at the *Times.*

When Romney woke up and saw the headline, he was angry, too—but mainly at Fehrnstrom.

Eric, never, ever, *ever* again will we let anyone write a headline without our approval, Romney repined. We've got to go out and communicate that *The New York Times* wrote this, not us.

We're never going to convince the American people that the newspaper writes the headline, Fehrnstrom replied. We're gonna have to live with it.

Well, then, let's get on the air so I can talk about the substance and people will see that I'm trying to *save* the industry, Romney pressed.

In the next forty-eight hours, Romney attempted to explain himself on CNN, Fox, CBS's *The Early Show,* and NBC's *Today.* His people assured him the furor would pass, that it would all blow over. Romney was not so sure. He had been mighty pleased about making his debut in the *Times,* but the Paper of Record had handed his opponents a gnarly club with which to whack him. And while the next election was four years away, he kept thinking about Michigan and Ohio, electorally critical states full of autoworkers, all believing that he wanted to put their employers—their lives—in liquidation.

"Guys, guys, guys—this could be it," he told his aides. "This could sink me."

RREPRESSIBLY AND UNSHAKABLY OPTIMISTIC about America and her prospects, Willard Mitt Romney was often panicky when it came to his own political circumstances—and dark, dark, dark. The first trait sprang from his devout Mormon faith, which held doctrinally that the United States was divinely inspired—not just the ideals of freedom and self-determination, but the design of the federal government and the Constitution itself. The second outlook owed at least in part to the experiences of his father, whom Romney revered.

In the sixties, George Romney had embodied the embattled strain of paternal progressivism in the GOP, championing civil rights and resisting extremism in all its forms. He waded into the 1968 presidential campaign as a front-runner for his party's nomination. But in attempting to explain his turn against the Vietnam War, he committed a fateful gaffe, telling an interviewer that his earlier support for the war had been the result of a "brainwashing" he received from generals he met with in Saigon in 1965. The word connoted weakness, paranoia, and naïveté, but Romney refused to take it back. Soon his candidacy was reduced to rubble. Trailing Richard Nixon by a five-to-one margin in the polls, he withdrew before the New Hampshire primary. In a letter to Mitt, then serving in France as a Mormon missionary, his father wrote, "Your mother and I are not personally distressed. As a matter of fact we are relieved." But four years later, when he resigned from the Nixon cabinet and more or less retired from public life, Romney ruefully told an aide, "Politics will break your heart."

The family never expected Mitt to run for office. Politics was not his passion growing up. But in 1994, shortly before his death, George Romney encouraged his son to challenge Senator Edward Kennedy. Eight years after being thrashed in that race, Romney won the Bay State's governorship, and four years later he launched his presidential bid—announcing it in Michigan, where he'd never lived as an adult, in front of a Nash Rambler, the car central to his father's turnaround of American Motors. The suspicion that Mitt was running to complete George's legacy was hard to avoid.

The political world assumed that Romney would take another shot at the White House in 2012. But as 2008 turned to 2009, his ambivalence about the prospect was abiding—and much of it came down to Ann.

Romney met Ann Davies, a pretty, perky, non-Mormon blonde, in high school and had been doting on her ever since. She converted to his religion, and they raised five strapping sons, all now married and with kids of their own. Ann put Mitt at ease and brought him a kind of contentment that he experienced nowhere else: not in business, not in politics, not with close friends, of which he had remarkably few. Obligation, aspiration, and curiosity compelled his forays into public life, but those adventures always seemed vaguely forced. Mitt truly felt at home only when Ann was by his side, which was where he wanted her as much as possible, ideally all the time. She was his comfort zone.

The worst day of Mitt's life was when Ann received her diagnosis of multiple sclerosis just before Thanksgiving 1998. For a time, she was desperate, scared, and very sick, but Mitt—and an array of treatments, from medication to reflexology, acupuncture, and craniosacral therapy—brought her back to health. She was far more outwardly emotional than her husband and took the loss in 2008 harder than he did. When it was over, they discussed whether he would run again. Absolutely not, she said.

Just a couple of weeks after Election Day 2008, Ann learned that she had breast cancer. The doctors had caught it at stage zero, but she was terrified, having lost her mother and grandmother to ovarian cancer and her great-grandmother to breast cancer. Elizabeth Edwards phoned to talk through her own experiences with the disease. Obama called, too, to wish her a speedy recovery, which impressed Mitt. "Ann and I have you in our prayers," he said.

Ann had a lumpectomy and received radiation treatment but was spared chemotherapy. Even so, her recovery that winter was slow. Her failure to snap back threw her husband and increased his sense that 2012 might not be in the cards. In the spring of 2009, they began a fresh chapter. They sold their hulking Colonial in Belmont, Massachusetts, their main residence for twenty years, and their chalet in Park City, Utah, leaving them with the places in La Jolla and Wolfeboro, New Hampshire—a home on each coast, both on the water, both idyllic.

The Romneys started talking about the new kind of life they could build around those abodes, especially the Wolfeboro compound. Mitt was sixty-two years old, with a couple hundred million dollars in the bank. He could imagine a mellow, cozy semi-retirement, surrounded by a swarm of kids, grandkids, cousins, nieces, and nephews in the high Mormon fashion. Three of his sons were entrepreneurs; he could dabble in their firms. (*I'll be an unpaid adviser*, he thought. *Or moderately paid.*) He took pleasure in the idea of being free of the responsibilities, anxieties, and colonoscopic scrutiny that politics entailed, not to mention the pressures of public performance, at which he floundered.

Exacerbating his ambivalence was the specter of another loss. *The odds of becoming your party's nominee are never as good as fifty-fifty,* he thought. *Beating an incumbent president is hard to do.* Coming out of 2008, the conventional wisdom was that Obama would marshal an awesome array of reelection assets: his grassroots army, inspirational flair, and ability to raise funds—maybe $1 billion. Like the president, Romney was a competitive guy who hated losing even more than he relished winning. He had no desire to dive headlong into a propeller.

But Romney had told Rath that he wanted to "preserve the option," and he meant it. For most of 2009, he retreated into semi-seclusion to write a book, as Rath suggested in his memo. Nothing bothered Mitt and Ann more than his having been painted a coreless opportunist during the campaign. Romney blamed himself for having failed to articulate his beliefs clearly and cleanly. The book would be a remedy for that blunder: a campaign manifesto if he ran again, pure catharsis if he didn't. Eschewing treacly personal anecdotes, Romney focused on international and economic issues, laying down his positions in a flurry of mini-lectures. There was also a hefty dose of censure for Obama, with Romney singing in harmony with the Palin/Limbaugh/Fox News choir that the president was "eager to note all of America's failings, real and perceived, and reluctant to speak out in defense of American values."

The book's working title was *The Pursuit of the Difficult,* which came from a bit of wisdom his father once imparted: "The pursuit of the difficult makes men stronger." But Romney was unsatisfied with it. One day at a meeting with his aides before the manuscript shipped to the printer, a staffer piped up with *No Apology*—and Mitt was instantly sold.

Hawking *No Apology* was a whole other production. Romney knew that Palin, with her 2009 memoir *Going Rogue,* made it to number one on the

Times best-seller list—and he was eager to match her. To get there, his people employed a variety of methods, some legit and many dodgy. His PAC set up a website, NoApology.com, to sell the book. On Romney's book tour, some venues were required to buy copies in large numbers. On the lecture circuit, he would forgo his fee and have clients put the money toward book purchases. Mormon groups bought *No Apology* in quantity; so did Romney's PAC. Mitt retained an expert who knew the tricks of the trade to shimmy a book onto the *Times* list.

The resulting fishy sales patterns did not go unnoticed. When a book's ranking was the result of bulk orders, the Paper of Record denoted that with a dagger symbol. When *No Apology* debuted at number one in March 2010, there were double daggers.

B Y THEN ROMNEY WAS doing more than writing to preserve the option. At the cramped, drab PAC headquarters in Lexington, he installed a passel of his top advisers from 2008. To run the shop, he tapped Rhoades, a thirty-six-year-old from upstate New York with a pronounced air of imperturbability but a temper below the surface. Rhoades's orientation was tactical and operational—he was a pure mechanic. He had earned his bones as a dirt-digger, running opposition research for the 2004 Bush-Cheney reelection campaign. He was famous for having a direct pipeline to Matt Drudge; colleagues claimed (only half-jokingly) that he had a chat window on his computer open 24/7 with the freak show's primo online impresario. Averse to publicity, allergic to appearing on TV, Rhoades had cultivated a Keyser Söze–ish mystique. Romney liked him for his loyalty, discipline, and intense focus.

The hiring of Rhoades was one sign that Romney was starting to cast an eye toward 2012, but there were others. He dispatched his close friend and former Bain partner Bob White to travel around the country and conduct more postmortems to glean lessons from the last campaign. Mitt had been despised by his 2008 rivals, not just McCain, for his slashing attacks and apparent lack of conviction. Now he reached out to Giuliani and Huckabee to mend fences (and subtly gauge their intentions about running again). That summer, Mitt trouped a parade of donors up to Wolfeboro, taking them on boat rides, feeding them crab salad, and telling them he wouldn't put in his own money this time—if he ran. He invited reporters to off-the-record barbecues by the lake and dinners in D.C. He knew they considered him distant and robotic, and he wanted to combat that perception. (Success rate: low.)

With the 2010 midterms ahead, Romney also tapped his donor network, turning his PAC into a powerhouse, establishing offshoots in New Hampshire and Iowa that allowed him to tiptoe around donation limits to local officials. Largely under the radar, he hit the trail on behalf of congressional and state-level candidates, doing more than a hundred events in thirty states, handing out hundreds of thousands of dollars to the likes of future governors Nikki Haley, in South Carolina, and Terry Branstad, in Iowa.

The ramp-up in Romney's political activities coincided with two developments, the first being his swelling sense of Obama's deficiencies. On policy, Romney disagreed with most of what the president had done, from the fatback-festooned stimulus to the heavy-handed Dodd-Frank reform. He disdained the fervidly partisan approach that the supposedly post-partisan Obama had taken on health care reform and so much else. And then there was the BP oil spill. As governor, Romney had always been hands-on, from micromanaging the plows when blizzards came to personally overseeing the crisis when a concrete panel collapsed in Boston's Fort Point Channel Tunnel in 2006. On learning that many weeks had passed after the Deepwater Horizon explosion without Obama calling BP's CEO, Romney barked, "He's the leader of the free world! He hasn't picked up the phone?"

The second development was the rise of the Tea Party. That January, Romney had been among the earliest supporters of Scott Brown, the Republican candidate in a special election to fill the Senate vacancy created by Ted Kennedy's death. With the Tea Party rallying to Brown's side and opposition to Obamacare at the center of his campaign, the Republican's victory was an indication of the president's vulnerability and the movement's gathering force. And while Romney was not in sync with its hot-eyed fury, he thought the Tea Party's focus on spending, deficits, and debt played to his strengths.

Yet Romney's ambivalence remained—unspooling in ways that would later haunt him. Out in La Jolla, he was planning a renovation of Fin de la Senda. It was by no means a mansion, at three thousand square feet and with three bedrooms, hardly enough room for his and Ann's sons, daughters-in-law, and sixteen grandkids to visit. On top of that, the house was at the end of a pinched cul-de-sac in a neighborhood virtually devoid of street parking. Romney wanted to bulldoze the structure and build a new one with nearly four times the space, including an expanded split-level garage with a hydraulic lift to move cars around inside.

Romney knew he would be criticized for the elaborateness of the construction when the plans became public, as they surely would—if he ran. And he knew that if he won the presidency, it would all be for naught, because the Secret Service could never protect the house: it was on a public beach. But when some of his aides, including Fehrnstrom and Rhoades, suggested he put the renovation on hold, Romney squirmed and went looking for the answer he wanted to hear, turning to Stuart Stevens.

Stevens had been a part of Romney's media team in 2008, providing an idiosyncratic voice that had often been drowned out. Since then, however, he increasingly had Mitt's ear.

"Should I not build this house?" Romney asked Stevens.

You don't know if you're gonna run, Stevens said. You know you're gonna be alive. There are a million reasons for people not to vote for you. If you run, they're gonna say you're rich. You *are* rich. If you want to build a house, you should build a house. "You've got to live your life," he said.

ROMNEY INVITED STEVENS AND his business partner, Russ Schriefer, to have lunch with him in Belmont, where he and Ann had recently purchased a modest townhouse in a condominium complex. (For more than a year after selling their old Belmont digs, the couple claimed a basement flat in their son Tagg's nearby home as their legal Massachusetts residence.) It was November 2, 2010, midterm Election Day, and Romney was starting to get antsy about making the decision he had put off for so long. He had a job offer to extend to the consultants—conditionally.

One of Romney's insights from his and White's autopsy of 2008 was that his campaign had been plagued by too much talent. He had approached his candidacy as if it were a Bain consulting project: throwing bodies and big brains at the endeavor. Romney didn't mind a cacophony of brilliant if conflicting voices. He liked to bring clever people together, let them duke it out at length. But he also had a tendency to vacillate, to want more data, to reprise every internal debate. Taken together, these elements had yielded paralysis, pettifoggery, and a terminally muddy message. This time (if there was a this time), Romney swore that his outfit would be lean and mean instead of top-heavy, and guided by a single and singular chief strategist.

The Svengali Romney wanted for 2012 was Mike Murphy, a rumpled, blond, forty-eight-year-old image maker based in Los Angeles. Murphy's résumé was replete with high-profile clients: John McCain, Jeb Bush, Arnold Schwarzenegger. In the sharp-elbowed world of political hired guns, he had as many detractors as admirers, but no one gainsaid his self-promotional chops. Glib and quotable, Murphy was a frequent TV presence, a kind of Republican James Carville—but with irony and sarcasm substituting for bug-eyed apoplexy. He cheerfully trumpeted his reputation as Murphy the Mudslinger; for a time, the vanity plates on his Porsche read GO NEG.

Murphy had masterminded Romney's successful 2002 gubernatorial campaign. But in 2008, with two former clients in the presidential hunt, he sat on the sidelines, to Romney's great regret. Ever since, in e-mails, phone calls, and in-person meetings, the governor had labored to draw Murphy back into the fold. Tagg Romney paid a recruiting visit to the consultant in L.A., double-teaming him.

Murphy was happy on the West Coast, working various Hollywood angles. The idea of moving to Boston struck him as a stone-cold bummer, but he gave the matter serious consideration. He liked Romney, thought he would make a good president. The trouble was that the governor had surrounded himself with mediocrities. Murphy told Romney that if he took the job, he would want to fire half of his team. Mitt blenched. Maybe you could find a way to work with everybody, he said weakly.

"I don't think I want to do this anyway," Murphy replied. "But no, I couldn't."

For most politicians, such a blunt rejection would have been the end of the story. Not Romney. His feelings for Murphy, the man who'd engineered the one political victory of his life, were slightly fetishistic. Romney would continue to seek out Murphy's counsel at critical junctures in the 2012 race, almost always keeping the communications secret—specifically from his second choice as chief strategist, with whom he was now having lunch.

Stuart Phineas Stevens was a decade older than Murphy and even more colorful. Mississippi-born, educated at Colorado College, Middlebury, Oxford, and UCLA film school, he was an ad maker, travel writer (*Feeding Frenzy*), TV writer (*Northern Exposure*), film consultant (*The Ides of March*), and extreme-sports fanatic who had skied to the North Pole, and ridden the Paris–Brest–Paris bicycle race while hopped up on steroids, chronicling his exploits for *Outside* magazine. Charming, flirty, and superficially laconic, yet capable of prickly combativeness, Stevens spoke in a lazy drawl that could devolve into a mumble or elevate to a wheeze. His political clients tended to be moderate Republicans such as Bob Dole and former Florida governor Charlie Crist, but there were notable exceptions: Stevens helped elect Bush 43 and prepared Dick Cheney for his 2004 vice-presidential debate with John Edwards.

Stevens, too, inspired animus in rival consultants, Murphy vehemently among them. ("It's not that we don't like each other," Murphy told friends. "I just think he's an idiot.") The lineage of their feud had been lost in the mists of time. But it was fueled by the fact that, looks aside—with Stevens a ringer for Thomas Haden Church and Murphy resembling Philip Seymour Hoffman—they had much in common, from galaxy-size egos (about their writing, celebrity shoulder-rubbing, bon mots, ad making, and facility at fricasseeing opponents) to Hollywood connections, unconventional lifestyles, and a propensity to procure real estate the way normal people acquire shoes.

Stevens had been in the running for the Romney account in 2002 until Murphy beat him out. But in 2007, after a brief spell working for McCain, he and Schriefer were appended to the bloated Boston talent roster and were now at the core of Romneyland. Stevens worked closely with Mitt on *No Apology*, and while they sometimes seemed to hail from different planets, and possibly even different species, they somehow clicked. Both were hyperliterate book and film junkies, introspective, watchful—and not entirely obsessed with politics. Their relationship was something like the one between the patrician Bush 41 and his southern-fried savant, Lee Atwater: odd, affectionate, respectful, sustained by mutual curiosity.

Now, in November 2010 in Belmont, Romney was ready to take the next step to cement their bond. For ninety minutes, they ran through the putative 2012 game plan, with Stevens ticking off a series of homespun maxims that would be the first principles of a second Romney campaign.

To begin with, Stevens said, Romney was "gonna have to steal the nomination." The Republican Party was increasingly a southern, populist, evangelical beast. Romney was northeastern, buttoned-down, and Mormon. Much of the base would see him as an establishment figure, even though the Beltway crowd, to which he had few ties, regarded him as an alien.

"The party will not drift to you," Stevens continued. You're going to have to win it over. And winning it over would be possible for one reason: the depth of the desire of Republican voters to oust Obama. If you can convince them you're the guy who can beat him, you can win.

In order to do that, Stevens said, "we gotta dig the ditch we're gonna die in." In 2008, Romney had essentially conducted multiple campaigns, each with its own tactics, to convince every important Republican faction that he was the most conservative candidate in the field. In 2012, they would focus squarely and almost exclusively on the economy and jobs, articulating a forceful critique of Obama's failed management and agenda—the same themes they would drive in the general election, assuming that they got there. You have to say, This is what I bring to the table; come eat at this table, Stevens argued.

Finally, Stevens said, "You have to be willing to lose to win, and you're going to lose a lot"—a lot of votes, a lot of states. "No one gets elected president without being humiliated. How you deal with the humiliation is the key."

Romney had never suffered public humiliation until the 2008 campaign. Enduring it then had been excruciating, but it had also hardened his shell—and that was only one of the ways in which having run last time would give him a leg up on any first-time candidates who challenged him this go-round. With the passage of time and plenty of postmorteming, he had come to understand the perils of chasing the news cycle and letting the freak show drag him down. And he had learned how damaging it could be to allow a negative meme to spread and fester, as it had with him on the question of flip-floppery.

He recognized that he was now in a straitjacket, with none of the latitude that other candidates had to shift or shade his positions. What he had said in 2008 and written in *No Apology* would be his gospel in 2012. The flip-flopper tattoo had left a scar; he did not intend to reopen the wound.

On all of these dimensions, Romney believed that having run once before equipped him to run better and smarter this time. But the question lingered: Did he really want to?

Over the Christmas holiday, the Romney family went on vacation on Maui. Four years earlier, when Mitt had polled his brood on whether he should run, the result was unanimously in favor. But now four of his sons were against the idea, with only Tagg voting aye. It's grueling, hard on your health, the majority said. You've written your book, said what you need to say—move on. Romney didn't disagree. "Why go through the process just to lose again?" he asked, only partly rhetorically.

There was, however, one other dissenter besides Mitt's eldest boy. In the more than two years since she'd expressed adamant opposition to another run, Ann Romney had gradually but inexorably shifted her position. Watching the news, she had become more and more alarmed by Obama and the deteriorating state of the nation.

Ann asked her husband if he thought he could fix the mess. Mitt said that he did. So why wasn't it obvious that he simply had to run? Why on earth was he dragging his feet?

Romney spent the next couple of weeks brooding some more about what to do. He'd answered Ann honestly: He believed that his background and skills placed him in a near-unique position to put America back on track. Just as important, he doubted that the other plausible entrants in the race could beat the incumbent.

Many insiders were high on Indiana governor Mitch Daniels. *Good record,* Romney thought, but Daniels lacked the requisite charisma. Others praised South Dakota senator John Thune. Romney had talked to him. *Terrific guy.* Didn't have what it took to win. Mississippi governor Haley Barbour was a favorite of the establishment, but his history as a lobbyist would make him toxic. Huckabee? *Good candidate,* Romney mused, but easily marginalized as a staunch evangelical. Tim Pawlenty? *Credible,* Romney thought, but too weak on the fund-raising side. Then there was Jeb Bush, whom Romney saw as the real deal. *Burdened by his family's name, but great record, great organization, great guy.* Romney talked to Jeb, too, however, and it seemed clear that the former Florida governor had no interest in running.

Romney understood his own limitations and vulnerabilities; he knew that capturing his party's nomination would be an uphill slog. But the more he considered the situation, the more apparent it was to him that he was the only Republican thinking of jumping in who possessed a genuine chance of unseating Obama—the only one who could save the country. Although Romney had no inferno raging in his gut, he realized that his wife was right: he simply had to run.

In mid-January 2011, in their living room in La Jolla, Romney told Ann he had come around, then he conveyed the news to his team. Ann was thrilled. So was the Lexington crew.

Up in L.A., Murphy shook his head. For two years, Romney had basically been asking himself, Am I crazy enough to put myself through this, take on this horrible mission? The answer turned out to be no. And yet—out of a mixture of duty, ambition, and self-aggrandizement—he was doing it anyway. In a sense, it was admirable, Murphy thought. But it was also a recipe for trouble, especially in light of one bracing fact: much of the Republican Party believed that Romney didn't stand a chance.

THE SOURCES OF THIS skepticism were many, but none was greater than the millstone around Mitt's neck known as Romneycare. In 2006, near the end of his gubernatorial tenure, Romney had enacted a sweeping reform of the Massachusetts health care system, the centerpiece of which was an individual mandate to buy insurance. The signing ceremony took place at Faneuil Hall and was elaborate and festive. "I want to express appreciation to Cecil B. DeMille for organizing this event," Romney joked, and then, with Ted Kennedy hovering over him, he put fourteen pens to paper to turn the bill into law.

In 2008, Romneycare didn't pose political difficulties for the candidate; quite the contrary. The individual mandate, with its roots at the Heritage

Foundation, was seen as a sound free-market idea for dealing with the problem of the uninsured driving up health care costs. Romney's having passed it through a Democratic legislature was seen as a sign of his legislative moxie. South Carolina's Jim DeMint, the farthest-right member of the Senate, singled out the achievement when he endorsed Romney for president. "He has demonstrated, when he stepped into government in a very difficult state, that he could work in a difficult partisan environment, take some good conservative ideas, like private health insurance, and apply them to the need to have everyone insured," DeMint said.

But Obamacare changed everything, rendering the individual mandate anathema and turning Romneycare into an albatross. In 2009, as the health care debate erupted in Washington and around the country, Mitt's earnest, bespectacled new pollster, Neil Newhouse, found that the Massachusetts law was the candidate's gravest liability among Republican primary voters in New Hampshire. In South Carolina, it came in second, after Romney's Mormonism.

The issue was equally noxious among Republican elites. All through 2010 and into 2011, Romney was pummeled with hostile health care questions by big-ticket donors—often waving copies of *The Wall Street Journal*, whose op-ed page was waging a serialized jihad against Romneycare. Paul Singer, a billionaire hedge-fund operator who was among the party's most sought-after bundlers, refused to sign on with Romney largely over the issue. Woody Johnson, the owner of the New York Jets, was on Romney's team but urged him repeatedly to repudiate the law and apologize for passing it. Karl Rove, with whom Romney had quietly nursed a phone and e-mail relationship, offered the same advice. You gotta disavow it, Rove told him. You gotta say, Look, we set out to do something, but it didn't work the way I wanted.

Thus was Romney faced with his first test of the Stevens axiom that he had to be willing to lose to win. At a meeting at the PAC in early 2011, Romney asked Newhouse if it would be better for him politically to walk away from the law. The pollster chuckled. Would it be better to change to a position that 95 percent of the party agrees with? he said. You're asking me this? Um, yes, it'd be better.

"Do you think it'll cost me the nomination if I don't switch?" Romney asked Stevens.

"I have no idea," Stevens replied. "Possibly."

But Romney was not going to back away from Romneycare. He still believed what he'd said when he signed the bill at Faneuil Hall: that it was "a Republican way of reforming the market," that "having thirty million people in this country without health insurance and having those people show up when they get sick, and expect someone else to pay, that's a Democratic approach." Romney had a wonky knowledge of health care policy. He thought the law worked in Massachusetts and that voters there were happy with it.

There was, however, another impetus for Romney's resoluteness. Switching his position on health care would be the flip-flop to end all flip-flops—and he would be rightly slaughtered for it. I am not going to let that happen, he said. I'm not going to backtrack one inch.

Romney's unwillingness to capitulate heartened Stevens and the rest of his outfit, but the political quandary remained. In Lexington that spring, his team deliberated endlessly over how Mitt could stand his ground without alienating the Republican base. With the help of Newhouse's focus groups, the Romneyites settled on a three-part strategy: stress that the Massachusetts plan was a state-level solution, not a federal takeover; point out that Romney's plan didn't raise taxes or increase the debt, unlike the president's; and pledge up and down that, if elected, the first thing Romney would do in office was repeal Obamacare.

No one was certain it would work. On the table was a proposal for him to make a major health care speech before he formally entered the race. Some of Romney's advisers were nervous about calling attention to the issue, but the candidate was gung ho. Romney had written a book called *No Apology,* and he wanted to let the world know he wouldn't be apologizing for a policy he was proud of.

Yet Romney's swagger went only so far. When the paperback version of his book hit shelves that February, observers noted that one line from the hardback, about the success of Romneycare, had been expunged: the author's hopeful boast that "we can accomplish the same thing for everyone in the country."

———

THE APARTMENT IN BOSTON's Back Bay belonged to Ron Kaufman, the longtime lobbyist who served as Romney's unofficial ambassador to the Beltway political class. Kaufman split his time between Washington and Boston. He had purchased this pad on Beacon Street years earlier from an aging Irish lady, in as-is condition—and left it that way. There were chintz-covered couches, plaid lampshades, floral wallpaper, a gaudy chandelier; the bookcases were still stocked with the biddy's books. The only personal touches were some pictures of Kaufman from his time in the Bush 41 White House, along with a bust of Winston Churchill on a marble pedestal.

It was the morning of April 8, 2011, opening day at Fenway Park, a few blocks away. Arrayed around Kaufman's living room were Mitt, Ann, and the members of the Romney high command. For the next few hours, they would run through pretty much everything about the campaign ahead, from message and money to calendar and competitors, actual and potential. Three days from now, they would announce the formation of a presidential exploratory committee, and soon after that shift their base of operations from Lexington to Boston's North End, where they had rented the same building on Commercial Street that had housed Romney's effort in 2008. Final check-off time was upon them.

Almost everyone in the room had served Romney since the last campaign or even further back. In addition to functioning as chief strategist, Stevens would oversee advertising along with Schriefer; Rhoades would manage the campaign. A trio of Bostonian arch-loyalists would act as senior advisers: Beth Myers, a seasoned jack-of-all-trades who had served as Mitt's statehouse chief of staff and run the 2008 campaign; Peter Flaherty, a former homicide prosecutor and a rare social conservative in Mitt's orbit (a devout Catholic, he kept a statue of the Virgin Mary on his desk); and Fehrnstrom. Bob White would play the role of personal counselor without portfolio. Zwick, a polished go-getter in his thirties who was sometimes described as the sixth Romney son, would oversee the finance operation. Lanhee Chen, a pugnacious wonk with four degrees from Harvard, would pilot the policy shop.

The degree of continuity was striking. In almost every other respect, Romney was consciously seeking to steer clear of the mistakes of 2008: he would embrace the Mr. Fix-It persona, as opposed to the Conservative for All Seasons; downplay cultural issues in favor of a laser-like economic focus; abandon fantasies of a fast nomination-fight knockout; and avoid flip-floppery as if it were Ebola. But when cementing his team, he was essentially sticking with his 2008 crew—and while the familiarity was likely to provide him with maximum comfort, the question was whether it would also yield maximum performance.

The well-worn discussions of message and money were dispensed with quickly. Stevens's back was acting up, so he circled the room while dispensing his adages. Everyone was grappling with the new financial terrain created by *Citizens United.* Zwick laid out his fund-raising targets for the next year: at least $50 million, but ideally $75 million. Romney reiterated his reluctance to pony up his own dough this time; he worried that self-funding would again spark accusations that he was trying to buy the brass ring. On the helpful side, Myers and Rhoades had recruited some former Romney aides to start a so-called super PAC to support his candidacy. On the disquieting side, a rumor was circulating that Team Obama planned to spend $100 million during the Republican nomination brawl specifically to batter Romney. "A hundred million is a lot of money!" Mitt exclaimed.

Rhoades spoke at length about the mechanics of securing the nomination. Historically, the GOP had relied mainly on winner-take-all primaries to select its standard-bearer. But in the lead-up to 2012, the Republican National Committee (RNC) changed the rules: the 2,286 delegates who would vote at the national convention the next summer in Tampa, Florida, would be allocated proportionally to a candidate's share of the vote in any given contest. This only heightened the campaign's conviction that the race would be a marathon, not a sprint.

Even so, four early-voting states—Iowa, New Hampshire, South Carolina, and Florida—would be critical. Romney was obsessed with the Granite State, to the point of insisting that his formal entry into the race occur before a debate scheduled to take place there in mid-June. We need to show New Hampshire it's special, he said; missing the debate would be disrespectful. He and his team saw Florida as fertile ground, too. More problematic, however, were Iowa and South Carolina, each with heavy concentrations of evangelical voters deeply suspicious of Mormonism.

Angst about Romney's faith and its political repercussions had suffused his campaign the last time. Among his advisers, it was a given that The Mormon Thing—which they shorthanded as TMT—hurt him badly with evangelicals, a significant number of whom regarded the religion as a cult. The sting was felt sharply by members of the Romney clan, particularly in Iowa. Both Tagg and Josh Romney talked emotionally about encountering outfront anti-Mormon prejudice when they toured the Hawkeye State in 2007. Mitt's brother, Scott, told the campaign team that if he ever had to drive from Michigan to Colorado, he would detour around Iowa. Zwick vividly recalled a meeting with a group of Christian leaders in Iowa at which one of them said, Look, we care about two things: this country and the salvation of souls. But the salvation of souls is more important than the temporary well-being of this country. We think Romney probably understands the economy. But if we vote for him, we're conceding that Mormons are Christians—and that's not going to happen.

Aside from his family, Romney cared about nothing more passionately than his faith. But he was painfully uncomfortable talking about it publicly, and refrained from doing so in 2008 until it was too late. The campaign's strategy this time would be, in effect, to pretend the issue didn't exist or pose a threat. (Meanwhile Zwick was quietly raising bushels of money from wealthy Mormons, whom Mitt's aides referred to as "the Mos.")

The question of whether to play to win in Iowa, though, couldn't be ignored. Stevens thought it was a sucker's game; so did Rath, who believed it was nearly impossible to win both Iowa and New Hampshire. But Romney sided with others who argued that a small investment in Iowa would allow them to defer the decision until later. For all the pain the state had caused him and his family, Mitt wanted, as usual, to preserve the option.

Ultimately, resolving the Iowa question would depend on who else was running. Thune had announced that he was out. Indiana congressman and conservative darling Mike Pence was also taking a pass. Newt Gingrich, Tim Pawlenty, and Herman Cain, an Atlanta talk radio host and former CEO of Godfather's Pizza, had formed exploratory committees; Minnesota congresswoman Michele Bachmann, Texas congressman Ron Paul, and former Pennsylvania senator Rick Santorum were about to do the same.

Gingrich would be a factor, the Romneyites allowed, but his checkered history and reflexive indiscipline would likely preclude him from winning the nomination. Zwick concurred with Romney that Pawlenty would be handicapped financially; others noted that his performance skills were untested. Bachmann, Cain, and Santorum provoked guffaws. Surveying the field as currently constituted, Romney's people thought the same thing that David Plouffe did when he looked at the Republicans: Our guy might not be perfect, but we'd rather be us than them.

The field, however, was almost certainly about to change. For months, the political world had been waiting on decisions from Barbour, Daniels, and Huckabee about whether they would heave themselves into the scrum. Each possessed estimable endowments: Barbour's fund-raising prowess and strategic sagacity, Daniels's executive experience and fiscal rectitude, Huckabee's abundant charm and evangelical ardor. And then there was Donald Trump, with his nearly infinite capacity to consume media oxygen, currently at or near the top of the polls and ostensibly weighing a run.

As the meeting at Kaufman's wound to a close, the Romneyites professed a lack of concern about this potpourri, while at the same time holding their breath. A bunch of them headed over to Fenway Park, hopes high at the start of the new season, and were treated to the sight of the Bosox battering the Yankees, 9–6.

Politics, like sports, was a superstitious business, and the portents here were cheery. But no one would have predicted the extreme good fortune headed Team Romney's way: that Mitt was about to hit a grand slam without even swinging the bat.

★ 6 ★

FOUR LITTLE INDIANS

K ARL ROVE CHECKED his in-box and saw another e-mail from Romney. It was April 12, the day after the candidate announced his exploratory committee. "Well, I took the next step to get in," Romney wrote to Rove. "It won't be an easy road . . . Any advice? Best, Mitt."

Rove had loads of advice for Romney. Of course he did—he was Rove. He thought of himself as an open-source consultant to the party now, offering brass-tacks tips or grandiloquent theories to any presidential candidate, actual or hypothetical, who reached out to him. And they all did. Twelve years after piloting Dubya into the White House and four years after exiting the building, Rove was back in the thick of the action. At sixty, he had emerged as the quintessential political entrepreneur, a wired-up, plugged-in, multi-platform presence whose blend of media and monetary clout made him arguably the central Republican figure of the 2012 election cycle.

His resurgence was an unexpected development. Rove's departure from the West Wing had come on the heels of five grand jury appearances in the Valerie Plame leak case and the Republican wipeout in the 2006 midterms, and was followed by Obama's election and the expansion of the Democratic majorities in the House and Senate—all of it seeming to signify a conclusive end to the Rovean era.

But Rove was a resourceful and resilient man. Bush's nickname for him, after all, was Turd Blossom—a flower that blooms from shit. And at the outset of Obama's reign, the GOP was certainly in the crapper. The party was without a unifying leader, de facto or de jure. Its freshest new face, Sarah Palin, had chosen celebrity over credibility when she quit the Alaska governorship before finishing her first term. The new RNC chairman, Michael Steele, had ridden into office declaring his intent to promote conservative principles in "hip-hop settings" and his belief that abortion was an "individual choice." Being neither blind nor stupid, Rove spied a power vacuum—and then systematically set about filling it.

Rove's first step was to build up his personal brand; for all his influence inside the Bush White House, he had never been its front man. Rove also was hungry for cash, with legal bills having tapped his coffers and a divorce in the offing. Aided by Washington superlawyer Bob Barnett, he landed twin gigs at Fox News and the op-ed page of *The Wall Street Journal,* inked a book deal, and hit the lecture circuit. When his memoir, *Courage and Consequence,* was published in March 2010, he embarked on a marathon promotional tour, barnstorming 111 cities in ninety days. Between January and November, he wrote sixty-one *Journal* columns, appeared on Fox News eighty-three times, and dashed off fourteen hundred tweets.

In parallel, Rove built the Crossroads empire. Even before *Citizens United,* he and his partner, Ed Gillespie, had been pitching donors on an outside group that would, in effect, supplant the RNC. Panicked by Obama's agenda and the sight of their party reeling around dazed and headless, the bundlers who had funded the Bush ascendancy flocked to Rove, who offered a track record of winning, a road map out of the wilderness, and even a willingness to take on the task without pay. Rove's outfits—American Crossroads and Crossroads GPS, the latter designated a "social welfare" organization under the tax code, allowing its donors to remain undisclosed—raised $71 million ahead of the midterms and flooded the airwaves with tens of thousands of ads in support of Republican candidates.

Rove had long been the bête noire of the left, but his new role provoked the wrath of the Tea Party as well. On the populist right, he was seen as the embodiment of the Republican establishment, despised for his backing of the Bush-initiated bank bailout and budget-busting Medicare prescription drug benefit, and resented for taking public swipes at Palin and Christine O'Donnell, the failed Senate candidate in Delaware. Yet Rove's dual portfolios—raising his profile on the one hand, raising cash for Cross-roads on the other—allowed him to mind-meld simultaneously with the grassroots (on his book tour and at speeches to activists and local party stalwarts) and the elites (at paid corporate talks and donor meetings). It placed him in a unique position to understand his party and its challenges while imbuing him with outsize influence.

Now, with 2012 approaching, Rove was working the levers to increase the odds of dethroning Obama, a prerequisite to reviving his long-held dream of a durable Republican majority. The fund-raising turned out to be the easy part; donors were handing over checks as fast as he could cash them. The hard part was finding a good horse to ride. Given the dismal economy and the unpopularity of Obama's policies, the presidency was ripe for the picking. But to Rove's eyes, the existing Republican field was a stable-ful of nags, and the front-runner destined to falter before the finish line.

In many ways, Romney was Rove's kind of candidate. Despite Mitt's un-derwhelming 2008 national debut, there was a sense that it was now his turn, no small thing in a party governed by primogeniture. Between his personal wealth and fund-raising network, Romney would never be shy of cash. His corporate experience would contrast nicely with Obama's oblivi-ousness about the private sector. And Romney had ingratiated himself with the Bushes; 41 and his wife, Barbara, enjoyed Mitt's company.

But Rove saw Romney's plasticity and inability to connect as substantial flaws. He considered Romneycare a high hurdle in the nomination race, and an insurmountable one in a general election; he was certain it would cause the Republican base to stay home and also alienate independents. He had advised Romney to repudiate it, but instead the candidate played the feder-alism card. *What you're saying,* Rove thought, *is "The Tenth Amendment guarantees that the federal government can't fuck up the country, but gives us the right to fuck up Massachusetts." Not exactly a compelling argument.*

Rove's feelings toward Romney truly were emblematic of the GOP estab-lishment. Among elected officials, strategists, and lobbyists in Washington, Romney wasn't liked *or* disliked—he was a stranger. Apart from Ron Kaufman, it was difficult to locate a soul who was energetically and unreservedly for him. Instead they were frantically casting about for a more palatable alternative.

To Rove and much of the establishment, the beau ideal was Jeb Bush. But the former Florida governor was telling everyone the same thing he'd told Romney: he planned to stay on the bench. It wasn't so much concerns about a Bush hangover that were keeping Jeb there. It was his bank account.

You don't understand, Bush would say to the Republican pooh-bahs begging him to run. I was in the real estate development business in my state. There was a huge bubble, but I missed out because I was governor for eight years. So I'm starting from scratch. If, God forbid, I'm in an accident tomorrow—I'm in a wheelchair drooling, saliva coming from my mouth—who's going to take care of me? What are my wife and kids going to do? I've got to look after my family. This is my chance to do it.

With Jeb determined to stay out, the establishment, like the Romney campaign, monitored the movements of Barbour, Daniels, and Huckabee, while rolling its collective eyes at the theatrics of Trump. The four shared little in common biographically, politically, or characterologically. But when it came to 2012, each held several truths to be self-evident: that if he sought the Republican nomination, the battle would boil down to him versus Romney; that when it did, he would prevail; and that, in a country evenly split, he would stand a fighting chance in a general election against Obama.

In presidential politics, this level of certainty was as rare as a patch of white truffles sprouting in the Bronx. Almost always, when someone who believed he *should* occupy the White House—that the country would be well served by his presence in the big chair—also saw victory as attainable, he took the plunge. That four such men would stand down in the same year was almost unthinkable.

ROVE, FOR ONE, was sure that Haley Barbour would dive in. The bulk of the political world agreed. On April 14, the Mississippi governor was meeting-and-greeting in New Hampshire. The next night he was in South Carolina, speaking to the Charleston County Republican Party and winning its presidential straw poll. A month earlier, he had stumped in Iowa, held finance meetings in California, and given a major economic address in

Chicago. Behind the scenes, he had enlisted an all-star cast of campaign hands in the early states; his Washington brain trust had drawn up plans for an announcement tour in the first week of May. To all outward and inward appearances, Barbour was go, go, go.

He had been a central player in his party for thirty-five years: in the eighties as an operative (political director in the Reagan White House); in the nineties as one of Washington's most powerful lobbyists and chair of the RNC; in the aughts, as the two-term chief executive of his native state. Barbour was sixty-three now, with the body of a cannonball, a taste for bourbon, and a strategic brain as acuminate as Rove's. His connections and fund-raising capacity were unrivaled, his candidate skills top-notch. He was beloved by reporters for doling out dictums dripping in his syrupy twang: "In politics, good gets better and bad gets worse"; "The main thing is to keep the main thing the main thing."

Barbour had considered entering the 2008 field. Less than halfway through his first term as governor, he convened a secret meeting in Jackson of his closest advisers and his wife, Marsha, to start planning a White House run. But then Hurricane Katrina hit in August 2005 and blew it all away. Barbour realized he had no choice but to seek a second gubernatorial term to complete the recovery efforts.

With Barbour's handling of Katrina having won wide praise, the presidential buzz began building around him four years later. Over breakfast at the governor's mansion in late 2009, Rove raised the subject with Haley. "Ain't no way the country's ready for a fat white southerner with an accent who's been a lobbyist," Barbour joked, seeming to brush Rove off.

But the following summer, Barbour took the first step toward putting the pieces in place for a 2012 bid. He tasked his friend Scott Reed, who had managed Dole's 1996 campaign, to undertake a study of his vulnerabilities—and dredge up any slime his opponents might strive to smear him with. Barbour was serving as chair of the Republican Governors Association, a perch he could turn into a presidential launching pad if the party's candidates scored in the midterms. But he was careful to avoid the perception that he was using the job for his own advancement; he and other governors resented Romney for having done just that as RGA chair in 2006.

To say Barbour and Romney were oil and water severely understated the case. Romney respected Barbour's political mind and instincts but was astonished by how much Haley drank. Barbour, meanwhile, respected almost nothing about Romney professionally, considered him self-centered, tin-eared, and inauthentic. "The guy's never said a sentence to me that's spontaneous," Barbour told his people. What bothered him even more were the implications of Romney as front-runner. He's got a ceiling of 30 percent support for the nomination, Barbour said. His weakness will attract a large, unruly field, and that'll be bad for the party.

Barbour's views were broadly shared by the other Republican governors. Two weeks after the midterms—in which the GOP's candidates nearly pulled off a sweep on the back of Haley's massive RGA fund-raising haul—they met in San Diego, where an animated conversation broke out in one of the working groups about the looming presidential campaign. "It can't be Mitt," yelped Ohio's Kasich. "He's terrible!" Rick Perry of Texas concurred. New Jersey's Chris Christie was more diplomatic but no less unenthused.

The governors wanted one of their breed to be the nominee. Barbour took several aside and said he was thinking of running, winning pledges of support from some, such as Kasich, on the spot. But Barbour was having another set of conversations, too—a three-way discourse with Jeb and Mitch Daniels, a close pal of Barbour's. Over the phone and in person, they agreed that Romney had to be stopped and that one of them should step up to do it. Barbour and Daniels urged Bush to set aside his hesitancy, telling him they would stay out if he got in. But Bush refused to reconsider. Meanwhile, Barbour and Daniels, whose friendship stretched back to the Reagan era, lobbied each other to assume the mantle. Their importunings had a certain *Alphonse and Gaston* flavor, with each man clucking over his own weaknesses, praising the other's strengths, and saying, in effect, *After you!*

By late December 2010, Barbour was sitting in his statehouse office reviewing the dirt on himself, dug up by Scott Reed. The self-opposition research file was bulky, filling up the better part of a banker's box. It contained a long list of unsavory lobbying clients, including repressive foreign governments in places such as Kazakhstan and Eritrea, for whom Barbour's firm had labored. It laid out the areas where Barbour, as governor, had failed to improve his state's cellar-level national rankings, such as health and education. (*This won't be a "Mississippi miracle" type of campaign,* Reed thought.)

The strategist also talked to Barbour about his personal life, which for years was rumored to be nearly as vivacious as Bill Clinton's; as Barbour's former lobbying partner Ed Rogers liked to put it, "There is no skeleton in Haley's closet, but there is a bag of bones."

Barbour was unfazed. The lobbying stuff was old news, he said, and the Mississippi record he could talk his way through. As for any charges about his personal comportment, Barbour said, "I can handle that." With the Mississippi legislative session scheduled to end in early April, the governor set himself a May 1 decision deadline.

Not everyone shared Barbour's devil-may-careness about his influence-peddling background. In the Romney and Obama camps, it was considered poisonous enough to make him unelectable. Rove thought Barbour might be able to surmount the lobbyist label in the nomination fight but would be killed for it in the general—and told Haley so in a private meeting at CPAC in February 2011, mentioning his former firm's work for foreign governments.

That weekend, Barbour appeared on *Fox News Sunday*. The host, Chris Wallace, questioned him twice on lobbying, including references to Kazakhstan and Eritrea. Barbour smelled a rat. He and Rove had never been close; they existed in a state of subtle but distinct competition for the title of Smartest Guy in the GOP. With Rove's ties to Fox, the idea that Wallace's line of questioning was a coincidence struck Barbour as absurd. *I may have been born at night, but it wasn't LAST night,* he thought.

Serious as the lobbying issue might become, Barbour had a more pressing predicament, which involved the topic of race. On the same December day as his meeting with Reed, the conservative *Weekly Standard* magazine published a Barbour profile in which he discussed his boyhood in Yazoo City, Mississippi. Asked why his hometown, unlike many in the state, had been able to integrate its schools without violence, Barbour replied, "Because the business community wouldn't stand for it. You heard of the Citizens' Councils? Up north they think it was like the KKK. Where I come from it was an organization of town leaders. In Yazoo City, they passed a resolution that said anybody who started a chapter of the Klan would get their ass run out of town."

As it happened, Stuart Stevens, just back from a three-week trip to the

Arctic Circle, was also in Jackson that day to see Barbour, an old friend for whom he had made ads. Stevens had come to see whether Haley was planning to run, warn him that his chances were scant, and let him know that if Barbour did get in, the consultant's conflicting loyalties would probably cause him to sit out 2012.

Being from the Magnolia State, Stevens knew that the Citizens' Councils weren't as benign as Barbour made them sound; that although they'd squelched Klan violence to protect local businesses, they had been formed specifically to oppose school integration. "This is gonna be a problem," Stevens said to Barbour. "What are you going to do about it?"

Haley waved him off. "Nah," he said, "I don't think it's gonna be a problem."

This wasn't the first dismissive comment Barbour had made in his career on matters racial. But after a day of scorching criticism on cable and the Web, he released a statement calling the Citizens' Council "indefensible, as is segregation."

Then, in February, another racial brouhaha erupted when Barbour rejected an appeal from the NAACP to denounce a southern heritage group's proposal for a state-issued license plate honoring an early KKK leader, Confederate general Nathan Bedford Forrest. "I don't go around denouncing people," Barbour said. "There's not a chance it will become law."

Barbour's advisers believed that Haley had a blind spot on the issue. Their greatest fear was that he would be portrayed as Boss Hogg. Thinking back on the way Clinton—Bill Clinton!—had been cast as a race-baiter in 2008 by the Obamans, they knew that Barbour was a quadruply juicy target for caricature. If Haley were running the campaign of a candidate identical to himself, he would have seen it, too, and enforced an exaggerated degree of racial sensitivity as a political shield. Instead he retreated into defensiveness, failing to grasp the divide between what he believed about himself—*I don't have a racist bone in my body*—and his public image.

He laid off the bourbon, losing twenty pounds, and slipped away to the Mayo Clinic in April to secure a clean bill of health. His trips to the early states were going well; he was receiving a warm reception for his stances on three big issues on which he planned to run to Romney's (and much of his party's) left: immigration reform, a fairly quick exit from Afghanistan, and cutting defense spending.

But he was starting to flag physically on the trail, and jovially complained about being subjected to his own Bataan Death March. By Easter weekend he had conferred extensively with his family—Marsha and their two sons, Reeves and Sterling. Even though all three said they were behind him, his wife had recently told a Biloxi TV reporter how she felt about Haley running. "It horrifies me," she admitted. Sterling, too, had said publicly, "I am a private person and don't want him to run."

For months, Barbour had seemed to be sprinting like a scalded dog toward yes. But all along, he was shadowed by doubt. He thought about former Tennessee senator and actor Fred Thompson, whose ballyhooed 2008 campaign had gone nowhere. He thought about Gingrich, whom he bumped into in Iowa, bubbling about the crowds coming to see him. (*Jesus, don't let me run just because I get so full of myself because everybody's listening*, Haley mused.) He thought about the general election—how winning could turn the endeavor into a ten-year commitment, with two on the trail, four in office, and four more if he were reelected. For a man his age, the presidency would amount to "a life sentence," he said. Did Haley really want that? What about Marsha? *When does she get her turn?* he wondered.

Then there was the likelihood that he'd lose. It would be hard for *anybody* from Mississippi to beat the first black president, Barbour told Daniels, who didn't disagree. And given the premium in the GOP on electability, that meant it would be difficult for a Mississippian to claim the nomination. Barbour thought back to 2008 and how Katrina had dashed his plans. In presidential politics, he believed, your time only comes around once, and maybe that was it—maybe, Haley thought, he'd missed his moment.

The next day, April 25, Barbour got on a conference call with his embryonic campaign team and pulled the plug. "I decided I don't have the fire in my belly to make this race," he said, choking up. "I hope I haven't misled you all, or disappointed you too much."

Actually, the people closest to Haley heaved a sigh of relief. Over the months of gearing up, most of them had become convinced that if he ran, he would be destroyed. Donors were already expressing misgivings about his race-related blunders. ("He didn't just touch the third rail," said one. "He hugged the motherfucker.") Sadly, reluctantly, Barbour's inner circle concluded that a drinking, drawling, corpulent ex-lobbyist stood little chance of being elected president in modern America. In other words, that Haley had been right all along.

BARBOUR'S BAILING OUT WAS good news for Huckabee in at least two ways. It left him as the only potential southern charmer in the field, and it opened up the possibility of Haley endorsing him, which Huckabee thought conceivable. A couple of weeks earlier, the two had chatted when Huckabee was down at Mississippi College for a speech. Huckabee's daughter, Sarah, a political operative, had been angling for a job on Haley's team, in case her dad chose not to run. The two men joked about that, and about Barbour becoming Huckabee's campaign chairman if the decision went the other way.

Beyond their regional roots, silver tongues, and bulging waistlines, Huck and Haley were as different as could be. The former Arkansas governor was unimpeachably pious, a long-serving Baptist pastor. In terms of his policies, personality, and barely concealed resentments, he was a populist to his core. At political banquets, he often observed, I've got more in common with the people working in the kitchen than the ones at the head table. And unlike Barbour, Huckabee inspired trepidation in the Romneyites (because of his potency in the early states and with evangelicals) and the Obamans (because of his likability, folksiness, and optimism).

In 2008, that combination of qualities had carried Huckabee further than anyone expected: to second place in terms of delegates. (It made him crazy when pundits called Romney the runner-up. "Excuse me? Can you *add*?" he fumed.) Yet Huckabee was dismissed by the party's big shots. His offers to campaign for McCain were ignored, and he wasn't shortlisted for VP. Not long before the Republican convention, Huckabee received a call from the organizers, offering a speaking slot—five minutes to talk about education at 5:00 p.m. on the opening day. *They might as well ask me to set up a hot dog cart in front of the arena,* he thought.

The campaign had left Huckabee more than bruised; he was also basically broke. To finance his bid, he had taken out a second mortgage on his house, cashed in his annuities, retirement plan, and life insurance, and run up a debt of nearly $100,000. So into Rove mode he went. In quick succession, Huckabee signed deals to be a political analyst and weekend host on Fox, do daily radio commentaries for ABC, and write a book. He started traveling constantly, Willy Loman style, giving speech after speech.

By the end of 2010, Huckabee Inc. had made him fiscally whole again—and then some. He and his wife, Janet, had grown up poor, and Huckabee had spent his adult life in the ministry and public service. For the first time, he had some bread in his basket and was enjoying the taste. Mike and Janet were building a reported $3 million beachside home down in Walton County, Florida, near Pensacola. When they inspected the property, they burst out giggling at their good fortune. The first apartment they shared had cost $40 a month, they reminded each other, and would have fit inside one of the closets of their manse-in-the-making.

All along, Huckabee was eyeing another presidential run—in 2016. But the events of 2010 caused him to revise his timetable. In Obamacare, Huckabee saw a defining moment of doom for the incumbent; in the Tea Party, he saw a populist rebellion in which many of those who were packing the pitchforks were also Christian conservatives. In his travels before the midterms, Huckabee was struck by the fame he had achieved by being on Fox. During the 2008 race, he rarely had been recognized in public except by political junkies. Now people were coming up to him on the street, in airports, and in restaurants, asking for his autograph or a photograph with him, telling him they loved what he said on the tube, beseeching him to run again.

The night after the midterms, Huckabee had dinner with Ed Rollins, who had been his 2008 campaign chairman, and told him he was raring to go. Rollins was a storied political strategist, the manager of Reagan's reelection campaign in 1984. Loquacious and pugnacious—Rollins titled his memoir *Bare Knuckles and Back Rooms* and posed on the cover wearing boxing gloves—he was sixty-seven but still appetent to be in the game.

Rollins saw a clear pathway to the nomination for Huck—and a last chance at glory for himself. A Reuters/Ipsos national poll at the end of 2010 ranked Huckabee as the most popular Republican in the country. He would be unstoppable in Iowa and South Carolina, and with those wins in the bag, he could close the sale in the Sunshine State, his soon-to-be home. Rollins imagined headquartering the campaign in Tampa, where the GOP convention would be held. He insisted on total control, telling Huckabee that he was too old to have it any other way. Huckabee said, I wouldn't do this without you, Ed.

Over the next several months, Huckabee, Rollins, and two other operatives met for dinner regularly to hash out the race. A forty-page memo on the field was prepared, which yielded a verdict that Rollins spelled out succinctly: "If you don't run, Romney is going to be the nominee," he said.

Huckabee's bitterness toward his 2008 rival was unsurpassed, and owed in part to personal grievance. On the night that Huckabee took Iowa, Romney failed to call to congratulate him; when Huckabee extended that courtesy to Romney after losing to him in Michigan, he felt Mitt brushed him off. For two years, Huckabee stewed, until one day Romney phoned during his mending-fences phase. I didn't do right by you, Mitt said. I apologize. I should have realized that's the way the game is played.

Huckabee thanked Romney, who seemed sincere enough. But he couldn't help suspecting that Mitt was thinking, *This guy is on television every week. He's on radio every day. A lot of Republican voters pay attention to him, and I don't want him telling everybody what a bum I am.*

Huckabee's bully Fox News pulpit had a major downside, though: his contract prevented him from taking any steps toward a candidacy. (In March 2011, Fox suspended Gingrich and Santorum, who also had deals with the network, for ramping up their campaigns.) So Huckabee had to keep his meetings on the down-low. In mid-April, when a dozen religious-right leaders flew to New York to exhort him to run and vow their support, Huckabee steered clear of the session, letting Rollins handle it.

The political world assumed he would pass, and that money was the reason. One day, Rove, who had a home of his own in Florida not far from where the Huckabees were building, drove over to take a peek at the construction project. *That ain't a $3 million house—that's a $6 million house,* Rove thought. And after doing some guesstimates regarding Huckabee Inc.'s revenues, Rove surmised, *No way he can afford to run.*

Money was indeed on Huckabee's mind, but the calculations were more complicated. He realized that if he ran, he would have to sell the Florida property. Although doing so would have been painful for him and Janet, they were willing to take that step. The greater personal financial obstacle was regular income. Unlike Romney and other candidates who could live off of dividends, Huckabee had no stocks or bonds. *Everything I do for a living, every dime I make, ends the minute I become a candidate,* he thought. *No more speaking engagements, radio, or TV. How will we make it for two years?*

Sometimes Rollins guilt-tripped Huckabee when he brought up these concerns. "God's calling to you was 'Go spend twenty years in a ministry and twelve years in a governorship, and you could be the first real moral man elected president,'" Rollins said. "You think God wants you just to go make money?" Other times he tried to placate his guy. "We'll figure something out," he said. But no solution was ever found to cover Mike and Janet's monthly nut.

Equally confounding was the other side of the financial equation, which involved fund-raising. As governor, Huckabee had taken some moderate positions that the far right hated; he also had granted clemencies to prisoners who committed violent crimes after their release. Huckabee took hits for all of this in 2008, but in the new world of super PACs, he assumed the pounding from Romney's allies would be much more brutal.

To equip himself to fight back, Huckabee believed he would have to raise $50 million for the nomination contest. But he abhorred asking rich people for money, and his populism had alienated business and Wall Street. What Huckabee needed was his own Spencer Zwick, a gangbusting finance chair. Recruiting such a person, however, would require a signal that he was getting in, which would jeopardize his Fox contract. Thus was Huckabee caught in a devilish catch-22: wary of sacrificing his livelihood without knowing that the support for a run would be in place, but unable to gauge how much support was there without risking that livelihood.

Even so, Huckabee was inching toward yes—until he and Rollins came a cropper. For months they had been arguing over how long they could wait before rendering a final decision, with Huckabee wanting to defer until September and Rollins insisting on June. In late April, Huckabee began seeing stories in the press about his increasing inclination toward a run, and they had Rollins's fingerprints all over them. When Huckabee confronted him, Rollins was unrepentant. Mike, I've got to do this to keep us in the conversation, he said.

Huckabee was furious. His situation with Fox was already delicate, and now he was being summoned to meet with the company's lawyers to explain away the stories. Huckabee's family was ticked off, too. Janet was enthusiastic about his running, and his three kids were on board. They viewed Rollins's blabbing as inexcusable.

Huckabee saw it as a kind of epiphany. While he had learned in 2008 that Rollins was sometimes indiscreet, Huckabee always believed he could trust the strategist. No longer. *And if you can't trust the people in your inner circle to keep their mouths shut, you can't run a campaign,* he thought. With no team in waiting, no confidence about the money, the gaze of the Fox attorneys on him, and the prospect of being pulped by Romney's super PACs ahead of him, Huckabee decided that there was no point in waiting until September.

On Friday, May 13, Fox released a statement saying that Huckabee would announce his intentions on his TV program the next night. He didn't alert Rollins as to his decision. He didn't tell his executive producer or his staff. Outside of his family, the only person Huckabee informed in advance was the one who mattered most: Fox News CEO Roger Ailes.

"I'm surprised," Ailes said. "I thought you were going to do it."

HUCKABEE FEATURED A SPECIAL guest star on his program that night, who appeared right after the host's sign-off. "I'm Donald Trump, and this is a special announcement," the besuited billionaire said. "Mike Huckabee is not going to be running for president. This might be considered by some people, not necessarily me, bad news, because he is a terrific guy—and frankly I think he would be a terrific president. But a lot of people are very happy that he will not be running, especially other candidates."

The two men had huddled in Trump's office a few weeks earlier. The Donald liked Pastor Mike, although he wasn't sure that Huckabee should be the person negotiating with the Chinese. (That was Trump's department.) Huckabee entered the meeting suspecting, as did many observers, that Trump's coquetry about running was a charade, a publicity stunt. But he left with a different opinion. *Gosh, he might really jump in,* Huckabee thought.

In the terrarium of American public life, Donald John Trump was an exotic specimen: famous and infamous, beloved and detested, lauded and mocked—but never ignored. His politics were promiscuously ecumenical. He had been a Republican, a Reform Party member, and a Democrat, and now he was a Republican again. On the left, he was excoriated as a racist for his promulgation of birtherism. On the right, he was scorned as a crank for espousing a variant of protectionism that bordered on mercantilism. Among many in the Beltway and Manhattan smart sets, he was derided as a bloviating braggart.

But there was no denying that Trump's political ledger was filled with items that any candidate would have killed for. He was at or near the top of the polls, both nationally and in the early states. He was filthy rich, with a net worth estimated by *Forbes* to be as high as $3 billion. He had two network television programs watched by millions every week, and while he would have to abandon them if he ran, he had unfettered access to the news media. (The network morning shows let Trump come on by phone, which was unheard of.) His speeches lured sell-out crowds with little promotion. Politicians of all stripes paid him homage. He was buddies with the Clintons, pals with Chris Christie, chummy with many others—not just because they wanted his money but because Trump was a hoot to hang with.

One way of seeing all of this was as a symptom of postmillennial decay, the degradation of public discourse, and the encroachment of celebrity worship into the arena of national affairs. Another way of looking at it was as an indication of the GOP's state of disarray. Then there was the way Trump perceived the thing: as a manifestation of his magnificence—and a prime opportunity.

Trump had vaguely considered running for president under the Reform Party banner in 2000. This time, his first apparent stirrings of interest came in early October 2010, when news broke about a mysterious telephone poll in New Hampshire that included thirty questions measuring his viability. Trump insisted he wasn't behind the survey, but two days later on Fox News he crowed, "I hear that the results are amazing . . . For the first time in my life, I'm actually thinking about it."

Four months later, Trump made his maiden appearance at CPAC. After telling the packed room he would decide by June whether he was running, Trump said America was becoming "the laughingstock of the world." Barely mentioning Obama, he spent much of his speech thundering about the need to get tough with China, India, and OPEC. (Also with Somali pirates: "Give me one good admiral and a couple of good ships, we'd blast them out of the water," Trump boomed.) The audience went wild.

Trump returned to New York luxuriating in his triumph, boasting about the size of the crowd and the enthusiasm of the response. Almost immediately, his numbers began to soar. A *Newsweek*/Daily Beast poll in February showed him neck and neck with Obama. An NBC News/*Wall Street Journal* survey that month gave him higher favorable ratings than Romney, Pawlenty, or Boehner.

To Trump, it only seemed right and proper. He was one of the great entrepreneurs of the age, with properties that spanned the globe. *(The greatest properties!* Trump thought. *I'm building things in Scotland that are unbelievable.)* Everyone wanted to hear what he had to say. *(I'm the highest-paid speaker in the world for success speeches!)* The fact that he wasn't a professional politician was the key to his appeal; his bracing stick-it-to-'em rhetoric was what drew voters to him. *It's not because they love me,* he thought. *They see the world as ripping us off, and they think: Trump is gonna stop it.*

They didn't think that about Romney, in Trump's opinion. He had never met the governor, best as he recalled, but his impressions from afar were unfavorable. He compared Romney to a Broadway play that opens to lackluster reviews: cursed before the curtain goes up. Trump was publicly sniffy about Romney as a capitalist, denigrating him as a "small-business guy," and privately disdainful of Bain. "They'd buy a company and fire everyone," he told his associates.

Trump's view of Obama had a more sinister hue, of course. Even beyond the birther stuff, he considered the president a failure and a fraud, horrible at governing and overrated as a campaigner. Trump believed it was luck and Bush fatigue that had allowed Obama to vanquish Hillary and McCain in 2008, and he dissed the president's oratorical skills. *(He's not bad—but great? No.)* He was convinced that Obama's memoir *Dreams from My Father* was actually written by Bill Ayers, the former Weather Underground member who was a source of controversy in the last campaign. And Trump was itching to probe Obama's academic history. *(Harvard Law Review? Bullshit! Nobody's ever seen his grades!)* But first Trump wanted to see his birth certificate.

Trump initially fastened on to birtherism in an interview on *Good Morning America* in March. The subsequent criticism came fast and fierce, and not only from liberals. "His full embrace of the birther issue means he's off there in the nutty right," Rove said on Fox News. "The guy is smarter than this . . . Making that the centerpiece of his campaign means that he is now, you know, a joke candidate."

Having written a $100,000 check to Crossroads in 2010, Trump was rip-shit with Rove. *He's a bully, just like Rosie O'Donnell,* the Donald thought. And Rove was also wrong, Trump asserted. Birtherism was just a part of his campaign; the press refused to pay attention to his other issues. But Trump also privately admitted that birtherism was a bonanza for him. The more he talked about Obama's genealogy, the better he polled—and the higher the ratings of *Celebrity Apprentice* climbed. Trump's office was inundated with letters from around the country imploring him to enter the race.

By the time Trump's Sikorsky helicopter was in descent into Portsmouth, New Hampshire, on April 27, he was running a strong second in the state, behind Romney. Just before touching down, the voice of Trump's adviser Michael Cohen cut through the roar of the chopper's engines, informing him that Obama was about to release his long-form birth certificate. *(Or another forgery,* thought Trump.) Stepping into an airplane hangar and facing a mob of reporters as the theory he had propounded was being ripped to shreds by Obama in real time, Trump might have been abashed. Instead, he basked in the attention. "I know what I think," Trump said later that day. "He only did it because of Trump!"

Amid talk from his camp that he would now be free to focus on other matters, Trump flew to Las Vegas. In a speech to an adoring throng at the Treasure Island Hotel, Trump addressed Iraq: "We build a school, we build a road, they blow up the school. We build another school, we build another road, they blow them up, we build again—and in the meantime we can't get a fucking school in Brooklyn!" And OPEC: "We have nobody in Washington that sits back and says, 'You're not going to raise that fucking price!'"

And the Chinese: "Listen, you motherfuckers, we're going to tax you 25 percent!"

The string of f-bombs made headlines and brought censure. Trump was only mildly chastened. *They're not even bad words—they're "emphasis words,"* he thought. *But would I do it again? No. I went to the Wharton School of Finance. I'm a very smart guy.*

Trump hopped back in his jet and made a beeline to D.C. for the White House Correspondents' dinner. Once again, he was swarmed—by the press, paparazzi, elected officials. *(It's the Academy Awards of politics, and I'm the hottest one in the room!)* Once again, he was spanked by Obama. And once again, in spite of the smoke that everyone near him saw emanating from his ears, Trump professed to be pleased as punch. "It was the greatest!" he told Cohen over the phone. "To have the president of the United States spend that amount of time talking about *me*—I loved it!"

All good things must come to an end, however, even for Trump. The reality hovering over his deliberations from the get-go was the future of the *Apprentice* franchise, which had to be resolved before May 16, when NBC would unveil its fall lineup at an event in New York for advertisers. Trump was under heavy pressure from his network bosses to close down the suspense.

Trump helicoptered to New Hampshire for a Nashua Chamber of Commerce lunch on May 11, then came back and conferred with his wife, Melania. *I like New Hampshire, New Hampshire likes me, I work well in New Hampshire,* Trump thought. *I like Iowa, South Carolina, and Nevada.* But he would be giving up a lot to run, especially financially. *(They pay me a fortune, and for what? It should be illegal.)* He was negotiating for a hundred acres in Miami, on which he planned to build a resort. He'd have to give that up, too. And a self-funded campaign would require a chunk of cheddar. *Rather than making a lot of money,* he thought, *I'd be spending a lot of money.*

On May 13, the same Friday that Huckabee put out word that he would announce his decision, Trump informed the NBC honchos he was choosing prime time over the pursuit of the presidency. It was a 50-50 call, Trump told his associates, and even after assuring the network he was staying, he had second thoughts—when he turned on the TV that Sunday morning and watched *Meet the Press*. The show's host, David Gregory, was discussing a new poll that put Trump in second place among Republicans nationally. The only person ahead of him was Huckabee, who had taken himself off the table the night before. Which made Trump the bona fide front-runner.

Am I the only guy in history at number one in the polls who got out? Trump asked himself. *Am I fucking crazy?* Then he thought again about what he'd be sacrificing to run, and about something that Melania once told him: he was already the biggest star in the world, bigger even than Tom Cruise.

Why would I do this? the Donald thought. *I already have an amazing life.*

MITCH DANIELS'S LIFE RESEMBLED Trump's as much as a plumber's resembled a porn star's. The Indiana governor had been married twice, but to the same woman, and his idea of decadent indulgence was a fried bologna sandwich. He stood five foot seven and wore a comb-over as reticent as Trump's hairstyle was rococo. He was averse to bluster, allergic to blarney, and drolly self-effacing. In a speech that spring, Daniels noted "all this favorable press I've been getting" about the possibility of his running. "Just listen to a quick sample: 'small,' 'stiff,' 'short,' 'pale,' 'unimposing,' 'unassuming,' 'uninspiring,' 'understated,' 'uncharismatic,' 'accountant-like,' 'non-telegenic,' 'boring,' 'balding,' 'blunt,' 'nerdy,' 'wooden,' 'wonky,' 'puny,' and 'pint-sized.' Really, it all points to one inescapable conclusion: it's destiny!"

The venue for that speech was the annual white-tie Gridiron Dinner in Washington, one of the Beltway upper echelon's haughtiest and hottest tickets. And Daniels's selection as the Republican toaster spoke volumes about his status on the national stage in early 2011. Far from being put off by his lack of magnetism, the GOP's potentates were coalescing around him, on the theory that Daniels would present the ideal contrast with the incumbent: he was the un-Obama.

The establishment attraction to Daniels was easy to understand. He had a gold-plated insider's résumé: staffer to Indiana senator Richard Lugar, Barbour's predecessor as Reagan's political director, top executive at the pharmaceutical giant Eli Lilly, head of OMB under Bush 43. He won the Indiana governorship narrowly in 2004 and by eighteen points in 2008, even as Obama became the first Democratic presidential candidate to carry the state since 1964. Daniels was a fiscal hawk and institutional reformer whose mixture of tough love and the common touch—he rambled around in an Indiana-made RV or on a Harley—earned him approval ratings north of 60 percent, even at the nadir of the recession.

Daniels's experiences as a candidate in the Hoosier State informed his dim view of Romney, whom he saw as the antithesis of authentic, a pre-programmed automaton. Former secretary of state Condoleezza Rice once told Daniels that when Mitt visited Stanford, where she had returned after her time in government, she watched astonished as he emitted a canned stump speech to a sophisticated, techie crowd—then repeated the faux pas at a small private dinner she hosted for him afterwards.

Even more problematic for Daniels was Romney's plutocratic demeanor. *If you wear the Republican uniform,* Daniels thought, *you have a stereotype stuck on you. You don't whine about it. You do something about it. You prove it isn't true—you prove that you're for the policies you're for because they're good for poor people, good for people on the way up.* And Daniels had done just that, winning 20 percent of the black vote and a majority of the youth vote in 2008. But when he looked at Romney, all he could think was *He's never going to get there.*

Daniels spent much of 2010 trying to recruit a Romney alternative. Besides making runs at Jeb and Haley, he pressed hard on two others: Fred Smith, the founder, chairman, and CEO of FedEx, and former Senate majority leader Bill Frist. But neither took the bait.

At the same time, a handful of Daniels's political and business cronies inspirited him to dangle his own toes in the water. Daniels believed the ballooning debt under Obama posed an existential threat to the country, and his friends maintained that he was the best person to defuse it. He had shrunk the government in Indiana, turning an inherited $200 million deficit into a $1.3 billion surplus, and his D.C. experience taught him where the bodies were buried in the federal budget. "Here's the thing," one of his buddies said. "Do you have any doubt you are competent to be president?"

Daniels had never aspired to occupy the Oval Office. "When I look in the mirror," he often said, "I don't see a president." But posing the question in terms of competence made him think differently. I don't know if anybody is ever really ready for that job, Daniels said, but I'm as ready as anybody.

Quietly, Daniels began holding private dinners in Indianapolis for donors, bundlers, and policy mavens while publicly floating a number of trial balloons that looked more like Hindenburgs. In a *Weekly Standard* profile, Daniels declared the need "to call a truce" on volatile social issues such as abortion and gay marriage. To *Newsweek*, he said that tax increases might be necessary to tame the deficit. In a speech in October, he talked favorably about a European-style value-added tax and tariffs on imported oil. Daniels anticipated that the reaction to these statements on the right might blow up the whole Mitch-for-president thing. But they detonated with only a dull pop—and even that sound was squelched by hosannas from other quarters.

By the end of 2010, Daniels had plenty of reasons to feel emboldened, but he also had a source of weighty discouragement, which had been there all along: his family. His wife, Cheri, was a private person who had been dead set against her husband running for governor. Mitch talked her into it with an ironclad promise: If we do this, I'll never ask you to go anywhere and sit there looking fawningly up at me; come or don't come to any event you want; it's my job, not yours. Cheri took him up on it, presiding as a popular but low-profile first lady. But Mitch couldn't guarantee similar seclusion in a presidential campaign. Her attitude toward the idea was *I don't even want to talk about this.*

There was another wellspring of Cheri's reluctance. In 1994, after sixteen years of marriage, she had left Mitch for a doctor in California with a wife and children of his own, breaking up that household and divorcing her husband. In the court proceedings, Mitch succeeded in keeping their four daughters, then ages eight to fourteen, in Indiana. Cheri married the doctor, then soon left *him* and reconciled with and remarried Mitch. In the years since, she had never spoken publicly about the turmoil, and Mitch had done so only once—pithily telling *The Indianapolis Star,* "If you like happy endings, you'll love our story."

Cheri dreaded the prospect of the intimacies of her marriage being dredged up and dissected by the freak show. She wanted a life filled with golf and grandchildren, not state dinners. The Daniels daughters were equally appalled by what a campaign would entail. And Mitch was no keener on the distortions and nastiness that would come. It was known that, as an undergraduate, he had spent two nights in jail for possession of marijuana.

But there was more to his infraction, including LSD and prescription drugs, which would be turned into tabloid fodder.

In early February 2011, Daniels flew down to Dallas for the weekend of the Super Bowl, which Indianapolis would be hosting the next year, and found himself summoned to a meeting with George W. Bush. The former president's purpose was clear: he wanted Mitch to run. You're nuts if you don't seize this opportunity, Bush said. The party ain't got much on the field; the nomination's yours for the taking. Now, I can't come out and support you. Not right for a former president to play that role. But my network, my people on the money side, will be with you, I'm sure of it.

When Daniels rattled off his and his family's qualms, Bush was dismissive. You're only looking at the downsides, 43 said. There are huge upsides, including for your family. You think Laura and the girls wanted me to run? Of course they didn't. But it all worked out great for them.

Six days later, Daniels took the podium at CPAC and delivered what sounded like a full-blown campaign speech. Devoted almost entirely to debt (which Daniels labeled "the new red menace, this time consisting of ink"), entitlements, and economic restoration, the address was adamantine in its conservatism. But it was also laced with calls for compromise, civility, and inclusion, and featured a gentle but unmistakable poke at the flying monkeys of the right-wing media circus. "We have learned in Indiana, big change requires big majorities," Daniels said. "We will need people who never tune in to Rush or Glenn [Beck] or Laura [Ingraham] or Sean [Hannity]."

Daniels's speech didn't light up the fire-breathers in the room the way that Trump's did. But outside the hall, cooler heads took notice. Over at the White House, Plouffe printed out a copy for Obama, who was impressed by Daniels's tone. "There's a reasonableness here," the president said. "I think I'd enjoy debating Daniels." Bill Clinton's ears pricked up, too. I know a lot of Republicans, and Daniels is one of the smart ones, he said publicly some time later—and told the governor privately, I watched that speech, and then I watched it again.

Seeing Daniels apparently teetering on the brink, the Republican establishment scurried to lasso and yank him in. Rove rang up to counsel him about placeholding with key fund-raisers and operatives. McCain called to convey a message similar to Bush's: As the previous nominee, I shouldn't endorse anyone—but you oughta run, and my people will be behind you. Christie, Jeb, and Wisconsin governor Scott Walker added their names to what Daniels thought of as his "fictional letterhead." Dick Cheney and Dick Armey, the former House majority leader now enmeshed in the Tea Party, were also phantom signatories, as was the august columnist George Will. Major league bundlers were beating a path to Mitch's door.

Daniels was candid with everyone: his family was still a problem—*the* problem, in fact. Which triggered a full-court press on Cheri from all directions. Inside the Daniels household, Mitch probed his daughters for any changes in his wife's thinking—"What's Mom said to you about it?" "Have you said any more to Mom?" Daniels's staff sent Cheri favorable press clips. The cronies who had originally induced him to test the waters sat down with her and pled their case. One day, the phone rang, Cheri picked it up, and W. and Laura Bush were together on the line, offering to address her concerns, attempting to wheedle her along. Cheri politely but firmly told them she didn't want to be pushed.

Then, out of nowhere, the Indiana Republican Party announced that Cheri would be keynoting its fund-raising dinner in Indianapolis on May 12. Mrs. Daniels had never given a high-profile political speech. More than a thousand people would be in attendance, along with much of the national media. Among politicos and the press, speculation was rampant that the speech represented a crack in the ice—or at least an attempt by Daniels's advisers to increase Cheri's comfort level in the spotlight, even as her appearance would smoke out unpleasant news stories about the couple's marital troubles.

Those stories arrived on schedule and en masse, popping up in newspapers and all over the Web days before the speech. Little information in the pieces was new or sordid, although an article in *The Washington Post* included an ominous sentence: "In exchange for anonymity, an official for another GOP prospect provided contact information for the ex-wife of the man Cheri Daniels married." (The ex-wife lashed out at Cheri to at least one reporter, calling her "vengeful" and a "narcissist.")

In the Daniels orbit, all fingers pointed at the Romney camp, and in particular at Rhoades, for shopping the ex-wife's cell-phone number and e-mail address to the press. Daniels didn't care—he already knew that the jig was up. For all the efforts at persuading his family, the sorority never budged. Unlike Ann Romney, Cheri didn't see her husband as some kind of savior. As for the Daniels girls, the idea of their father being president held zero attraction. "Dad, you don't get it," his daughter Meredith said. "We're not afraid that you'll lose. We're afraid that you'll win."

On Saturday, May 21, Daniels arranged a conference call with his cronies. He told them he had prepared a statement to release to *The Indianapolis Star* saying that he would not run. Like Barbour, Daniels rarely let his emotions show; but just as Barbour's voice had broken when he bailed out, so Daniels's did now. "Look, guys, I know you don't agree, and you're disappointed, and I'm sorry I've let you down," he said. "I love my country, but I love my family more."

One of Daniels's friends on the call suggested he include that last bit in his statement to the *Star*. Mitch agreed, and a few hours later the line was in, the word was out, and the fourth little Indian was gone.

MANY MONTHS WOULD PASS before the implications of the wave of Republican nolo contenderes in the spring of 2011 were fully visible. But even in the moment, it was clear they had yielded a freakish historical anomaly. With a vulnerable Democrat in the White House and a winnable election on the horizon, many of the GOP's most adept and accomplished potential candidates had decided not to bother. Their reasons were by turns political, personal, financial, generic, and idiosyncratic, but the upshot of their insufficient appetites was undeniable: the weakest Republican field in modern times—and an unloved, unsteady, unlikely front-runner blessed with a degree of blind shithouse luck that would make a Vegas gambler weep.

But Romney wasn't feeling as if he'd hit the jackpot. After months of internal back-and-forth in Lexington, his big speech on health care had been scheduled to take place at the University of Michigan, in Ann Arbor. Romney was deeply and fussily immersed in preparing the presentation. Lapsing into full Bain mode, he wanted to build his address around a PowerPoint deck, as he had sometimes done in the 2008 campaign. After asking his policy maven Lanhee Chen to put together the slides, Mitt looked them over, tossed them out, and then sketched out a new set on his own, by hand.

On the mid-May morning of the speech, Mitt woke up to find that *The Wall Street Journal* editorial page was at it again—with a scathing and supersize prebuttal of his defense of Romneycare, under the headline OBAMA'S RUNNING MATE. Mitt had been trying to win over Rupert Murdoch, the *Journal*'s owner, since the 2008 campaign. But Murdoch thought Romney was unconvincing and wooden from the get-go. And his resistance was revved up by the *Journal*'s editorial-page editor, Paul Gigot, who considered Romney the epitome of fraudulence and led the paper's fatwa against him.

"Have you read this?" Romney asked Chen in their Ann Arbor hotel.

"Yeah, it's not good," Chen replied.

"It's *really* not good," Romney said—and things would go downhill from there as the reviews of the speech came back and were as bad, politically and substantively, as the *Journal*'s preview. The left and the right agreed that calling Romneycare common sense and Obamacare lunacy was "a logical contradiction," as *National Review* put it. The lampoonery of Mitt's reliance on PowerPoint was so pervasive—especially among conservatives, who ritually chided Obama for his dependence on a teleprompter—that Romney would never use it again in the campaign.

On June 2, Romney made his candidacy official with another speech, this one at Bittersweet Farm, in Stratham, New Hampshire. The setting was bucolic and gorgeous, but there were two problems with it. Bittersweet was a hay farm, and Romney suffered from hay fever; and the farmhouse was filled with cats, to which he was also allergic.

While Romney's mortified traveling aides scrambled for drops to salve his rheumy eyes, he and the rest of his team discussed another unwanted distraction of the day: the intrusion of Sarah Palin. A week earlier, Palin had embarked on a haphazard bus tour of historic sites along the Eastern Seaboard. That morning, Team Romney learned that she would be pitching up later in the day at a clambake in Seabrook, New Hampshire, a site of no historic import that just happened to be a mere twelve miles from Bittersweet Farm.

Some of Romney's aides were irate about what they saw as an obvious attempt by Palin to step on Mitt's headlines. (Just before his announcement,

Palin addressed reporters on Bunker Hill and attacked Romneycare.) Ann Romney shared their irritation, grousing around the farmhouse that Palin's incursion was "classless."

The candidate himself shrugged Palin off. Sure, she was angling for attention. Sure, she was a pest. *But how annoyed can you get at Sarah Palin?* Romney thought. All that mattered was that there was no way she was going to run—Romney was sure of it. He had plenty of real things to worry about and wasn't going to let himself be distracted by shiny objects. But he wasn't particularly pleased by what he saw in the *New Hampshire Union Leader* the next morning: a huge front-page photo of Palin, with the story about his formal entry in the race tucked inside on page A3.

Romney was still absorbing that affront when he sat down for an interview via satellite that same morning with CBS's *The Early Show* as part of his announcement tour. Obama was headed to Toledo, Ohio, that day to tour a Chrysler plant and trumpet the news that the company would be paying back its $7.6 billion government loan in full and ahead of schedule. The program's anchor, Erica Hill, asked Romney about his 2008 *Times* op-ed, citing its provocative headline. Wasn't he wrong to have advocated allowing Detroit to go bankrupt?

"Bankruptcy, as you understand, is not liquidation of an enterprise," Romney replied. "It's allowing an enterprise to go through the bankruptcy court so that they can reorganize and come out stronger. And that's precisely what finally happened . . . The president recognized I was right . . . and the company finally went through bankruptcy, went through a managed bankruptcy, came out of bankruptcy, and now is recovering."

Hill seemed unsatisfied with Mitt's answer. She kept trying to interrupt as he continued to explain. "But, sir," Hill said, breaking through at last, "the company actually had to go through bankruptcy before that bailout."

To Romney, the anchor's comment was, on its face, at once redundant and a non sequitur; Hill was playing back his precise argument to him as if she were challenging his logic.

Romney paused, blinked his eyes twice, raised his eyebrows, and smiled tightly.

"Yeah, that's, that's exactly what I said," Mitt replied, his voice betraying annoyance. "The headline you read, which said 'Let Detroit Go Bankrupt,' points out that those companies needed to go through bankruptcy to shed those costs."

The interview went on in this vein for another few minutes—Hill still pressing, Romney ever more irritated. ("Erica, I think you're misunderstanding.") But the damage was already done. All along, Romney knew that the politically problematic aspect of his op-ed was not the content but the headline. And yet now he had committed the grave faux pas of repeating the four poisonous words on camera.

Romney realized the mistake would almost certainly come back to bite him. That he would see that footage again someday in ad after ad, assuming that he made it to the general election. The prospects of his getting there had been improved by so many heavy hitters deciding to stay on the sidelines—about that there could be no doubt. But even now, Romney continued to suspect that someone else would inevitably suit up. There was talk of Paul Ryan, talk of Rick Perry, and talk of Chris Christie, all of whom would be formidable.

And then there was the talk about that other guy, who actually *was* about to enter the race—a guy who possessed the rare capacity to make Romney's blood boil.

THE TEST-TUBE CANDIDATE

J ON AND MARY KAYE HUNTSMAN, decked out in tuxedo and gown, sashayed down the steps of their new townhouse just north of Dupont Circle and strolled across Connecticut Avenue to the Washington Hilton. They were headed to the White House Correspondents' Dinner. This would be the night Obama dismembered Trump, but for them April 30 would be memorable for more than that. Forty-eight hours earlier, the Huntsmans had returned to America after spending much of the past two years in Beijing, where Jon served as ambassador to China. Tonight would be a welcome home and a coming-out party—and the start of a misadventure as strange and surreal as any in the annals of presidential politics.

Surreal was the word that kept running through Jon's head as he and his wife swept into the hotel ballroom that Saturday night. In Beijing, Huntsman had been subsumed into a world of lusterless confinement, surrounded by military intelligence officers in an embassy so secure it felt like a prison, about as distant as one could be from the Beltway hurly-burly. Now here he was, smack-dab in the middle of the most glamorous, garish event on the Washington social calendar. And, making matters infinitely weirder, everyone wanted . . . to talk to him.

Huntsman had been to the Correspondents' Dinner before, when he was governor of Utah. He and Mary Kaye strutted down the red carpet and were ignored (as flashbulbs popped for Madeleine Albright). As ambassador, he'd been just as anonymous. But since January, when Huntsman dropped an unsubtle hint in a *Newsweek* interview, speculation had been raging that he was coming back to the United States to seek the Republican nomination—and, ultimately, a face-off with his current boss and benefactor.

Huntsman knew that the presidential buzz about him was building, but he hadn't expected it to transform him into the belle of this particular ball. Colin Powell came up, all smiley and chatty, and said hello. David Gregory asked him to appear on *Meet the Press*. (*Really?* thought Huntsman. *Never been invited on someone's show before.*) Even Trump shook his hand and welcomed him to the race. *My gosh—Don Trump, the guy I read about,* Huntsman mused. *Maybe this thing is real.*

As guests of Mike Bloomberg, Jon and Mary Kaye arrived at their table, where they were seated with Valerie Jarrett. Dealings with the Obamans had been fraught since the conjecture started that Huntsman might be aiming to unseat POTUS. Jarrett greeted the Huntsmans with iciness, through clenched teeth. Obama, in his routine onstage, took a gentle jab at Jon's fluency in Mandarin, suggesting English was his second language. Seated at an adjacent table, Axelrod leaned over, eyebrow arched, and said, "Welcome back. I see you have a big speech coming up"—a commencement address in the key Republican primary state of South Carolina.

"Well, if you have any suggestions for me, let me know," Huntsman awkwardly replied.

"I'm sure you have *plenty* of help," Axelrod said.

Everyone in politics was aware of who was helping Huntsman: a fifty-two-year-old Texan strategist named John Weaver, who had guided McCain's outside-the-box campaign in 2000. A longtime rival of Rove, Weaver had a large network of loyalists and a matrix of enemies just as extensive. He was tall and disheveled, murmuring and furtive. By his account, he had taken a flier and assembled a campaign-in-waiting for Huntsman's return, raising issues of both legality and appearances. The Hatch Act, on the federal books since 1939, restricted election activities by executive-branch officials; by custom and tradition, those involved in foreign policy and national security abstained absolutely from domestic politics. Weaver publicly insisted that there had been no coordination or even contact between him and Huntsman about a 2012 bid. But the Obamans assumed there was more to the tale. Much more.

Weaver was at the Hilton, too. He had run into the Huntsmans on the way in, but shooed them off in a mild panic. ("Governor, please keep walking.") Arriving at his table, Weaver discovered that one of his seatmates was Plouffe.

"I just met my candidate," Weaver said innocently.

Plouffe rolled his eyes.

When the dinner was over, Weaver repaired to the hotel bar with a posse of operatives he had recruited to the campaign-in-waiting. No one was certain whether Huntsman was actually running; they hoped to meet with him Monday to find out.

Midnight had passed, amber liquor was flowing, and Weaver's crew was on its way to seeing double—when the strategist checked his e-mail and scurried out of the bar. Minutes later he returned, phone in hand, and gathered his belongings.

"Guys, I gotta go," Weaver said. "He wants to see me first thing tomorrow morning."

THE REPATRIATION OF Jon Meade Huntsman Jr. was an irresistible story. He was fifty-one years old, with a charming spouse, seven attractive children, oodles of foreign policy expertise, and a glittering résumé that included stints in the administrations of Reagan and both Bushes, as well as experience as an executive at his family's chemical firm. Elected governor of the Beehive State in 2004 and reelected four years later in a landslide, he was fiscally conservative, pro-gun, and anti-abortion, but moderate on issues such as the environment, immigration, and gay rights. The heterodoxy was one element of what made him intriguing. Another was the impudence of turning on Obama. But most compelling were his ties to the man he would have to roll over to claim the Republican nomination.

As former governors, multimillionaires, and members of the Church of Jesus Christ of Latter-day Saints, Huntsman and Romney had much in common. With their lean frames, chiseled features, ramrod postures, and salon-model hair, they looked as if they were related—and were, in fact, distant cousins. They were scions of what one scholar of their religion described as "two royal families of Mormonism," two clans entwined for generations, once warmly but no longer.

The bonds stretched back to the faith's founding. Parley Pratt, a contemporary of the Mormon prophet Joseph Smith and one of the church's earliest missionaries, was Huntsman's great-great-great-grandfather and Romney's great-great-grandfather. Huntsman's mother, Karen, roomed at the University of Utah with Mitt's sister, Jane. Karen's father, David Haight, was the boyhood best friend of Mitt's dad, George, with whom Huntsman's father served in the Nixon administration.

Jon Huntsman Sr. kept a lower profile than Romney père, never holding elective office. But he amassed a far greater fortune, founding a packaging company that invented the clamshell box for the Big Mac, then building the conglomerate that made him a billionaire and one of the wealthiest Mormons on the planet. Gruff, impressive, philanthropically munificent, he had a mind-bogglingly ecumenical array of friends: Margaret Thatcher, Dick Cheney, Harry Reid, Warren Buffett, Michael Moore, and Glenn Beck, who once described him as having "the character of George Washington." Senior's eldest boy and namesake, whom he called Jonny, was the apple of his eye.

With the help of the father's political connections, the son rode the fast track. Under Bush 41, Jon was named ambassador to Singapore at thirty-two, making him the youngest U.S. plenipotentiary in a century. But in 1999, his next aspiration—to be the rescuer of the scandal-ridden Winter Olympics in Salt Lake City—was derailed. In seeking the job, Jon squared off against Mitt, whom (incredibly) he had never met. Huntsman Sr. pushed hard for Jonny. The Romney forces fought back with an intense lobbying campaign, accusing the Huntsmans of pursuing the plum to advance Jon's political ambitions, and reportedly enlisting the Mormon church hierarchy in Mitt's cause.

Utah governor Mike Leavitt led the search committee, and his decision to pick Romney left the Huntsman family livid. In *The Salt Lake Tribune*, Huntsman Sr. assailed Mitt as "politically driven" and "very, very slick and fast-talking," comparing him to Bill Clinton. Huntsman Jr. would complain for years thereafter that he'd been "used" to make a closed process look open, that Romney's selection was "precooked."

By the time Romney was gearing up for his 2008 run, the storm seemed to have blown over. Mitt began consulting Jon about foreign policy and trade. Huntsman Sr. signed on as a finance chair to Romney's PAC. In mid-2005, Huntsman Jr. was quoted in a Salt Lake City newspaper saying, "I'll do whatever I can" for Romney. "Mitt would make an excellent [presidential] candidate. I'm probably the only governor who has come out this early." Face to face, he assured Romney of his support.

Yet Huntsman soon started feeling taken for granted, as though he wasn't part of Mitt's inner circle. He complained to his gubernatorial chief of staff, Jason Chaffetz, that Romney was just going through the motions— that if Mitt won the White House, he would feel inhibited about naming a fellow Mormon as secretary of state, a job for which Huntsman pined.

McCain, by contrast, was courting Jon like crazy, inviting him on a trip to Iraq in March 2006. When Huntsman returned, Romney, who had picked up murmurs that Jon might be wavering, called to check in. Jon told him all was well. But a few weeks later, with no warning, Huntsman announced that he was backing McCain, joining the Arizonan's team as a national co-chair.

When Romney heard the news, he hit the roof. Perfidy was a part of politics—Mitt knew that—but he expected better from a Huntsman. He thought of Haight, Jon's late maternal grandfather and a Mormon apostle, one of the church's high elders. Mitt had helped him raise money for Brigham Young University; Haight was a giant. What would he have said about this?

Romney got Huntsman on the phone and told him what he thought, hissing the nastiest personal insult he could conjure: "Your grandfather would be ashamed of you!"

Mitt wasn't finished—his next angry call was to Huntsman Sr.

Your son betrayed us, Romney said. We brought him inside, shared strategy with him. He said he was on our team. Now he's done this without even having the decency to call me first.

The Huntsmans proffered all manner of justifications for the about-face.

Jon Jr. argued that 2008 was shaping up to be a national security election, and that McCain was the better candidate to prosecute those issues. Jon Sr. complained that his son had been kept out of the Romney loop.

Give me a break, Mitt thought. Jon had flipped because he'd decided McCain was more likely to win. It was that simple, and that craven.

From that moment on, Mitt emitted nothing but bile about Huntsman. He was a man of no accomplishments. He had inherited his money, not earned it. He was in politics only because his father had concluded that he had no aptitude for business, and he had become governor only because of Senior's throw weight and the strength of the family name in Utah. Moreover, Huntsman was a "Jack Mormon," the equivalent of a Catholic who forgoes mass. (Jon and Mary Kaye were known to enjoy their white wine— more than a glass, every night.) Ann Romney was equally contemptuous, calling Huntsman "cold and arrogant."

The Huntsmans vice versa'd the vitriol. Their family had built their fortune by making stuff; Mitt got rich by shuffling paper. The Huntsmans were worldly and open-minded when it came to religion; the Romneys were parochial and dogmatic. Jon was in politics for the sake of public service; Mitt was in it for the sake of Mitt. Watching Romney's performance in 2008—the flips, the flops, the ceaseless attacks on McCain and the other Republicans—Huntsman thanked heaven he had jumped ship.

Being on board the USS McCain was good for Huntsman in other ways, too. It earned him a featured slot at the GOP convention, where he gave the nominating speech for Palin (clumsily, but still). It placed him on the campaign trail around the country that fall, raising his national profile. And it introduced him to Weaver, who had exited McCainworld during a fractious period in the campaign, but not before striking up a friendship with Jon.

The two men discovered they shared a sense that their party had veered off track, which was only reinforced by McCain's drubbing by Obama. Huntsman and Weaver agreed that Republicans had to appeal to young voters and Hispanics or risk irrelevance. That meant putting a halt to the party's hard line on social issues, denialism on climate change, and restrictionism on immigration. Huntsman had been moving in this direction already in Utah; now he and Weaver started talking about taking his act to the big stage.

Within days of Obama's victory—and Huntsman's Utah reelection, with 78 percent of the vote—Jon was out there showing leg to the national press. In February, at Weaver's instigation, he took a trip to South Carolina; a visit to Michigan was scheduled for May. Romney was still lying low, but everyone assumed that he wouldn't be for long. The Mormon rivals appeared to be on a collision course for 2012, with all of the drama that implied.

"They're Cain and Abel," a Republican strategist told a reporter. "Two brothers, so similar, but also willing to do anything to get at each other. And in the end, one of them winds up dead."

The Obamans, however, had a different idea about the timing of the funeral.

JEFF BADER PONDERED THE QUESTION for a moment before offering an answer. It was the last week of April 2009, and Bader, the senior Asia hand on Obama's National Security Council staff, was being asked by a White House personnel officer if he had any bright ideas for filling the ambassadorship to China. "Well," Bader said, "let me suggest a Hail Mary for you: Jon Huntsman."

"Who's Jon Huntsman?" came the reply.

Bader had struck up a friendship with Huntsman in 2001, when they both worked in the U.S. Trade Representative's office under Bush 43. Now Bader ran through Huntsman's vitae, noting that Jon was a serious Sinophile, fluent in Mandarin. Okay, the personnel officer said, let me run the idea up the chain of command. An hour later, Bader was told that Rahm Emanuel was eager to pursue it.

Emanuel had two unimpeachable reasons to be excited about sending Huntsman to Beijing: he was eminently qualified for the job, and it would be a symbol of bipartisanship. But the chief of staff also saw a bonus benefit: eliminating a potential 2012 rival. Emanuel and Messina doubted that Huntsman could gain the approval of the GOP nominating electorate, but if he did, the guy could be trouble—so why not pack him off to the other side of the planet?

Emanuel reached Huntsman by phone on May 2 while Jon was in Michigan flashing his gams to Republican voters. Weaver was steaming ahead with plans to set up a PAC for Huntsman and recruiting operatives in the early states. But when Emanuel proposed the Middle Kingdom mission, Jon was intrigued, and even more so when Obama called personally and offered him the job three days later.

Just as the White House had mixed motives for wanting him in China, Huntsman was animated by impulses that were by turns idealistic and calculating. He had long dreamed of holding the Beijing post. Both Huntsman and his wife had been smitten with Obama since they first met three years earlier at Coretta Scott King's funeral. (When Jon and Barack clasped palms, Mary Kaye stargazed, *Somewhere, somehow, you two will come together again.*) The idea of being part of a Lincolnian team of rivals with 44 was intoxicating to Huntsman.

Still, he also gamed out the opportunity in terms of his presidential ambitions. With one of his closest Salt Lake City confidants, Zions Bank CEO Scott Anderson, Huntsman raised the concern that joining the administration would mark him with a scarlet O among conservatives. Yeah, it might, Anderson said. But moderates and independents will like the idea that you put aside party to serve your country. And presiding over America's most important geopolitical relationship was a surer route to national prominence and credibility than being governor of Utah. "You don't get many Jimmy Carters who come along from a small state and win the White House," Anderson said.

Four days after Obama's call, Huntsman huddled with the president at the White House and accepted the job—then immediately called Weaver. "I apologize for wasting your time," Huntsman said. "We'll see what happens when I come back. I don't know when that will be."

Weaver assumed that Huntsman 2012 was a dead deal. The rest of Washington presumed the same, hailing the Obamans for their shrewdness in dispatching a nascent threat. "They Shanghaied the bastard!" Chris Matthews cried on *Hardball.* "Isn't that smart?"

Huntsman decamped for China that August, sending a gushing letter to Obama ("You are a remarkable leader") on his departure. The next time the two men saw each other was in November—in Shanghai, funnily enough. The White House aides accompanying Obama, including Axelrod, Bader, and Jarrett, noted Huntsman's keenness at schmoozing the press corps, but they thought nothing of it. In public, Jon expansively praised the president, and in private he was still more effusive. Remarking on the ferocity of the Republican opposition to Obamacare, he said, "I don't recognize my party."

For the next year, the Obamans were happy as clams with Huntsman, whose ambassadorial performance they considered superb. The only question was how long he would stay in the job.

The answer came in the first week of October 2010, when Huntsman notified the White House that he would be returning sometime in the middle of 2011. Emanuel had just exited the building, so Huntsman told Jarrett instead. The Chinese capital was wearing on his family; two years there would be long enough.

"Oh, that's too bad," said Jarrett. "What do you think you're going to do next?"

Huntsman said he wasn't sure.

"Would you still be interested in government service?" Jarrett asked. "We'd hate to lose you."

Actually, yes, Huntsman said. "I might have some ideas of doing government service."

"Where are you going to live?"

"I'll probably be in Washington."

"When you settle back here, come see us," Jarrett said. "Because we'd love to have you."

THE NEW TOWNHOUSE WAS one sign that Jon's planning was more advanced than he was letting on. A four-story, five-bedroom, Federal-style beauty in the tony Kalorama neighborhood, it had served as the set for *Top Chef: D.C.* The Huntsmans had purchased the place for $3.6 million back in June but kept the transaction quiet. It wasn't the only thing they were keeping that way.

Contrary to everyone else's assumptions, Huntsman never believed that accepting Beijing took 2012 off the table. In his conversations with Anderson before he left, he was clear-eyed that the White House was, in part, attempting to sideline him. Anderson suggested that, if "the stars aligned,"

Jon could come back after two years and run. "If you win, that's fabulous, and if you lose, it sets you up well for 2016," his friend contended. Huntsman agreed.

I won't let myself be written off by going over there, he said. I can play this game.

His gamesmanship had begun even before he set off abroad. Approached by an Academy Award–winning producer about making the Huntsman family's excursion the focus of a documentary on U.S.-China relations, Jon and Mary Kaye were delighted and provided extraordinary access. The cameras shot them surrounded by packed boxes in their house in Utah and unpacking in Beijing; the crew made eight trips to China to gather footage. Huntsman saw the movie as a way to maintain his visibility back home. His hope was that it would debut at the Sundance Film Festival—in January 2012.

Even seven thousand miles away from Washington, the looming campaign found its way to his doorstep. The American CEOs who turned up at the embassy all wanted to talk politics. Their growing disdain for Obama was matched by their revulsion at the hair-on-fire rantings of the Tea Party. They were lukewarm on the cold fish Romney and desperate for a temperate internationalist to save them. You should run, they said to Huntsman. Business would stand behind you.

If the blandishments turned Huntsman's head, the caliber of the blandishers inflated it like a balloon. To his family and intimates, he excitedly recounted their names: Jeff Immelt, Henry Kravis, and Jamie Dimon, who, Jon reported, was especially passionate about his taking on Obama.

The encouragement of his family mattered even more. Huntsman's three twentysomething daughters—Mary Anne, Abby, and Liddy—thought Romney was a sham and wanted their dad to make a run at him. Mary Kaye amplified their sentiments. Ever since the Salt Lake City Olympics uproar, she had considered Mitt a clammy creature of the Mormon mafia. (Her family was Episcopalian.) The idea of Romney as the Republican nominee struck her as intolerable, especially when her husband was available.

Jon held his cards close even with his family; as ambassador, his phone calls and e-mail were under surveillance, his residence possibly bugged. But in the fall of 2010, Mary Kaye began e-mailing Weaver and asking about

2012. Sometimes two or three times a day the missives hit his inbox: What's the state of the race? Who's in? Who's out? What do you think? She referred to her husband as "HE," a code that probably would not have provided much protection had the communications been exposed. Weaver knew how close the couple was. He assumed that Jon was using his wife as a proxy and a backchannel, especially as her messages became more pointed: that they were planning to return in the spring, that her man might have "another run in him."

Weaver had never given up the ghost on Huntsman. That August, he had helped Anderson set up a Utah-based fund-raising entity called R-PAC, thinking more about 2016 than 2012. But Mary Kaye's e-mails suggested a new timetable—and so did an invitation to meet with her and Jon the week before Christmas in Washington, when the couple would be bunking in their new home on a holiday break from Beijing.

Weaver wasn't the only top-shelf national strategist to receive such a summons. On December 17, the Huntsmans sat down in their D.C. living room with Nick Ayers, an up-and-coming young operative who had spent the previous four years as executive director of the Republican Governors Association—and was now on the hunt for a presidential campaign to manage. Mary Kaye did most of the talking; Jon was more circumspect, pointing out to Ayers that he had to "be careful how I do what I do and even what I say to you." But he also made clear that he was seriously considering a run.

The next morning, Weaver replaced Ayers amid the cardboard boxes in the Huntsman abode. Having researched the Hatch Act, Weaver wasn't surprised that Mary Kaye took the lead. But Jon was more forthcoming than he'd been the day before. He talked about his view of the field: that it amounted to Romney and a bunch of Tea Party yahoos. He talked about his respect for Barbour and Daniels, asking Weaver if he thought either would get in. (No.) He talked about timing, about staffing, about money, about how to deal politically with his service to Obama. While Huntsman prefaced many of his comments in the conditional—"If I decide to move forward"—he was signaling about as subtly as an airport ramper waving orange batons.

Weaver got the message. Two days later he was on a flight to Salt Lake City for meetings with Huntsman's chief of staff from Beijing, Neil Ashdown, and with Anderson about R-PAC, which would now be converted into a vehicle for a shadow campaign until Jon's return stateside.

Back in Washington, however, Huntsman's semaphoring was spinning out of control. With Weaver's voice still echoing in his living room, Jon conducted an interview with a *Newsweek* reporter, who asked about his presidential intentions. "I'm really focused on what we're doing in our current position," Huntsman said. "But we won't do this forever, and I think we may have one final run left in our bones." Pressed to rule out 2012, he "decline[d] to comment," said the magazine.

The *Newsweek* piece appeared on January 1. The West Wing instantly erupted. In seventeen days, Chinese president Hu Jintao was coming to Washington for a state visit; Huntsman was slated to attend the state dinner feting him. Now America's ambassador to China was indicating he might be quitting his job to challenge Obama. The story was bound to stir up all the wrong kind of interest.

Jeff Bader was baffled and concerned. A few months earlier, over dinner in Beijing, Huntsman had employed a similar one-more-race-in-me locution—but specifically said he was referring to 2016. Bader picked up the phone and rang Huntsman, who was now back in China. What's this story about? Bader asked. It's going to get attention. We need to know what to say.

"I can't help what people write," Huntsman said. "I'm just saying 'No comment,' and you should say 'No comment.'"

"Jon, look, we can't just say 'No comment,'" Bader replied. "That's just not gonna fly."

"Well, if people don't want me to come back for the state visit, so be it. I won't come back."

Bader was unsettled; he had never heard his friend sound so defensive. The next day, he called NSC director Tom Donilon and said, "Tom, I know Jon pretty well. It's clear to me that there's something going on here. You may want to talk to him."

Donilon took the matter to Obama first. The president's reaction was relaxed but unequivocal. Look, he said, I have no problem with people running for president. But they can't run for president while they're working as ambassadors in this administration. It's either-or.

Donilon conveyed that message to Huntsman. Makes perfect sense to me, Jon said. As long as I'm your ambassador, I'm your ambassador and nothing else.

The Obamans were right that the press would find the topic too titillating to avoid during the state visit. At a joint press conference of the two presidents in the East Room on January 19, the AP's Ben Feller, standing right behind Huntsman, asked Obama what he made of the speculation that "the gentleman in front of me . . . might run against you in 2012."

As Huntsman shriveled in his seat, Obama gently twisted the knife. "I couldn't be happier with the ambassador's service, and I'm sure he will be very successful in whatever endeavors he chooses in the future," the president said. "And I'm sure that him having worked so well for me will be a great asset in any Republican primary."

Some of the Obamans were even sharper. At the state dinner that night, Axelrod sidled up to Huntsman and probed him. Huntsman squirmed and said, "Well, this is all blown way out of proportion"—a non-denial that annoyed Axelrod for its shiftiness. For months thereafter, Axe would stalk into the Oval Office, brandishing stories about Huntsman 2012, braying to Obama, Have you seen what this guy has done now?

Bill Daley, at this point new to his job as chief of staff, was even less amused. On January 27, after reading a *Washington Post* article on Huntsman's inner circle, including Weaver, Anderson, and Ashdown—"a team of political operatives and fundraisers [that] have begun informal talks and outreach to ensure he could rapidly ramp up"—Daley phoned Huntsman in the middle of the night in Beijing.

"This is a pretty shitty way to treat someone who gave you the opportunity of a lifetime," Daley flared. Huntsman stammered something about being unaware of what all the fuss was about.

"Go down the hall and ask your chief of staff," Daley grumbled, and hung up.

Two nights later, the Huntsmans were back in Washington for the annual Alfalfa Club Dinner. From the stage, Daley went after Jon again, this time with humor rather than the hammer. "It's also good to see . . . our ambassador to China," Daley needled. "Or as we call him around the White House: the Manchurian Candidate."

Jon was abashed; Mary Kaye, mortified. The situation was becoming untenable. On January 31, they had lunch with Bader and his wife at Cafe Milano, in Georgetown. Huntsman handed his friend his letter of resignation, effective May 1, to submit to the White House.

Obama expressed no surprise, and little irritation. Huntsman was doubtless being disloyal, the president told his aides, but more striking was the fancifulness of the quest on which the ambassador was embarking. Among the potential GOP challengers, Obama remarked to Plouffe, "he's the sanest of the group." But how could that be an asset in seeking the nomination of *this* Republican Party?

HUNTSMAN'S SANITY WAS the least of Weaver's problems. From a standing start, the strategist had three months to assemble an organization, create momentum, and begin fashioning a national brand for a candidate who was virtually unknown to the Republican electorate. A candidate who lived on the other side of the world, who hadn't firmly committed to running, and with whom Weaver was effectively prohibited from conferring. Man.

Weaver didn't shrink from the task. He sank his canines in deep. Though the press fixated on his brooding idealism, Weaver was at bottom a hardboiled operator. He knew the game, the players, the secret passageways, and the way to win, even if he didn't always reach the finish line. He had no compunction about bending the rules; those who played strictly by the book were suckers, he thought. In 2000, McCain's operation saw itself as a pirate ship, and Weaver was its remorseless captain. (He referred to himself as "the icy hand of death.") Now a different metaphor applied. In the absence of a candidate, he and his acolytes were building a test-tube campaign, with Weaver as the chief mad scientist.

Their laboratory announced that it was open for business on February 22, with the launch of a website for the newly rechristened Horizon PAC. While making no mention of Huntsman, the site's home page featured a bright red H and the coy slogan MAYBE SOMEDAY. Its unveiling was accompanied by an e-mail to reporters from a PAC staffer describing the committee as a "campaign-in-waiting."

The site stirred up a flurry of stories raising thorny questions about whether it was proper for such a PAC, which could accept unlimited contributions, to be financing what appeared to be the precursor of a presidential campaign; about the possibility that, if Huntsman was encouraging the outfit's activities, he was violating the Hatch Act. Weaver insisted that Horizon PAC's purpose was to raise money for a new generation of conservative candidates. As for Huntsman, the strategist told Politico that his last contact with the diplomat had come in the form of a Christmas card. "There's no other channel, there's no Wo Fat from *Hawaii Five-O,* there's no carrier pigeons," he said. "None of that."

In truth, Horizon PAC was doing nothing to identify like-minded candidates to fund (and never would); its function was to pay the salaries of Weaver's crew and lock up consultants for a Huntsman presidential campaign. While there were no carrier pigeons roosting on Weaver's window, by February he was talking regularly with Huntsman Sr., who said that he communicated with his son every day—and who visited him in China that spring and discussed the impending race. I'm a riverboat gambler, the elder Jon told the younger. Romney will be the favorite, but I like your odds.

The test-tubers also had other open channels to Beijing. They started an e-mail list for the daily distribution of news clips about the shadow campaign; among the recipients were Ashdown and Mary Kaye. Mrs. Huntsman monitored the clips closely, continuing to pepper Weaver with e-mails about the race to come. After Politico ran a story about Jon's youthful dabblings in a rock band, she indicated that the ambassador was "a bit worried about" the piece. She pushed to enlist elite opinion-mongers to Jon's cause. ("Peggy Noonan would be a good one to write something," she suggested.) She kept Weaver abreast of efforts to set up a meeting between her husband and David Gergen. She worked with the team to finalize arrangements for Jon's commencement address in South Carolina in May.

The clips Mary Kaye was receiving showed that the test-tubers were doing a bang-up job of generating buzz. The doubts about Romney and the nonexistence of exciting alternatives had created a vacuum, and Weaver's lab mates aggressively stepped in to fill it. Press hand Tim Miller massaged the Beltway media, whispering scooplets to Politico and tweeting Huntsman tidbits. Adman Fred Davis toured the country, urging donors to hold off on Mitt until Jon's return. Turning Huntsman's status as a missing person to their advantage, they stoked the image of him as international man of mystery.

The careful burnishing of the Huntsman brand seemed to falter only once—with the April revelation, by the conservative Daily Caller, of the "remarkable leader" letter he sent to Obama when he set off for China. Many assumed that the missive had been leaked by the administration, but it was actually the work of the test-tubers. Having dug the letter up in Huntsman's gubernatorial archive in Utah, they wanted to lance the boil before his return.

In Beijing, Mary Kaye was upset at the reaction to the story on the right. ("The uniqueness about HE is his civility and respect for others," she e-mailed Weaver. "He is tough but diplomatic. The fact that one is criticized for being gracious, instead of filled with hate for someone who might be of a different party, is very sad.") But in the White House, Plouffe was struck by the savviness of the move. *Where the hell did that letter come from?* he thought. Followed by, *This son of a bitch is pretty smart.*

All the while, Weaver was scaling up the campaign-in-waiting at a breakneck pace. To make up for Romney's head start, Team Huntsman had to get big fast. By the end of April there were a dozen staffers, five outside firms, and thirty-two fund-raising consultants (including one dedicated solely to raising money from the gay community) on the Horizon PAC payroll.

Weaver was legendary for his capacity to burn through cash; his profligacy had been one cause of his split with McCain. But he assured his crew that finances would be no problem this time. In his talks with Huntsman Sr., Weaver said, the old man had flatly declared, "My son will not lose because of money," pledging that he would plow big bucks into the PAC and eventually into a pro-Huntsman super PAC. He also promised that he would be the campaign's de facto finance chair, tapping his millionaire and billionaire pals, and claimed that dozens of Huntsman relatives would open their checkbooks, too. And all of that was apart from Jon Jr. himself, who Weaver asserted was worth north of $100 million and ready to pony up for his campaign.

Most of Weaver's lab assistants had never laid eyes on Huntsman. Their labors on his behalf required a willing suspension of disbelief—which was enabled by the dancing dollar signs before their eyes. The shadow campaign's fund-raiser, Jim McCray, conceived of "Daddy Huntsman," as they all called him, as a latter-day Joe Kennedy. *We're gonna fly around the country in his G5,* McCray fantasized. *We're just going to fucking crush it.*

For the press and the rest of the political realm, the Huntsman family's loadedness lent Jon's putative candidacy a final measure of credibility—further fueling the aura of anticipation that awaited him at the Correspondents' Dinner. He was handsome, he was smart, he was raring to go. And by self-funding his campaign, he could match Romney dollar for dollar.

The morning after the dinner, Weaver and one of his people, Susie Wiles, walked over from the Hilton to Huntsman's home and rang the bell. Jon answered the door in a flannel shirt and jeans.

"Hi, I'm Susie," Wiles chirped, extending her hand. "I'm gonna manage your campaign."

And with that, the test-tube phase abruptly ended—and something even more bizarre began.

APART FROM A QUICK breakfast with Rupert Murdoch, Huntsman spent his first day in years as a private citizen in a marathon meeting with his soon-to-be campaign team. Brutally jet-lagged but hot to trot, he signed the paperwork to form an exploratory committee. "We've decided we want to do this," he announced.

Huntsman had never worked with consultants or operatives back in Utah, let alone high-end hired guns. He was dimly aware of Weaver's reputation as a mercurial fomenter of internal strife; Cindy McCain had recently passed through Beijing and warned him and Mary Kaye to watch their backsides. But Huntsman had already placed a lot of faith in Weaver, and the team assembled in his living room seemed first-rate. He accepted them lock, stock, and barrel, with no questions asked, and issued several directives: that his campaign be civil, substantive, and have "no drama."

The next three weeks were a parade of public triumphs for Huntsman, as supply met pent-up demand. In Washington, he paid courtesy calls on Capitol Hill and found senators stacked up to meet him; receptions with lobbyists and young D.C. professionals were standing room only. In New York, he was greeted by a receiving line of the business elite: Kravis, Ron Perelman,

Herb and Jeanne Siegel, Jimmy Lee. His foray to South Carolina on May 7 was a resounding hit. "'The consensus was, *Holy crap, this guy looks like a president,'* said one [insider]," CNN's Peter Hamby wrote. "'I have never seen anybody sweep into this state . . . and get as much accomplished in forty-eight hours.'"

Eleven days later, a swarm of boom mics and cameras trailed Huntsman on a five-day swing through New Hampshire: to a Harley-Davidson dealer in Manchester, where he bemoaned his lack of time lately on his own hog; to a gun shop in Hooksett, where, when asked what he liked to hunt, he replied "large varmints" (a sly shot at Romney, who in 2008 offered that his favored prey was rodents and rabbits, "small varmints, if you will"); and all the way to Kennebunkport, in next-door Maine, where he was warmly received by 41 and Barbara Bush. The coverage was as ample and consistently glowing as any Republican received in all of 2011.

Huntsman was in his hotel room in New Hampshire when Daniels announced that he wouldn't run. Catching the news on MSNBC, he was dumbfounded to hear the anchor mention his name first among the viable candidates left standing. *I can't get my mind around this,* Jon thought. What he would have found even harder to fathom was that, unwittingly and indirectly, he had played a role in the Daniels saga: it was his own communications-director-to-be, Matt David, and not Romney's Matt Rhoades, who had shopped the cell-phone number of the ex-wife of Cheri Daniels's ex-husband to reporters.

The Daniels decision only fed the perception that everything was falling into place for Huntsman with astonishing swiftness. But just beneath the surface of the boomlet, doubts were creeping in among Weaver's crew. After several meetings with the candidate, Fred Davis noted in a journal he kept that the candidate was "a tad too sheepish and way too self-effacing." Huntsman relentlessly referred to himself as "we"—"I" was a four-letter word for Jon. Meeting members of Congress, he was too reticent to ask for support, fund-raising rosters, or volunteer lists; instead of saying he was running, he would hedge, "We're kicking the tires." ("What was *that* about?" one member of Congress texted Huntsman's Capitol Hill sherpa, Al Shofe.) With potential bundlers and contributors, Huntsman would say, "We don't want your money right now. We just want you to be our friend."

The failure to close the deal with donors would have been worrying enough on its own. But it was coupled with three money-related messages that threw Weaver's crew for a loop. First, Huntsman told them, "My net worth is a lot smaller than you all think." Second, he indicated that he had no intention of self-funding. And third, he said, "If I run, I want to do it without my father's help."

Almost immediately, the campaign was thrust into a state of abject financial panic. On the premise that money would be no object, Weaver was building an operation that was "a Cadillac, not a Kia," as Davis put it. The initial budget the two men drafted called for spending an astronomical $110 million from May 2011 through March 2012. There were already twenty paid staffers in New Hampshire. A lease had been signed for office space to house a headquarters in Orlando, Florida, to the tune of $66,000 a month. Due largely to the size of the Huntsman family road contingent, the campaign was blowing through $25,000 a week in travel expenses. And almost nothing was coming in.

In conversations with McCray, Huntsman Sr. offered to write a $5 million check; Huntsman Jr. not only ordered that it be turned down but said he didn't want his father involved in any way in raising money. With the launch of Huntsman's exploratory committee, a new federal PAC had been created to help finance the operation: HPAC. By the end of May it had $500,000 in bills to pay and no way to cover them.

In Orange County, on a West Coast fund-raising swing, McCray corralled Huntsman in the lobby of the health care company Allergan. Given Jon's unwillingness to let his father be involved and his refusal to make hard asks of donors, self-funding was the only option. You're going to need to loan HPAC $2 million, McCray told him, and then infuse the campaign, once you officially announce, with another $5 million.

"*Nobody* had this conversation with me," Huntsman said icily. "I am not going to mortgage my family's future for this presidential race."

Davis was along on the West Coast sojourn, and Huntsman asked him to take a drive. A shaggily silver-haired Oklahoman who plied his trade in the Hollywood Hills, Davis had worked on scores of Senate and gubernatorial campaigns, Dan Quayle's presidential exploratory bid in 2000, and McCain-Palin in 2008. He was responsible for many of the most outré political ads and videos of recent vintage, from Carly Fiorina's "demon sheep" to Christine O'Donnell's "I am not a witch." Davis had been impressed by Huntsman in 2007, when they first met on a shoot for an Environmental Defense Fund spot, but he was starting to think that Jon was lazy and entitled. (The provisional title of the adman's personal campaign journal was *Kicking and Screaming*.) Huntsman called Davis "creative" in a way that sounded like he meant "freaky-deaky."

They pulled up to the Balboa Bay Club in Newport Beach and headed for the sand. For the next two hours they sat in the sun, sweating, their ties cinched up. Huntsman was fairly out of sorts, having second thoughts about getting in. Is this really what running for president is supposed to be like? he asked. He had questions about his team, about the spending, and, pointedly, about Weaver. Is he the right guy for this? Is he doing a good job? Huntsman wondered if maybe 2016 made more sense than 2012.

Davis vouched for Weaver's savvy as a strategist and attempted to soothe Huntsman. There are always hiccups, Davis said. This is the right year, the right race for you. There's a path to victory.

"What did you tell Dan Quayle *his* path to victory was in 2000?" Huntsman asked snarkily.

Huntsman's announcement was scheduled to take place in a month, on June 21. Yet Davis couldn't tell whether his candidate was in or out. Huntsman flew to Utah with McCray, where they met with Senior, who demanded to see the campaign budget. The document hadn't yet been finalized, but McCray coughed up what numbers he could. Huntsman Sr. considered the spending obscene, and suspected that Weaver was as interested in milking the family as in electing his son president. Huntsman Jr. didn't disagree, but he thought that Weaver could be managed—and that firing him would cause the campaign to collapse.

A few days later, at an emergency meeting in Houston, Huntsman agreed to loan HPAC the $2 million that McCray had requested, though not happily. (His team was shocked to discover that Jon Jr.'s net worth was just $11 million, including real estate.) McCray suggested that Huntsman Sr. could ease the burden by offering his son an unsecured loan. Huntsman declared again, with a trace of petulance, "My father is not going to be involved in this. I'm doing it on my own."

The relationship between father and son was a central riddle of the Huntsman campaign—as was the question of how the expectations of Weaver's crew had ended up so far out of line with reality. One theory was that Jon Jr. had massive daddy issues. Another was that Weaver was playing a con, saying what was necessary to get the train rolling and hoping that, one way or the other, there would be gravy on it. Still another was that Huntsman Sr. wasn't as wealthy (or liquid) as people thought, that he was making promises he couldn't keep, and that his son was straining to protect him. And yet another was that the Huntsmans had bluffed Weaver, gambling that the illusion of self-funding would get Jon's late entry off the ground and that once it had taken flight, the campaign could be financed through normal channels.

Whatever the case, father and son were together with the entire family a month later when Jon Jr. reached the starting line: his announcement in Liberty State Park, New Jersey, the same venue from which Reagan had launched his general election campaign in 1980, with the big copper lady as its backdrop.

The event was a mess in almost every way, starting with Huntsman's speech. His advisers were determined that, to assuage concerns among the base about his moderate stances on some issues, the address present him as a conservative, and that it include a direct contrast with Obama, to lessen the political drag of his tenure with the administration. Huntsman refused to countenance either insertion. He detested the impugning of the president on the right. The furthest he would go was to say, "He and I have a difference of opinion on how to help a country we both love." And in draft after draft of the speech, he struck the word "conservative." *Never used it before,* he thought, *and I'm not about to.*

The logistics were more glaringly awful. The crowd was tiny, with nearly as many reporters on hand as supporters—most of whom were bused-in college Republicans. The credentials for guests and the press misspelled the candidate's name as "John." The generators died just before the speech, only coming back to life in the nick of time. The buses ferrying the Huntsmans, their staff, and the press to Newark airport for a flight to New Hampshire were held at the gateway to the tarmac for half an hour. Finally let through, they drove first to the wrong plane and then to the right one, which had no pilot.

Huntsman Sr. was furious, demanding that someone be fired immediately. Huntsman Jr., who had worked as an advance man in the Reagan White House, was humiliated. When he saw the sparse crowd, his heart sank. In a restroom at the airport hangar, he stared into the mirror and thought, *Most important day of my life politically, and we're in shambles.* While on the plane to New Hampshire, with his father ballistic, he sat shaking silently in his seat. Mary Kaye leaned over, squeezed his arm, and whispered in his ear.

"They let you down," she said.

THE CLOWNS IN ORANGE WIGS, the person in the gopher costume, and the Uncle Sam on stilts had already ambled down Boston Post Road when the main sideshow at the Amherst, New Hampshire, Fourth of July parade took place: Huntsman and Romney meeting face-to-face for the first time since Jon entered the race. As they prepared to start marching, Mitt spotted Huntsman, jogged over, clasped his hand, patted his shoulder—and then stuck in the shiv.

"Welcome to New Hampshire!" Romney trilled, as if greeting a foreign tourist. "It's not Beijing, but it's lovely!"

"The air is breathable," Huntsman muttered in reply.

Afterwards, a reporter asked him about the colloquy, inducing an outlandish lie. "It was a nice exchange," Huntsman said. "A nice greeting, wishing each other luck, and being friends."

Romney's staff had tried to keep him away from Huntsman; they didn't want pictures of the two together in the paper. But Romney couldn't resist, and didn't really want to. Huntsman's headlong dive into the race had only ratcheted up Romney's level of contempt for what he saw as shameless opportunism. Huntsman had dumped Mitt for McCain in 2008 when that seemed the safe bet; then he abandoned the Republican Party and joined up with Democrats when it appeared Obama would be a two-term president; and now that the incumbent was vulnerable, he was running to replace him.

Boston's Mormon regiment—the Romneys, Zwick, and Mike Leavitt, who after the Olympics had become a close friend and adviser to the candidate—also suspected that part of Jon Jr.'s and (especially) Jon Sr.'s motivation was simply to toss a monkey wrench into Mitt's plans.

The non-Mormon Romneyites found the feud as impenetrable as a Tolkien subplot rendered in Elvish. Rhoades, Myers, Fehrnstrom, Flaherty: none of them took Huntsman remotely seriously as a threat. Stevens was most dismissive of all, telling Romney, "Mitt, don't even think about it. The two words Republican voters hate most are 'Obama' and 'China.' And this is a guy who has been *working* for Obama—in China. *It's absurd.*"

But no amount of logic could dislodge Huntsman from Romney's craw. In recruiting support in the Granite State and elsewhere, Mitt made it clear that there would be no hard feelings toward those who chose to back another Republican—as long as it wasn't Jon. Of all the endorsements Mitt snared, few pleased him more than that of Jason Chaffetz, Huntsman's former chief of staff and now a Utah congressman.

Huntsman had choice words for Chaffetz when he learned that his former protégé was backing Mitt. "Asshole" was one of them. "Liar" was another. "Backstabber" was a third.

To the dismay of Weaver's crew, however, Huntsman could never summon sufficient ire to rip into Romney himself. As with asking for money, he and Mary Kaye seemed to believe that hitting his opponents was beneath his dignity. In July, at a donor event in Utah, Davis unveiled an ad contrasting Huntsman's job-creation record in Utah with Romney's in Massachusetts, featuring a beat-up baseball glove as a metaphor for Mitt. In front of several dozen contributors, Mary Kaye objected. That's *way* too negative! she exclaimed. That's not who we are. We're going to run on Jon's positive message for America.

Weaver's team had started out thinking that Mary Kaye was a gamer. By midsummer they had decided that she reinforced the worst aspects of her husband's personality, of which they felt there were quite a few. The candidate was slothful, incessantly lobbying to lighten his schedule. He suffered from severe dark spells, especially in the morning. He and Mary Kaye were both like candle-drawn moths to the liberal glitterati; the approval of Tina

Brown and Diane Von Furstenberg made them swoon. One day, Mary Kaye called Miller and bubbled, "Arianna Huffington wants to help!"

Mary Kaye, honestly, said Miller, if Arianna Huffington wants to help, you should tell her to book herself on television right now and talk about how she has misjudged Jon Huntsman—he's far too conservative.

As the summer wore on, it was becoming clear that the Huntsman cause was in fact beyond help. The financial woes of the campaign were only getting worse. On July 12, Weaver, after studying the latest fund-raising projections, dispatched a morose e-mail to Wiles: "We should fold our tent. What has happened is malpractice."

Nine days later, Wiles was replaced by Matt David as campaign manager. After the horror show of an announcement, Huntsman had lost faith in her; she considered him weak and hopeless. Around the same time, Weaver threatened to leave the campaign, together with Davis, to run the long-discussed pro-Huntsman super PAC. Jon Jr. and Jon Sr. were both sick to death of Weaver; they were privately considering replacements such as Rove or Scott Reed. But the younger Huntsman still believed that losing Weaver might be too destabilizing to survive, especially coming on top of Wiles's departure.

A story in Politico on August 4 revealed some of the turmoil swirling in Huntslandia. With Jon readying himself for his first debate appearance a week later, in Ames, Iowa, Weaver's crew was disconsolate. A candidate they had believed was a Triple Crown thoroughbred had turned out to be a neddy. Brooding over their misjudgment, they speculated that Huntsman had been pushed into running by his father and Mary Kaye—or that, having lived a life where so much had come so easy, he found the sheer difficulty of the pursuit of the presidency more than he'd bargained for. Whatever the case, the test-tubers shared a unified view, which was summed up by Davis: "Everything was a hundred percent positive . . . until he came back."

Huntsman's assessment of the situation was nearly as grim. Having wanted little more than an enterprise free of drama, he was drowning in it. Three months after his return to the States, his support stood at 2 percent in the national polls, and it was scarcely better in the early states. Huntsman endeavored to keep his chin up, reassuring himself that at least he'd conducted himself with dignity and swearing that he would continue to do so for as long as he was in the race. The pressure to veer from principle, to pander, was ever present. He knew it would be upon him on the debate stage at Ames. He vowed to resist. *I've always stood tall, I'm the man that I am, I've got the record I've got,* he thought.

Making his debut alongside his rivals on the night of August 11 in Iowa— a state where Huntsman wasn't even planning to compete because of the right-wingness of the caucus electorate—he tried to muddle through. Huntsman hated the artificiality of debating, the enforced brevity, the tyranny of the thirty-second timer. At just around the halfway point, one of the moderators, Bret Baier of Fox News, asked a gimmicky but revealing question of the nine Republican candidates.

Say you had a budget deal that contained ten dollars in spending cuts for every one dollar in tax increases, Baier said. "Who on this stage would walk away from that deal? Can you raise your hand if you feel so strongly about not raising taxes, you'd walk away on a ten-to-one deal?"

Huntsman had no doubt about what he believed. Of course he wouldn't walk away from that deal—and neither would Ronald Reagan. But another thought raced through his mind as well: *Oh shit. If I don't raise my hand, the anti-tax hounds will dog me for the rest of my campaign. I can either tell the truth or just sleaze by.*

With only a split second to make up his mind, Huntsman took the hindmost. Poking his hand in the air, he felt regret and not a little shame—as it dawned him that he was just another candidate after all.

★ 8 ★

F'D UP

ROMNEY HAD NO HESITATION or regrets about raising his hand at the Ames debate. He stuck it up and then glanced over at the candidates immediately to his left: Michele Bachmann and Tim Pawlenty. Mitt was keeping his eye on those two, and for the same reason. Bachmann and Pawlenty—despite Romney's ostensible front-runner status—had taken up a lot of space in the race that summer. While one was rising and the other falling, both were in a position to stake a robust claim in Iowa. For Romney, it remained an open question as to how vigorously he would compete in the Hawkeye State. And the answer hinged to no small extent on the viability of the Minnesotans.

Bachmann was actually born in Iowa, but in her teens she moved to a town not far outside the Twin Cities; Pawlenty was raised in the meatpacking burg of South Saint Paul. Bachmann was elected to Congress in 2006, the year that Pawlenty won his second term as governor of the North Star State. They shared a reverent evangelical faith and a biting distaste for each other. (Bachmann considered Pawlenty a weak-kneed fraud; he disparaged her as "dangerous" and "insane.") But in 2012, what would bind them together was their emergence as twin illustrations of a verity of presidential politics: that a single aberrant moment can demolish a candidacy—if the candidate is sufficiently fragile.

Pawlenty hadn't appeared flimsy in the run-up to the race. In 2008, he was McCain's second choice for the VP slot, after Palin. He had governed successfully in a Democratic state, balancing the budget and enacting a market-friendly health care law. With a blue-collar background (his dad drove a milk truck) and regular-guy tastes ("I'm pro-beer and pro-hockey"), he had a natural connection to Sam's Club Republicans. He ritually watched clips from *Talladega Nights* on an iPad, and mimicked Will Ferrell's Ricky Bobby on the stump. "I'm very thankful for my red-hot smoking wife, the first lady of Minnesota," he would say.

But Pawlenty never seemed comfortable with his image or identity as a presidential contender. He was consumed by the search for pithy concepts to match each moment, which he called "swing thoughts." He bristled when pundits knocked him as plain vanilla, hiring speech and style advisers. In his introductory campaign video, he struck the pose of a hero in a Michael Bay action movie; in early forays on the trail, he seemed to affect a southern accent. And he was roundly mocked for both.

Republican elites and the national press corps liked Pawlenty. But his early travails made them skeptical of his ability to hit big-league pitching. His operation had a small-time feel and labored to lift off. Fund-raising was tough, especially after T-Paw's finance chairman moved to China. He had trouble luring top talent to Minnesota. When he finally landed Nick Ayers as his campaign manager, tension arose between Ayers and Pawlenty's wife, Mary, who was intimately involved in her husband's political strategizing and placed a high value on his "Minnesota nice" reputation.

After months of fits and starts, Pawlenty gained a modicum of traction in late May. His official announcement, in which he cast himself as a truth teller, went decently. His economic plan received favorable notices, including a glowing editorial in *The Wall Street Journal*. With the Republican field presumed closed, Pawlenty had a chance to seize the status of Romney alternative if he could dispel the suspicion that he was soft. And he had an ideal setting to do so: a CNN-sponsored debate in New Hampshire on Monday, June 13, where Romney would make his first appearance alongside his rivals.

The Friday before the debate, Pawlenty and his squad mulled a plan to hit Romney where it hurt—on health care. Pawlenty suggested conjoining Romney's and Obama's reforms in a single word: Obamneycare.

Pawlenty was jazzed up. *(Great swing thought!)* So were Ayers and the rest of his advisers. Bachmann would also be making her debut that night, even before she formally entered the contest. Her presence posed another challenge to Pawlenty, as she threatened to siphon off some of the Iowan and evangelical support on which T-Paw was counting. But if Pawlenty executed the Romney smackdown, it would be the lead story of the debate, elevating him and smothering Bachmann in one swoop.

Team Pawlenty agreed that the candidate would preview the attack in an appearance that weekend on *Fox News Sunday*. It would all but guarantee that the debate moderator the next night, CNN's John King, would then ask a question about the new coinage. And that was what Pawlenty did, delivering the line with relish to Fox's Chris Wallace.

Twenty-four hours later, however, Pawlenty began backpedaling. When a reporter on Monday asked whether he would invoke Obamneycare at the debate, T-Paw replied, "Probably not."

Ayers wigged out, knowing that if his man failed to deliver the punch he had telegraphed, it would reinforce all the doubts about his muscle. When T-Paw's advisers reminded him that afternoon about the imperative of following through, Pawlenty shut the conversation down, putting on his headphones, turning up his music, and staring off into the distance.

In the holding room not long before the debate began, after some rousing country music and a quiet prayer, Pawlenty retreated into a corner for a call with Mary, whose dismay at her husband's advisers had been growing steadily. She was angry with them for manipulating Tim and just as peeved at her husband's docility in allowing them to do it. She hadn't come to New Hampshire for the debate and was out of the loop on the Obamneycare plan. Now, on the phone with her spouse for the first time in days, Mary was surprised at the gambit and expressed pointed reservations about hitting Mitt. When he got off the call, Pawlenty seemed pensive and flaccid to his aides.

Before showtime, as the candidates waited to go onstage, Romney approached Pawlenty. Mitt was expecting the Obamneycare hit, of course; in preparing for the debate, his advisers had urged him to counterpunch, and hard. But Romney was planning a smother-him-in-sweetness move for when the time came in the debate, and laid the groundwork now. He greeted Pawlenty like a long-lost brother: Hey, Tiiiiim! How've you been? How's Mary?

By the time the cameras went live, T-Paw's head was screwed on sideways. King asked him about Obamneycare. Pawlenty let the pitch go by. King asked again. Strike two. Practically placing the ball on a tee, King tried one last time—and Pawlenty whiffed again.

Pawlenty would spend the next few days in denial about his strikeout. But the political world's umpires rendered a swift, definitive ruling. The media decried him as feckless and fainthearted. Prominent pols who had been talking to Ayers about endorsing Pawlenty foreclosed the option. Already skittish potential donors simply shut down.

Team Pawlenty maintained that their guy could bounce back in August with strong showings at the Ames debate and straw poll. But from the New Hampshire debacle forward, T-Paw's star was in steep descent—and eclipsed by a supernova that burned more brightly but flamed out just as quickly.

CLASSIC PAWLENTY," Bachmann said, smirking over T-Paw's Obamney-care fluff. She had no respect for shrinking from a fight. Bachmann was plenty nervous herself before the debate, bordering on terrified. First impressions mattered, particularly for a woman, most particularly for her. But she'd spent a full week, at least a hundred hours, prepping for that night. In the green room, she prayed with her husband, Marcus, for a long while. Then she walked onstage, announced that she had filed her papers to run, and proceeded to steal the show with her verve, composure, and sharp sound bites.

Bachmann's poise made it clear that she was a kind of performance artist. In her brief time on Capitol Hill, she had achieved little besides a reputation for churning through staffers as if they were disposable razors. But her pyretic opposition to Obama—whom she accused of holding "anti-American views"—and camera-ready flair made her a Tea Party darling. Long before she entered professional politics, Bachmann was splashing in the conservative media puddle, gamely trying to call in to Rush Limbaugh's show as an ordinary dittohead. Yet mere months after being rebuffed in her bid to join the House Republican leadership in late 2010, she found herself receiving encouragement to run for the White House from the yakkers she idolized and who had hoisted her to prominence: Sean Hannity, Mark Levin, and even Rush himself.

Bachmann knew zilch about the presidential process, but she was keenly aware that she needed a badge of credibility. To captain her campaign, she turned to Ed Rollins, who was at loose ends after the Huckabee eschewal. Up until that point, Rollins had been an avowed Bachmann skeptic. But the lure of being in the mix (and getting a paycheck) proved too enticing for Ed to resist.

Rollins understood that Bachmann's image needed softening, which meant a focus on her biography as a mother of five, as well as a foster mother to twenty-three children over the years. More essential, she had to quash widespread perceptions that she was dim-witted, nuts, or both, which were often twinned with comparisons to Sarah Palin. Rollins and Bachmann's other new advisers were surprised to discover how bookish, frugal, and un-diva-like she was. (She paid $19 to have her hair styled at Fantastic Sams.) For her part, Bachmann considered the Palin analogies far-fetched. She often observed, modestly, that Sister Sarah was much prettier than she was. On the other hand, Bachmann, a tax attorney, saw herself as brainier than Palin. *Name three Supreme Court cases I disagree with?* Bachmann thought. *No problem!*

But Bachmann's efforts to strut her IQ were undermined by gaffes galore. In New Hampshire, she hailed the state for being "where the shot was heard round the world in Lexington and Concord." (That blast emanated from Massachusetts.) On June 27, the day of her official announcement in her hometown of Waterloo, Iowa, Bachmann proclaimed in a Fox News interview that "John Wayne was from Waterloo." (Wayne was in fact from Winterset, Iowa; serial killer John Wayne Gacy was from Waterloo.) From now on, her son Lucas razzed his mother, "you can't say George Washington was the first president unless we Google that shit first."

THEN THERE WAS THE COMPLICATION of Bachmann's headaches, which were no laughing matter. In July, the Daily Caller reported that she suffered from chronic, stress-induced migraines, which "occur once a week on average and can 'incapacitate' her for days at time" and had landed her in the hospital at least three times. Bachmann's response was to put out a statement shooing away the story: her "ability to function effectively [had] never been impeded" by her condition, it said.

Blowing past controversies was Bachmann's way. Unless they penetrated the Fox News cocoon, they were like gnats to be waved off. Instead she focused on her rapid rise in the polls, especially in Iowa, where she was suddenly leading the field—and where she saw a chance for another big score at the straw poll. Rollins advised her to stay out of it, to hoard her resources. Between cash left over from her congressional race and funds she had raised since June, she had nearly $4 million in the bank. But Bachmann was willing to spend pretty much every penny to pistol-whip Pawlenty, for whom the straw poll was now a make-or-break event.

In preparing for the Ames debate, Bachmann received some sub-rosa assistance from Boston, which still saw T-Paw as the real threat. Through back channels, Rhoades's research minions slipped a file to Bachmann's people—a dossier detailing Pawlenty's deviations from conservative orthodoxy as governor.

The day before the debate, however, panic struck the Bachmannsphere. The candidate was lying in the dark in her hotel in the fetal position, trying to ward off an intracranial onslaught. A doctor was placed on standby. A hospital was notified. A hefty dose of drugs was obtained and administered—and, glory be, the meds worked.

On the debate stage, Bachmann deployed the Romney-supplied oppo to tear into Pawlenty. Two days later, August 13, the strength of her performance carried over to the straw poll. She became the first woman ever to win it, edging out Ron Paul and consigning Pawlenty to a distant third. On her campaign bus, Bachmann wept tears of joy. The next morning, her happiness was magnified a thousandfold when Pawlenty announced that he was dropping out of the race.

Bachmann was fluttering like a Japanese kite, telling Rollins that she was on her way to the nomination, that it was what God intended. But she was also exhausted, having risen at 3:00 a.m. to do five morning shows, and she had a long day ahead. She would stop by a hospital to visit a woman who had been injured at the straw poll. She would ride two hours to Waterloo, check in on an aging relative, then speak at the Black Hawk County Republican Party's Lincoln Day Dinner. There she would come face-to-face with Rick Perry, who had announced his candidacy in Charleston, South Carolina, the day before while the straw poll was taking place in Iowa.

Bachmann had originally turned down an invitation to the dinner, but when her staff learned it was part of Perry's announcement tour, they muscled her in. The Texas governor was entering the race to much fanfare; a sizable contingent of the national press corps would be tailing him in Bachmann's hometown. Rollins wanted her to defend her turf and take the wind out of Perry's sails. The manly Lone Star Stater had been a "yell leader" in college at Texas A&M; Bachmann had waved the pom-poms in high school. So Rollins crafted a playful but edgy greeting for his candidate to deliver: "From one former cheerleader to another, welcome to Iowa!"

Bachmann at first embraced the gambit, but when her bus pulled up outside the Electric Park Ballroom, her feistiness deserted her. She seemed flustered, intimidated. While Perry was inside addressing the crowd, Bachmann was telling her aides that she preferred to stay in her coach until he left. "I don't want to be in the room with him," she said. She wished she hadn't come at all. And she wasn't going to say the cheerleader line.

Meanwhile, in the auditorium, Bachmann was being introduced over the loudspeakers. Her butt remained planted on the bus. The announcer intoned her name again. Still no Bachmann.

Finally, one of her aides cajoled her out of her crouch, telling her that Perry had made his exit. But when Bachmann reached the rostrum, she looked out in the crowd—and there he was, beaming at her from a table in the front. Noticeably flinching, she scooted over to move out of Perry's line of sight. Distressed and discombobulated, she meandered through a disjointed version of her stump speech. Rather than mingling with voters in the audience when she finished, Bachmann remained onstage, leaning down to scribble some autographs, before being escorted out by a phalanx of factotums.

Bachmann knew immediately how dreadfully she'd done, that the show-down had become a rout. "Worst speech I've ever given," she told Rollins afterwards. "I just totally freaked."

In the space of twenty-four hours, Bachmann had plunged from the heights to the depths, and she would never gain altitude again. The coverage of Waterloo was bruising; she absorbed it all. She followed up her victory in the straw poll by taking a vacation, vanishing from the campaign trail. Her fund-raising dried up on the spot. Her poll numbers started falling. Her relationship with Rollins was poisoned; he quit three weeks later. And the media that inflated her bubble in the first place shut off the helium spigot. The press was bored with Bachmann and, more to the point, entranced by a new bauble—the tough-talking stud in a ten-gallon Stetson, whom Bill Clinton called a "good-lookin' rascal."

RICK PERRY'S PULCHRITUDE WAS beyond dispute, but it accounted for only part of the Republican fascination with him. Born in the West Texas town of Paint Creek, raised in a house without indoor plumbing, he was folksy and swaggering at sixty-one, a natural populist who boasted about packing "a Ruger .380 with laser sights and loaded with hollow-point bullets," and once using it to fell a coyote that crossed his path. Lone Star State liberals mocked Perry as a nimrod; the late columnist Molly Ivins dubbed him Governor Goodhair. But since 1984, he had stood in ten contested elections—for state representative, agriculture commissioner, lieutenant governor, and governor—and won them all. Having secured his third statehouse term in 2010, Perry was the longest-serving governor in the country and in Texas history.

It was Perry's recent reelection that brought him national attention. Confronted with a stiff primary challenge from U.S. senator Kay Bailey Hutchison, Perry tapped into the energy of the Tea Party in its formative stages. At three massive anti-tax rallies, in Austin, Arlington, and Fort Worth on April 15, 2009, he decried the federal government's stranglehold on the states. Asked by a reporter about a fringe conservative call for Texas to secede, Perry replied, "We've got a great union. There's absolutely no reason to dissolve it. But if Washington continues to thumb their nose at the American people, you know, who knows what might come out of that?"

Hutchison thought Perry's flirtation with secession would doom him, but instead it roused the right. A year later, he thrashed her by twenty points and his general election opponent by thirteen. The day after the midterms, he flew to New York to promote a new book he had written. Entitled *Fed Up! Our Fight to Save America from Washington,* it contended that Social Security was a "Ponzi scheme" and that the Sixteenth and Seventeenth Amendments—which allow for the federal government's collection of income taxes and the direct election of senators, respectively—were mistakes. On NBC's *Today* show, he declared that *Fed Up!* was proof positive he wasn't running for president.

Perry privately told everyone around him the same thing. Even as speculation to the contrary grew in the spring of 2011, with a Draft Perry movement popping up and Limbaugh virtually begging him on the air to dive in, Perry kept insisting that he had no interest in immigrating to Washington, a town he despised. His chief political strategist, Dave Carney, and his 2010 campaign manager, Rob Johnson, had joined Gingrich's campaign, with Perry's blessing. His plan was to complete the Texas legislative session and then have surgery to fix a malformation in his lower back, which had nagged at him for years and lately worsened.

But as the legislative term wound to a close, Perry's stance began to waver. At a bill-signing ceremony in Austin on May 27, he said for the first time, "I'm going to think about [running]"—but then quickly added, "I think about a lot of things."

Even Perry's closest aides were shocked. Carney, a gruff, bearlike, reclusive presence who had been Perry's sage for thirteen years, called him up and asked if it was true. Perry, noting the apparent groundswell beneath him, said it would be silly not to explore whether a late entry was feasible. Two weeks later, amid turbulence on the Gingrich campaign, Carney and Johnson left Newt and started gaming out a plan for the governor.

To Perry's mind, the logic behind his putative candidacy was impeccable. In a race that would center on the economy, his record in Texas, which had led the nation in job creation during the downturn, gave him a terrific story to tell. His business boosterism and home-state eminence provided him with a mighty donor base. Between his southernness, his Tea Party credentials, and his avid evangelical faith, he presented a package more complete and better tailored to the Republican electorate than anyone in the field. And he was a hell of a talker—a man "able to communicate to people in a boardroom, people in a pool hall, and people in a church pew," in the words of one of his aides. And thus a man capable of stomping the bejesus out of Romney.

Perry's wife, Anita, agreed that her husband had the White House goods, and that mattered more than anyone knew. Protective of their two adult children and her family's privacy, Anita generally kept her distance from Rick's political doings. But at the RGA meeting in November 2010 where anti-Romney sentiments boiled over and Barbour told his fellow governors he was considering a bid, Anita urged her husband to go for it, saying, *You're* the one who should think about running. A nurse, Anita objected to Obamacare and believed that the president had to be defeated. She also knew that her husband thought Romney was a hollow conniver, and a yellow-bellied punk.

Perry's distaste for the front-runner stemmed from an altercation between them in 2006. As RGA head, Romney had employed a consultant, Alex Castellanos, who was working at the same time for an independent candidate challenging Perry. The incumbent considered this an outrageous conflict—a sort of RGA subsidy to his opponent. In a heated meeting at the governor's mansion in Austin, with Carney looking on, Perry demanded that Romney stop paying Castellanos or send Perry additional funding to even the score. Romney's reaction struck Perry as disingenuous, defensive, thin-skinned, and limp; after one sharp exchange, Romney stood up as if to storm out, then shrunk back in his seat and sulked.

When the meeting was over, Perry snorted to Carney, "How's he going to deal with Putin if he can't deal with this?" (Romney thought Perry was acting like a bully, and started referring to Carney as "Jabba the Hutt.")

On July 1, Perry underwent his scheduled back surgery. Two weeks later, Carney, Johnson, and Perry's statehouse chief of staff, Ray Sullivan, came to the governor's residence to meet with the Perrys and "scare them straight," as one adviser put it, about the realities of what a run would mean. Given the extreme lateness of Perry's start, his schedule would be punishing. Assuming a mid-August launch, he would face three crucial debates in September while at the same time having to rake in a whopping pile of cash to demonstrate his fund-raising strength by the end of the third quarter.

The Perrys had been subjected to invasive scrutiny in the past, including over a raft of rumors in 2004 that Rick was gay. Anita had hated that episode, and it left her husband disgusted and prone to passive-aggressive tangles with the press. A presidential campaign would be exponentially worse, his advisers warned the couple. Carney cited the stories about the Daniels marriage, which Perry's people (like everyone else) assumed had been driven by the Romney campaign. They're ruthless, Carney said, and the national press would be jackals. "There will be people following you, people following your family," Johnson added. "Your lives will change forever."

Nothing Perry's advisers were saying struck him as new information. *I've been in this business long enough to understand the seedy underbelly of politics,* he thought. *Sure, they play rough and hit hard in the NFL. But Texas football ain't exactly powder-puff.*

The Perrys told Carney and Johnson that they understood the dangers. The couple was ready to make their decision.

"Don't say yes now," Carney cautioned. "You need to think about this."

The next day, Perry phoned his lead strategist and said firmly that he was in. The degree of his confidence was stratospheric—and rooted in delusion about how prepared he and his team actually were.

Less than a month before Perry's presidential announcement, his entire operation consisted of fewer than a dozen people. They had held precisely one full-blown planning meeting. They had not done a speck of polling or other survey research. There had been no thorough examination of Perry's record in Texas or analysis of how it might play nationally. Nor did his team have an accurate understanding of the surgery Perry had just undergone. His spokesman had described it publicly as a "minor medical procedure," and that was what the governor told his advisers, too. In fact, Perry's doctors had performed a partial spinal fusion and nerve decompression, as well as injections of his own stem cells, an experimental therapy not approved by the FDA. In the fortnight after going under the knife, as he prepared to embark on the most demanding physical and mental excursion of his life, Perry was ingesting painkillers and having trouble sustaining his attention during meetings with potential bundlers and policy experts. Ever taciturn, ever macho, he told his people he was fine—and not one of them pressed him for more information or seemed to give it a second thought.

For a little while, none of this looked like political malpractice. Perry burst into the race as if he had been shot out of a cannon. On August 6, he hosted a prayer rally in Houston called "The Response"; some thirty thousand Christians filled Reliant Stadium to hear him sermonize. A week later, he drew comparisons to Reagan for the announcement stem-winder he delivered in Charleston. And then it was on to New Hampshire, Iowa, and the decimation of Bachmann.

The morning after Waterloo, August 15, Perry showed up at the Iowa State Fair, in Des Moines. In an open-necked blue shirt and khaki pants held up by a silver-tipped belt, he looked right at home amid the livestock pens, deep-fried butter treats, and pork chops on sticks—and sounded delighted to unsheathe his populist hatchet and hack his main competitor to pieces.

Earlier that day, across the country in New Hampshire, Romney had taken a thinly veiled jab at Perry, suggesting he didn't comprehend "the real economy" because he wasn't a businessman. Perry fired back: "I was in the private sector for thirteen years after I left the Air Force. You know, I wasn't on Wall Street, I wasn't working at Bain Capital, but the principles of the free market, they work whether you're in a farm field in Iowa or whether you're on Wall Street."

Later, a reporter pressed the point: Romney says his background makes him more qualified to create jobs. What about that?

Perry smiled wryly, blew a kiss to the camera, and said, "Give him my love. Give him my love."

FOURTEEN HUNDRED MILES AWAY on Commercial Street, Perry's facetiously tender display of amour elicited a torrent of f-bombs from Rhoades and a forced laugh from Romney. For nearly a year, the default front-runner had been waiting for the other shoe to drop—and now a giant ostrich-skinned cowboy boot had come crashing down on his head.

Everything about Perry made Romney anxious. The frenzied Bible-thumping of The Response struck him as a bizarre way to kick off a campaign, but *thirty thousand people*? Hoo, boy. Romney's calls to his bundlers to scope out Perry's fund-raising potential did nothing to reassure him, and neither did Zwick's assessment: We're going to lose market share with donors. Then there was Perry's instant rise to the top of the polls. Forty-eight hours after his announcement, Rasmussen Reports had Perry at 29, eleven points ahead of Mitt. For the first time this cycle, Romney gazed at a rival and thought, *This guy could be the nominee.*

On August 17, Romney sent an e-mail to his inner circle with the subject line "the road ahead," the rally-the-troops intent of which was undercut by its tone of rattled apprehension:

Hi team,

It didn't take a PhD to figure that Rick would get a rocket boost in the polls when he finally got in. The media has been begging for his entry for months, with folks like Rush and Fox among the most passionate suitors. What's it mean for us? . . .

Of course, we will not shrink from a fight, as conflict is sure to be brought our way. And in the meantime, we will ready our forces—financial, intellectual, strategic, political. The intensity of the coming campaign will sharpen us for the contest with President Obama.

We should not burden the days ahead with heavy seriousness and worry. We are in the middle of one of the most animated features of a democratic republic—a campaign for the presidency. It should be fun, and at the least, it should be instructive. We will grow from the experience, and if we take care to hue [sic] to our values and vision, it will enrich the nation as well, win or not win. But winning would be better . . .

Lately, in my stump speeches, I've been quoting a New Hampshire 19th century poet. His poem was written to capture the spirit needed to overcome the challenges that faced the pioneers of America's West. In some ways, it may apply to us. "Bring me men to match my mountains, / Bring me men to match my plains. / Men with empires in their purpose, / And new eras in their brains."

Mountains ahead,

Best, Mitt

Romney wasn't the only one spooked by Perry's ascent. The entire GOP establishment was in a tizzy, and nowhere was the alarm greater than in Bushworld, which had helped spawn the creature it now considered a sort of Frankenstein.

Perry had begun his political career as a Democrat, but in 1989 Rove persuaded him to switch parties and then ran his campaign for Texas agriculture commissioner. Eight years later, when Perry sought the lieutenant governorship, the Bush machine was behind him. Since Rove was working full-time for W. on his gubernatorial reelection and nascent presidential effort, he installed Carney as Perry's lead strategist. But the consultants wound up clashing bitterly over tactics, with Rove at one point threatening to withhold use of an ad in which Bush 41 endorsed Perry. Carney capitulated and Perry eked out a win, but the too-close-for-comfort margin left a nasty aftertaste on both sides.

Feuding consultants are as commonplace in politics as camera hoggery, but in the years that followed, Perry personally escalated the noisomeness as he sought to distance himself from a patrician dynasty with which he felt scant kinship. In 2002 he opposed the appointment of Robert Gates, Bush père's CIA director, as president of Texas A&M, annoying 41 and Barbara, and then publicly attacked their son. Campaigning for Giuliani in 2007, Perry volunteered that 43 "was never a fiscal conservative" in Texas—"I mean, '95, '97, '99, George Bush was spending money." Lashing back, Bush the Elder and his wife endorsed Hutchison in her primary challenge to Perry, as did several of their son's lieutenants, including Rove, who had come to view his former protégé as an ungrateful clown.

As Perry stepped into the presidential race, Rove was ready to pounce at the first opportunity. In short order, out in Iowa, Perry provided two: an intemperate eruption regarding Fed chairman Ben Bernanke ("If this guy prints more money between now and the election, I dunno what y'all would do to him in Iowa, but we would treat him pretty ugly down in Texas") and an unsubtle poke at Dubya's privileged breeding ("I went to Texas A&M; he went to Yale"). The next day on Fox, Rove unloaded, calling Perry's Bernanke comments "over-the-top" and "not presidential" and adding that "this pattern of sounding like he's being dismissive of the former president is not smart politics."

Jeb Bush sought to squelch the story that his clan was at war with his brother's successor. "I've never heard anybody in my family say anything but good things about Rick Perry," he told Fox News, which suggested Jeb was either deaf or not listening carefully. Up in Kennebunkport, his mother was hyperventilating over Perry. His brother was steaming, too. At a dinner party in Washington, the forty-third president vented to a Romney ally. "You can't take Perry seriously," Bush said. "He's a chicken-shit guy."

The Romneyites, like their boss, were taking Perry very seriously. Heading into Labor Day, he had established himself as the front-runner, seizing the lead in nine consecutive national polls, by as much as nineteen points. Scouring his Texas record, Romney's researchers noted that Perry supported letting the children of undocumented immigrants pay in-state tuition rates at public colleges—a lethal position in GOP primaries around the country. But when Newhouse tested the issue in Iowa focus groups, the reaction was disturbing: Republican voters were so enamored of Perry that they refused to believe he could hold such a liberal position.

Amid the chorus of concern in Boston, Stevens was a lone dissenter. Though he'd been worried about Pawlenty, Perry looked like a paper tiger to him. *He's a guy running against government who has been a government employee for most of his life,* Stevens thought. Perry grabbing credit for prosperity in his home state? What a joke. Texas was a business paradise long before Perry took office, and the unemployment rate was lower on the day he was sworn in than it was now. On social issues, Perry would be nailed from the right by Bachmann; on foreign policy, he was clueless.

And that was before Stevens had a chance to read *Fed Up!* Once he did, he changed his view of Perry from paper tiger to clay pigeon. The book's assertion that Social Security was unconstitutional, the equivalent of a pyramid scheme, caught Stevens's attention first. And the more he studied the text, the more wacky stuff he found. At headquarters, on plane rides, on the bus, with his colleagues and with Romney, Stevens obsessively whipped out his Kindle and read passages aloud. The guy wants to legalize marijuana! he bayed. He thinks Obamacare is somehow connected to the *Dred Scott* decision!

Soon everyone in the Commercial Street headquarters was poring over the book. On the cover of his copy, Rhoades placed a yellow Post-it on which he'd scribbled an apostrophe so that the title read *F'd Up!*

Romney found his staff's preoccupation with *Effed Up,* as they referred to it in conversation, sort of funny. But he assumed that they were gilding the lily in describing some of Perry's positions. "You're just paraphrasing," Romney would say. "Come on." He was especially disbelieving that Perry's views on Social Security were as out-there as Stevens claimed—until his strategist sat him down and made him watch a Perry TV appearance that proved the point.

But none of it really served to soothe Romney's fears. When he heard about Perry's Bernanke comments, he said, "I bet the base will love that."

On September 6, in an effort to parry Perry on jobs, Romney unveiled in Nevada a tract of his own that was considerably more sober than *Fed Up!*: a 161-page "business plan for the American economy" containing fifty-nine discrete policy proposals. From there he flew on to California, where he would go toe-to-toe with Perry for the first time, at a debate at the Reagan Presidential Library, in Simi Valley, not far from where Ann Romney engaged in one of her hobbies—dressage horseback riding.

The morning of the debate, the Romneys, Stevens, and a handful of other aides gathered for a final round of prep at a guesthouse on the stable grounds where Ann kept her horses. Rhoades and other staffers in Boston were piped in via speakerphone. Stevens was happy to be past what he dubbed the "snakes on a plane" free-for-all dynamic of the early debates, and confident to the point of cockiness about Mitt's ability to win a "strength versus strength" showdown with Perry.

Romney remained unpacified, his innate political pessimism running rampant. He's hitting me hard, he's scoring points, Mitt said. We keep talking about the problems, about his weaknesses, but we never get specific about how I'm supposed to respond. I want model answers. We don't have them. And the debate's a few hours away.

Stevens could see that Perry was in Romney's head, and tried to calm him down.

Don't let him psych you out, Stevens said. You're so much better than he is. You're gonna kill him.

Don't tell me that, Romney snapped. He's a natural. He was great at the Iowa State Fair.

Give me a break, Stevens said, his voice rising. He's an agriculture commissioner who went to an ag fair! He's an accidental governor! Just go out there and be the hunter!

You keep telling me this race is all about jobs and the economy, Romney retorted. He's got a great jobs record in Texas. He's got a great narrative. Don't underestimate him!

He's the guy George Bush thinks is an idiot! Stevens said, now shouting.

Romney pushed back from the table and walked out of the room. Stuart was making him crazy; Romney needed to cool off. Rhoades dispatched an e-mail to Stevens: Did Mitt just leave? Did you really just yell at him? Is that what's happening there? *What the fuck is going on?*

Mitt's just worried about Perry, Ann said, breaking an awkward silence in the room.

He's gonna kill him, Stevens repeated. It won't be close.

By the time the debate started, Romney had regained his composure. He slapped at Perry for being a career politician. Citing *Fed Up!*, he smacked him on Social Security. And, most aggressively, he sought to undermine him on jobs. "Texas has zero income tax," Romney said. "Texas has a right-to-work state, a Republican legislature, a Republican supreme court. Texas has a lot of oil and gas in the ground. Those are wonderful things, but Governor Perry doesn't believe that he created those things. If he tried to say that, well, it would be like Al Gore saying he invented the Internet."

Perry wasted no time in hitting back: "Michael Dukakis created jobs three times faster than you did, Mitt." But Romney was ready for him: "Well, as a matter of fact, George Bush and his predecessor created jobs at a faster rate than you did, Governor."

Romney wasn't alone in bashing away at Perry; by the middle of the debate, the newcomer had been socked so often by his rivals that he was moved to exclaim, "I kinda feel like the piñata here." When one of the moderators asked about a fresh criticism from Rove, who had said that day on *Good Morning America* that Perry's likening of Social Security to a Ponzi scheme was "toxic," Perry strayed far from any imaginable script and took a pop at his tormentor. "Karl has been over-the-top for a long time in some of his remarks," Perry groused. "I'm not responsible for Karl anymore."

The media verdict on the debate was that Perry had started out strong but sagged visibly partway through. Romney thought Perry had done okay, but just okay; the Texan could be had.

"See?" Stevens said. "The guy's not in your league."

But for Romney's strategist, the memory that stuck from the evening wasn't what took place on television. It was something Stevens said he'd witnessed on-site before the debate: Perry, clearly in pain, requiring help from two members of his security detail to get up a short flight of steps.

"There's something wrong with him," Stevens told Romney.

"What do you think?" asked Mitt.

"I don't know," Stevens said. "But I'm glad it's not me."

PERRY HEADED SOUTH from Simi Valley to San Diego for a fund-raiser the next morning. Then back north to Newport Beach, Los Angeles, Bakersfield, Palo Alto, and Fresno—for more fund-raisers. Chasing dollars was job one for Perry at this point. There wasn't time for much else. He had to put a big third-quarter number on the board, and was well on his way to the $17 million he would report at the end of September. In addition, six pro-Perry super PACs had been formed, including one pledging to spend $55 million on his behalf. With cash pouring in and poll numbers aloft, a middling debate debut seemed survivable.

But out of public view, both Perry and Perryville were melting down. Ten days earlier, Perry had attended a closed-door meeting with many of the country's most prominent evangelical leaders at a ranch in central Texas, where he was pointedly questioned about the persistent rumors that he was gay. "I can assure you that there is nothing that will embarrass you if you decide to support me," Perry told them.

What Perry didn't reveal was that his campaign had just received an e-mail filled with detailed and incendiary allegations from a Huffington Post reporter who had been pursuing the story doggedly all summer. Perry's aides believed the charges were ridiculous but feared that their airing at the moment the candidate was introducing himself to the country could be devastating. So Austin lawyered up, hiring the famed libel attorney Lin Wood to send a letter to HuffPo's owner, AOL, threatening to sue if the story was published.

Perry was all for firing a loud shot across the website's bow. *If you're gonna try to destroy my reputation,* he thought, *you better be certain that you've got your information extremely correct.* Flagrant as the story was, his opponents were sure to flog the daylights out of the charges. *Last thing we need is two weeks of doing nothing but responding to a bunch of fabrications.*

Just dealing with the HuffPo inquiries was a considerable distraction. Perry's aides were engaged in a furious scramble—pulling schedules and personnel records, since some of the allegations involved interns—to prove a negative. The process consumed huge amounts of staff time and energy that otherwise would have been devoted to dealing with the real issues Perry faced, of which there were many.

The most serious was his health. Since Perry's surgery, he had been in constant discomfort. A complication of his nerve decompression emerged almost immediately. First his right foot started tingling, then the tingle spread up his leg and the feeling changed to something more like burning. He was strapped in a brace to deal with lingering back pain. He was wearing orthopedic shoes. He couldn't sit still or stand stationary for too long. Most debilitating, he was no longer able to go running, and that in turn was causing him to suffer from insomnia.

Perry had sleep issues going back to the early seventies; he found it hard to shut his mind down at night. In the eighties, he took up jogging to ease his stress—and once he started jogging, he started sleeping. The virtuous cycle had turned him into a fiend for roadwork. If there was one addiction Perry had in life, he often said, it was to his daily run.

Robbed of that capacity, Perry was now like any addict deprived of his fix: sleepless and strung out. To try to stop the burning in his foot and leg, he took Lyrica. It didn't work. To try to shuttle himself into shut-eye, he tried warm baths. No luck there, either. On some nights, Perry's slumber was fitful. On others, he didn't sleep at all; he just lay there, staring at the ceiling.

Perry was well wired into his state's medical community. At the evangelical summit, a doctor friend of his from Tyler, Texas, slipped into his tent, examined him, and recommended that he visit a sleep lab.

The weekend after the Reagan Library debate, Perry checked himself in for a stay at a facility in Austin. The doctors strapped probes to him and monitored his behavior overnight. The result was a diagnosis of apnea—blockages of the upper airways that caused temporary lapses in breathing, robbing him of REM sleep. Perry doubted the diagnosis but assented to the prescription: a CPAP (continuous positive airway pressure) machine, which involved placing a plastic mask over his mouth and nose at night. But that was a washout, too; Perry's wakefulness continued. His campaign was less than a month old, and he was already comprehensively out of gas.

The question for Carney and Johnson was what do about it. The next two weeks held in store a pair of debates in Florida, the first sponsored by the Tea Party in Tampa and the second in Orlando in conjunction with the Presidency 5 straw poll, which the campaign was pushing to win. If Perry was able to run this gauntlet successfully, Carney thought, they could dial back his schedule and deal with the sleep issue properly.

But the plan went awry immediately. At the Tampa debate, on September 12, Perry was once again manhandled by the entire field. This time he turned in a performance glaringly more unsteady than the one in Simi Valley. With the stakes for the Orlando debate now appreciably higher, most political observers assumed that Perry would devote much of the next ten days to preparing himself. Instead he returned to the fund-raising circuit, traveling from Florida to Massachusetts to Virginia to New York to Iowa and then back to New York.

While Perry was in Gotham, he met with Trump, who introduced him to Kim Kardashian. He also did an interview with *Parade* magazine, which would not be published until October, in which his sit-down with the Donald reared its head. After saying, "I don't have a definitive answer" as to whether Obama had been born in the United States, Perry went on to note that "I had dinner with Donald Trump the other night . . . He doesn't think [Obama's birth certificate] is real." And what did Perry think? "I don't have any idea. It doesn't matter. He's the president of the United States. He's elected. It's a distractive issue."

When Perry arrived back in Orlando, he was a mess. In advance of the straw poll, his Florida team had set up a string of meetings with delegates, donors, activists, and legislators. But Perry was so distant, unfocused, and uncommunicative that most of the meetings had to be canceled—and his debate prep sessions, though lengthy, were scattered and ineffective.

By now Carney was on the phone almost daily with Perry's doctors, including sleep specialists consulting on how to address the problem. But the exercise in futility continued. The morning of the debate, September 22, Perry's team learned he hadn't caught a wink the night before. In the holding room, Carney and Johnson girded for trouble. What they got was a disaster.

It arrived midway through the debate, when Romney went after him on the issue of in-state tuition benefits. "If you're a United States citizen from any one of the other forty-nine states, you have to pay $100,000 more" than the child of an "illegal alien" for four years at the University of Texas, Romney said. "That doesn't make sense to me."

Perry had been copiously prepared for this attack, which had come up in Tampa, too. And the start of his answer, touting his commitment to border security, was uncontroversial. But then Perry went further, blurting out a sentiment that none of his aides had ever heard him enunciate before. "If you say that we should not educate children who have come into our state for no other reason than they've been brought there by no fault of their own," he said, "I don't think you have a heart."

For Perry's advisers, the debate was now effectively over. Providing in-state tuition to the kids of undocumented workers was a defensible position, if not a popular one among Republican primary voters. But calling those who disagreed heartless was an act of political suicide.

Perry wasn't quite finished committing verbal seppuku, however. Toward the end of the debate, after Romney offered a defense of his Massachusetts health care law, Perry attempted to slam his rival as a flip-flopper, a rejoinder he had been rehearsing for at least a week. In fact, he had it written out on a piece of paper in front of him, but it came out sounding like the ravings of a drunk:

"I think Americans just don't know sometimes which Mitt Romney they're dealing with. Is it the Mitt Romney that was on the side of, against the Second Amendment before he was for the Second Amendment? Was it, was before, he was before the social programs from the standpoint of—he was for standing up for *Roe vs. Wade* before he was against first *Roe vs. Wade*? He was for Race to the Top. He's for Obamacare and now he's against it. I mean, we'll wait until tomorrow and, and, and see which Mitt Romney we're really talking to tonight."

The next day in the halls of the P5 event, Perry's pratfalls were all anyone could talk about. A day earlier, he was primed to claim victory at the straw poll; now his erstwhile supporters were defecting in droves. Twenty-four hours later, he was walloped by Herman Cain, who took 37 percent of the vote to Perry's 15.

Nothing would ever be the same for Perry after Orlando. Republican elites, circumspect about him from the get-go, dug a grave for him and covered it with a metric ton of scorn. In *The Weekly Standard,* William Kristol pronounced the debate performance "close to a disqualifying two hours." On *Fox News Sunday,* Brit Hume observed that "Perry really did throw up all over himself" and was "half a step away from almost total collapse."

The Republican base was no kinder. For the first time, Boston saw movement in its polling and focus groups away from Perry, almost entirely over immigration. Romney demonstrated no reluctance about exploiting the issue. As part of his rightward repositioning on social and cultural matters in 2008, Mitt had become an immigration hawk, denouncing Giuliani for turning New York into a "sanctuary city" for illegals and hoisting Huckabee on the in-state-tuition petard. (Romney had vetoed a similar bill in Massachusetts.) While Mitt wanted to stay focused on the economy this time around, what he wanted more was to win—and immigration was looking like Perry's Achilles' heel.

Coming out of Orlando, Team Romney pounded away at the Texan on the issue for a solid month. When Perry next visited New Hampshire, Rhoades and one of the campaign's Granite State operatives arranged to have him greeted by protesters, including one who was wearing a sombrero and holding a placard that read THANKS FOR THE IN-STATE TUITION.

From the announcement of his candidacy until the second Florida debate, Perry had topped every national poll, sixteen of them. From Orlando onward, he would never lead again. As was the case with Pawlenty after Obamneycare and Bachmann after Waterloo, Perry was now the walking dead—a victim of a hair-trigger Republican electorate, a hyper-drive media, and his own catastrophic foibles.

The governor's people knew he had inflicted awful damage on himself. But like Bruce Willis in *The Sixth Sense,* they weren't aware that their cause had passed from the land of the living. Perry was still armed with millions of dollars in the bank and half a dozen super PACs on his side, along with a conviction that someone would emerge as the conservative alternative to Romney. For a little while, that alternative had been Perry himself. What the Texan couldn't fathom was why it couldn't be again.

9

BIG BOY

THE BILLIONAIRES' CLUB NEVER thought much of Governor Goodhair. Perched at the pinnacle of the Republican donor pyramid, the club comprised a loose affiliation of financial titans, industrial tycoons, and media machers. They were for the most part northern sophisticates, urban and urbane. They were adamantly conservative on matters of taxes, spending, and regulation, decidedly moderate on social issues, uniformly repelled by evangelical fervor and dum-dum populism of any flavor. They found the holy-rollerism of The Response hideous, and the rough talk about Bernanke preposterous. But they agreed with Perry about one thing: Romney just wouldn't do.

The billionaires' reluctance to rally around Mitt was surprising but undeniable. Nearly four months after his official entry into the race, many of the party's most bodacious bundlers remained seated on their hands: hedge-fund goliaths Stanley Druckenmiller, Ken Griffin, Dan Loeb, Paul Singer, Paul Tudor Jones, and David Tepper; über-financiers Steve Schwarzman and Charles Schwab; Home Depot founder Ken Langone. Romney was hungry for the support of them all. None found him objectionable: he was a member of their tribe, sound on economic policy, and infinitely preferable to Obama—all in all, a stand-up guy. But even now, in late September, the billionaires were still looking for more than that. They were looking for *the* guy. A candidate without any phoniness about him. A candidate with a pair of clanging brass balls you could hear from around the corner. A candidate they were sure could win.

Christopher James Christie was the man they had in mind, and he made for an unlikely object of desire. He was not yet fifty, less than two years into his first term as governor of New Jersey, suave as sandpaper, and morbidly obese. He was also one of the most intriguing figures in American politics.

Christie's ascent to this rarefied air had been rapid and unexpected. Born in Newark, he spent the nineties as a lawyer-lobbyist, serving on the Morris County Board of Chosen Freeholders and losing a bid for the New Jersey General Assembly. In 2000, he cast his lot early with George W. Bush, visiting Austin three times, becoming acquainted with the candidate and Rove. His prodigious fund-raising earned him an appointment as his state's U.S. attorney and a signature W. nickname: Big Boy.

In 2009, after a six-year stint in law enforcement, Christie hurled himself at the governorship, which was occupied by Democratic multimillionaire Jon Corzine. The race was tight, obstreperous, and mean. Corzine ran ads swiping at Christie for "throwing his weight around." Christie showcased a capacious personality and a coriaceous hide ("If you're going to do it, at least man up and say I'm fat") but presented mainly platitudes and no clear agenda. The *Wall Street Journal* editorial page predicted that if he won, he would "arrive in Trenton with a mandate to do what he campaigned on—nothing."

Christie's victory was narrow, by less than four points, but the dervish-like governance that followed confounded every expectation. He capped local property taxes, slashed spending, and laid off state workers. He waged pitched battles with the Democratic legislature over a ballooning budget shortfall and with public-sector unions over unfunded pension liabilities. His style was equal parts take-no-prisoners and take-no-shit. He ritually sparred with voters and the press in public forums, exchanges captured on video by his staff and filed in the library of smackdowns that was his YouTube channel. (To a constituent asking him to justify cutting funds for public education while sending his kids to private school: "Hey, Gail, you know what, first off it's none of your business." To a reporter noting his confrontational tone: "You should really see me when I'm pissed.")

Less than a year into his tenure, Christie had emerged as a certified shooting star, beloved by conservatives, moderates, and populists alike. In the run-up to the 2010 midterms, he was besieged by questions about a White House run in 2012. His answers were unvarying and emphatic. "Short of suicide, I don't really know what I'd have to do to convince you people that I'm not running," he told reporters in Trenton the day after the Republicans retook control of the House. "I've said I don't want to. I'm not going to. There is zero chance I will. I don't feel like I'm ready to be president."

What Christie was ready to do, however, was flex his newfound national muscle. With the help of his two main political advisers, Bill Palatucci and Mike DuHaime, he convened a series of intimate dinners at Drumthwacket, the grand nineteenth-century mansion in Princeton that served as the New Jersey governor's official residence. On the guest list were the presidential aspirants deemed worthy by Team Trenton. On the table was Christie's endorsement, along with access to New Jersey's copious crop of rich Republican donors, over whom he exercised ironclad control.

Romney arrived one night in late January, the first to be granted an audition. He and Christie weren't personally close, but the ties between their worlds ran deep. Schriefer and Stevens had served as consultants and ad makers on Christie's campaign; Rhoades's girlfriend was a Christie appointee; DuHaime and Romney's political director, Rich Beeson, were pals; and Jets owner Woody Johnson was mates with both Mitt and Chris. When Christie had faced a primary challenge in 2009, Romney endorsed him and heaped money in his coffers. Now Mitt was hoping for a payoff on that investment.

Packing into Drumthwacket's formal dining room were a couple dozen of Christie's associates; Romney brought with him Johnson and Spencer Zwick. The case Mitt made over the meal was forceful and direct. His 2008 bid had taught him invaluable lessons; he wouldn't make the same mistakes again. He would run an all-economy-all-the-time campaign, hammering Obama for his fecklessness and failures. Only he had the business background and sagacity to fix the mess that the country was in. Only he would have a fund-raising operation capable of matching the president's. He was far and away the party's likeliest standard-bearer and best chance to reclaim the White House.

Romney was even more aggressive after dinner, when he and Christie repaired to the library for a private talk. I am going to be the nominee, Mitt declared. You should get on board now, before anybody else. The earlier you give your endorsement, the more it will mean.

Christie told Romney he wasn't going to back anyone in the near future. It's too soon, he said, I'm not ready. (What Christie thought was less diplomatic: *This guy will be delighted with my endorsement whenever I decide to make it.*) He also told Romney something else—that until Christie made up his mind, he wanted none of the candidates, including Mitt, to raise money in New Jersey.

Romney found the stipulation galling, and voiced his displeasure. As Christie dug in his heels, the atmosphere got tense. Look, Christie said, when I decide to support someone, it will be more powerful if I bring everyone along with me. Just be patient; it'll be fine. But let's be clear: if you jump the gun and start raising money here, you can almost certainly kiss my support good-bye.

Romney left Drumthwacket incredulous at Christie's diktat and the backroom delivery—it was like something out of *The Sopranos. Are you kidding me?* Mitt thought. *He's going to do that?*

Up in Boston, Stevens was equally astonished at Christie's imperiousness. There were plenty of New Jersey donors who'd given money to Mitt in 2008; now Chris was trying to impose a gag order on talking to them? "He sounds like the biggest asshole in the world," Stuart griped to his partner, Russ, about their mid-Atlantic client.

Rhoades was no more pleased with the prohibition, but he counseled prudence. The earlier we get Christie, the better—but better late than not at all, he said. When members of Zwick's finance team complained about being blocked from pockets of ready Garden State cash, Rhoades always offered the same verbal slap upside the head: Shut the fuck up. Don't go into Jersey. We have plenty of time.

But as winter turned to spring and spring turned to summer, with no Christie endorsement in sight, doubts crept in on Commercial Street. Although the governor continued to issue denials of any 2012 ambitions, his comments were increasingly freighted with self-regard. In late June, he appeared on *Meet the Press,* where David Gregory asked him who in the current field might garner his support.

"Any one of them could if they're willing to be authentic," Christie said. "That's what allows you to do the big things like we're doing in New Jersey. It's not that I'm universally loved; we know I'm not in New Jersey. But what they do say in New Jersey is 'We like him and we think he's telling us the truth.' I think we need to have that type of politics on the national level."

Romney's luck regarding would-be rivals had been miraculous so far. The later it got, the less likely it was that anyone plausible would jump in. But Mitt worried that Christie might be an exception. The establishment loved him. The Tea Party adored him. The punditocracy pined for him. And then there were the blandishments of the billionaires' club—which even politicians with smaller egos than Big Boy's would find difficult to ignore.

O N THE SAME JUNE Sunday that Christie made his latest turn on *Meet the Press,* three hundred of the fantastically rich and colossally conservative were waiting for him in Beaver Creek, Colorado. The plutocrats were gathered at the Ritz-Carlton, Bachelor Gulch, for a secret retreat hosted by the Koch brothers. Christie was jetting in from Washington to deliver the coveted dinnertime keynote.

That afternoon, the attendees heard from Perry, who at that point was still weighing whether to enter the race and had managed to wangle a speaking slot. The billionaires and millionaires were curious about this character who was ginning up so much chatter. But by the end of the speech, the air had gone out of the room. Instead of laying out a vision for the nation, Perry boasted ceaselessly about Texas. Raising five fingers, he declared that he had a four-point plan to solve something or other; after ticking off its planks, he was left with one digit extended awkwardly in the air. In the back of the room, one of the Kochs' political advisers thought, *If this dude runs, he'll be done after the second debate.*

The contrast with Christie could not have been more striking. After being introduced lavishly by David Koch—who called him a "true political hero," professed to being "inspired by this man," and declared him to be "my kind of guy"—Christie spoke for nearly an hour and had the crowd in the palm of his hand. He regaled the group with tales of his battles with the unions. In the Q&A, he drew laughs with references to MTV's *Jersey Shore* and some sly mockery of the Lone Star State (and, by implication, its governor): "We all love Texas, okay? The greatest place in the world, it's wonderful, it's fabulous, it's amazing. We all love Texas. Great. So we dispense with that first."

The Koch retreat was Christie's first stop on a summer tour of mogulfests. Two weeks later, he was in Sun Valley, Idaho, for the annual Allen & Company media-and-technology conference. Interviewed onstage by Tom Brokaw, Christie blew the room away again, eliciting kudos not just from Republicans but from Democrats, independents, and the studiously apolitical members of the info-royalty.

One sovereign in particular left Sun Valley burbling about Big Boy: Rupert Murdoch. Still sour on Romney and un-enamored of the rest of the field, News Corp's chairman returned to New York determined to draw Christie into the race. He's energetic, sure-footed, and electable, Murdoch gushed to a confidant of many years—who had never seen the old man with such a crush on a candidate. Murdoch knew that Roger Ailes had been urging Christie to run for months and had gotten nowhere. But Rupert also knew someone who seemed to be making more progress.

That someone was Ken Langone, who had appointed himself as the unofficial chief of the Draft Christie conspiracy. Seventy-five years old, Langone, the son of a plumber, had bootstrapped himself to the top of a financial empire, playing in venture capital and investment banking. Blustery and impatient, with a quick temper and a gutter mouth, he was conservative but idiosyncratically so. In 1992, he had been a key backer of Ross Perot, a close friend. In 1996, he raised dollars for Dole but ended up being happy that Clinton prevailed. In 2000 and 2004, he favored Bush, but only because he saw Gore and Kerry as so much worse.

Although Langone had nominally supported McCain, he greeted Obama's presidency with high hopes. Langone was passionate about education reform and chaired a charter school in Harlem. On election night in 2008, he went to bed thinking, *Isn't this wonderful? Minority kids have a new role model—not a football player, not a rapper, but a president of the United States.* But to Langone, it was all downhill from there as Obama revealed himself to be a rank ideologue, demonizing wealth to divide the electorate to his political advantage. *If it wasn't for us fat cats and the endowments that we fund,* Langone thought, *every university in the country would be fucked.*

In contemplating who should replace Obama, Langone had latched on to Christie in 2010. He loved the governor's clashes with the teachers' unions, his aversion to political correctness, and his penchant for telling critics to shove it—not least when Christie caught flak from some on the right for appointing a Muslim American judge. Comparatively, Romney was a yawn. At a meeting in Langone's office that summer, the billionaire told Mitt that he would support him, but only in the breach. "Governor, I'll make it easy," Langone said. "If my guy doesn't run, as I look at what else is out there, you're it."

By then Langone had been cajoling Christie for months, in person and by phone, and enlisting Murdoch and others to do the same. *This is a gang bang,* Langone thought. *The more the merrier.*

The apotheosis of Langone's lobbying took place on July 19 at the Racquet and Tennis Club, on Park Avenue. The financier had invited Christie to meet with a few folks who wanted to make their case to him directly about why he should run—a full-scale rollout of the Draft Christie brigade in all its moneyed glory. Druckenmiller, Schwab, Schwarzman, real estate magnate Mort Zuckerman, and former New York Stock Exchange chairman Richard Grasso were in the house (with a combined net worth of more than $20 billion). Patched in via speakerphone were Singer, Jones, David Koch, Carl Icahn, former GE chairman Jack Welch, former AIG head Hank Greenberg, and former Morgan Stanley CEO John Mack.

When Christie arrived with his wife, Mary Pat, seventeen-year-old son Andrew, and DuHaime, they were startled and staggered by the firepower on display. Christie told the group he was there to listen. They had a great deal to say. Langone pledged that everyone in the room would be behind him, and that money would be no object. Druckenmiller and others argued that the fate of the American economy rested on Christie's shoulders.

But perhaps the most powerful plea came from a non-billionaire who was also present. Henry Kissinger had been taken with Christie since they first met at a Yankees game a year earlier. The foreign policy éminence grise had then invited the governor to dinner. Rising now with the aid of his cane, Kissinger said, "If you ask me whether Governor Christie knows anything about foreign policy, I'd have to say he doesn't know anything about foreign policy. But if you ask me whether he should run, I think we need a candidate with character and courage—and I think he's got both."

Christie was rarely at a loss for words, but this silenced him. Listen, he said finally, I don't want to mislead you. The overwhelming likelihood is that I won't do this. But I can't tell you I'm not moved by what I have heard just now. And after everything you all have said, I can't walk out of here and not at least consider this thing. So Mary Pat and I are going to take some time and figure out what we think.

No one in the room was deluded enough to believe that Christie had undergone a conversion, or foolish enough to dismiss his reticence. But few doubted that, for the first time, he had left the door ajar—which was enough for Langone to leave the meeting thinking, *Mission accomplished*.

WORD OF THE CHRISTIE-LANGONE powwow leaked to Politico almost immediately. The governor was asked about it at a press conference in Trenton later that afternoon. "There are some people who believe that I should leave this job and go for another one," Christie said. "I'm always willing to sit and listen to folks who want to make that argument to me, but I said nothing different to [Langone and Co.] today than I've said to other folks in the past."

Disingenuous though it was, Christie's public posture wouldn't waver for the next ten weeks: Nothing has changed, I'm not considering a run, and please get off my back. But behind the scenes, the period was fraught and frantic with deliberations, to-ing and fro-ing, and solicitations of advice.

Mary Pat Christie's main focus was the impact on her four children, all under age eighteen, but she also had less motherly concerns. An investment banker at Cantor Fitzgerald, she was politically astute and protective of her husband's public image and long-range potential. She feared that if he ran and failed to win the nomination, the setback would imperil his reelection as governor—and thus his future on the national stage. Embedded professionally in the financial sector, she had savvy questions about the fundraising hurdles Chris would have to surmount. New Jersey had "pay-to-play" restrictions limiting the contributions he could collect from Wall Street, which had handicapped him in his war with Corzine. What effect would those rules have on a national bid? Were Langone and his crew really good for the astronomical sums they were promising?

The governor had a lot of questions, too. In getting a handle on the logistics and mechanics of a late entry—the filing deadlines, debates, prospective travel schedules—he could rely on DuHaime and Palatucci. Christie's sharpies were receiving oodles of unsolicited intel from party bigwigs, name-brand strategists, and early-state operatives. They also had presidential experience of their own: Palatucci with Bush 41 in 1992, and DuHaime with Bush 43 in 2004 and Rudy Giuliani in 2008.

But Christie's consultations extended far beyond his immediate orbit. He talked to Barbour, Kasich, and Giuliani, all of whom pledged their support. He talked to Paul Ryan, who was himself receiving presidential entreaties from members of the billionaires' club. He talked to Ken Mehlman, manager of Bush's 2004 operation and later chair of the RNC, who told him his pugnacity and reform-mindedness were ideally suited to the political moment. And he talked to the fellow Mehlman had helped steer to reelection: calling from Kennebunkport one August day, Dubya jawed with Christie for forty-five minutes, playing sounding board as the governor ran through the pluses and minuses of a run.

Mary Pat's phone rang at her desk at Cantor Fitzgerald some days later. Barbara Bush was on the line, offering encouraging words detailing the kid-friendliness of White House life. After hard-edged conversations about buck-raking and consultations with Mehlman (independent of Chris) regarding the prospects for a race, Mary Pat found chatting with the GOP's First Grandma a breath of soothing fresh air.

Rare was the colloquy of any consequence in Bushworld that didn't get back to Rove. And rare was the day he didn't receive at least one call from a palpitating Langone. On August 15, Rove turned up on *Hannity* and touted—teasingly, tantalizingly—what he knew to be true about the altered state of Christie's disposition.

"I talked to a number of people who had picked up the phone and called

Christie to tell him they thought that he ought to run," Rove said. "I'm starting to pick up some sort of vibrations that these kinds of conversations are
causing Christie . . . to tell the people who are calling him, 'Well, you know
what, I owe it to you. I think I will take a look at it.'"

On cable, on the Web, and in the political world writ large, Rove's vague
pronouncement stirred up a fuss. Two days later, Christie was asked about
it at another Trenton press event. Feigning bafflement, he replied, "I listened
to that four or five times . . . because I was interested to hear what he was
saying . . . [My] answer isn't changing and I don't see any reason why it
would."

Christie was indeed interested in hearing what Rove had to say about
his entering the race. So interested that the two already had a meeting inked
in their calendars. For the day after tomorrow.

Rove rolled up in a town car in front of Christie's family home in Mend-
ham on the evening of August 19. He came directly from Fox, where he had
pretaped a segment of *The O'Reilly Factor* in which he again talked up a
Christie run. Now, as he took a seat at the kitchen table at 46 Corey Lane,
Rove doffed his pundit's beanie and donned his strategist's chapeau—and
spent the next three hours with the Christies, DuHaime, and Palatucci, running the traps on a Big Boy bid.

Rove addressed the central question first: Was it too late for Christie to
get in? Not at all, Rove argued. In fact, it would probably be better to wait
until late September, when there was a lull after the first three Republican
debates. But, look, he went on, you can't spend the next month sitting here
like a monk, cloistered in the abbey. You need to spend the time in a way
that lays down a predicate: consulting policy experts, setting in the foundation for a finance operation, reaching out to players in the early states.

Beyond that, Rove explained, Christie had to do more to stoke the rising
fever among his fans. "You need to keep this thing fluid," he said. Every day
that goes by, bundlers, operatives, and electeds are making commitments to
other candidates; to the degree people think that you might be getting in, it
keeps them from signing on with someone else. "So put a little gasoline on
the campfire," Rove counseled. "Make certain the blaze is bright enough so
that people can see it back in the woods."

Christie asked Rove about Romney point-blank: Can I take him?

I think you can, Rove said. But this won't be about winning any one state or picking off votes here and there. For you to win, you have to galvanize people around the country. "You've got to blow a couple of pylons off of the edifice called Romney by being a northeastern governor who actually has confidence, consistency, compassion, and energy," Rove said. You can do it by just being yourself: the tough-talking straight shooter who took on the teachers' union in New Jersey. And if you pull that off, you can be credible in Iowa, New Hampshire, South Carolina, Florida—and everywhere else.

Christie hoisted up his and Mary Pat's reservations. Rove shot them down one by one. On fund-raising: "Langone is a bullshit artist," Karl said affectionately, but he's a significant guy who can raise a lot, and money's not going to be your problem anyway. On betraying New Jersey voters by abandoning them to chase a grander ambition: Clinton did it, Bush did it, Perry's doing it now; voters are in on that joke. On the fear that if Christie ran and lost, it would make his reelection in the Garden State tougher: Sure, Rove said, but there's a solution to that: "Don't run and lose!"

Rove had the sense that Mary Pat was warming to the idea, but that DuHaime and Palatucci were wary. As for Christie himself, Karl couldn't quite tell. When Rove went to leave, the governor accompanied him to the door, and they stood talking on the porch for another half an hour. I think I understand why all this is happening, Christie said. People keep telling me that our country is at risk and I'm the one who can save it. But I gotta say, I'm not sure I'm ready.

I get that, Rove said. But we're talking about the presidency here. "There's a difference between feeling like you're *ready* for the job and that you can *do* the job. Do you think you can do the job?"

"Probably," Christie replied.

"Well, the guy we've got in there now is clearly not up to it," Rove said. "And you'd be a hell of a lot better than him."

THE LOCUS OF ROVE'S LOW regard landed at Newark airport, disembarked from Air Force One, and met Christie on the tarmac. It was September 4, the Sunday of Labor Day weekend, and Obama was in New Jersey to survey the damage from Hurricane Irene, which had torn its way up the East Coast at the end of August. Four days earlier, the president had declared the Garden State a disaster area. More than $1 billion in damage had been inflicted on 200,000 homes and buildings, making Irene the costliest natural calamity in New Jersey history.

Obama and Christie hadn't spent much time together, but they greeted each other warmly, locking arms and patting shoulders. The picture they presented was a study in physical and political contrasts. Next to Christie, Obama resembled a stick figure; next to Obama, Christie looked like a dirigible: On the heels of the debt-ceiling fracas, Obama's popularity and potency were at low ebb; in the midst of the will-he-or-won't-he guessing game, Christie's were at new heights. Christie thought Obama was an atrocious chief executive, passive and disengaged, but he knew that the president's caginess and magnetism would make him tough to beat. Obama had devoted less thought to his companion as a potential opponent, but his advisers saw the dangers in Christie's blue-collar-friendly charisma. Though Plouffe believed that an entry this late would be absurd, Messina thought there was no harm in being prepared. From Corzine's old team he cadged a hard drive filled with Christie oppo—and the stuff was pure gold.

As Obama and Christie toured the flood-ravaged towns of Paterson and Wayne, they fell into an easy repartee. Born a year apart, both were clever, able to charm at will, and irritated by pointless posturing. Publicly praising each other, they privately kibitzed about their kids. (Christie's daughters, Sarah and Bridget, were close in age to Sasha and Malia.) After being ferried from spot to spot on Marine One for four hours, they returned to Newark, and Christie walked Obama to Air Force One.

"You're not coming on there with me, too, are you?" the president inquired teasingly.

"Only if you ask," Christie said.

"No, you can finish here," Obama teased again, then flew back to Washington. When his aides wanted to know what he made of Christie, Obama grinned and said, "He's a *big* man."

The blanket coverage of the president and the governor in tandem only pumped more air into the rapidly inflating Christie boomlet. And so did Christie's latest viral sensation: a video of him as the storm bore down, scolding seaside residents who were ignoring orders to evacuate. "Get the

hell off the beach in Asbury Park!" he commanded. "It's four thirty—you've
maximized your tan. Get. Off. The. Beach."

With reporters on the lookout for any small shard of Christie-related
news, a rather large one plopped into their laps: an announcement by the
Reagan Library that the governor would be delivering a major speech there
on September 27. The appearance, in fact, had been on Christie's schedule since April, when he received a handwritten invitation from Nancy Reagan. But that was beside the point. Rove had advised Christie to sprinkle
some gas on the campfire. With Perry stumbling through the three September debates and anti-Romney Republicans fanning the embers, Big Boy's
library address was tantamount to a hogshead of petrol.

On September 24, the *New York Post* declared that Christie was "thinking about becoming the new face in the race" and quoted a Republican
source asserting, "He'll decide this week." Former New Jersey governor Tom
Kean, who decades earlier had mentored a teenage Christie and was now
one of his informal advisers, told *National Review*, "It's real. He's giving it a
lot of thought. I think the odds are a lot better now than they were a couple
weeks ago."

The billionaires' club was getting the same impression from its closed-
door talks with Christie. A few days before the Reagan Library event, Christie sat down with Langone, Druckenmiller, and Joel Klein, the former New
York City schools chancellor who was now one of Murdoch's top lieutenants. The clock was ticking, Christie said. Given the hubbub surrounding
the speech, he would need to decide soon after. The kinds of questions he
was asking, his tone and body language, left his suitors feeling optimistic.
Back at News Corp, Klein told Murdoch, I think he's gonna play.

With word leaking out that Christie's speech would be not about New
Jersey but about America's role in the world, speculation mounted that he
might announce his candidacy then and there. His hosts at the library hoped
that it was true. Even in her nineties, Mrs. Reagan remained a canny ob-
server of the political scene and voracious consumer of political gossip.
Christie's strength and take-charge attitude had impressed her from afar
(and she was not easily impressed). The library's executive director, John
Heubusch, a former Republican operative and Capitol Hill staffer, orches-
trated the proceedings to give Christie a gentle nudge toward making news.

On the appointed day, the Christies arrived a bit early for a tour of the museum, beaming and holding hands. Lacking time for the full circuit, Heubusch made sure to plant them in the Legacy Theater to view the three-and-a-half-minute film on Reagan—a slick and emotional distillation of his life. The fortieth president was the first Christie had voted for, as a freshman in college; his reverence for Dutch was deep. As Christie exited the theater, Heubusch was pleased to see tears in his eyes. He ushered the governor to sit with Mrs. Reagan, whose well-practiced flattery bowled her guest over.

Before the speech, Heubusch, who would moderate the Q&A afterwards, asked Christie if he should kick things off by posing the obvious query.

Nah, Christie answered after thinking for a second. If it's going to happen, it's going to happen naturally. Just let it come from the audience.

Christie's speech, titled "Real American Exceptionalism," was bracing and solid, including a brisk critique of Obama as "a bystander in the Oval Office." But the Q&A session was something else. The second question was the inevitable one; Christie brushed it off, encouraging the audience to visit Politico's website, where a video compendium of his expressions of lack of presidential interest had been compiled. The last questioner, however, raised the topic again—from the balcony, with great feeling.

"We can't wait another four years to 2016," said a middle-aged woman, her daughter beside her. "I really implore you, as a citizen of this country, to please, sir, to reconsider. Go home and really think about it. Please. Do it for my daughter, do it for our grandchildren, do it for our sons."

The audience sprang to its feet and roared applause. At the podium, Christie dropped his head and faintly buckled in the face of that rarest thing in politics: a genuine, spontaneous moment.

"I hear exactly what you're saying, and I feel the passion with which you say it, and it touches me," Christie said. "It's extraordinarily flattering. But by the same token, that heartfelt message you gave me is also not a reason for me to do it. That reason has to reside inside me."

CHRISTIE'S DANCE OF the seven hundred veils was starting to wear on Boston. Nervous all along watching the Big Boy shuffle, the Romneyites had taken comfort in the judgment of Schriefer, who talked regularly with

Christie and his people and heard nothing but mollifying mewling. Now, though, between the press reports he was reading and subtle telephonic wavering from Trenton, Russ slipped into doubt. After months of maintaining regular contact, Beeson's friend DuHaime suddenly had gone dark.

Christie's behavior had long rankled Stevens the most, and now it was working his last nerve. A few days after the governor's Simi Valley samba, Stuart phoned Palatucci in a huff.

What's the governor of New Jersey doing at the Reagan Library? Stevens demanded to know.

He was asked by Mrs. Reagan, Palatucci replied. And when she asks, you have to go.

"The fuck you have to go!" cried Stevens. This is the problem with your whole operation. You're sitting in Jim McGreevey's seat, Christie Whitman's seat, Jim Florio's seat, Jon Corzine's seat. And where are they now? "He's the governor of *New Jersey*," Stevens said. "There will be another governor of New Jersey."

Stevens had been certain from the start that Christie would not run. That the flirtation was a charade, an exercise in self-pleasuring. If Christie gets in the race, Stevens told Palatucci, he'll be out by the Super Bowl. And if he isn't going to run, he's doing needless damage to his brand.

"You're killing Chris Christie," Stevens said. You're turning him into Mario Cuomo—Hamlet on the other side of the Hudson.

When Palatucci told the governor of Stevens's tirade, Christie scoffed. He barely knew Stuart and didn't much like him; Schriefer was his guy. And while Russ was also arguing, if more tactfully, that it was inadvisable for Christie to run, he dismissed those views, too. *No shit they think it's a bad idea if I get in!* Christie thought. *They work for Romney. It's a bad idea for them if I get in!*

Before returning from California, Christie told Palatucci he planned to lie low for the weekend ahead, October 1–2, and think through his decision. Tell people they shouldn't call me or bother me or ask for updates—just leave me alone, Christie said.

In measuring the pros and cons, Christie faced a divided household on Corey Lane. None of his four children were in favor of him running; only Andrew expressed even the slightest openness to it. But in the weeks since the Langone meeting, Mary Pat's apprehensions had abated. Early one recent morning, Chris had awoken from a sound sleep to find her wide awake, staring at him. "What's up? What's wrong?" he asked. And out of her mouth popped something she had never said before: if he was in, she was, too. "Don't worry about me and the kids," she said. "It'll be hard, but we'll be okay."

There were other powerful factors on the positive side of the ledger. With Langone and his billionaire brethren behind him, Christie believed that, one way or the other, he could clear the money bar. With Murdoch and Ailes squarely in his corner, he had already won the Fox Primary without even entering the race. Rove had told him that clear paths to the nomination were a thing of the past, and Christie agreed. But after gleaning so much information from his weeks of explorations, he could see a route that was distinctly marked and mapped. His head told him he could win.

What was holding Christie back wasn't intellectual, however. It was instinctual. There was his failed General Assembly bid in 1995, when he tried to jump to a state legislative seat after just a few months as a local official; he had stuck his chin out too far, too soon, and wound up on the canvas. Not wanting to repeat the error, he resisted pleas to run for governor in 2005, and his patience was rewarded four years later. *To run for president, you have to know deep down it's the right time,* he thought. *Because if you don't, when things go sideways—and they always do—you're going to be sitting there kicking yourself and saying, "I shoulda trusted my gut."*

Christie had hoped to have reached a decision by Sunday night. But when Monday dawned, his gut and his head were still at war—as every word he'd heard from office holders, party leaders, strategists, and billionaires raced through his mind. All day at work, he was in a muddle, not focused on his job. Being driven home, he finally reached his breaking point. *You know what? Screw it? I'm not doing this,* he thought. The burden lifted, he reclined his seat—and promptly fell asleep. Arriving at his house, he walked in and announced to his family, "Listen, guys, Dad's made a decision: I'm not running." Mary Pat smiled, and all four kids burst into applause.

The next day, Christie called a midday news conference at his office in Trenton and pulled the plug. "Over the last few weeks I've thought long and hard about this decision," he said, acknowledging publicly for the first time that he had seriously considered it at all. "In the end, what I've always felt was the right decision remains the right decision today. Now is not my time . . . So New Jersey, whether you like it or not, you're stuck with me."

Christie then phoned Romney and suggested they get together soon. Four days later, Ann and Mitt arrived for lunch on Corey Lane. After two hours of idle chat and goofing around with two of the Christie kids on the patio, Romney asked what he needed to do to finally bring the governor on board.

"Nothing," Christie said. "I'm in."

Gobsmacked, Mitt turned to Ann and said, "Wow—Christmas in October."

Smiling brightly, Ann said gratefully to Christie, "Governor, you don't know how important and big this is."

Actually, Christie said, "I do."

For Christie, the ease of the endorsement reflected mainly the grimness of the other options. Bachmann, Cain, Gingrich, Huntsman, Paul, Perry, Santorum: if those were the seven brides, Christie would abstain from being a brother.

Romney was at least a serious person, with an outside chance of winning—though Christie doubted his capacity to tackle Obama. Behind Mitt's back, Chris mocked his Fred MacMurray affect and antiquated vocabulary. On the night after the Romneys came for lunch, *Saturday Night Live* did a cold-open sketch about Mitt and Chris, in which Jason Sudeikis portrayed Romney as an uptight priss ("Heck it all to fudge!") and Bobby Moynihan played Christie as a coarsely charming favorite of the press ("After this poor bastard loses, I'll get a nice head start, I'll run in four years, it'll be great—fat president, come on, it writes itself!"). Christie promptly memorized the skit and performed his part at private functions all over the country.

Three days later, on October 11, Christie flew up to Hanover, New Hampshire, to bestow his blessing publicly on Mitt. Romney was eager to unveil the endorsement before the next Republican debate, that night at Dartmouth—in particular because he hoped that it would rattle Perry. In a conference room at a small hotel crammed with national reporters, Christie delivered such a big, bold performance that it made Boston's long wait since

Drumthwacket well worth the angst. "America cannot survive another four years of Barack Obama," Christie proclaimed. "Mitt Romney's the man we need to lead America, and we need him now."

After the endorsement, Christie delivered in another way. On a pair of conference calls arranged by Zwick—one with the campaign's national finance committee, another with donors who had written checks for less than the full legal limit—Christie threw his financial support to Romney. Mary Pat and I have just written personal maxed-out checks, Christie announced to the contributors on the second call. You should do the same.

The move was pure theater, pure symbolism, but the gesture was a rarity among elected officials, and it packed a terrific wallop. In the days ahead, as Christie called around to the members of the billionaires' club who had courted him so ardently, he urged them, too, to cast their lot with Mitt. The disappointment of the billionaires with Christie's decision was acute. But one by one, they began their inexorable migration. Druckenmiller, Griffin, Loeb, Singer, Jones, Tepper: within weeks they would all be bundling for Romney, with many also writing massive checks to Restore Our Future. Leading the way was Ken Langone, who kept his word and jumped in with Mitt the moment Chris was out.

"Looks like we know who the horse is gonna be," Langone told a friend. "Now all we gotta do is get the horse to finish the race."

10

THE DATING GAME

OMNEY HAD EVERY REASON to feel emboldened by the Christie endorsement. In a normal race, in a normal year, it would have been a landmark moment in his march to the nomination. With twelve weeks to go before the caucuses in Iowa, he had been spared a potentially destabilizing October surprise, and the donors who worshipped the New Jersey governor had seen the writing on the wall. It was Bill Clinton who once pithily captured the contrast between the two parties when it came to selecting a presidential standard-bearer: "Democrats want to fall in love; Republicans just fall in line." Now, finally, the GOP establishment seemed prepared to pile in behind Romney.

But Republican voters in the 2012 cycle were behaving like Democrats of yore. Even after their party's most eligible bachelors had declined to enter the dating pool, they continued to resist a marriage of convenience to Mitt—they were still searching for true romance. Over the course of the next two months, they would engage in torrid flings with a pair of new paramours, each an unlikely leading man. And such fickleness would encourage the spurned suitors to stick around, hoping for another roll in the hay.

The first heartthrob on deck was Cain, the former pizza-peddling CEO who stood out from the pack for his self-promotional exuberance and the color of his skin. On the stump, Cain blessed his audiences with what he called "The Hermanator Experience," a phrase he legally trademarked, and took delight in winking references to himself as the "dark horse" candidate.

Brassiness had brought Cain his first national notice back in 1994, when, as a member of the audience at a televised presidential town hall, he had challenged Bill Clinton over the contention that restaurateurs with part-time employees would bear little new cost under Clintoncare. ("With all due respect, your calculation on what the impact would do, quite honestly, is incorrect," Citizen Cain brusquely informed 42.) From there it was on to a failed U.S. Senate run in Georgia, a successful stint as an Atlanta talk radio host, and a sprint into the arms of the Tea Party.

Cain approached public policy in much the same way he did pepperoni pies: with a greater concern for marketing than nutrition. His campaign's signature economic proposal was developed by a Cleveland-based Wells Fargo wealth management adviser with no training in economics, who wanted to scrap the existing federal tax code and replace it with three 8.7 percent taxes, on sales, personal income, and business transactions. "Goddammit!" Cain bellowed. "Nobody's gonna remember 8.7, 8.7, 8.7. We're rounding it up—it's 9-9-9!"

Bolstered by the catchy simplicity of 9-9-9 and a series of flamboyant debate performances, Cain rose to the top of the polls nationally and in Iowa by the middle of October. On Fox News, Sarah Palin offered complimentary words about the new star, while also pegging him as "the flavor of the week" (and repeatedly referring to him as "Herb"). But Cain rejected the notion that he was a passing fancy. "I happen to believe that there's ice milk and there's Häagen-Dazs," he told Jay Leno. "I'm Häagen-Dazs Black Walnut. It lasts longer than a week."

Cain's candidacy began to melt under the glare of scrutiny almost as soon as those words left his lips. "I'm ready for the 'gotcha' questions," he told one TV interviewer. "When they ask me who is the president of Ubeki-beki-beki-beki-stan-stan, I'm gonna say, 'You know, I don't know.'" More troubling to conservatives was Cain's position on abortion, which he conveyed to CNN's Piers Morgan as being essentially the same as (if less coherently formulated than) Mario Cuomo's: personal opposition to the procedure but also to the government doing anything to prohibit it.

What reduced Cain to a puddle on the floor were personal accusations dating back to his tenure in the nineties as head of the National Restaurant Association. Alumni of the group remembered Cain as a flagrant tomcat who had been accused of sexual harassment. When he began climbing in the polls, they assumed the tales (there were many) would get out, and sure enough, they did. On October 31, Politico reported that two women had received financial settlements after lodging complaints that he had behaved inappropriately toward them. A few days later, a story about a third woman surfaced, and then a fourth, and then a fifth—the last alleging that she'd had a thirteen-year affair with Cain.

Publicly and privately, Cain denied it all, though his inconstant memory and evasive answers strained credulity even among his sympathizers. When he told former RNC chair Michael Steele that his wife was "upset, but she understands," Steele upbraided Cain: "Herman, you're married to a sister. You're going to sit here and tell me she's just finding this out and she's cool with it? Come on, man!"

Cain insisted he was being taken down by an organized plot. His acrimony toward the establishment had always been high. ("Don't trust the bastards in Washington," he said to his staff; also, the media is "out to slash my tires.") But now he directed his paranoia at his GOP rivals. Cain's top adviser, Mark Block, went on Fox and accused Team Perry of "despicabl[y]" instigating the scandal. "This is one of the actions in America that is the reason people don't get involved in politics," Block said. "Rick Perry and his campaign owe Herman Cain and his family an apology."

PERRY DIDN'T OWE HERMAN anything but a swift kick in the teeth, he thought. Team Perry had had nothing to do with the stories, and Cain had been a burr under the Texas governor's saddle for some time. In early October, shortly after the Orlando debate debacle, *The Washington Post* had published a piece about a hunting camp leased by the Perry family, which for years had a rock by its entrance that bore the ranch's appellation, "Niggerhead." Perry claimed his father had painted over the word in the early eighties. But Cain, who had already declared that Perry was the one Republican he could not support as his party's nominee, went on TV and accused him of racial "insensitivity" anyway. Perry couldn't figure out what he'd done to turn Cain into Al Sharpton.

The Perry campaign was nurturing plenty of other resentments for its misfortunes. Carney was certain that Rove had planted the Niggerhead story, and not long after, Anita Perry complained publicly that her husband was being "brutalized by our opponents and our party" because of the depth of his faith. When Perry delivered an antic speech in New Hampshire in which he appeared soused, stoned, or both, clips of it went viral on YouTube; his advisers, who swore he was sober (if a tad hyper-exuberant), bitterly blamed liberal websites for editing the video unfairly.

Perry and his team hoped they could turn the corner by unveiling a comprehensive economic plan with a flat tax as its centerpiece. But the roll-out, in late October, got overshadowed when, two days prior, *Parade* published its September interview with Perry. Although his birtherish comments provoked the most controversy, what caught the attention of Bushworld was his response when asked to explain the differences between himself and Dubya: "We grew up differently. We have different value sets."

It wasn't long before Rove heard that Barbara Bush, having taken the quote as an affront to her parenting, was on the verge of going nuclear on Perry. Rove called Ray Sullivan and read him the riot act. "There's a gray-haired little old lady who spends half the year in Kennebunkport and half the year in Houston, and I'm giving you fair warning that she is no longer under control," Rove said. "I've spent nearly forty years trying to stay on her good side. You think you'll win a battle with Barbara Bush? You go ahead."

Watching Perry lurch from one PR disaster to another, his debate performances still desultory, Romney was baffled. "Why is he running if he doesn't want to do this?" Mitt asked his advisers. Boston was befuddled, too, but had no intention of removing its boot from Perry's throat. With his cash in the bank and evangelical support, Perry could still stage a comeback in Iowa—and if he did, he might pose a real threat in South Carolina and beyond.

By the time Perry arrived in Auburn Hills, Michigan, for the next debate on November 9, his organization was in something close to complete disarray. At Anita's urging, he had shaken up his campaign staff, bringing in a pack of Washington hired guns known internally as "the consulterati," along with a Bush veteran, Joe Allbaugh, to put the train back on the rails and get it running on time. Perry's old hands from Austin were chafing under Allbaugh and bickering with the consulterati. Carney, feeling sidelined, was about to quit. The candidate himself, dealing with a new debate prep system, let the mushrooming chaos go unchecked, which further rattled his team.

Despite all this, Perry's performance was unusually adept for much of the night, as he touted the Texas economic record and his new flat tax plan. But when he tried to pivot to institutional reform, he got his mental shoelaces tangled. "I will tell you," Perry said, "it's three agencies of government, when I get there, that are gone: Commerce, Education, and the, uh, uhm . . . what's the third one there? Let's see . . ."

"You need five!" Ron Paul interjected, splaying his bony fingers in the air.

Perry tried again: "Commerce, Education, and the, uhm, uh, ahh . . ."

"EPA?" Romney chimed in helpfully.

"EPA! There you go!" Perry said, waving a hand at Mitt. "No . . ."

The audience was in hysterics now, but the moderator, John Harwood of CNBC, would not let go. "Seriously?" Harwood asked. "Is EPA the one you were talking about?"

"No, sir. No, sir," Perry admitted.

"You can't name the third one?"

"The third agency of government," Perry said, shoulders sagging, staring at his lectern, defeat washing over him. "I would do away with the Education, the, uh, Commerce, and, let's see . . . I can't, the third, I can't, sorry." Perry paused briefly, tilted his head, and said, "Oops."

In the Perry staff room, all noggins sank in unison. Sullivan whispered to one of his colleagues, "I don't know if we can recover from this." The Romneyites (and everyone else in America watching on the tube) concurred. For weeks, Perry had been the walking dead. Now, rigor mortis was setting in.

Afterwards, Romney again expressed surprise at Perry's incapacity. "I don't understand why he didn't take my lifeline," Mitt said.

Someone pointed out that he had provided Perry with the wrong answer; the right one was the Department of Energy.

Who cares? Romney said. "He should have just taken it and bluffed."

JON AND MARY KAYE HUNTSMAN felt awful for Perry. They had been friends with Rick and Anita before the campaign and were even closer now—especially the wives, who spent the debates texting words of encouragement to each other as their husbands flailed around onstage. After Perry expectorated his "oops," Mary Kaye glanced over and caught Anita's eye; the look on her face said, *Oh, no.*

The Huntsmans' level of sympathy for Cain was a good deal less heightened. When Jon gazed across any debate stage, he could scarcely believe the mediocre caliber of his competitors. *It's the B-list,* Huntsman thought—and the Hermanator barely rated a gentleman's C. As Cain rose to the top of the polls, Huntsman puzzled over what had gone awry with his party. His campaign, though, had a more active thought: Let's take Cain out.

After getting a tip from a donor, Huntsman's researchers had dug into Cain's past, discovered the first two sexual harassment claims, and fed the story to Politico. Not that Cain was seen by Team Huntsman as a particular barrier to their man. But the Utahan's people were increasingly desperate, looking for any opportunity to upend the prevailing dynamic. Also, their attitude was: Any bullet left in the chamber is a bullet wasted.

The perfidy here was thick and double-barreled. Huntsman put himself forward as a clean-hands candidate, owing to his almost pathological refusal to criticize his opponents. And his operation was panned among political pros as flawed and faulty. But, as the cases of Cain and Daniels demonstrated, Weaver's crew was ruthlessly efficient at one thing: serving as a secret conveyor belt for the kind of dirt the candidate claimed he could not abide. As they waited for Politico to turn their tip into a story, members of Huntsman's circle asked each other when the "high heel" was going to drop on Cain.

Huntsman, however, had more problems of his own. In late September, running low on cash and mired at 1 or 2 percent in national polls, Huntsman had shut down his Florida headquarters and switched focus exclusively to New Hampshire. By then his alienation from Weaver and the rest of his advisers had become corrosive. They fought about debate prep. (Huntsman simultaneously thought himself too good for the exercise and irremediably terrible at it.) They clashed over media strategy. (Huntsman cared more about Manhattan glossies than the conservative press.) The squabbling over money only worsened (with Weaver and David at one point enlisting Huntsman's daughter Abby to beg her dad to write another check). As autumn unfolded, Huntsman's advisers finally, fully came to dismiss their candidate as a lazy, whiny wuss. Huntsman came to disdain his adjutants as soulless mercenaries.

Gradually, Huntsman retreated into the embrace of his family, relying more and more on his wife and daughters for political advice. And this, in turn, produced another layer of friction with the professionals. Mary Kaye was forever scouring the Web for fresh poll numbers or blog posts about Jon, reading them back to him instantly, even if they were harshly negative (as they often were), threatening his mood and focus. Eventually Huntsman's advisers banned her from debate prep.

The Huntsman girls, meanwhile, became pseudo celebrities; they had a joint Twitter feed and released a series of cheeky videos. Their final effort had to be quashed by the campaign. A spoof on Fox News morning show *Fox and Friends,* the clip was entitled "Foxes and Friends" and featured the lasses gussied up in blond wigs, interviewing a Romney bobblehead doll.

But the biggest source of tension between Huntsman's family and his advisers revolved around a less trivial matter: the possibility that Jon might quit the Republican Party and wage an independent bid for president.

Huntsman had first placed the idea on the table immediately after the Tea Party debate in Tampa. Beforehand, he was skittish about the crowd. "These aren't my people," he told David. "They're going to boo me."

Seated in the audience, Mary Kaye and Abby were aghast at the right-wing chatter they heard all around them. When the debate was over, they came into the green room, Huntsman's wife in tears, Abby shocked and offended. As David drove home from Tampa to Orlando, his cell phone rang.

"I want to go independent," Huntsman said. "I think we should do it sooner than later."

For some time, a number of Huntsman's supporters in New York had been encouraging him to hop in the vehicle being built by a new group called Americans Elect. Formed and partly funded by Peter Ackerman, a wealthy financier and majority shareholder in Web-based grocer Fresh-Direct, Americans Elect was spending millions to gain ballot access in all fifty states for an independent "unity" ticket to be chosen through an online nominating convention in June 2012.

That much was public knowledge. But Ackerman and his associates were also secretly meeting with potential big-name candidates including former Democratic senator and presidential candidate Bill Bradley, retired army generals Stanley McChrystal and David Petraeus, and Starbucks CEO Howard Schultz. The group had its eye on Huntsman, too.

Jon's advisers told him that hooking up with Americans Elect defied reason. The outfit seems legit, they admitted. But Ackerman and his buddies are only going to secure ballot access for their nominee; they're not going to finance the campaign. If you can't raise money for *this* campaign, what makes you think you could raise it for an independent run?

Huntsman could see their point, but he couldn't let the idea go. Mary Kaye and his daughters kept prodding him: You're not yourself. You're not happy in this campaign. You don't do red meat, you don't pander, you're stuck at 2 percent in the polls. This is not your party. People come up to you all the time—liberals, conservatives, moderates—saying you should run as an independent. Why not do it? You could do it. You should be yourself.

On Friday, November 18, the Huntsmans traveled to New York City so that Jon could appear on *Saturday Night Live* the next day. That evening, they met Mike Bloomberg and Diana Taylor, his significant other, for dinner at one of the mayor's favorite restaurants, Gabriel's, just off Columbus Circle. Huntsman queried the mayor about his past noodlings over an independent bid. Bloomberg said that the hurdles remained formidable, that he had never been able to discern a path to the White House taking that route. Even so, the idea remained seductive, Bloomberg went on, then dropped a flattery bomb on Huntsman. You're the embodiment of the perfect independent candidate, he said.

In a few days, Huntsman was supposed to deliver a major speech on American's "trust deficit." Returning home to Washington, he called David and said that the independent plan was back on. "The trust speech is perfect for this," Huntsman said. "That's where I'm going to make the announcement."

"What the fuck are you talking about?" Weaver asked when he got Huntsman on the phone. If you do this, Weaver continued, you'll be doing it alone; pretty much everyone who works for you will quit. Huntsman had no real plan. He told Weaver he would continue to campaign in New Hampshire, even though he would not be competing in the primary there. It was senseless. Weaver and others pointed out that switching would make Huntsman look weak and petulant, as if he were leaving his party because he was getting creamed. You can still finish second in New Hampshire, they told him. If you do, you can use that as a launching pad for an independent run—if the idea is still appealing then.

Huntsman thought it over. His daughter Abby was wavering on the wisdom of his leaving the GOP. His father was adamantly against it. Jon was still young; whatever happened in 2012, he had a viable future as a Republican. Huntsman grudgingly agreed. Maybe it was more reasonable to try to reform his party from within.

Ackerman and Americans Elect ran up against that kind of logic every day. More than ballot access, more than money, it was by a wide margin the greatest hindrance to getting an independent bid off the ground. Ackerman had on his side an array of heavy-hitting allies: former and current senators David Boren, William Cohen, Chuck Hagel, Ben Nelson, Alan Simpson, and Sam Nunn; former White House chief of staff Erskine Bowles; and former New Jersey governor Christie Todd Whitman. All were concerned that the two-party duopoly had run its course, that the Republican and Democratic parties were so tightly in the grip of the far right and the far left that good governance had become impossible. What they wanted to see in 2012 was a campaign that would drag the political conversation to the sensible center. What they had witnessed so far in the Republican race filled them with dread that the opposite would occur. Huntsman's inability to gain traction was one worrying sign. Romney's tenuous standing was another. But scariest of all was the identity of the new front-runner—a man to whom a zillion different adjectives had been applied, but "sensible" and "centrist" certainly not among them.

NEWTON LEROY GINGRICH NEVER aspired to be president of the United States, which wasn't to say that his political goals were any less grandiose. From the time he was in college, Gingrich wanted to be speaker of the House and a transformational historical figure. And in his pyrotechnic twenty-year congressional career, he achieved both aims, not only leading Republicans to control of the lower chamber for the first time in forty years but also doing more than any other individual to refashion American politics around the principle of total war.

Gingrich felt the bite of the presidential bug in 1995, the initial heady year of his speakership, but shrugged it off. In 2000, two years after he was driven ignominiously from office, the political and personal wounds were still too fresh for him to run. In 2008, he briefly mulled the concept, but for the first time in his life he was making serious money (through a web of consulting and grassroots advocacy enterprises) and wading gingerly into the waters of bipartisanship (collaborating with Hillary Clinton on a health care initiative, appearing in a climate change TV ad with Nancy Pelosi). In 2012, though, he would be sixty-eight years old. This was his last chance.

Gingrich's political makeup seemed to accord with the laws of Newtonian physics: every salutary attribute was balanced by an equal and opposite toxicity. He was at once articulate and verbose, unusually fluent in policy and painfully didactic, refreshingly spontaneous and chronically undisciplined, and also consumed by insatiable appetites and a need for perpetual attention. ("I'm a hot dog," he would say.) Like his nemesis from the nineties, Bill Clinton, with whom he shared a great many of these yin-yang qualities, Gingrich lived a life governed by a ceaseless cycle of triumph, disgrace, and rejuvenation—up and down, up and down, wash, rinse, and repeat.

Or at least the old Newt Gingrich did. Heading into 2012, the people closest to him swore that there was a new incarnation in the house—not displacing but coexisting with the original. The Old Newt might still occasionally snarl at Obama over his Kenyan, anticolonial leanings, or label him the "food stamp president," but the New Newt was less gruff, less grandiloquent, more contemplative and self-aware. Nearly seven decades of brashness, bomb throwing, and priapism had tuckered him out. The New Newt was a churchgoing grandfather of two who required naps to stay sharp.

The catalytic element in the creation of the New Newt was his third wife, Callista, whom he married in 2000 after they carried on a six-year affair. Callista was forty-five, with a helmet of platinum blond hair and unblinking ice-blue eyes, and Newt was gaga for her. He draped her in opulent jewelry from Tiffany, where the couple maintained a $500,000 interest-free line of credit. He lavished her with expensive travel. She was a Catholic; he converted. ("One of the happiest moments of my life," she said.) She loved opera; he joined the Kennedy Center. She played golf; he took up the game.

Callista, while a devoted spouse, wanted no part of a presidential campaign. She worried about the financial impact of Newt abandoning his lucrative ventures. She fretted over the intrusions of the press. Most of all, she quivered—with both fear and rage—at their marital history being picked over. (She detested being referred to as Newt's former mistress and third wife; "I've only been married once," she protested again and again.) Gingrich's close friend and longest-serving political adviser, Joe Gaylord, cautioned him against a run. Gingrich's personal and political baggage was so heavy, Gaylord argued, that lugging it down the road would be mighty painful and likely lead nowhere good.

But Gingrich ignored the flashing yellow lights, playing down the fact that Gaylord and many other aides from his speakership days declined to join the campaign. He hired consultants, including Dave Carney and Rob Johnson, to join another longtime adviser, Sam Dawson, in running his operation. He wheedled Callista into acquiescence, promising that he would accommodate her priorities.

Gingrich wasn't blind to his vulnerabilities, including the disintegration of his first marriage in circumstances strikingly similar to the dissolution of his second. *I've made mistakes, I'm fallible, I'm a Christian who has asked forgiveness,* he thought. *It's all out there. There will be no surprises. This will be exhilarating.*

The lark-like tenor of Gingrich's approach to his campaign became apparent before his run officially began. In a March 2011 appearance on the

Christian Broadcasting Network, he was asked obliquely about his serial infidelities. Gingrich answered as if he had never given the question an ounce of thought, with a lengthy disquisition that included the suggestion that his indiscretions had been driven by a combination of exhaustion and excessive patriotism. "There's no question at times in my life, partially driven by how passionately I felt about this country, that I worked too hard and things happened in my life that were not appropriate," he said.

Two months later, on May 9, Gingrich announced his candidacy via Twitter. When the tweet went out, he was on a plane with Callista and some staff, on the tarmac in Atlanta, dozing in his seat. Hey, Newt, we just did it! his staffers cried, trying to rouse him. Gingrich remained slumped in his chair, snoozing like a hibernating bear.

The passage from slumber to life support took just four weeks. On May 15, Gingrich went on *Meet the Press* and described Paul Ryan's proposal to turn Medicare into a voucher system as "right-wing social engineering," infuriating Rush Limbaugh, Ryan himself, and conservatives around the country. Two days later, Politico broke the story about the half-million-dollar charge account at Tiffany. (When Dawson investigated, he found that the bill the couple had run up over the years made half a million dollars seem small beer.) At the end of May, with his campaign reeling, Gingrich set off with Callista on a luxury cruise in the Greek isles. His team had begged him not to go, but Callista put her foot down. When the couple returned in early June, virtually all of Gingrich's top people quit, with Carney and Johnson making their return to Austin to launch Perry.

"This is suicide," Dawson told Newt. "And I'm not going to be a part of an assisted suicide."

Gingrich would later call the next two months "the hardest in my career." Bereft of backing, unable to raise money, he was deemed effectively defunct by the political class. But with Gingrich's national name recognition, red-meat policy theories, and savvy about scaring up free media, he was able to live off the land in a way that a candidate such as Pawlenty never could. Gingrich saw the packed schedule of debates in the late summer and fall as an opportunity to resurrect himself. And he was further buoyed by what he perceived as Romney's multifarious and mortal weaknesses.

For all the denigration of the Bay Stater by his fellow Republicans, Gingrich's critique stood out as the purest distillation of the form. Newt had been observing Mitt since 1994. He had met with Romney in Boston and Washington and talked to Huckabee and others about his conduct in 2008. Gingrich thought Romney was intelligent and a fund-raising machine. But he also thought Mitt was burdened with nonexistent people skills, a religious faith he refused to talk about, and a record in Massachusetts he was unable to explain—especially a health care plan that put him at daggers drawn with the core of his party. (That Gingrich glossed over his own past backing of an individual mandate only proved the Old Newt was alive and kicking.) Gingrich's cumulative judgment wasn't that Romney faced long odds of winning; it was that there was zero chance of him becoming the nominee.

Gingrich was right about the rejuvenating effect of the debate stage on his candidacy. In Ames, at the Reagan Library, and in the two Florida forensic scrums, he turned in a series of bracing performances. Gingrich intuitively understood that there were two surefire techniques for stimulating the erogenous zones of the Republican base: taking the wood ferociously to Obama and whaling on the media. His genius was in divining ways to do both at once, and on occasion even including a third tickle—a pious, Reaganesque call for Republican unity—in the bargain.

A classic instance occurred in Simi Valley when one of the debate moderators, John Harris of Politico, attempted to draw Gingrich into a squabble between Perry and Romney over the individual mandate. "Well, I'm frankly not interested in your effort to get Republicans fighting each other," Gingrich began. (Loud applause.) "You would like to puff this up into some giant thing," Gingrich went on. "The fact is, every person up here understands Obamacare is a disaster. It is a disaster procedurally. It was rammed through after they lost Teddy Kennedy's seat in Massachusetts. It was written badly, it was never reconciled. It can't be implemented. It is killing this economy. And if this president had any concern for working Americans, he'd walk in Thursday night and ask us to repeal it because it's a monstrosity. Every person up here agrees with that." (Wild applause.) And let me just say, since I still have a little time left . . . I, for one, and I hope all of my friends up here, am going to repudiate every effort of the news media to get

Republicans to fight each other to protect Barack Obama, who deserves to be defeated. And all of us are committed as a team—whoever the nominee is—we are all for defeating Barack Obama." (Deafening applause.)

By the early autumn, Gingrich's premonition about gaining a second life was starting to seem prescient, at least to him. With Perry in free fall, Newt's poll numbers were edging upward. After paying a visit to Governor Haley in South Carolina on October 4, Gingrich walked out on the statehouse grounds and phoned his old friend Vin Weber. A former Minnesota congressman who was one of Newt's leading lieutenants in the nineties, Weber had championed Romney in 2008 and Pawlenty early in this cycle; now he was back with Mitt.

"Perry's not going to come back, and Cain is going to collapse," Gingrich prophesied. "And I'm going to be the main competitor to Romney by the middle of November."

"Well, you might be," Weber replied. He had long thought that Newt could be a credible candidate, and was surprised by his summer implosion (although, knowing Gingrich as he did, not totally surprised). He also thought Newt was one of the most farsighted politicians he had ever met.

"I know what the Romney campaign is capable of—I've watched them," Gingrich continued. "I respect Mitt Romney. But I want you to tell them that if they try to do anything to me and Callista, I will destroy him."

GINGRICH'S COMEBACK PREDICTION CAME FULLY TO fruition on precisely the schedule he had forecast. Heading into Thanksgiving, on the heels of Perry's "oops" and in the midst of the cascading Cain accusations, four national polls in a row put Newt in first place, narrowly ahead of Romney, and he had surged to double-digit leads in Iowa and South Carolina.

Despite his speakership, Gingrich never considered himself a member of the Republican establishment. The feeling was mutual. The party's grandees greeted his climb to the top of the polls with manifest incredulity, dismissing him as an impetuous flake. On a speaking jaunt to Chicago, Rove ran into a local business honcho who asserted categorically that Gingrich could never win the nomination. When Rove asked why, the muckety-muck cited a recent visit by Newt to the Windy City during which, instead of fund-raising or politicking, he frittered away much of a Saturday touring the Field Museum's dinosaur collection.

Rove found the tale astonishing, and repeated it on Greta Van Susteren's program on Fox. Soon after, he received a chippy e-mail from Gingrich: "How many days did George W. spend at the ranch? Reagan spent one year out of eight at the ranch. I don't have a ranch. Half day at the Field Museum cleared my mind. Just a thought. Newt."

Now even more incredulous, Rove fired off a sharp reply: "With all due respect, I don't remember Bush taking a Saturday off in September of 1999 to visit a museum in a state that holds a late primary, nor a Greek cruise that summer. Field Museum board member had been inclined to support you until he heard about your excursion and concluded you weren't serious . . . When you get to be president, you can have the schedule of Nixon, Reagan, 41, or 43, and you'll find the job doesn't leave you at the ranch, or Kennebunkport, or Camp David. It just follows you."

Rove was all but certain that Gingrich's temper and unruliness would inevitably cause him to self-destruct—the only question was when. But some of Rove's establishment chums were less sanguine. Fabled lobbyist and McCain adviser Charlie Black was warning anyone who would listen that Gingrich's hold on conservative activists was deep and durable. At receptions and in network green rooms, senior Republicans fretted that Boehner would lose the speakership if Newt was their standard-bearer.

Up in Boston, Romney shook his head. He regarded Newt as a font of provocative policies, a galvanizing orator, and an agile debater. But Gingrich's campaign was a one-man band, his world topsy-turvy, and his personal life more sordid than Romney cared to contemplate. The Republican speed-dating tournament was starting to weigh on Mitt. *First it's Perry, then it's Cain, now it's Newt,* Romney thought. *What's wrong with me? Why not me?*

Stevens stoked Romney's sense of disbelief at Newt's front-runner status. To a farcical degree, Stevens was the most Panglossian of the Romneyites; no matter how horrific the development, he would declare it a boon for Boston. Newt's rising? Great for us! said Stevens, who professed, even after "oops," to be more concerned about Perry. Of Gingrich he said, Are you kidding me? The party's going to nominate *him?* Be real.

The lenses Rhoades peered through, by contrast, were less rose-tinted. He saw Gingrich's rise as a real threat, as did the rest of Team Romney. The reason was Iowa. Assuming Romney carried New Hampshire, where he held a commanding lead, he was well financed and well organized enough to withstand losses in the other three early states—unless one person swept those other three. And a thumping victory for Gingrich in the Hawkeye State would set him up to do just that, propelling him powerfully into South Carolina and Florida. Stevens's partner, Schriefer, even worried that a Newt win in Iowa would imperil New Hampshire for Romney. On November 27, the *New Hampshire Union Leader* endorsed the former speaker, lending ballast to that nightmare scenario.

In the days before and after Thanksgiving, the Romneyites held a series of meetings at the Boston HQ to figure out their play in the Iowa caucuses, which were scheduled for January 3. All year long, the campaign had been keeping its powder dry, maintaining just a skeleton crew in the Hawkeye State, delaying a decision about how aggressively to compete. Not one TV ad had been aired, and the candidate had stumped there on only three occasions.

Newhouse's polling suggested that Romney would be hard-pressed to garner more than 25 percent of the Iowa vote, the same as his 2008 total and probably not enough for a first-place finish. Yet to Boston's way of thinking now, claiming the number-one spot was not the point. The point was to keep Gingrich from prevailing by a stonking margin, and to inflict serious damage on him in the process. We probably can't catch him in Iowa, Rhoades said, but we can make sure that he comes out battered. Stevens disagreed. Not only can we catch Newt, the strategist said, but he's gonna finish third.

In the end, the decision came down to Romney. He and Ann remained wary of Iowa and The Mormon Thing. Yet his people in the state reported that there was little anti-LDS chicanery taking place that they could detect. At the same time, Romney was itching to move past the anarchy of the past months. The *Union Leader* endorsement of Newt unnerved him. After 2008, he had vowed to resist the allure of the quick-knockout strategy in 2012. But he was thinking anew about the virtues of trying to shut this deal down early.

On December 1, the Romney campaign announced that it was going on the air in Iowa with TV ads. The news came amid a torrent of bad headlines for Mitt. Two days earlier, in an interview with Bret Baier on Fox, Romney had turned testy and sarcastic when asked about having changed his stances over the years on climate change, abortion, gay rights, and immigration. ("Well, Bret, your list is just not accurate. So, one, we're going to have to be better informed about my views on issues.") Romney's face was plastered on the cover of *Time;* the headline read WHY DON'T THEY LIKE ME? A new Rasmussen poll put him behind Gingrich by twenty-one points nationally; a fresh Public Policy Polling (PPP) survey had him trailing by thirty in Florida.

Gingrich was out in Des Moines, absorbing the same streams of data, floating on cloud nine. "I am going to be the nominee," he proclaimed in an interview with ABC News's Jake Tapper. "And, by the way, I don't object if people want to attack me. That's their right. All I'm suggesting is that it's not going to be very effective and that people are going to get sick of it very fast."

Gingrich's declaration was bald and bold, and his mind unshadowed by doubt. Before the caucuses, there would be two debates in Iowa—two more chances for him to shine. His pollster, Kellyanne Conway, told him that he was "in Romney's head." Boston's decision to start advertising seemed to confirm the analysis: Mitt was running scared.

Gingrich would come to regret having put prudence aside and run his mouth so hubristically with Tapper. Newt freely admitted he had said plenty of asinine things in his career, yet this was one of the dumbest. Looking back on it months later, he thought, *When the other guy has a ton of money and you have none, it's not smart to paint a bull's-eye on your back.*

11

MAN ON FIRE

THEY WERE ARMING THE missiles for launch in Boston even as Gingrich was declaring his nomination a fait accompli. As they had done for Pawlenty and Perry before him, the Romneyites convened a series of "Kill Newt" meetings on Commercial Street. On a whiteboard, they drew up a list of potentially fruitful lines of attack on Gingrich's record, résumé, and character. Before long, the whiteboard looked like John Nash's equation-crammed window in *A Beautiful Mind*.

Even setting aside his personal peccadilloes, Gingrich made for a target-rich environment. In a recent debate, he had argued for a "humane" approach to immigration that would forswear the hard-right solution of mass deportation of illegals; Romney, picking up where he left off with Perry, was already denouncing Newt for offering a "new doorway to amnesty."

Gingrich's "right-wing social engineering" crack about the Ryan Medicare plan was another vulnerability. So was his global warming ad with Pelosi, which not only costarred the dreaded San Francisco lefty but was part of a campaign led by the demonic Al Gore. Gingrich had been the first speaker ever to receive a formal ethics reprimand and had been compelled to reimburse the House $300,000 for its investigation of him. After leaving Congress, he earned millions for what could be portrayed as nefarious logrolling. Among his clients was the housing-bubble villain Freddie Mac, from which Newt had collected $1.6 million—for providing services as "a historian," he now maintained.

One Sunday morning, Romney sat in on a Kill Newt meeting and added his two cents. Mitt was perfectly happy to strafe the speaker until he was a human colander. But in 2008 Romney had learned all about the distaste of Iowa voters for candidate-on-candidate violence. He preferred to leave his staff and surrogates to man the rocket launchers, though he had no compunction about taking potshots at Newt's soft spots.

Gingrich had a storied record of tantrums under pressure. Everyone in politics remembered his admission that he had propelled the federal government shutdown in 1995 in part because of his seating assignment in the rear of Air Force One on a trip to Israel with Bill Clinton—a conniption memorialized in a front-page illustration in the New York *Daily News* of the speaker in diapers, under the massive-point headline CRY BABY. In Boston, the hope was that, with a bit of provocative psyops, the campaign could light the fuse that would lead to one of Newt's patented acts of self-immolation.

The morning after Gingrich's exercise in braggadocio on ABC, Romney kicked things off with an appearance on *Fox and Friends,* where he dinged Newt for making "self-aggrandizing statements" and being a Washington lifer. A week later, on December 8, Boston cranked the acrimony up a notch. On a Romney campaign conference call with reporters, former Missouri senator Jim Talent, who had served with Newt in the House, slapped him around as "not a reliable or trustworthy leader," while former New Hampshire governor John Sununu called his dis of the Ryan plan "self-serving" and "anti-conservative."

Team Romney went up with a new TV ad called "Leader" that same day. As sepia-hued footage from home movies unspooled, showing Mitt and Ann doting on their young children, the soundtrack featured Romney speaking proudly of having been "married to the same woman for . . . forty-two years" and "in the same church my entire life." The commercial never mentioned Gingrich. It didn't have to. The implicit contrasts were about as subtle as a mallet to the forehead.

The next day's offensive had all the delicacy of an atomic blast: a sixty-second spot spitting out many of the issues from the Boston whiteboard in rat-a-tat succession. It was just the first in a fusillade of similarly themed commercials that would dominate the airwaves for the next three and a half weeks.

The ads were the work of the pro-Romney super PAC Restore Our Future, which meant that, technically speaking, Boston had nothing to do with them, since by law the campaign was barred from coordinating with Restore. The reality was more complicated. Although Restore was operationally independent from Team Romney, in every historical, genetic, and practical sense it was a subsidiary of the campaign.

The inspiration for Restore arose out of the ashes of 2008. In Iowa, Romney had been assailed over abortion and other issues by automated telephone push polls and television ads funded by a third-party outfit supporting Mike Huckabee. With no outside gang of his own, Romney was caught flat-footed and defenseless. His people were convinced that it had cost him dearly—Beth Myers, who managed the campaign, most of all.

Myers was a planner. She swore to herself that if her boss ran again, Boston would have an affiliated outside spending organization riding shotgun. In the summer of 2009, she began doing legal diligence on how to set up such a group. After the *Citizens United* decision a few months later, Myers realized that what she had in mind was, in effect, the first-ever presidential super PAC—and aptly code-named her embryonic project Avatar.

Rhoades concurred wholeheartedly regarding the need for Avatar. He and Myers shared a theory about how to build it. Avatar would be run by people who knew Mitt and his world intimately, who were attuned to Romneyland's strategic and tactical proclivities, so that when the two sides were legally forced to curtail communications, they would be as much in sync as possible.

By the fall of 2010, Myers and Rhoades had recruited a threesome that perfectly fit that bill: Carl Forti, Romney's 2008 political director; Charlie Spies, his 2008 general counsel; and Larry McCarthy, a key member of the 2008 media team. This isn't a throwaway—it's integral, Rhoades told them. We're asking you because we've gotta have the A-Team on the super PAC. We're asking because "you're part of the Romney family."

From then until the following summer, the triumvirate was in regular contact with the Boston high command. Campaign law dictated that they would need to cease all discussions 120 days before the super PAC, now operating under its official Restore banner, put up its first ads. While it was far from certain that Romney would be playing in Iowa, they agreed that they should start the clock ticking in early August so that Restore could go on the air in early December if need be. They also agreed that, although it would be fine for Mitt to bemoan outside spending in broad strokes publicly, he should never repudiate the group or its ads, lest any supporters get skittish about contributing—and that, before the Chinese wall between the sides was imposed, Romney had to send a neon signal to donors that Restore bore his imprimatur.

The Washington Post first reported the existence of Restore in June 2011. That month and the next, Romney attended three of the group's fund-raising events: at the Four Seasons in Boston, in the penthouse apartment of real estate magnate Stephen Ross in New York, and at the Beverly Hills Hotel. Romney was the warm-up act at each, delivering a brief stump speech, bestowing his blessing on Restore and its troika, and making his exit. Charlie Spies then performed a ritual that would become standard at countless donor dog-and-pony shows over the next year: after starting his PowerPoint presentation with a slide that explained what a super PAC was, he put up another highlighting the trio's roles and titles in the 2008 campaign—a blunt way of telegraphing that, yes, indeed, they were part of the Romney family.

In the first five months of 2011, before the press or most Republicans even knew it existed, Restore had raised $8 million. After Romney's laying on of hands, it doubled that total in June and July, in chunks ranging from $100,000 to $1,000,000—and there was more help on the way. In early August, right before the Chinese wall went up, Team Romney dispatched its lead fund-raiser, Steve Roche, to join Restore, armed with the campaign's invaluable donor lists of mega-rich loyalists. At a final meeting at the Washington offices of Romney's campaign lawyer, Ben Ginsberg, the Restore boys and the Boston brain trust held a closing discussion of the road ahead. When it was over and they got up to leave, Myers went to hug McCarthy— then pulled up short.

"Oh, my God," she said. "I just realized I'm not going to see you guys for a year and a half!"

McCarthy chuckled. After more than twenty years of honing his craft in the shadowy world of independent expenditure committees, the adman was all too familiar with the weirdness of mandated non-communication.

With a sparse gray beard, glasses, and a Washington Nationals cap ever present on his head, the fifty-nine-year-old McCarthy looked uncannily like Steven Spielberg. In political circles, he was most famous (or infamous) for a piece of work less uplifting than *E.T.* but as scary and effective as *Jaws*: the 1988 Willie Horton commercial that helped destroy Mike Dukakis. Equally potent was another McCarthy spot, "Ashley's Story" from 2004, which showed President Bush comforting a teenage girl whose mother had been killed on 9/11. ("He's the most powerful man in the world, and all he wants to do is make sure I'm safe," Ashley said.) "The ad was pretty close to decisive in Ohio," John Kerry's chief strategist, Bob Shrum, contended later. "And Ohio was the whole thing."

McCarthy had commissioned no research on Gingrich until November; before that, like pretty much everyone else, he assumed Newt was toast. Scrambling to do last-minute ad testing and focus groups, McCarthy discovered that Republican voters were fairly clueless about Newt's past. They liked him, thought he was smart, that he would give Obama what-for in the debates. When confronted with discrete pieces of negative information about Gingrich, they tended to give him the benefit of the doubt. His reputation as a conservative leader outweighed almost all else.

But not everything. McCarthy also found that voters had a loose, undefined sense that Gingrich was saddled with "baggage" related to his personal life. They used that word, "baggage," and used it a lot, which surprised McCarthy. *(Normal people talk that way? Huh.)* To McCarthy's eye, the term had the makings of an umbrella under which he could assemble an assortment of Gingrich's substantive liabilities, alluding to his serial infidelities without invoking them directly. Presented that way, in aggregate, Gingrich's flaws gave voters pause.

The sixty-second ad that hit the air in Iowa on December 9 opened with a picture of a grinning Obama. "Why is this man smiling?" the female narrator asked. Because he was tickled pink about facing Gingrich as the Republican nominee. "Newt has a ton of baggage," the ad went on, and then marched through the dizzying panoply of charges against him: ethics, Freddie Mac, Pelosi-Gore, amnesty for illegals, his support for an individual mandate in health care, etc. "Maybe that's why George Will called Gingrich 'the least conservative candidate,'" the ad concluded.

Gingrich's initial reaction to the start of the air war and Team Romney's efforts to get under his skin was a cheery dismissal. On the afternoon of December 10, a few hours before the next debate, he paid a visit to his newly opened (and still largely empty) Iowa headquarters, just outside Des Moines. "My campaign will be relentlessly positive," Gingrich said as Callista beamed in the front row. "We're not going to be tearing people down." He regaled the assembled staff and reporters with an account of the advice being rendered by his two "debate coaches": his pre-teenage grandchildren.

The debate that night at Drake University was the first to not include Cain, who had departed the race days earlier. Its most memorable moment came from Romney: his tone-deaf offer to bet Perry $10,000 as they wrangled over the accusation that the paperback of *No Apology* had been edited to remove the suggestion that Romneycare was a national model. ("I'm not in the bettin' business, but I'll show you the book," replied Perry slyly.)

The rest of the night was devoted almost entirely to broadsides directed at Gingrich. Romney jeered at his "idea to have a lunar colony that would mine minerals from the moon," and again took after him for being in favor of "a form of amnesty" that would be "another magnet that draws people into our country illegally." Paul poked Gingrich on Freddie Mac. Bachmann ridiculed him for making his living on K Street, the "Rodeo Drive of Washington, D.C." And Perry went there on the question of monogamy: "If you cheat on your wife, you'll cheat on your business partner, so I think that issue of fidelity is important."

The Drake debate was but a gentle preview of the pile-on that lay ahead for Gingrich. At the next debate, five days later in Sioux City, Bachmann inveighed against him for "influence-peddling" and being insufficiently pro-life. On TV, Paul's campaign and the pro-Perry super PAC Make Us Great Again pulped him with negative ads.

Boston, meanwhile, continued to pummel Gingrich from every conceivable direction, but especially on the Ryan plan, including with a one-minute campaign video resurrecting his May *Meet the Press* interview. Romney moved into full mockery mode: demanding that Newt return the money he'd earned from Freddie Mac, blowing raspberries at his claim that he wasn't a lobbyist ("That would make him the highest-paid historian in history"), and deeming him "zany" in *The New York Times*. "Zany," Romney said, "is not what we need in a president."

Yet all of these were Circus Iowus sideshows compared with what was going on under the big top: the continued bombardment of Gingrich by Restore. A few days after putting up its initial sixty-second "baggage" spot, the group released a thirty-second version—and soon followed that with another sixty, this one enlivening the motif with visuals of suitcases on an airport luggage carousel (with a green valise labeled FREDDIE MAC popping open and expelling a flurry of hundred-dollar bills).

The money behind Restore's assault was enormous: roughly $3 million, triple the amount that Gingrich was spending in Iowa, more than double Team Romney's outlay. In focus groups that Boston and Restore were each conducting, the effects were immediately apparent. The pre-ad blitz mentions of Newt's "baggage" had turned into a thundering chorus. McCarthy was flabbergasted by how fast the ads were working; he'd seen nothing like it in years. Myers was relieved and delighted; her handiwork was paying off. *This is a very good thing,* she thought.

It was becoming apparent to one and all that Gingrich's incineration was the story in Iowa. The network newscasts played it prominently, night after night. His poll numbers were plunging. Two weeks earlier, Gingrich had been scoring in the low thirties; now he was in the teens and trailing both Romney and Paul. On December 17, *The Des Moines Register* gave Newt the back of its hand and conferred its endorsement on Mitt.

The *Register*'s blessing was a coveted commodity, and Romney was thrilled to have it. The question was what Gingrich was thinking, and that was difficult to discern. With the caucuses approaching in two weeks, his rivals humping the hustings, and his front-runner status being shredded, Newt was literally a thousand miles away—with his mind on other matters.

GINGRICH TOOK HIS SEAT in the fourth row at a high school auditorium in the Virginia suburbs of Washington, awaiting a holiday concert by the City of Fairfax Band. Perched onstage behind a thicket of red poinsettias, Callista, who played French horn, smiled brightly and waved to her husband as the lights went down. At that moment, the news of the *Register* endorsement was lighting up Twitter, but Gingrich's BlackBerry was shut off and tucked away. By the time the band eased into "Silent Night," he had drifted into a peaceful doze.

It had been a full day for Newt. In the morning, he'd conducted a long-distance conference call with Iowa voters in which he addressed some of the charges against him and made a plea for support on caucus night. ("I'd be very, very grateful if you'd be willing to be a precinct captain by pressing 2," he said.) In the afternoon, he spent two hours in Mount Vernon, sitting next to Callista as she signed copies of her new children's book, *Sweet Land of Liberty,* and mugging for the cameras with a man dressed up as Ellis the Elephant, the cartoon hero of his wife's tome.

In print, on cable, and on the Web, Gingrich's decision to occupy himself this way on the last non-holiday weekend before the caucuses brought forth waves of derision. The reaction galled him, especially coming from Fox; he had expected better from his former employer than being subjected to an absurd double standard. *Romney can go off to one of his fancy houses and it's a non-event,* Newt thought. *But the media kills me for going home for a Christmas concert for my wife. In a different world, you can imagine people saying, "Gee, what an awfully nice thing to do."*

Gingrich had spent the first half of December behaving as if that fantasy realm was real. He had entered the race expecting that Romney and his allies would say anything to nuke him, but he did nothing to prepare a robust defense. He thought it would be a sufficient rebuttal to denounce the attacks as "lies," "distortions," or "grotesqueries," because that plainly was what they were. When he insisted he would run a "relentlessly positive" campaign, he assumed he would be taken seriously. One thing the Old Newt had rarely been accused of was naïveté. The New Newt was firmly in its grip.

Gingrich had also imposed a paralytic degree of caution on himself. He knew as well as anyone his propensity for self-inflicted damage. Whenever he was asked about his latest successor as speaker, Newt compared Boehner to Woody Hayes: three yards and a cloud of dust. Gingrich, by contrast, saw himself as a gunslinging quarterback, rolling out of the pocket and heaving the ball upfield. His style had produced its share of touchdowns over the years but also plenty of interceptions. (Watching the 2002 NFL playoff game when Brett Favre was picked off six times, Gingrich thought, *That's me.*) With Romney and his abettors trying to get into his head, Newt had been trying to run out the clock rather than drive for the end zone—and instead had managed to fumble the ball on his own ten-yard line.

After his weekend in Virginia, Gingrich returned to Iowa and attempted to get back on offense. On December 20, after appearing at a factory in Ottumwa, Gingrich once again decried his rivals for their negativity. When a voter asked about a radio ad that called him a "globalist," Newt snapped, "I think these guys hire consultants who just sit around, get drunk, and write really stupid ads. I am just so fed up with this stuff."

But it was Romney who seemed to have pushed Gingrich over the edge. Earlier that day, on *Morning Joe,* Mitt had been questioned about Restore. Following to the letter the script that his and the group's advisers had drafted over the summer, Romney grumbled, "Campaign finance law has made a mockery of our political campaign season. We really ought to let campaigns raise the money they need and just get rid of these super PACs." Asked if he would tell Restore to stop its anti-Newt onslaught, Mitt replied, "I'm not allowed to communicate with a super PAC in any way, shape, or form . . . If we coordinate in any way whatsoever, we go to the big house."

Gingrich knew enough about Restore to spot the hypocrisy on display. And he knew that the laws against coordination contained no prohibition against a candidate disavowing, or calling for a super PAC to take down, any ad. Marching into a press conference after his Ottumwa event, Gingrich brandished a transcript of Romney's remarks. "His comments today are palpably misleading, clearly false, and are politics in its worst form," Gingrich thundered. "Understand, these are his people, running his ads, doing his dirty work while he pretends to be above it."

Gingrich had always despised what he called the "consultant class," and the mass resignation of his own hired guns in June had only deepened the animus. Newt also had little affection for the Bush family, so he wasn't surprised the next day when 41 declared his support for Romney. The endorsement came on the heels of that of Bob Dole, who confided to Boston that he believed if Gingrich were the nominee, it would guarantee a blowout for Obama on the scale of Reagan's in 1984.

Newt never expected to be the candidate of the Beltway, but to see the establishment rushing to the ramparts took him aback. More and more of his former House colleagues were on TV slamming him gratuitously, questioning his character, not his policies, alluding to his personal life. It left him bewildered, hurt his feelings. The same was true of his treatment by Fox, which Gingrich saw as having turned on him viciously and inexplicably. The on-air talent was pumping the pom-poms so feverishly for Romney that Newt wondered if their arms were getting tired. He assumed that Rupert Murdoch must have taken a shine to Mitt. (In Boston they thought, *If only.*)

Gingrich's woes deepened on Christmas Eve, when the Virginia Republican Party notified the campaign that it had failed to submit the required signatures to qualify for the March 6 GOP primary. For Gingrich, a loud devotee of management fads such as Lean Six Sigma, the rudimentary screwup was a huge embarrassment. On Facebook, his campaign director called it an "unexpected setback" similar to "December 1941"—thus providing Romney with another opportunity for burlesque. "He compared that to Pearl Harbor," Mitt quipped. "I think it's more like Lucille Ball at the chocolate factory."

Gingrich returned to Iowa after Christmas for the caucus home-stretch, setting off on a nine-day bus tour of the state. The schedule originally called for forty-four stops, but that number had already been cut in half. As he traipsed from town to town, Newt seemed determined to avoid anything resembling a consistent message, rambling from one arcane disquisition—on the history of the transcontinental railroad, the threats posed by pandemics and electromagnetic pulses, his status as an "amateur paleontologist"—to the next. In a nod to Romney (and Lucy), he visited a sweet shop in Algona.

"Now that I have the courage to come to the chocolate factory," Newt said, "I hope Governor Romney has the courage to debate me one-on-one and defend his negative ads."

By December 30, Gingrich was entirely out of sorts. At a morning event billed as a "mom town hall," he took to the stage looking exhausted, his face pale and puffy. The moderator was pollster Frank Luntz, who had helped Gingrich devise the Contract with America in 1994. Luntz asked Gingrich about the candidate's own late mother: "What special moments come to mind?" Almost instantly, Gingrich's eyes welled up, and soon tears were streaming down his cheeks.

Gingrich often became emotional at the memory of his mother, who was physically abused by his biological father and suffered under the household tyranny of her second husband, Newt's adoptive father. But another factor was in play here: Gingrich was sick as a dog that day—vomiting, diarrhea, severe dehydration. When Newt's staff learned how ill he was, they knew he needed some attention. But taking him to a hospital would be impossible without the press corps blowing the whistle. R. C. Hammond, Gingrich's press secretary, had an idea. He smuggled Newt into a local fire station, where he was administered fluids through an IV.

Gingrich spent the next two days in wretched shape. His New Year's Eve was a bowl of broth and a quiet family vigil anticipating the news of the night.

By tradition in Iowa, every four years the political world waited on tenterhooks for the results of the final *Des Moines Register* pre-caucus poll. The stats gurus at the paper were highly esteemed, with a long-held reputation for producing surveys of startling accuracy. Four years earlier, the *Register* had shocked everyone by not merely calling Obama's victory but correctly forecasting an unprecedented turnout on caucus night. And while this year's numbers were less eye-popping, they confirmed just how disastrously far Gingrich had fallen: all the way to fourth place—behind Romney, Ron Paul, and Rick Santorum—with a meager 12 percent.

New Year's morning was a Sunday, and Newt and Callista started the day by attending mass at St. Ambrose Cathedral, in Des Moines. From there they drove thirty-five miles north to Ames, to a media-swarmed event at the West Towne Pub, and from there another forty miles due east to the Junction Sports Bar and Grill, in Marshalltown. Gingrich still wasn't feeling well, but his discomfort did little to blunt his outrage over what had befallen him. After chatting and taking pictures with voters for an hour, he commandeered a back room and staged an impromptu media availability. Among those present was Chris Matthews, who more or less took control of the proceedings, goading Newt by suggesting that he had allowed Romney to "kick the shit" out of him.

"I've been Romney-boated," Gingrich said emphatically, then slipped into the past tense. "If I could have done anything different, I would have pulled the plug on Romney's PAC. I probably should have responded faster and more aggressively . . . If you have somebody spend $3.5 million lying about you, you have some obligation to come back and set the record straight."

Gingrich had been complaining about Restore like this for days, but his tone was different now—less theatrical, less hyperbolic, more genuinely seething. While Newt spoke, Callista was in an adjacent room, taking in the spectacle on a live TV feed, her chair pulled up right next to the monitor, her face a few inches from the screen. Bringing his rant to a conclusion, Newt offered a stinging coda aimed directly at Romney: "Someone who will lie to you to get to be president will lie to you when they *are* president."

Sitting next door, Callista nodded solemnly, silently mouthing the word "yes."

R ICK SANTORUM'S SUNDAY was a happier affair, kicking off with an appearance on *Meet the Press* that marked his sudden arrival in the top tier. The media had sensed a swell coming up under Santorum for several days. The *Register* poll made it official—and there was even better news for him buried in the fine print. Looking at the data from all four days that the paper surveyed voters, Santo was in third place. But counting only the sampling from the last two days put him in second, with 21 percent, three points ahead of Paul and three behind Romney. Out of nowhere, Santo had snagged the Big Mo.

From the moment he entered the race, Santorum was seen less as a long shot than a no shot, and duly ignored. A former two-term senator from Pennsylvania, Santorum had been turfed out of office in 2006, losing his reelection bid by a chasmal eighteen-point margin. To the extent that he was known nationally, it was for the extremity of his socially conservative convictions: opposition to abortion even in cases of rape and incest, condemnation of contraception, and such a fierce revulsion toward homosexuality that he once compared it to "man-on-child, man-on-dog" relations. Among many of his former colleagues, he was seen as arrogant, headstrong, preachy, and puerile. Nebraska Democrat Bob Kerrey summed up the prevailing upper-chamber opinion in five words: "Santorum—that's Latin for 'asshole.'"

But Santorum proved to be synonymous with something else in Iowa: persistence. He worked the state tirelessly, appearing at 381 events over the course of two years. As a retail pol, Santorum still left much to be desired. He was windy, dour, and digressive—senatorial in all respects. But his crushing defeat in 2006 seemed to have imbued him with a degree of humility, and he exhibited none of the slickness, phoniness, or cartoonishness of some of his rivals.

Santorum and his wife, Karen, both devout Catholics, had seven children, all of them homeschooled. Their youngest daughter, Bella, suffered from a rare genetic condition known as trisomy 18 that meant she was frequently in and out of the hospital. Wearing lapel buttons with Bella's picture, the other Santorum kids often appeared on the campaign trail with their mom and dad. The family picture they presented was cozy and appealing, especially to religious conservatives.

And yet Santorum remained little better than an asterisk in the Iowa polling—until mid-December, when he appeared at a pro-life forum sponsored by Huckabee at the Hoyt Sherman Place theater, in Des Moines. Casting aside his suit, Santorum donned a sweater-vest and delivered a tub-thumping speech that blew the room away. To that point, evangelical voters had been split among Bachmann, Perry, Cain, and Gingrich. But as each of those candidates collapsed in sequence, the religious-right bloc remained up for grabs, with Santorum the last man still standing erect and capable of seizing it.

All along, Rick had clung to a thin reed of hope. If he could break into double digits in just one poll before Christmas, Santorum believed he could parlay that into a strong Iowa close. When he flew home to Virginia for the holiday weekend, it hadn't happened yet—even after he had picked up the support that week of two of Iowa's leading social conservatives. Santorum thought he was through.

Then came a bolt from the blue: a new Public Policy Polling (PPP) survey on December 23 that put him at 10 percent. Santorum boisterously relayed the news to his family. To his daughter Elizabeth, he predicted, "This is going to change the race—we're going to win."

Santorum's confidence was based on two suppositions: that the lateness of his rise would make it impossible for any of his rivals to obliterate him with a barrage of negative ads; and that he would be bathed in the glow of national media attention when the media bigfeet arrived in Iowa for the homestretch, compensating for the fact that he had barely two nickels to rub together for TV advertising.

The *Register* poll left Santorum looking like Nostradamus. On January 2, at his penultimate stop on the day before the caucuses, he arrived at a Pizza Ranch restaurant in Boone, twenty minutes west of Ames, to find a hundred voters and almost as many media personages crammed into the small dining room.

After giving a brief speech, Santorum took questions from the crowd for the better part of an hour. Toward the end, a woman asked for his reaction to liberal Fox commentator Alan Colmes, who earlier that day had criticized the way Santorum and his wife handled the death of their infant son Gabriel in 1996. "Get a load of some of the crazy things [Santorum has] said and done," Colmes said. "Like taking his two-hour-old baby when it died right after childbirth home."

The essence of what Colmes said was true. After Karen miscarried, the couple refused to let the morgue claim Gabriel's corpse, slept with the body between them that night in the hospital, and then took him back to their house the next day. Santorum recounted this story at the Pizza Ranch, choking up as he did, explaining that "we brought [the body] home so our children could see him"; that it was important for them to "know they had a brother."

Standing a few feet from her husband, Karen began to weep. "This is just so inappropriate," she blurted out. Santorum held back his own tears, building to a ringing chastisement of Colmes. "To some who don't recognize the dignity of all human life," he said, "recognizing the humanity of your son is somehow weird, somehow odd, and should be subject to ridicule."

Even observers with no sympathy for the Santorums' ardent pro-life views or how they chose to process their grief were struck by his sincerity and depth of feeling—a humanity that was central to Santorum's appeal on the eve of the caucuses.

That night, the story of Santorum's Pizza Ranch moment received wide coverage on local news. The possibility that he might steal the caucuses was growing with each passing hour. Ten days earlier, Santorum had been reckoning with the prospect that his candidacy might soon be kaput. Now he thought, *In twenty-four hours, I may be giving the most important speech of my life.*

ROMNEY GREETED THE MORNING of the caucuses at peace with that potential outcome—and everything else about Iowa. In the final days before the voting, Mitt had reverted to his preferred form: floating above the fray and training his fire on Obama. The speech in which he presented his closing argument sounded more like a general election address. He had stopped attacking Gingrich entirely. No need to kick a man already lying crumpled on the ground.

In a holding room at a Des Moines hotel as he waited to do a TV interview, Romney leaned back in his chair and reflected on how different the caucuses were for him this time than the last. *All that money, time, and effort in 2008—and for what?* he thought. *Heartbreak.* A loss that left him referring to Iowa as "the La Brea Tar Pits of politics."

But now he had changed his tune. *The people know me better, I know them better, and we played the thing so much smarter,* he mused. *No matter what happens tonight, there's one thing I know: that it won't lead to my extinction.*

Of course Romney wanted the victory. Of course he wanted to slay the dragon. But in a way, he had already won. His late headlong leap into Iowa had been designed to thwart Gingrich and put down Perry, and both were accomplished. A victory by Santorum, on the other hand, would be nearly meaningless. Santorum had no money, no organization outside the Hawkeye State, no national profile. As for Ron Paul, his radical libertarianism, out-front isolationism, and just plain kookiness—from his abhorrence of paper money to his ties to the John Birch Society—made him more likely to end up on a park bench feeding stale bread to the squirrels than become the Republican nominee.

Gingrich was a few blocks away doing an interview of his own on CBS News's *The Early Show.* His last comment in Marshalltown the day before had been intended to provoke a follow-up. He was aching to be asked point-blank if he considered Romney—not his surrogates, not his allies, not the people behind Restore, but Romney himself—a falsifier, a prevaricator, a dissimulator. Now, anchor Norah O'Donnell obliged him.

"You scolded Mitt Romney, his friends who are running this super PAC," O'Donnell said. "I have to ask you: Are you calling Mitt Romney a liar?"

"Yes," Gingrich replied without hesitation or emotion.

"You're calling Mitt Romney a liar?"

"You seem shocked by it," Gingrich said, and then repeated calmly, "Yes."

What followed was an extraordinary anti-Romney screed, focused on Mitt's unsuitability for the Republican Party of 2012. "He's not telling the American people the truth," Gingrich said. "Here's a Massachusetts moderate who has tax-paid abortions in Romneycare, puts Planned Parenthood in Romneycare, raises hundreds of millions of dollars of taxes on businesses, appoints liberal judges to appease Democrats, and wants the rest of us to believe somehow he's magically a conservative."

There was no suspense for Gingrich that night when the caucus results began rolling in around seven o'clock. His fourth-place finish was quickly set in stone. He wondered if he should simply skip New Hampshire and fly directly to South Carolina. His advisers told him he couldn't do it—he had to get to the Granite State. That's where the media will be, his pollster Conway said, and you need them for oxygen.

Bachmann's fate was sealed early, too: she came in last. Five months after her straw poll coup, she had picked up only an additional thousand votes. Sitting in her campaign bus, in the same seat where she cried with joy in August, she now sobbed over her drubbing. "God, I'm a loser," Bachmann said. "God, I turn people off." With two debates ahead in New Hampshire, some of her advisers thought she should consider staying in the race. Bachmann wanted no part of it. Let's draft a withdrawal speech for tomorrow, she said.

Perry was leaning the same way. In his suite in the Sheraton West Des Moines, around eight o'clock, he learned that he would likely finish fifth. He still had $4 million in the bank, but that seemed immaterial. I think this is

Romney's race to lose now, Perry said to Allbaugh, Sullivan, and his son, Griffin. Perry's advisers exited the room thinking it was over, though in his concession speech he left a little wiggle room: "I've decided to return to Texas to assess the results of tonight's caucuses and determine whether there is a path forward for myself in this race," Perry said.

Romney, Santorum, and their teams were living in an orthogonal reality—smack in the heat of the tightest nip-and-tuck tussle for first place in Iowa caucus history. In the jam-packed Romney boiler room in the Hotel Fort Des Moines, Mitt paced back and forth as the results came in by phone from the caucus sites. He and Santorum each had approximately 25 percent, but the lead kept seesawing. 10:38 p.m.: Santorum up by thirteen votes (out of some sixty thousand cast). 10:45: Romney up by eighty-five. 11:12: Santorum up by twenty-eight.

"This is ridiculous!" Romney said, and burst out laughing.

Santorum and his shoestring operation were at the Stoney Creek Inn, in Johnston, just outside Des Moines. They had no field team, no real war room; they were getting their information from CNN and Fox. Like Romney, Santorum was cackling as he watched the advantage bounce back and forth, partly out of pure elation: he had taken on the party's most likely nominee and come away with a virtual tie at worst.

The question was when to take the stage. Around 11:00 p.m., Santorum overheard one of the Fox talking heads say, If I were Rick Santorum, I'd get out there and declare victory—now.

And so Santorum did. Ditching the sweater-vest that had fast become his trademark, he took the podium and spoke with neither a teleprompter nor a full text—just a set of bullet points. As an introduction to a national audience, the address could scarcely have been more poised or savvy, with its emphasis on biography, family, and principle, its invocation of Santorum's blue-collar immigrant roots and his ancestors' coal-mining past. And it contained one indelible stanza: "I'll never forget the first time I saw someone who had died. It was my grandfather. And I knelt next to his coffin, and all I could do at eye level was look at his hands. They were enormous hands. And all I could think was: *Those hands dug freedom for me.*"

Stevens had stayed up most of the previous night writing a speech for Romney. But after he and Mitt saw Santorum speaking without a prompter, they ditched the text in favor of Romney's standard stump speech—including a recitation of bits of "America the Beautiful" and accompanying textual commentary. ("'O beautiful for heroes proved in liberating strife, who more than self their country loved, and mercy more than life,'" Romney said. "Do we have any veterans in the room tonight?") Even his staunchest allies considered the effort stilted, and somewhat embarrassing.

When Romney returned to his suite, the race was still too close to call. But just before 1:00 a.m., his political director, Rich Beeson, concluded that Mitt was going to lose—by six votes. Romney's top advance man, Will Ritter, called the candidate's cell phone and told him he had lost. Beeson headed to his hotel room; he had an early flight to catch. When he got there, just after 2:00 a.m., his phone rang. Rhoades was on the line.

"Do you believe in miracles?"

"Are you fucking kidding me?" Beeson asked.

"We won!" Rhoades exulted.

Beeson called Romney with the good news. "Great—on to New Hampshire!" Romney said.

The Iowa Republican Party had no comprehensible explanation for the discovery of late ballots that turned a narrow loss for Romney into an eight-vote victory. If the members of Santorum's team hadn't been so tired, giddy, and ill-equipped, they would have challenged the result on the spot. But Santorum himself believed that, in the end, it wouldn't matter. Whether he prevailed by six votes or lost by eight was immaterial. He was the night's big winner, and he was sure the press would cover it that way. *By God!* thought Santorum. *We spent no money! We had no money! But we dueled Romney, with millions behind him, to a draw. Talk about a miracle story!*

As Romney set off for New Hampshire the next morning, his ostensible triumph seemed equally total to him. Bachmann was gone. Perry would soon be gone. Gingrich had been crippled. The other caucus prizewinners, Santorum and Paul, were profoundly flawed. Restore had played precisely the role that Romney and his people had designed it to. And Mitt had put to rest the Iowan ghosts of 2008. The state he once thought of as a tar pit had been transformed into a springboard.

But in the Iowa cornfields Romney had also planted seeds that would sprout in unfortunate ways. He had taken positions—on immigration, on the Ryan plan—that had the Obamans gleeful. In allowing Santorum to rise and dismissing his future viability, Boston had underestimated his potential appeal as the conservative alternative to Mitt. And then there was Gingrich.

From the start, Newt had believed that South Carolina was the place where he would make his stand. His cremation by Restore had roused a powerful financial force that was about to come to his aid. Most fatefully, Romney and his allies had dangerously altered Gingrich's mental state. The New Newt might have been a teddy bear, as his friends kept saying, but now the teddy bear was angry. On arriving in New Hampshire, he informed his aides of a shift in strategy that was at once unequivocal and unrepentant: "We have to make Romney radioactive."

★ 12 ★

MITT HAPPENS

ROMNEY FLEW OUT OF DES MOINES that Wednesday morning, January 4, arrived in Manchester before noon, and headed to a rally at a nearby high school gym. As his blue-and-white campaign bus deposited him at the entrance, Romney was bedraggled from lack of sleep but upbeat about being back on home turf. In the Granite State as in no other, he had led in the polls from the start, and by a country mile. No non-incumbent Republican had ever carried the caucuses and the first-in-the-nation primary in the same year. Now, after months of seeing his front-runner status serially usurped by Pierrots and pretenders, Mitt was poised to make history when the votes were counted six days later.

The event at Central High was designed to cement his position in the catbird seat. With Romney onstage was John McCain, there to confer his endorsement. Four years earlier, the idea of McCain standing behind Romney—unless he was preparing to slit his throat—would have seemed as likely as a terrier reciting Tennyson. And some awkwardness was still apparent. After offering his approbation of Romney, McCain couldn't resist disgorging a morsel of sarcasm: "By the way, we forgot to congratulate [Mitt] on his landslide victory last night!"

Like most of McCain's political judgments, his endorsement was based on a mixture of caprice, calculation, and comparative chagrin. Huntsman he disdained for his service to the president ("Why the fuck would he do that?" he asked Weaver) and going soft on Afghanistan. Newt he detested for being "a moron." Santorum he despised not only for backing Romney in 2008 but also for recording robocalls that ripped McCain for lacking presidential "temperament." All of which left Mitt, among the extant options, on the bottom rung of McCain's pecking order of pique. And Romney alone had a prayer of beating Obama—who was, of course, at the top.

Still, the strangeness of the situation wasn't lost on either man. Afterwards, on Romney's bus, McCain cracked wise about it. "The choice in the Republican Party has come down to the dog-on-roof guy or the man-on-dog guy?" he said. "I'm with the dog-on-roof guy."

Romney spent the next twenty-four hours with McCain, traipsing with him from Manchester to Peterborough to Salem, agog at his inability to complete three sentences without dropping an f-bomb. (Romney employed prim substitutes for profanities: "blooming" for "fucking," "grunt" for "shit.")

The oddity of their coupling notwithstanding, Romney took comfort in having the 2000 and 2008 New Hampshire winner at his side. Since his final push in Iowa, Romney had been working his worry beads over how a victory there might come back to bite him in the next contest. He recalled a theory his Granite State guru, Tom Rath, had propounded: that Live Free or Die voters were congenitally incapable of rubber-stamping the results of the caucuses. Romney would never forget the way Obama had come flying out of Iowa four years earlier, only to be greeted by an extended middle finger in New Hampshire, as the state simultaneously flipped the bird to Mitt.

To the extent that his nervousness had a tangible focus, it was Huntsman. After months of camping out in the Granite State, the Utahan's poll numbers had ticked up into double digits, though he remained twenty points off the lead. Stevens kept telling his candidate to ignore Huntsman. But Romney, having restrained himself for months, was itching to pop his Mormon rival in the puss.

The opportunity presented itself that Saturday night, in a debate at Saint Anselm College, outside Manchester, when Huntsman scolded Romney for being jejune about China.

"I'm sorry, Governor," Romney shot back. "You were, the last two years, implementing the policies of this administration in China. The rest of us on this stage were doing our best to get Republicans elected across the country and stop the policies of this president from being put forward."

Huntsman's retort was literally incomprehensible: he gibbered something in Mandarin.

After the debate, Huntsman's aides were beside themselves, and this time the candidate was, too. Stung by McCain's endorsement of Romney—which, given Huntsman's abandonment of Mitt for Mac in 2006, struck Jon as a piquant betrayal—he retreated to his hotel and engaged in a fit of full-bodied self-flagellation. By a quirk of the schedule, the candidates would meet again for a debate the next morning in Concord. Huntsman's wife and daughters, along with his advisers, all agreed: for the sake of his dignity, if nothing else, Huntsman needed to come out swinging.

The next morning, Stevens warned Romney, "He's gonna come after you," and Huntsman did. "I was criticized last night by Governor Romney," Jon said. "While he was out raising money, [I was] serving my country—yes, under a Democrat, like my two sons are doing in the United States Navy. They're not asking what political affiliation the president is. I want to be very clear with the people here in New Hampshire and this country: I will always put my country first."

For Huntsman and his team, the moment represented the high point of his campaign: a flash of principle and a flogging of Mitt, with McCain's 2008 campaign slogan thrown in for added oomph. When the debate was over, Stevens reminded Romney, "I *told you* he was gonna come after you."

"It was worth it," Mitt merrily replied.

Less easily laughed off was a line of attack pushed by Gingrich in the debates that weekend, assaulting Romney's record in private equity. The former speaker had taken a glancing swipe at Mitt's Bain background a few weeks earlier, then let the matter lie. But now came news that the billionaire casino mogul Sheldon Adelson had written a $5 million check to the pro-Newt super PAC Winning Our Future, which had just bought the rights to

Michelle and Barack Obama. The first lady, hugely popular with the American public, was a formidable force inside the White House and out on the campaign trail.

Mitt and Ann Romney. Famously devoted to his wife of four decades, Mitt felt most comfortable and confident when Ann was at his side, prompting his team to adjust her campaign schedule accordingly.

Photography by Christopher Anderson

Jon Huntsman, with his wife, Mary Kaye and daughters, Liddy (left) and Abby (right). The former Utah governor and Obama's ambassador to China entered the race with loads of promise, but his campaign collapsed in a mass of contradictions and confusion.

Michele Bachmann. The congresswoman from Minnesota dazzled in early debates but saw her efforts crumble when Rick Perry joined the race.

Newt and Callista Gingrich. The former House speaker and 1990s GOP icon, mellowed by marriage to Callista, was unnerved by Romney's massive money machine and reverted to his prickly, irrepressible disposition in the face of the onslaught.

Rick Santorum. Operating on a shoestring budget, the former senator from Pennsylvania enjoyed a sudden burst of momentum and press attention that led to a surprise victory in the Iowa caucuses.

Herman Cain. With his charming affect and zingy 9-9-9 tax slogan, the former Godfather's Pizza CEO had a brief run at first place in the polls but was brought down by scandal.

Rick Perry. As a presidential contender, the handsome Texas governor seemed to have it all—until he declared his candidacy and stepped onto the debate stage.

Chris Christie. The New Jersey governor was nicknamed "Big Boy" by George W. Bush—reflecting his outsize personality, physicality, and political potential. Christie considered his own 2012 presidential bid before endorsing Romney.

Paul Ryan. Mitt Romney tapped the young Wisconsin congressman as his running mate for his keen intelligence, Capitol Hill experience, and ability to energize conservative voters.

Mitt Romney. Romney began preparing for his October debates against Obama in June—and the hard work paid off with a game-changing performance in Denver.

Joe Biden. Vice President Biden cultivated a warm personal rapport with Obama but still had to fight for a bigger role in the campaign.

Barack Obama and Bill Clinton. Overcoming the mutual rancor of the 2008 campaign, the Big Dog made a strong case for Obama's reelection on the stage at the Democratic National Convention in Charlotte.

Mitt Romney. The Republican nominee had high hopes for his convention in Tampa, until it was rocked by a hurricane, speechwriting bedlam, and Clint Eastwood's unexpected Dadaistic presentation.

Barack Obama. At an election-eve rally in Des Moines, Iowa, an emotional Obama returned to the state that launched his 2008 campaign.

Mitt Romney. After decades of personal and professional success, Romney believed it was his patriotic duty to run for president. Up until the final hours of Election Day, he thought he would pull off a win.

Barack Obama. Obama considered his reelection victory in 2012 a far more satisfying and significant achievement than his win in 2008.

a twenty-eight-minute video, *King of Bain: When Mitt Romney Came to Town,* and reserved half-hour blocks of airtime to run it in South Carolina.

Gingrich didn't distance himself from the charges in the video, which depicted Romney as a greedy, job-killing corporate raider. Instead, over the next forty-eight hours, he amplified them as if through a bullhorn, describing Bain's endeavors as "rich people figuring out clever legal ways to loot a company." Down in South Carolina, Perry, who had surprised everyone the morning after Iowa and decided to stay in the race, chimed in on Bain—comparing firms such as Romney's to "vultures."

Romney had always expected to be assailed on Bain, just not so soon, and not by Republicans. Stevens was surprised, too, but not terribly concerned. History told the strategist that when incendiary issues were aired out during a nomination fight, they tended to fade away before the general election. *Think of Reverend Wright,* Stevens mused. *Think of Gennifer Flowers. Better that we go through this now against Gingrich than later against Obama.*

There were other reasons for the Bain broadsides not to bother Boston. They distracted Mitt's opponents from harping on Romneycare and presented Mitt with a chance to seize the conservative high ground. With Gingrich and Perry sounding more like Daily Kos commenters than Republicans, Romney could champion the glories of market capitalism, rallying the right (for once) to his cause.

Executing this jujitsu move required a dexterity that Romney had rarely evinced. Starting that summer, when he'd cheerfully referred to himself as "unemployed" at a Florida coffee shop and blurted out in Iowa that "corporations are people," and continuing through his proposed $10,000 bet with Perry, the candidate had shown a propensity for faux pas when talking about money. Now, in the waning hours before the New Hampshire vote, he coughed up two more gems: his claim that, in his vaunted private sector career, "there were a couple of times I wondered whether I was gonna get a pink slip"; and his comment, in discussing the virtues of shopping around for health care purveyors, that "I like being able to fire people who provide services to me."

Boston collectively blanched. Gingrich, Perry, and Huntsman pounced. And yet, when the results tumbled in that Tuesday night, January 10, none of it seemed to matter. All week long, the flashbacks from four years earlier had been vivid in Mitt's mind: the stricken look on Ann's face as the exit polls arrived, the sense of being kicked in the teeth by Iowa and then punched in the gut by . . . his neighbors. But not tonight. In the campaign's war room at Southern New Hampshire University, the Romneys were as much relieved as ebullient when they learned the final tally: with 39 percent of the vote, Mitt had whipped Ron Paul by sixteen points and Huntsman by twenty-two.

For his victory speech, Romney's advance team wanted an image of him solo in the arena, surrounded by a teeming crowd—a shot announcing, *This is over.* But Romney insisted his family join him on the podium. Flanked by Ann and his five sons, he offered his indictment of Gingrich and Perry with a clarity that eluded him in less carefully scripted settings. "President Obama wants to put free enterprise on trial," Romney said. "In the last few days, we have seen some desperate Republicans join forces with him. This is such a mistake for our party and for our nation. This country already has a leader who divides us with the bitter politics of envy."

Half an hour later, Huntsman delivered his concession speech at the Black Brimmer bar, in Manchester. Since the Concord debate, Jon had been bolstered by a sense of momentum that convinced him he could finish a close second. Mary Kaye saw a promo ad on MSNBC that echoed her husband's new "country first" message and was sure that Jon had inspired the spot. Huntsman Sr. was talking to Weaver and Davis about putting $10 million into the super PAC, though Jonny continued to resist. (In the end, the father contributed just over $2 million to Our Destiny.)

The distant third crushed the Huntsman family's spirits; Mary Kaye and the girls were in tears. Onstage, Jon proclaimed, "I'd say third place is a ticket to ride—hello, South Carolina!" But no one believed it. When Abby Huntsman brought the New Hampshire exit polls to her father, she could tell from the look on his face that it was over. Six days later, he dropped out and anemically endorsed Mitt.

The morning after New Hampshire, at the Westin Boston Waterfront, Zwick gathered three hundred donors to hear from Romney, Newhouse, and Mike Leavitt about the road ahead. For a year, the campaign had stressed again and again that securing the nomination would require a long slog, and Leavitt's presentation on the path to the required 1,144 dele-gates, repeated the point.

In that heady moment, however, many in the room dismissed Leavitt's sobriety as perfunctory kill-joyism. With Romney's back-to-back victories, he had achieved the unprecedented. Gingrich had campaigned like crazy in New Hampshire and placed fourth again. Santorum, receiving no lift from Iowa, had come in fifth. The South Carolina primary, the winner of which had gone on to claim the Republican nomination in every election since 1980, was ten days away. And while the Palmetto State—with its intensely conservative and evangelical electorate—had always been Romney's weak-est link among the first four contests, Newhouse informed the crowd that Mitt had surged to a healthy lead both there and in the Sunshine State.

All of a sudden, the triumphal speech from the night before seemed like more than spin. All of a sudden, everyone was thinking Romney had a chance to run the table, and even Mitt allowed himself to drift into reverie. *If I can win South Carolina and Florida, it's game over,* he thought.

But when Romney was told how far ahead Boston's polling had him—34 percent to 15 over Newt in South Carolina, 45 to 15 in Florida—his usual doubts crept in. *The numbers are too good to be true,* he fretted. The ques-tion was what Gingrich would do next. Romney hadn't a clue, but he feared it would not be pretty. As a Republican senator had said to him recently about Newt, "When that watermelon falls to earth, you don't want to be anywhere around."

GINGRICH HIT THE PAVEMENT in South Carolina with a splat, shaken to his core, and not just by his second straight rout. Romney's defense of free enterprise had turned the conservative echo chamber into an amen corner. Limbaugh likened Newt to Elizabeth Warren and Oliver Stone. Giuliani compared him to Saul Alinsky. Even Romney's nemeses at *The Wall Street Journal* weighed in against Gingrich and Perry. "These candidates are des-perate," noted the paper's editorial page, "but do they have to sound like Michael Moore?"

Being compared to this lineup of left-wing loonies blew Newt's mind. But with South Carolina now "make it or break it" for him, as he put it to

Callista, he was more convinced than ever that he had to render Romney septic, and that tarring the front-runner as an out-of-touch plutocrat remained his best chance. In a tactical retreat, Newt slunk away from his Bain attacks, calling on Winning Our Future to soften or take down its video—while in the next breath calling for Mitt to release his tax returns.

Romney's personal finances were less the elephant in the room than a full herd of pachyderms. Since the start of his Massachusetts governorship, in 2003, most of Mitt's assets had resided in blind trusts he set up for himself, Ann, and his sons. His fortune was not only staggering in size but Byzantine in structure: some $250 million or more wrapped up in a maze-like assemblage of holdings. There were stakes in more than a dozen Bain funds domiciled in the Cayman Islands; foreign accounts in other exotic locales—Switzerland, Luxembourg, Bermuda—that were notorious as tax havens; investments in offshore shell companies and so-called blocker corporations; an IRA that had somehow swollen in value to as much as $100 million.

Overseeing Romney's trust was Brad Malt, the chairman of Boston's largest law firm, Ropes & Gray, and Mitt's personal attorney. Malt had great expertise in the area of private equity. (He and Mitt had met through Bain.) But he had no political background or orientation; he saw his responsibility as maximizing his client's wealth, not protecting his public image. In 2007, when Romney's foreign holdings first came to light, Malt told the *Los Angeles Times,* "I don't care whether it's the Caymans or Mars, if it's organized in the Netherlands Antilles or the Jersey Islands. That means nothing to me. All I care about is whether it's a good fund or a bad fund."

Romney expressed no qualms about Malt's management of his money or its potential political implications. He knew that his offshore investments and Swiss bank account would be targeted by the Democrats if he won the nomination. But Romney believed there was nothing untoward about the Swiss account, on which he paid full taxes. As for the Cayman, Bermudan, and other Bain-related vehicles, not only did they produce prodigious returns, but Romney (as a former partner in the firm) was allowed to invest in them without paying a management fee. *Just because someone is going to be critical, I'm going to pass up a deal that good?* Romney thought. *No, sir.*

In 2007 and 2011, Romney had filed the personal financial disclosure statements required by federal law. But they provided nowhere near as clear a picture as would his taxes, which he had refused to make public all throughout his political career. With Democrats agitating on the topic, Romney was asked in separate appearances on MSNBC in December if he would release his returns. "I don't intend to," he told Chuck Todd; questioned by Andrea Mitchell, he declined to commit to doing so even if he became president. For Chicago, those replies were chum in the water. From Obama's official Twitter account came a tweet—"Why won't Mitt Romney release his tax returns?"—with a link to a DNC video entitled "What Is Mitt Romney Hiding?"

Romney's private stance was a bit more yielding than his public one. If he became his party's standard-bearer, he told Malt, Bob White, and Rhoades, he would feel compelled to release at least a summary of some of his tax returns. But he and Ann (who was even more emphatic about the privacy issue than her husband) wanted to reveal as little as possible as late as possible, and certainly nothing unless and until he had the nomination sewn up. In Rhoades's mind, that translated to *Let's get to April.*

What Romney hadn't counted on was that his Republican rivals would take up the Democratic banner on his returns, just as some of them had done on Bain. In the run-up to a Fox News debate in Myrtle Beach on Monday, January 16, Santorum joined Gingrich in seizing on the issue, and at the first opportunity onstage, Perry raised it unprompted. "Mitt, we need for you to release your income tax so the people of this country can see how you made your money," he said. "We cannot fire our nominee in September. We need to know now."

Romney's debate prep on the tax question had been weak and inconclusive—and it showed. "I looked at what has been done in campaigns in the past with Senator McCain and President George W. Bush and others," Mitt said when asked the question. "They have tended to release tax records in April, or tax season. I hadn't planned on releasing tax records, because the law requires us to release all of our assets, all the things we own. That I have already released. It's a pretty full disclosure. But, you know, if that's been the tradition and I'm not opposed to doing that, time will tell. But I anticipate that most likely I am going to get asked to do that around the April time period, and I'll keep that open."

While Mitt was serving up a mile-high stack of waffles, Gingrich was tossing chunks of raw red meat to the well-lubricated crowd, which had availed itself of cocktails aplenty at the pre-debate receptions. Discussing the merits of negotiating with the Taliban, Gingrich blood-lustily invoked a favorite son of the Palmetto State: "Andrew Jackson had a good idea what to do with our enemies—kill them." He argued that Obama aimed "to maximize dependency" and did not believe "work is good."

Gingrich was challenged by the African American moderator, Juan Williams, who asked if he could understand how some of his rhetoric, including his suggestion that poor kids be put to work as janitors, might be seen "as insulting to all Americans, but particularly to black Americans." Newt replied sternly, "No, I don't see that," and launched into a soliloquy that ended with the claim that "only the elites despise earning money."

Williams brought up Gingrich's frequent references to Obama as "the food-stamp president" and suggested that "it sounds as if you are seeking to belittle people."

Newt's eyes flashed like twinkle lights on a Christmas tree. "Well, first of all, *Juan*," he said in a tone dripping with condescension, "the fact is that more people have been put on food stamps by Barack Obama than any president in American history." The crowd roared approval. "Now, I know among the politically correct, you're not supposed to use facts that are uncomfortable," he went on, lecturing Williams for another sixty seconds. The audience hooted, hollered, and delivered Gingrich two standing ovations.

Looking down from the stage, Newt saw the bodies rising from the back of the hall and rippling toward him like a wave. In his years at the intersection of politics and performance art, Gingrich had encountered his share of wonders. But he had never witnessed anything like the scene at Myrtle Beach—and he found it hard to imagine that he ever would again.

R OMNEY HAD NEVER SEEN anything like it, either. Afterwards, Stevens told Mitt he thought that Gingrich's mau-mauing of Williams played to an ugly side of politics. Romney didn't disagree, but he knew that Newt's onstage fireworks exhibition was bound to affect the polls; on Fox News, they were already calling the debate a "game changer."

Mitt woke up grouchy the next day. On his schedule was an early-morning rally in Florence, a long bus ride away. Arriving at the Florence Civic Center, he found a cavernous room and a sparse crowd—space for a thousand, fewer than a hundred in attendance. Romney cooled his heels backstage as his traveling crew scurried to prevent photographers from capturing a bird's-eye view of the embarrassing turnout. (A photograph in the next day's *New York Times* testified to the futility of their efforts.)

After his speech, Romney met the press by his bus—and was immediately hit with a question about his taxes. What was the effective rate he paid? a reporter asked. "It's probably closer to the 15 percent rate than anything," he answered, going on to explain that his income came mainly from investments. "And then I get speaker's fees from time to time, but not very much."

In Boston, Rhoades was monitoring the proceedings on a live feed, with a mounting sense of horror. Fearing that the tax questions would just keep on coming, he started frantically texting and calling the troops on the ground: Kill it! Kill it now!

By Wednesday morning, Romney's riches had eclipsed all else in the headlines and on the trail. The press seized on Mitt's definition of "not very much" regarding his speaking fees: $374,327.62 in the past year. On *Today* and *Morning Joe,* Chris Christie was offering unsolicited advice: Mitt should release his tax returns, as Big Boy always had. Meanwhile, the fallout from Myrtle Beach was showing up in Boston's internal polling—and starkly. When Romney had walked onstage that night, he was ten points ahead of Gingrich. Thirty-six hours later, he was narrowly behind.

Romney would have a chance to stop the slide on Thursday, when the next debate was set to take place in Charleston. Instead, the dawn greeted him with another sharp stick in the eye: a call from Iowa notifying him that he was no longer the winner of the caucuses. After a recount, it appeared that Santorum had won more votes, though the situation was sufficiently unclear that the Republican Party in the Hawkeye State wanted to declare the contest a tie. Romney considered that ridiculous and called Santorum, leaving a message on his cell phone, conceding, "You came out on top, so nice work."

With Romney attempting to resist a downward spiral, Gingrich was joyfully hanging ten atop a breaker. That morning, Perry at last called it quits and tossed his support to Newt. Around the same time, ABC News put out word that it had snared a scoop: Newt's second wife, Marianne, was claiming that in 1999, while he was engaged in his affair with Callista, he had asked for an "open marriage." But that night on the debate stage, Gingrich spun the sewage into sunshine, lacerating the moderator, CNN's John King, when the newsman led off with a question about the story.

"The destructive, vicious, negative nature of much of the news media makes it harder to govern this country, harder to attract decent people to run for public office," Gingrich thundered. "And I am appalled that you would begin a presidential debate on a topic like that."

As Gingrich piled on the adjectives and the crowd went bonkers, à la Myrtle Beach, Mitt and Ann caught each other's eyes and exchanged knowing nods. *Yet another moderator giving Newt exactly what he wants,* Romney thought.

Mitt was waiting for the inevitable question about his taxes, having finally spent some time in debate prep rehearsing his answer. When King introduced the topic, Romney answered with more aplomb than he ever had before: "When they're completed this year in April, I'll release my returns in April and probably for other years as well."

But King would not let go. "In 1967, your father set . . . a groundbreaking standard in American politics," the moderator reminded Mitt. "He released his tax return. He released them for not one year, but for twelve years. And when he did that, he said this: 'One year could be a fluke, perhaps done for show.' When you release yours, will you follow your father's example?"

"Maybe," Romney replied with a forced laugh and a forged smile. The crowd jeered.

Watching on Commercial Street, Rhoades couldn't avoid the thought: *We're not going to make it to April.* Unlike Stevens, with his what-me-worry optimism and ability always to find a pony in there somewhere, Rhoades was Boston's designated realist and bearer of bad news. When potentially troubling stories flared up, Rhoades instantly placed them into one of two categories: they were either nothingburgers or shitburgers. To his mind, the tax-return dustup was inescapably the latter.

Later that night, after the debate, Rhoades and White got on the phone with Mitt. Guv, this issue isn't going away, Rhoades said. We need to lance the boil. With White in agreement, Romney relented, assigning his former Bain partner to oversee the readying of the release of at least one year of returns.

The next morning, White assembled a small team in Boston to tackle the monumental task. Dozens of bankers' boxes were hauled into a single office and put under lock and key. For the next seventy-two hours, the team was neck-deep in documents, combing through hundreds upon hundreds of pages. Most Americans had never seen anything resembling the Romney tax returns—the blindingly complex paperwork of extreme wealth. The members of the White task force were almost inured to it by now, having worked on Romney's previous financial disclosure forms. Even so, they were stunned by the number of eyebrow raisers and potential political vulnerabilities that the tax returns presented. Every page raising an issue was flagged with a Post-it note. Soon enough, the room they were working in looked like a confetti factory.

In South Carolina, the Romneys were reconciling themselves to what seemed a certain loss. Ann was more upset than Mitt at Newt's efflorescence. She thought he was hotheaded, manipulative, impetuous, and immoral. That there was prejudice against her and Mitt's faith among evangelicals was not news to her, but she took Gingrich's surge as a galling reminder: the so-called values voters of South Carolina apparently hated Mormons so much that they preferred a serial philanderer.

Mitt was less emotional than his wife, but not entirely composed. His schedule for the Saturday morning of the primary, January 21, included a meet-and-greet at Tommy's Country Ham House, in Greenville. By sheer coincidence, Gingrich was expected to be there at the same time. When Romney learned this, he ordered his team to move up his arrival time, telling them, "I don't want to see Newt Gingrich." The press immediately tagged it the "Ham House Showdown" and declared Mitt the loser. On Romney's staff, the humiliation was given another name: Hamageddon.

Such apocalyptic phrase-making seemed all the more apt a few hours later, when the results of the primary rolled in. The trouncing Romney suffered was greater than expected: 40–28. It was also comprehensive, with Gingrich pummeling him soundly across the board: 42–26 with men and 38–29 with women; by nine or more points in every age cohort; by double digits in every educational segment except voters with postgraduate study (which Romney won by a bare two points); among both married and unmarried voters; among the poor, the middle class, and the rich; among Republicans and independents; among the very conservative and somewhat conservative; among voters most concerned about beating Barack Obama; among late deciders and early deciders; and, especially dramatically, among those for whom the debates were important.

The sweep and scale of his loss took Romney aback. The political implications were all too clear. Ten days earlier, Mitt had seemed to be on his way to a historic sweep. Now, after having the Iowa tiara snatched from his head and South Carolina blow up in his face, he was heading into Florida with just one notch in his belt. That so many voters—any voters, really—would pull the lever for Newt struck him as incomprehensible. *What can they be thinking?* Romney wondered.

What Mitt was thinking was that he needed to reboot, and fast. A few hours after the primary results were in, he got on a conference call with Boston to discuss his tax returns. White's task force walked everyone through the minefield of what they'd found: the offshore accounts, the IRA, the tax rates, the works.

A plan was set for Romney to appear the next morning on *Fox News Sunday* and announce his intention to release his 2010 return and an estimate for 2011. They would do the deed on January 24, when Obama would be giving his State of the Union address, which might help to distract attention and lessen the media firestorm. Romney was quiet for much of the call, just listening to the task force and his media team hash it out, taking it all in. As the call was wrapping up, he thanked everyone—and then, in a tone of resignation, said, Well, I guess this is going to be a real shitburger I have to eat.

Little as Romney relished the prospect, he realized that Rhoades and White were right—and even more so in light of the South Carolina loss. *Gingrich is now the front-runner,* Romney thought. *He could be the nominee.* To stop him, Mitt knew that Boston would need to be on offense, and with a vengeance. But as long as the tax-return controversy was out there, Romney would be playing defense.

No one agreed more wholeheartedly with that than Christie. "End this stupid issue," the New Jersey governor told Romney by phone later that night. Mitt, the cat's out of the bag. You're rich. Okay? Let's use it as a strength, not as a weakness. You've been successful. You want other Americans to have the chance to be successful like you are. And by the way, you didn't make your money by being an influence peddler on Capitol Hill like Gingrich made his money. So let's start talking about that.

"Get out of your crouch and kick the shit out of this guy," Christie said. "That's what you should do. He's a joke. And you're allowing him to be taken seriously."

None of this was news to Romney, but it was good to hear. The ten-day stretch between now and the vote in Florida on January 31 would be to Mitt what South Carolina had been to Newt: make or break. The next morning on a conference call with Boston, Romney was resolute.

Guys, he said flatly. No messing around. We've got to shoot to kill here.

T HE NEW, guns-blazing Romney hit the debate stage the next night, January 23, in Tampa, and encountered an exhausted and lethargic Gingrich, who suddenly seemed every bit his age. Mitt showed no mercy. He tore into Newt, attacking his character, raising questions about his ability to govern. On Freddie Mac, Romney took a cue from Christie and branded Newt an "influence peddler in Washington." Cutting even closer to the bone was his denigration of Gingrich's speakership. "The speaker was given an opportunity to be the leader of our party in 1994," Romney said. "And at the end of four years, he had to resign in disgrace."

While their man was letting fly in the debate, Boston was walking reporters through Romney's taxes in preparation for their release the next day. The returns would show that Mitt had an effective tax rate of 14 percent for 2010, on $21.7 million in income, paying $3 million in federal taxes (after $3 million in charitable deductions), with roughly the same picture for 2011.

The shitburger Romney had been expecting was duly served up by the press, which zeroed in on the special sauce of his Swiss bank account. In a heartbeat, the DNC put up a Web video—"What is Mitt Romney hiding? And where is he hiding it?"—that laid out a litany of abuses connected with

Swiss-banking secrecy and featured audio of Malt explaining that the $3 million Romney had stashed at UBS was "a bank account, nothing more, nothing less. An ordinary bank account."

Much as the release of the tax returns delighted the Democratic opposition, it also sucked the air out of the issue in the primary—and allowed Boston to train its fire on Newt. The scorching assault was like Iowa times ten. Until now, the Romneyites had refrained from running negative ads against Gingrich, leaving Restore Our Future to do that dirty work. Now both the campaign and the super PAC unloaded on Newt from the air. On conference calls with reporters, Boston scratched and clawed at Gingrich's claim of having been in the vanguard of the Reagan Revolution. A parade of establishment grandees—led by McCain and Dole—marched through Florida, dumping on Newt. The long-standing Rhoades pipeline to Matt Drudge became a viaduct; for several days, Drudge's home page consisted of almost nothing but anti-Newt headlines linking to Boston-sourced nuggets. Taking the Hawkeye State psyops strategy to new heights, Romney surrogates started showing up at Gingrich's events, providing a counter-narrative to reporters and occasionally even tangling with his press secretary as the TV news cameras rolled.

On the debate stage again in Jacksonville, on January 26, Mitt reprised his Tampa takedown. Days earlier, Gingrich had visited the Florida Space Coast to talk some more about his passion for a lunar colony—over which Romney witheringly mocked him. "I spent twenty-five years in business," Mitt said. "If I had a business executive come to me and say they wanted to spend a few hundred billion dollars to put a colony on the moon, I'd say, 'You're fired.'"

Once again, the angry teddy bear of the South Carolina debates was replaced by a sleepy, sedated beast. When he attempted to go after the moderator, CNN's Wolf Blitzer, the ensuing ursid-on-canid action left Gingrich deflated as Blitzer calmly stood his ground. When Gingrich clipped Romney for having investments in Fannie Mae and Freddie Mac and with Goldman Sachs—"which is today foreclosing on Floridians," Newt noted—a well-prepped Romney lowered the boom. "Mr. Speaker, I know that sounds like an enormous revelation, but have you checked your own investments?"

Mitt asked. "You also have investments through mutual funds that also invest in Fannie Mae and Freddie Mac."

Gingrich frowned. "All right," he said meekly.

Romney reveled in the post-debate commentary. *Newt's the pussycat and I'm the aggressor, they say,* he thought. *The press says I proved I'm tough.* Mitt loved that. In Tampa, Gingrich had complained that the audience was too quiet; in Jacksonville, he whined that Boston had stacked the hall (which it had) and the audience was too loud. Romney found it hilarious, and vaguely pathetic.

This guy is like Goldilocks, Mitt thought. *Has to have everything just right—or he falls apart.*

GINGRICH'S DISINTEGRATION LOOKED more like dismemberment two days after Jacksonville, when his bus pulled up outside the Centro Internacional de la Familia church, in Orlando. He was there for what had been billed as a Hispanic town hall meeting. Inside the church, there was row after row of vacant pews and forty-two voters. For an hour after the scheduled starting time, Newt and Callista remained cloistered on the bus. When they finally entered, it was announced that the event was no longer a town hall; the candidate would speak briefly, then take pictures with the scant few voters who'd turned up. Standing behind a Lucite lectern, Gingrich talked for a bare eight minutes and eleven seconds.

The vertigo that Newt was experiencing was extreme. Coming out of South Carolina, he'd been greeted in Florida by massive crowds—six thousand in Naples, four thousand in Sarasota—and gotten news that Sheldon Adelson was bestowing another $5 million on Winning Our Future. Gingrich's plan was to spend his week-plus in Florida talking about little except Romneycare and Obamacare. But the strategy was ripped up by the taunts of Team Romney, which provoked him into defensiveness and endless relitigation of issues that tormented him, especially the invective about how he exited his speakership under an ethical cloud.

The "resign in disgrace" line echoed in Newt's ears louder than anything else. His time in the speaker's chair was the crowning achievement of his life. And here Romney and his lackeys were crapping all over it. To his friend Vin Weber, the only Mitt adviser Gingrich really knew or trusted, he sent text after text, e-mail after e-mail, lodging fierce complaints.

Weber thought Gingrich had a point. The speakership attacks were unfair, untrue, and, in fact, overkill. Weber was the rare Romneyite with a window into Newt's psyche. He realized that killing Gingrich was necessary for Mitt to win. But there was a difference, Vin believed, between a dignified assassination and a public drawing and quartering. More than once, Weber warned Rhoades and others in Boston that some of their attacks were digging at Newt in a bad way. You're at risk of making him not just mad but crazy, Weber said. And crazy people can be really dangerous.

For Gingrich, the line between fuming and full-on berserk was thin— and a story that he read on January 29 threatened to push him across it. The piece was in that Sunday's *New York Times*. Its headline read FACING SECOND LOSS TO GINGRICH, ROMNEY WENT ON WARPATH. The article chronicled in vivid detail Boston's consultations the day after South Carolina, describing the Romneyites' plan to "eviscerate" Gingrich in Florida by "mak[ing] Newt mad and Mitt meaner."

The word "eviscerate" seemed to flip a switch inside Newt and Callista. They repeated it over and over to each other: "eviscerate." Everything they despised about Romney was embedded in that word: the premeditation, the soullessness, the malignancy, the arid amorality.

That morning the couple attended services at the Exciting Idlewild Baptist Church, in Lutz, just north of Tampa, a megachurch so mega that it had its own Starbucks in the lobby. Afterwards, Gingrich stood in the parking lot with the media and unleashed a spree of rhetorical violence that made Weber seem prescient. Calling Romney a "pro-abortion, pro-gun-control, pro-tax-increase moderate from Massachusetts" using "money from Wall Street" to spread pernicious lies—"as big an outrage as I've had in my career"—Newt predicted that Mitt would be unable to secure the requisite number of delegates to claim his party's nomination. "When you add the two conservatives together," Gingrich maintained, referring to himself and Santorum, "we clearly beat Romney." He vowed to spend the months ahead waging a "straight-out contest" that would go on all the way to Tampa.

Gingrich's invocation of Santorum would likely have surprised the former senator—had he been around to hear it. But not only was Santorum not in Lutz, he was on his way out of Florida that day, heading home to suburban Virginia.

Since Iowa, almost nothing had gone right for Rick. His assumption that a virtual tie would provide a boost had proved badly mistaken. After his fifth-place finish in New Hampshire, he entered South Carolina broke and disorganized. He secured the endorsement of a group of prominent evangelicals but was able to do nothing with it. By the time the news arrived that he had beaten Romney in the Hawkeye State, the media had moved on. In the Palmetto State, he finished third, with just 17 percent of the vote. The one bright spot was that his performances in the Florida debates were strong, propelled by a searing critique of Romneycare—that it would render Mitt unable to prosecute the president on Obamacare. "Your mandate is no different than Barack Obama's mandate," he said in Jacksonville. "Folks, we can't give this issue away in this election."

But the depletion of Santorum's kitty made it impossible for him to be a factor in such a vast and vastly expensive state. Sagging again in the polls, absent from his own bed for a month, Santorum had another reason for going home: having challenged Mitt to release his tax returns, he felt obligated to do the same. Unlike Romney, however, Santorum had no task force in the wings to put his finances in order. All he had was his home computer and TurboTax.

ON JANUARY 30, ROMNEY held his last event on the eve of the Florida primary: a massive rally at the Villages. Everything about the Villages was massive, truth be told. A sprawling retirement community fifty miles northwest of Orlando, it had nearly 100,000 residents, 63 recreation centers, 540 holes of golf, and a conservative political bent. Owned by Gary Morse, a co-chair of Romney's Sunshine State campaign, the Villages had given a corporate donation of $250,000 to Restore Our Future; Morse's wife, Renee, had written the super PAC a matching personal check. If any place in Florida was Romney Country, this was it.

As the campaign bus rolled toward the event in the early evening, White and Romney were gabbing in the back. Mitt's recitation of "America the

Beautiful" had become a standard trope of his stump speech—roundly derided by the press, cringed at by some of his own donors, but beloved by the candidate and his pal Bob. Hey, White said. Why don't you *sing* it tonight?

Really? Romney's young trip director, Charlie Pearce, thought—as visions of Mike Dukakis in the tank, looking like Rocky the Flying Squirrel, raced through his mind.

Um, I'm not sure about that, Bob, Pearce said. Can the governor actually sing?

At Pearce's urging, Romney rendered a muted, a capella audition right there on the bus.

Not bad, Pearce said.

Not bad at all, White agreed.

The serenade Romney offered from the stage was slightly off-key. The five-thousand-strong crowd didn't seem bothered; plenty of them sang along. The video hit YouTube instantly and went viral just as quickly. Any mockery slid off Romney's back. He had a ball doing it; he considered himself quite the crooner.

The victory Romney racked up the next day was every bit as impressive as Gingrich's had been ten days earlier. The top-line totals—46 for Mitt, 32 percent for Newt, 13 for Santorum—told only some of the story. In addition to whipping his main rival within the constituencies that were part of Romney's bedrock electoral coalition (the affluent, the educated, the moderate, the non-evangelical), Mitt carried conservatives and Tea Party supporters, and tied Newt among Christian conservatives.

That Romney had won big in the Sunshine State was beyond dispute. But there was no denying that he also had won ugly. The degree of the unprettiness was causing qualms among GOP leaders, who feared that the damage Mitt and Newt were inflicting on each other might prove hard to heal in time for the general election.

In his victory speech in Tampa, Romney sought to allay those concerns. "Primary contests are not easy," he declared. "As this primary unfolds, our opponents in the other party have been watching, and they like to comfort themselves with the thought that a competitive campaign will leave us divided and weak. But I've got news for them. A competitive primary does not divide us—it prepares us, and we will win. And when we gather back here in Tampa seven months from now for our convention, ours will be a united party with a winning ticket for America."

Yet the Republican establishment's jitters about Romney were rooted in more than the harsh tone of the Florida contest. In the last three primaries, Mitt's core claim—electability in the fall—had taken a beating. A new NBC News/*Wall Street Journal* poll found that his unfavorability rating among independent voters had risen twenty points, from 22 to 42 percent, since December. Two months earlier, Romney had been beating Obama 47–34 among those voters. Now the numbers were reversed: Obama was besting Mitt 44–36.

Some of that damage was attributable to the Gingrich and Perry broadsides on Mitt's Bain tenure and his income taxes. But much of it had been self-inflicted, most notably by the string of flubs—from his fear of pink slips to his enjoyment of firing people to his "not very much" in speaker's fees—which gave the impression he suffered from a hybrid of affluenza and Tourette's. At the debate in Tampa, Romney had piled one more brick on his back: his statement that, when it came to immigration, "the answer is self-deportation." And the morning after the primary, he added yet another.

Making his victory lap on the morning shows, Romney was asked by CNN's Soledad O'Brien if he understood the "needs of average Americans."

"I'm in this race because I care about Americans," Romney said. "I'm not concerned about the very poor; we have a safety net there. If it needs repair, I'll fix it. I'm not concerned about the very rich; they're doing just fine. I'm concerned about the very heart of America, the 90 to 95 percent of Americans who right now are struggling."

With his ostensible dismissal of "the very poor," Romney hadn't quite snatched defeat from the jaws of victory. The triumph in Florida was still real enough: the nomination was within his grasp now—everyone knew that. Later that day, he would become the first Republican candidate to receive Secret Service protection; his code name would be Javelin; Ann's would be Jockey.

But in Boston, no one doubted that "very poor" would leave a mark. There was nothing to be done. The candidate's stumbles and fumbles were a part of the environment, like oxygen. Faced with a choice between wringing their hands or keeping their eyes on the prize, his people picked the latter. Rhoades had even developed a catchphrase to ward off frustration with his guy's gaffes. Whenever the candidate stuck his foot in his mouth, the campaign manager would shrug and say, "Mitt happens."

13

FEAR AND LOATHING IN THE MOTOR CITY

AGAINST A BACKDROP OF royal blue drapes, flanked by American flags, the Romneys stood before a swarm of reporters just off the lobby of the Trump International Hotel Las Vegas. It was February 2, two days after Florida and two days before the Nevada caucuses, and Mitt was there to receive a prize he had sought with ardor but also ambivalence: the endorsement of the Donald.

Since his decision to forgo a pursuit of the presidency in favor of his TV paycheck, Trump had played a noisy—and, in the view of many establishmentarians, noisome—role in the race. He had tried in December to moderate his own Republican debate, which fell apart for lack of interest. He had switched his political affiliation to independent and was fulminating about waging a third-party bid. But none of this had kept most of the GOP candidates, actual and potential, from queuing up outside Trump Tower to kiss his ring. Palin, Huckabee, Bachmann, Perry, Gingrich, Cain: all had called or met with the Donald in search of his favor.

And so had Romney, first paying a visit to Trump in New York in September and then staying in touch by phone. The Donald took a shine to Mitt, who struck him as looser and funnier than he came across on TV. And Romney liked Trump, too. For a man of such extreme squareness, Romney

took curious pleasure in the company of oddballs and showboats. After en-
counters with Trump, he would say to his aides, "Isn't he fun?"

Jollity wasn't the only motivating factor in Romney's romancing of
Trump. The Donald was a Tea Party favorite and a potential fund-raising
dynamo. (Some in Boston wondered whether Trump could be to Romney
what George Clooney was to Obama.) He had also been endowed by the
freak show with a puissant bully pulpit—and Romney preferred to see
Trump bullying Mitt's rivals rather than him.

But Romney was aware that hitching his wagon to Trump entailed political risks. The birther issue was nothing but trouble, Mitt thought: ludicrous on the merits, repellent to swing voters, and a needless distraction
from Obama's real vulnerabilities. *(If we stay focused on the economy, we can
beat this guy; shut up about Kenya, please.)* And Romney knew that many
New York donors and members of the mainstream media considered Trump
a punch line. For the Mitt-Donald meeting in Gotham, Rhoades had Will
Ritter fly down from Boston to execute one firm directive: "No fucking pictures." So Ritter played decoy, holding court with the press outside Trump
Tower—standing by the wrong entrance so that Romney could enter and
exit through a different door, undetected and unmolested.

Boston tried to approach the endorsement itself with similar delicacy.
When Romney learned he had won the Trump Primary, it was a few days
before the vote in Florida. The Donald suggested he bestow the honor there,
but Newhouse polled the matter and found that it made more sense to wait
until Nevada; that Trump wasn't popular in either place, but he was less
unpopular in the Silver State. Trump pushed for a splashy event at his hotel
just off the Strip—*Tallest building in Las Vegas!*—but Boston seized control
of the logistics. Fearing an iconic rich-guy photo in front of a gaudy water-
fall or gold-encrusted columns, Ritter spent a bundle to install a setup that
was as drab as possible. (Trump later deemed it "gorgeous.")

Yet even as the stagehands were at work, Romney and Rhoades were
wondering if they were being played. The night before, a number of top-
shelf media outlets—from *The New York Times* and *The Wall Street Journal*
to CNN—reported that the Trump endorsement was going to Gingrich.
Rhoades couldn't believe Trump would have the gall to set them up that

way. On the other hand, the campaign manager thought, *This is a circus, and Trump's an entertainer.*

Romney's doubts didn't fully abate until he and Ann saw Trump in the flesh in his hotel suite that morning. Trump had been waxing exuberant to Romney's staff about the media horde on hand. ("Biggest crowd of press you've ever gotten!") He was eager to take questions from the reporters after the endorsement. Envisioning a birtherfest, Boston wanted no part of it. Three times already, Trump had tried to cajole Mitt's press secretary, Andrea Saul, into having a Q&A. Three times, she waved him off. Now, in the elevator on the way downstairs, Trump implored Romney, We're going to take questions, right?

"I'm not taking questions," Mitt replied, digging in his heels. "*You* can take questions."

Trump could live with that.

Team Romney had no idea what Trump was going to say as he took the podium. Mitt and Ann gazed on, arms stiff at their sides, frozen half smiles on their faces. Watching the spectacle on TV in Boston, Gail Gitcho, the campaign's communications director, shook her head and thought, *This looks like a hostage situation.*

Liberation came quickly, at least. Trump's comments consumed less than two minutes. Mitt's remarks took three minutes—and included a pair of the most candid sentences of 2012. "There are some things that you just can't imagine happening in your life," he said. "This is one of them."

J UST AROUND THE CORNER on the Strip, Gingrich was bunkered in a hotel owned by a different billionaire—*his* billionaire, Sheldon Adelson—wondering why anyone ever thought he was about to receive the Donald's blessing. Newt and Callista were members of Trump National Golf Club, in Virginia. They considered its proprietor a friend. But that was irrelevant. "Trump plays the odds," Newt told his aides, and the odds were obviously in Romney's favor.

After Florida, Gingrich felt he needed to regroup. So he had pitched up at the Palazzo and convened an extended retreat with his consultants, major donors, and the ragtag crew that made up his campaign staff. For the better part of four full days, while Romney was beating the bushes for votes in Nevada, Gingrich and his allies were tucked away in windowless warrens and private dining rooms, eating and drinking, scheming and dreaming, and yak-yak-yakking.

Gingrich himself spent most of the first two days grousing and griping. The anger that started bubbling in Iowa and simmered through Florida had now reached a boil. Over and over, Newt berated Romney and his henchmen as a pack of lying liars whose level of mendacity he could scarcely comprehend. He also lashed out at his own people, yelling at them, insulting them ("That's a stupid thing to say"), ridiculing their suggestions ("You think that we're going to find the votes we need in *Maine*?"). Newt's staff averted their eyes. Never had they seen him quite so seethingly out of sorts.

At a dinner with donors on Friday, the night before the caucuses, Gingrich's mood began to brighten. Adelson rose and offered him a heartfelt tribute, talking about what a great friend to Israel he had been, how he would make "a fantastic president."

By the next morning, Gingrich was convinced he saw a route to his third resurrection: a long march through the South and the industrial Midwest to the Texas primary that spring. There he would emerge again as the frontrunner as Romney buckled under the weight of his Massachusetts record. Newt was sure that Santo would be gone by then. The guy had more children than campaign staff; he wasn't built for the long haul. Facing off one-on-one against Mitt, Newt would deny him a majority of delegates. Then the two of them would duke it out at the Republican convention.

The scenario now sustaining Gingrich was implausible, but it struck those who knew him best as all too typical. In trying to explain his old friend's behavior to Boston, Vin Weber often observed that Newt saw himself as the hero of an epic historical film unspooling in his mind. Gingrich was too smart not to grasp the damage that Romney and Restore had done to him in Iowa and Florida. But there would be nothing doughty about dropping out and throwing his support to Mitt. What Newt's psyche required was a fittingly dramatic end to his story arc. A convention-floor brawl for the heart and soul of the party would surely qualify.

Gingrich provided a public preview of the blockbuster brewing in his head late that Saturday night. The results of the caucuses were still rolling in, but it was clear he had been crushed by Romney. Rather than deliver a concession speech, Newt conducted a press conference—a twenty-two-minute montage of sarcasm, contumely, and free disassociation. He emphatically denied rumors that he was withdrawing from the race. He predicted his resurgence and its timing with demented certitude. He pledged to march all the way to Tampa. And then he applied his rhetorical mace to Mitt.

After listening to Newt mash his rival in florid terms yet again, *The New York Times*'s Jeff Zeleny asked him, "Can you be successful going forward if Mitt Romney is still in your head?" Scowling, sneering, Gingrich answered, "I'm not sure Mitt Romney is in my head . . . I'm sure that with a psychiatric degree, that will get you a tremendous opportunity to have new clients." Then he returned to lambasting Romney, calling him "substantially dishonest," "blatantly dishonest," and "fundamentally dishonest."

Even among a political class inured to over-the-top rhetoric from Gingrich, his unhingedness in Vegas caused mandibles to drop to sternums—and nowhere more so than in Boston. Thinking Gingrich was still a threat, Romney had devoted the better part of three straight days to defending his position in the Silver State. But his final victory margin was a whopping twenty-nine points.

After New Hampshire, Boston had believed the race might be over. After Nevada, certainty took hold. While Gingrich might stick around, encouraged by Adelson's largesse and the prospect of another debate scheduled for later in the month, the Romneyites were convinced that Newt was plainly cooked and possibly crackers. (Gingrich would win just one more primary—in his home state, Georgia.) As for Santorum, he wasn't even in Nevada. How could someone who had ceded the field ever be any sort of threat?

IT WAS A MIRACLE, in a way, that Santorum was still in the race at all. His special-needs daughter, Bella, had caught a cold while he was in South Carolina, and by the time he left the trail in Florida, her condition was spiraling downward. Rick and Karen had been dealing with Bella's fragile health since the day she born; they had a makeshift ICU in their home. But after a long night in which her heart rate kept rising and her breathing became more labored, they rushed her to the hospital, where the doctors diagnosed her with pneumonia. The last time Bella had been this bad off, she was on a ventilator for five weeks and almost died. If that situation repeated itself now, Santorum's campaign would be over.

Bella usually didn't react quickly to treatment. This time, she did. Twenty-four hours later, her lungs were nearly clear and her doctors at a loss to explain the rapidity of her recovery. The Santorums put it down to prayer. In any case, the scare had passed—and Rick bounded back into the fray. But rather than making a beeline for Nevada, he headed to Missouri, Minnesota, and Colorado, where the next set of contests would take place on February 7.

The leapfrogging strategy was a brainchild of his campaign manager, Mike Biundo. After three straight finishes near the bottom of the pack, Santorum was running out of cash. The media was writing him off. Nevada was a lost cause. (*Vegas isn't my town,* thought Rick.) If he didn't win something, somewhere, somehow, Santo was finished.

Biundo believed that victory was readily obtainable in Missouri, where Gingrich had failed to qualify for the primary ballot, and that the electorate in Minnesota's caucuses would be conservative enough that Santorum could prevail in them, too. While Colorado would be a dicier proposition, pulling off a shocker there wasn't out of the question. Though all three contests were nonbinding in terms of delegates, Biundo reckoned that if Santorum brought home two wins, the media narrative might shift to Rick's reemergence as the anti-Mitt. If he pulled off the trifecta, all the better. It's time to make a stand, Biundo told his boss.

Santorum sensed a new kind of energy when he returned to the hustings. In Colorado Springs, he made a surprise appearance with James Dobson, the prominent evangelical leader whose organization, Focus on the Family, was based in the state and influential with politically active conservatives. In Colorado and Missouri, he was accompanied by Foster Friess, the multimillionaire mutual fund manager who had emerged as Santo's super-PAC sugar daddy.

But it was the outpouring of concern over Bella that most inspired Santorum. His retreat from the trail to tend to his girl received wide media coverage, and now he was regularly being approached on rope lines by voters asking after her—especially by those with special-needs kids of their own. At one event, he noticed a father standing with his young daughter, who had Down syndrome, holding up a sign reading I'M FOR BELLA'S DAD. Santorum's momentum in the February 7 states seemed to be growing every day. He wondered if he would have chosen this path if he hadn't been pulled abruptly off the trail and compelled to take stock of his campaign. *Everything happens for a reason,* he thought.

Before Nevada, Team Romney did next to nothing to counter Santorum's moves. Missouri was as hopeless for Mitt as Nevada was for Rick—and Beeson and Weber agreed that Minnesota was a goner as well. But the campaign was confident about the outlook in Colorado, which Romney had carried in 2008. Having spent a ton of dough in Florida, Boston wasn't eager to pour dollars or Romney's precious time into a contest with no delegates at stake that Mitt was likely to win in any event. Beeson was a native of Colorado, knew its politics backward and forward. Don't worry, he kept saying. Santorum and Gingrich will split the evangelical vote, and we'll run right up the middle.

But Newt's tour de farce Vegas press conference, and the full-scale collapse it epitomized, had an unexpected spillover effect. On Super Bowl Sunday, February 5, Newhouse's polling started picking up a migration of Gingrich voters to Santorum in Colorado. Suddenly Boston's decision to have Romney camp out in Nevada was looking iffy—though Mitt remained unworried. Arriving in Colorado on Monday, he was greeted by big crowds; three thousand showed up to see him that night in Centennial.

Romney woke up the next morning to snow on the ground—the first bad sign of many he would encounter on February 7. The weather made him late to his first event. (Nothing rankled Mitt more than being off schedule.) His body man, Garrett Jackson, had picked up a stomach bug and stayed behind in Nevada—leaving Romney without his human security blanket. The Santorum-friendly polling trend from Sunday had accelerated Monday. The staff was bickering. Beeson's confidence was ebbing.

That morning, the political director sent out a preemptive memo to the press dismissing the importance of the three races that day because they would award no delegates. "John McCain lost 19 states in 2008, and we expect our opponents to notch a few wins too," Beeson wrote. But "it is diffi-cult to see what [they] can do to change the dynamics of the race."

In Denver, Romney retreated to his hotel room to rest up for his election night speech, telling his traveling team he wanted an on-time departure. But when the hour arrived, Mitt was still in his suite. He's watching the early returns on TV, Stevens told Charlie Pearce. He's spooked.

"Have you seen these numbers?" Romney asked Stevens a few minutes later in the suite.

"They suck," Stevens replied.

"We're going to lose Colorado," Romney said.

"Yeah, we are. It's not going to matter in the long run, but it's gonna be a pain in the ass."

The numbers, in fact, were extremely close, but the closeness only infu-riated Mitt. "Why didn't I come here more?" he asked. "We could've won."

Before his speech at the Tivoli Student Union, Romney stood three feet from a giant plasma screen backstage, still glued to the cable coverage. He had lost Missouri and Minnesota, as expected, but the final results weren't in yet for Colorado. As Pearce alerted him to the two-minute warning, a CNN reporter, broadcasting live from the event, appeared on the monitor and remarked on the meagerness of the crowd on hand.

Shooting daggers at Pearce, Romney snipped, "Did you hear that?"

"Guv, we've got as many as we're gonna get," Pearce said. "Let's get this over with."

Back at his hotel afterwards, Romney learned from Beeson that he had in fact lost all three contests. For the first time, Beeson entertained the pos-sibility that Mitt might not be the nominee—that GOP voters might be about to cast aside electability in favor of purity, driving the party off a cliff.

"This thing could be about to go *Thelma and Louise* on us," he said to his war room colleagues.

Up in his suite, Romney was equally funked. *Rick will surge now—he's far less damaged than Newt,* Mitt thought. *And I'll be starting all over again.* Romney puzzled through the potential reasons he had been swept: *We didn't visit or spend dollars in these states. Rick did a great deal. My "poor" state-ment. The Mormon Thing, Romneycare, unanswered attacks. I'm seen as the moderate, and he's the conservative alternative.*

Santorum's speech in Saint Charles, Missouri, sought to reinforce exactly that perception. "Tonight was a victory for the voices of our party, conservatives and Tea Party people, who are out there every single day in the vineyards building the conservative movement in this country," he said. "[On] health care, the environment, cap-and-trade, and on the Wall Street bailouts, Mitt Romney has the same positions as Barack Obama." Positioning himself as a populist antidote to Romney, he touted his vision of "supply side economics for the working man" and added, "I care about 100 percent of America." But he also injected a dose of God talk in the mix, taking Obama to task for "impos[ing] his secular values" on Catholics with his newly unveiled contraceptive mandate.

Like Romney, Santorum took the podium before he knew the outcome of Colorado for certain. When CNN called the state for him, he and Karen were so thrilled that they started snapping pictures of the TV screen. Santorum wrapped his arms around Biundo in a bear hug. Against the odds, they had gone all in and pulled off the trifecta. "This is going to be a game changer," Santorum said.

THE ROMNEYITES TRIED TO make the case to the contrary the next morning on a conference call with Mitt. They repeated their talking points about delegates, the long haul, and yadda, yadda, yadda. The candidate wasn't buying it. You guys can talk about that stuff all you want, he said. But for normal people just seeing the news, they're not going to say, Oh, those were just beauty contests. They're going to say, Wow, this Santorum guy has a little bit of something in him.

Romney was right about the tenor of the coverage. Biundo's bet that the press would treat Santo as the ultracon comeback kid had paid off. Eager to shift the storyline, Mitt held a press conference that day in Atlanta in which he inveighed against Obama on contraception and attacked Santorum from the right on spending. But Romney's splashier opportunity for a reset would come forty-eight hours later in Washington, where he was slated to appear at the annual meeting of CPAC.

Highly anticipated addresses were always a source of angst and agita in Romneyland—because Mitt's speechwriting operation really wasn't an operation at all. Romney considered himself an able pen; given his druthers, he would have handled all his wordsmithing himself. That being impractical, he had forged an authorial bond with Stevens. But Stuart had a great many other responsibilities, so their joint rhetorical endeavors were often shambolic and last-minute. In an effort to make the process less of a two-man show, Myers had brought on board a talented young writer, Lindsay Hayes, who had worked for Sarah Palin in 2008. It was Hayes to whom responsibility fell for drafting the Friday CPAC speech.

When Mitt got a look on Thursday morning at what Hayes had put on paper, he wasn't happy. *It's too light,* he thought. *I want a serious tone and lots of substance.*

After spending two hours with Stevens, Fehrnstrom, Flaherty, Chen, and Hayes debating how to change the speech, Mitt set off for the Virginia suburbs, where he had a fund-raising dinner and another speech to give the next morning before CPAC. He soldiered through the supper, which included taking 450 photos with donors, then went back to his hotel expecting a new draft to be waiting. Nope. Around 11:00 p.m., he convened a conference call with his people for another two hours. *No draft, no time in the morning—and why am I speaking in Virginia?* Romney unhappily thought. Exhausted, he called Ann at around 1:00 a.m., took a sleeping pill, and passed out.

Stevens and Hayes, working in shifts, pulled an all-night revision session. When Mitt showed up at the hotel where CPAC was being held, Stevens was still editing the speech. Romney had just one chance to practice it on the prompter, and even then, his people were still tweaking it as he did so.

To Romney, the point of the address was to explain that, while he wasn't a classic movement conservative, he had come to the creed through experience and now embraced it deeply. And for the first few minutes, he was cruising. "Not everyone has taken the same path to get here," he told the audience of activists. "My guess is some of you got here by reading Burke and Hayek. When I was your age, you could've told me that they were infielders for the Detroit Tigers."

But when Romney pivoted to defending his record in Massachusetts, his delivery seemed a mite awkward—in the manner of a speaker not completely comfortable or familiar with his text. "I fought against long odds in a deep-blue state," he said. "But I was a *severely* conservative Republican governor."

"Severely" was nowhere in Romney's script. The moment the modifier escaped his lips, Flaherty and Chen, seated in the front row, turned and gaped at each other, silently mouthing the offending word at the same time. Flaherty was Mitt's designated liaison to the right. He found the adjective superfluous and odd, and knew others would, too. *It's like in* A Few Good Men, *when Demi Moore gets up and says, "I strenuously object!"* he thought. *You either object or you don't object—there are no gradations.*

Romney fed himself happy talk about his performance. *Five standing ovations, glowing media reports—the speech was a hit,* Mitt thought. "Severely conservative" didn't trouble him too much. *I meant "severely" in the sense of "strictly." What a silly kerfuffle.*

The Obamans were certainly pleased to be provided with video of Romney touting the severity of his right-wingery. But Flaherty was correct that the reaction among conservatives would be equally strong. Among establishmentarians such as Rove, Romney's employment of the qualifier was a sign of his lack of confidence in his connection to the animating spirit of the party. To fire-breathers such as Limbaugh, it was an occasion for more mockery. "I may be a little giddy here," Rush chortled on his show that day. "I have never heard anybody say, 'I am *severely* conservative.' No, I've *never* heard anybody *say* it!"

Frazzled, fried, and missing his wife, Romney wanted a respite—a weekend jaunt to La Jolla to see Ann and collect himself. It had been a month since he'd spent a night in any of his homes. But the next day in Maine, there were caucuses happening, and Romney decided he couldn't afford a fourth straight loss in one week. From CPAC, he flew up to Portland for a hastily arranged town hall meeting that night and visits to a pair of caucus sites on Saturday. His plan was to bug out to California from there—but that itinerary was thwarted by an emergency strategy meeting called by Rhoades for Sunday in Boston.

Romney and his inner circle gathered in the third-floor conference room on Commercial Street at noon. Their mood was by turns dispirited, clear-eyed, and suffused with a sense of urgency. On the back of his trifecta,

Santorum had seized the momentum in the race; in the first national poll taken since his wins, he had jumped to an eye-popping fifteen-point lead. As the sole survivor, Santorum was now in a position to consolidate the large bloc of anti-Romney GOP voters behind him. Rhoades was adamant that if Santorum caught fire, he could be the nominee. Everyone agreed that the fuse had been lit—and they had to douse it immediately.

The next two contests were primaries in Michigan and Arizona on February 28, two weeks away. While the latter was safe territory for Romney, the former was not. Before the trifecta, Newhouse's polls had him up by ten points in the Wolverine State. But that lead had already evaporated, as Santo stormed ahead. Given Mitt's historical Michigan ties, the expectations of his winning there would be sky-high—and the reaction if he lost all the more debilitating.

Romney was under no illusions about his status in the state. Sure, he was the scion of George Romney. Sure, he was a Michigan native. Sure, he had won the primary there in 2008. On the other hand, Mitt hadn't lived in Michigan in forty years. He had been the governor of another state. Almost all of the voters who had supported his father were now dead. Then there was "Let Detroit Go Bankrupt," which had already been a problem with Motor City donors and over which he suspected he would take major flak in the primary. The state's Republican electorate had swung hard to the right; the Tea Party was ascendant. Though Mitt wasn't pleased to be running behind Santo, he wasn't shocked, either.

None of which made the prospect of losing Michigan any less daunting to him, or the scale of the challenges he faced any less dismaying. Before the meeting, he had raised with Stevens the possibility of skipping Michigan. "Is this winnable?" Mitt asked. "Because if it's not, we shouldn't go in there and spend millions of dollars just to lose."

Team Romney was certain that Michigan was winnable, and over the next several hours they laid out a plan to win it. Deputy campaign manager Katie Packer Gage, who was also a native of the state, proposed that they treat the two weeks before the primary as if it were a gubernatorial race— reminding Michiganders of Mitt and Ann's roots there, keeping them both stumping hard on the ground as much as humanly possible. As for dealing with Santorum, his years in Washington and his record on matters ranging from earmarks to spending presented plenty of juicy targets. Just as they had strafed Gingrich in Florida, they would carpet-bomb Santorum in Michigan.

Romney headed to the airport, where he hopped a small private jet with his Secret Service detail for La Jolla. Flying private was less an indulgence than an indignity. With the cost of the nomination fight now stretching the campaign's finances thin, he had decided to pay for his flight home out of his pocket, leaving his staff and the media behind.

He was resolved to do what was necessary to halt the Santo surge. *If I lose Michigan, I'll lose Ohio,* he thought. *If I lose Michigan and Ohio, I'll lose Illinois and Wisconsin. Then it's game over.*

Romney took a dim view of Santorum. *He's sanctimonious, severe, and strange,* Mitt thought. But he believed that Santorum was now as likely to be the nominee as he was. Between the trifecta, the contraception issue coming to the fore, and Mitt's vulnerability on health care, Santo was positioned to seize the momentum and send Romney packing. *At least it's not Newt,* Romney thought, recalling with a chuckle a recent line by Dick Armey, who said that Gingrich's "second-rate campaign has become a first-rate vendetta."

On the flight to California, Romney thought about what losing to Santo would mean. *La Jolla, family, and horses for Ann—not a bad outcome. I'm resigned to whatever happens. I know it'll be hard to get up for campaigning if I'm behind in the polls and my prospects don't look great, but I'll follow the course wherever it leads. And I won't stay in the race beyond the point of being able to win. If we can't reasonably get there, I'll exit the race to give Rick the best chance of beating Barack.*

For many in the Republican establishment, the specter of a Santorum coronation was too horrid to contemplate. But watching a flawed and faltering Romney struggle to put away the nomination was enflaming fears that his elevation might prove nearly as awful. In the wake of the trifecta, the salons of the Beltway's right-leaning potentates and pundits were abuzz with speculation about an alternative scenario. About the possibility of a white-knight candidate galloping onto the nominating field for a handful of contests late in the spring. About the desirability of a brokered convention that summer.

Mitt had heard the mutterings and dismissed them out of hand. *This talk of a brokered convention is nuts,* he thought—and maybe it was. But it was also getting louder and emanating from some serious sets of lips.

HALEY BARBOUR PICKED UP the phone and called Scott Reed to bewail the state of the race. That Romney was proving an inept candidate—incapable of connecting with voters, inspiring conservatives, or restraining himself from planting his penny loafers in his piehole—was no surprise. What troubled them more was that Mitt was winning only by burying his rivals in an avalanche of money and manure. On his present course, Romney seemed destined to implode or emerge from the nomination fight so grievously injured that he would be easy pickings for Obama.

Barbour and Reed started gaming out the white-knight scenario. They agreed that if Mitt won Michigan and fared well on Super Tuesday, a week later, there would be no denying him the prize. But they were unconvinced he would do either. The key question, then, was how many primary and caucus ballots a late entrant could still qualify for after March 6. Reed did the research and discovered that the answer was seven—including those in the mega-states of California, New Jersey, and Texas. If a white knight ran the table, he could collect about five hundred delegates—far short of 1,144, but enough to deny that number to Romney or Santorum and then take the fight to Tampa.

Dole's former campaign manager wasn't the only A-list GOP operator digging into such details. Ballot-access spreadsheets were circulating like samizdat all over the capital. Stan Anderson, a senior U.S. Chamber of Commerce official who had worked for Goldwater, Nixon, and Reagan, had put together a similar document and provided it to eager governors, congresspeople, and fund-raisers. In the Senate and the House, on K Street and at the RNC, the phone lines were burning up with chatter about the who, when, and how of enlisting a savior if Romney continued to stumble.

Barbour was doing more than kibitzing. He had taken on the mantle of the establishment's de facto white-knight headhunter. Among those who had considered running and declined in 2011, there were two Haley thought had the cachet required to sweep the party off its feet: Christie and Daniels.

In the days leading up to Michigan, Barbour sat down with each in Washington and beseeched him to step forward.

Christie was again receiving entreaties from far and wide, and he could understand why. If Santorum were the nominee, he thought, the race would be over the day after the convention. Gingrich was the worst human being he had ever met in politics. Romney, by contrast, he had come to like—though he believed that Mitt had been too guarded and timid, that he might not be edgy enough for the mood of the party or the country.

But Christie, after consulting with his political wizard DuHaime about the filing deadlines and dynamics of a brokered convention, evinced little interest in picking up a lance at this late date. The task of knocking Romney off his steed, saddling up in Tampa, then putting together and funding a campaign in the sixty-seven days between the convention and November 6—against Obama's $1 billion machine—sounded to him like career suicide.

Daniels was less dismissive of the idea, more in sync with his friend Haley and others about how wretched the race had been and how piss-poor Romney's performance. (*As I predicted,* Mitch thought.) Daniels had delivered the Republican State of the Union response in late January, at Boehner's behest. The speaker had been briefed on the mechanics of a white-knight entry, and was increasingly warm to the notion. He made sure Daniels knew he wanted the Hoosier to reconsider his 2011 abjuration, while at the same time encouraging Paul Ryan to step into the fray.

Mitch consulted his daughters to see whether there had been a change of heart, once again making the case that he was being asked to run for the good of the country. But the Daniels sorority was no more open to the idea than it had been a year earlier.

Foiled once again, Daniels turned his attention to some white-knight recruiting of his own. His two favored candidates were Jeb (with whom he got nowhere) and Ryan, who Daniels knew had doubts about Romney. The Wisconsin congressman kept talking about how he was trying to "fix" Mitt, prod him into being more substantive and ideologically rigorous. But so far, no dice.

One day, amid the alternative-hunting flurry, Daniels sent a text message to Ryan: "When you get a minute, give me a call."

A few seconds later, Daniels's phone rang.

"Paul! Oh, hey! Didn't expect you so quick!" Daniels said, then launched into his white-knight pitch. When Mitch paused to take a breath, he heard Ryan sigh.

"Well, shit," Ryan said—I thought you texted to tell me that *you* were going to do it!

Boston was barely aware of the mid-February scramble. Only Ron Kaufman and Wayne Berman—a Republican strategist and bundler who had become Romney's other key Beltway wise man—had even an inkling of the establishment's consternation. For now, the maneuvering hardly mattered; it was a big circle jerk. The question was whether it would remain so after February 28.

If Mitt falls apart in Michigan, Reed said, we might be in business.

ROMNEY STRODE OUT OF the vomitory at Ford Field, in Detroit, and took in the vomitous scene. Near the twenty-yard line of the football stadium was the stage from which he would deliver what his aides had billed as a major economic address. In front of it were twelve hundred folding chairs, not all of them filled; behind it, acres of empty AstroTurf; and, surrounding that, 65,000 vacant seats.

It was just before noon on February 24, the Friday before the primary on Tuesday. The Ford Field event was supposed to be the kickoff for Romney's sprint to the finish line, but it had morphed into a logistical nightmare. A few days earlier, the Detroit Economic Club, which was hosting the lunchtime speech, had switched the venue from the stadium's atrium to the field—raising alarms in Boston that went unheeded on the ground in Michigan. When Rhoades, at HQ, saw the setting on cable, he yelled, "Motherfucker!" and hurled a water bottle at the TV.

The drafting of the speech had been a replay of CPAC, only worse. The version Romney saw that morning was such a mess, it lacked any mention of the auto industry. After madly making edits on the bus ride to the stadium, Stevens printed out the pages on a balky portable printer while Romney sat in the hold room wondering where the final text was. With no time for a run-through, he took the stage and opened with an ad-lib. "This feels good, being back in Michigan," he said. "I like the fact that most of the cars I see are Detroit-made automobiles. I drive a Mustang and a Chevy pickup truck. Ann drives a couple of Cadillacs, actually."

The combination of the atrocious visuals and another Richie Rich gaffe turned Ford Field into a debacle for Romney—one Democrats did their level best to abet. The white-knight plotters' fear that Mitt would be hobbled by an ugly and protracted nomination fight was the Obamans' dearest hope. To stir the pot, the DNC had mobilized a spirited demonstration outside the stadium, with union workers marching and chanting in protest of Romney's stance on the auto bailout. A circling truck bore a huge sign with a menacing picture of Mitt and the message LET ROMNEY GO BANKRUPT.

Even more than Romney anticipated, his *Times* op-ed had shadowed him from the moment he arrived in Michigan. An editorial-board meeting with the *Detroit Free Press* was the nastiest he'd ever endured. Everywhere he went, even outside the Motor City, the bailout was all reporters wanted to cross-examine him about. True to form, Romney instructed them to read the op-ed and ignore the title, but it was no use. "That headline is killing me," he told Rhoades.

The first ad the campaign aired in the state slapped the favorite-son card on the table. Behind the wheel as he tooled around Detroit, Romney reminisced about attending the city's auto show as a boy with his father. (The tagline: "Michigan's been my home, and this is personal.") But in Newhouse's focus groups, the spot's theme backfired. voters either didn't care he was a Wolverine State native, didn't believe it, or resented the suggestion—asking, in effect, If you're from here, where have you been?

Michigan presented Romney with a vexing confluence of circumstances and imperatives. The need to win the primary. The hope of putting the state in play in the general election. The backlash against him on the bailout. The emotional resonance for him and Ann of returning to the place they were born and raised, surrounded by relatives, old friends, and free-floating ghosts. The cumulative force of it all cracked Mitt's shell of hyperrationality. A week out from the primary, undone by the coldness and hostility he was encountering, Romney threw up his hands. "Why are we even wasting our time?" he asked Gage. "Maybe we should just pull out."

And that was before Ford Field—and what followed two days later. On a quick trip to Florida for the Daytona 500, Romney got drenched with rain, was booed by fans, and made three comments for which he was roundly mocked by the press: a declaration of his love for "cars and sport"; his chiding of some onlookers for their ponchos, which he called "fancy raincoats . . . you really sprung for the big bucks"; and a Richie Rich reference to his "great friends who are Nascar team owners."

Back in Michigan, Ann Romney was steaming at the coverage Mitt was receiving. "All of us in this room know the media loves Barack Obama—they don't want anyone who has a chance of defeating him," she said at a luncheon in Midland. "I am so mad at the press, I could just strangle them!"

But even as the Romneys were teetering emotionally, Mitt was pulling even with Santorum in the state polls. From the air, Boston was bombarding its foe for supporting "billions in earmarks," while Restore blitzed him with a series of spots, including one that Larry McCarthy regarded as the cycle's toughest. Called "Values," it went after Santorum for voting to increase the debt limit (five times), supporting the notorious Bridge to Nowhere, and siding with Hillary Clinton about "let[ting] convicted felons regain the right to vote."

The attacks were "disgusting," Santo told his team. But, unlike Newt, he could withstand them. "I'm not Gingrich," he said. He knew his own record. He was proud of his record. He could defend his record, every jot and tittle of it, and damn well intended to. His media adviser, John Brabender, was used to these traits of Rick's: the chip on the shoulder, the compulsion to litigate, to forget about driving a message and instead behave like he was chairing a Senate subcommittee hearing. There was nothing to be done about it, Brabender thought. But, boy, it could be a pain.

The scale of the problem had become clear a few days earlier at the twentieth (and final) debate of the nomination fight, in Mesa, Arizona. For the first time, Santorum was in the crosshairs of his rivals. Rattled by the boisterous disapproval of the crowd, which had been stacked by Team Romney, he was snappy, equivocal, and deep in the Washington weeds. Explaining his vote for a provision that funded Planned Parenthood in spite of his "moral objection" to the program, he said it was part of "a large appropriation bill that includes a whole host of other things." Of his vote for No Child Left Behind, he argued that it was important to President Bush and that "sometimes you take one for the team." When Ron Paul labeled him a "fake," he protested, "I'm real, I'm real, I'm real."

Santorum thought the debate went fine. His advisers thought it was a disaster—as did Karen, who had been frustrated for some time by her husband's refusal to do debate prep. *(I know my record!)* Now she was furious with him. After letting her cool down, Rick asked for her opinion, and she minced no words.

"You blew it," she said.

Santorum had been blowing it for a while. He had started out in Michigan intent on delivering an economic message (*blue-collar, bailouts, manufacturing,* he thought). But, like an iron filing to a magnet, Santorum couldn't resist being drawn to social issues. In the days before the debate, he found himself defending past statements (that "the Father of Lies has his sights" on America), making newly controversial ones (that Obama's policies were not "based on the Bible"), and carping about contraceptives. Now, on the eve of the primary, he attacked Obama for "wanting everybody in America to go to college—what a snob!" Asked by ABC News's George Stephanopoulos about his reaction to JFK's famous 1960 speech on the separation of church and state, he said it made him want "to throw up."

Santorum's unforced errors dominated the closing hours of coverage before Michigan. When his advisers pointed out that attacking JFK wasn't exactly a wise strategy for luring Catholic Democrats and independents (who could vote in the open primary), Santorum shrugged. "They're not real Catholics," he said. When his team upbraided him for his lack of discipline, he shrugged again. Speaking his mind, no matter how inconvenient or impolitic it was, had gotten Santorum this far; he wasn't about to hold back now. Even if he could will himself to do so, which he manifestly couldn't.

"I'm the Popeye candidate," he told Brabender. "I am what I am."

WHAT SANTORUM WAS ON February 28 was the loser of Michigan, and Romney its survivor. The last hours were tense for Mitt and Ann, who surrounded themselves with dozens of relatives and friends to wait for the results at the Diamond Center, in suburban Detroit. Newhouse's final poll had the candidate up by just a point or two; Beeson believed that if the vote had taken place a day earlier, Romney would have lost. Instead he narrowly edged Santorum, 41 to 38 percent. "We didn't win by a lot, but we won by enough," Mitt said in his victory speech. "And that's all that counts."

The next morning, Romney flew to Ohio, where he sat down for a local TV interview. Two weeks earlier, Obama, seeking to defuse the fury over the birth control mandate, had offered a compromise along the lines of the Hawaii model that the president had initially been told was unworkable. In the Senate, a number of conservative counterproposals had been offered that were about to be voted on, including one submitted by Missouri senator Roy Blunt, which would have allowed employers to refuse to include contraception in health care coverage if it violated their religious or moral beliefs.

"Blunt-Rubio is being debated, I believe, later this week," the interviewer asked Romney, confusingly. (A less sweeping contraceptive proposal had been put forward by Florida senator Marco Rubio, which Blunt supported separately from his own.) "Have you taken a position on it?"

"I'm not for the bill," Romney replied. "The idea of presidential candidates getting into questions about contraception within a relationship between a man and a woman, husband and wife, I'm not going there."

Romney had never been asked a question about the Blunt provision publicly before. That he was hearing it now was no accident. All throughout the GOP nomination fight, Lis Smith, the Obama campaign's director of rapid response, had been feeding questions to reporters to pose to Romney, with the aim of inducing him to tack to the right—and that was what had happened here. But Mitt's response disappointed Chicago. Apparently, he was already beginning to pivot toward the center and into general election mode.

The moment the news broke, Flaherty's phone began ringing in Boston. The right was riled up. Flaherty knew that Romney was, in fact, in favor of the Blunt amendment; he'd simply been beclouded by it being called Blunt-Rubio. Moving quickly to clean up the mess, the campaign set up an interview for Mitt with Beantown radio host Howie Carr. "I didn't understand his question," the candidate said. "Of course I support the Blunt amendment."

Champagne corks popped in Chicago: Mitt could now be hit not only for conservative extremism but for flip-flopping too. And soon he would be open to charges of poltroonery on a related controversy. On the same day as the Blunt back-and-forth, Rush Limbaugh had taken a spin down the low road and attacked Sandra Fluke—a Georgetown law school student who testified before Congress in favor of employers being required to provide contraception in their health care plans, regardless of religious objections—as a "slut" and a "prostitute" who "wanted taxpayers to pay her to have sex." When Romney was asked about the remarks, he replied wanly, "It's not the language I would have used."

Romney's former guru Mike Murphy had e-mailed Mitt and urged him to take on Rush, whom Murphy saw as a paper tiger and a good foil—the perfect target for a "Sister Souljah moment." (The reference was to a famous incident in 1992, when Bill Clinton criticized an intemperate rapper to signal to centrist voters his willingness to confront extreme elements of his party's base.) Murphy received no reply from Romney, who was squeamish about the issue and wished it would just go away. His Boston brain trust, meanwhile, believed that taking on any prominent conservative was too risky for a candidate who was struggling to win the nomination and whose ideological bona fides were forever in doubt.

Struggling was how the Romneyites saw themselves, even as the outside world assumed Mitt had the nomination sewn up. They were staring down the barrel of eleven more contests on Super Tuesday, March 6, with polling that showed Mitt behind Santorum in many states. They were looking at a system of proportional delegate allocation that could make the climb to 1,144 agonizingly slow and painful. In Santo, they were facing a rival more in tune with large swaths of the GOP base. And in Newt, a maniac who might hang around indefinitely just to spite them.

"We could still lose this nomination!" Rhoades barked out at a strategy meeting at HQ in early March, startling Mitt. "We gotta break their fucking backs! We gotta break their will to win!"

The breaking of Santorum and Gingrich would take just a little more than a month—but it was not an easy stretch. Romney only narrowly beat Santorum in Ohio on Super Tuesday, and then was defeated by him in Alabama and Mississippi. But with a double-digit victory in Illinois on March 20, Mitt began to pull away. The next day, Jeb Bush endorsed him; a week later, Rubio climbed on board. A few days before the Wisconsin primary, on April 3, Ryan did the same and linked arms with Romney on the campaign trail. "I'm just convinced now that if we drag this thing on through the summer," Ryan told Fox News, "it's going to make it that much harder to defeat Barack Obama."

Few Republicans would have disagreed—and yet the doubts about Romney that had troubled so many for so long had not disappeared. The nomination fight had laid bare many weaknesses of Mitt's, some long known, others brand spanking new. From Bain and his tax returns to his array of Richie Rich gaffes, Romney's public image had taken a hellacious beating. His campaign had shown itself to be capable enough, but also insular and thoroughly tactical. His fund-raising operation was impressive but spent, and the campaign was running on fumes. The Republican base remained wary of him; independents thought far worse. Maybe most problematic, the man who set out to run as Mr. Fix-It on the economy had saddled himself with far-right positions on a panoply of social and cultural issues that put him in a bad way with critical voting blocs: women, Latinos, young voters.

Boston professed no worries about any of this. The nomination fight was over. A new world lay ahead. "I think you hit a reset button for the fall campaign," Fehrnstrom told CNN the morning after the Illinois primary. "Everything changes. It's almost like an Etch A Sketch. You can kind of shake it up and restart all over again."

Fehrnstrom's gaffe was greeted with gales of derision, but no surprise. That Romney needed to reset was plain for all to see. That he would sprint to the center was taken for granted. What no one imagined was that the candidate didn't see it that way at all—that what Romney had in mind wasn't to Etch A Sketch but instead to double down.

PART THREE

14

THE PUGNACITY OF HOPE

BARACK OBAMA ARRIVED AT the Marriott Wardman Park hotel, in Washington, bouncing on the balls of his feet and bearing the eye of the tiger. It was April 4, the day of the Republican primary in Wisconsin, and Obama had ventured three miles from the White House to address a lunch hosted by the Associated Press. He'd been looking forward to this speech, not least because journalistic protocol dictated that there would be no applause. He had an argument to make and wanted to make it without interruption. The speech was a reprise of the one he delivered in Osawatomie, only hotter and more partisan. His two main targets, Mitt Romney and Paul Ryan, were in the Badger State, still scavenging for primary votes for Mitt. But for Obama, the general election started now—with a bang and not a whimper.

He refrained from assailing Ryan by name, but he blistered the newly released Republican House budget, of which the congressman was the chief architect. "A Trojan horse," he called it. "Thinly veiled social Darwinism." "So far to the right it makes the Contract with America look like the New Deal." Turning to his soon-to-be opponent, Obama continued, "Governor Romney has said he hoped a similar version of this plan from last year would be introduced as a bill on day one of his presidency. He even called it 'marvelous'—which is a word you don't often hear when it comes to describing a budget." The audience laughed, and Obama added drily, "It's a word you don't often hear generally."

Though Obama had never seen Romney in the best light, Mitt's performance as he scrabbled to the nomination had ratcheted down the dimmer switch. Before, Obama perceived Romney the way many others did: as a man with no compass or true north, whose only convictions were that wealth was good and being wealthy qualified him to be president. But watching Romney extol the Ryan budget, toe the hard-right line on immigration, and refrain from Sister Souljahing anyone—not Limbaugh, not Trump—made Obama wonder. "Maybe he really believes these things," he said to Plouffe.

Obama was alternately heartened and sobered by Mitt's difficulties in dispatching his cloddish rivals. His first thought was: *They're not exactly Hillary Clinton.* His second was: *And yet he could still beat me.* The juxtaposition caused him to shake and scratch his head. He said in amazement to his aides, "This guy's having trouble with Rick Santorum, but I could still lose to him."

Chicago and the West Wing agreed, and lived every day in fear. Their boss's position had improved appreciably since its autumn nadir, but not enough for any kind of comfort. The president's approval rating had inched up to 47 percent—decent, yet still shy of the 50 percent required for an incumbent to feel secure. The economy remained a ten-ton anvil around Obama's neck. His people had been praying for the kind of slow but steady improvement on the jobs front that would let them run an updated version of Reagan's "Morning in America" campaign. Instead they had been handed a succession of fits, starts, and false dawns, in which respectable jobs reports were followed by anemic ones, creating in the electorate a widespread, free-floating angst—with just a third of voters saying the economy was improving and two-thirds believing the country remained on the wrong track. Gas prices were rising. European banks were teetering. The Middle East was a mess. Plouffe constantly wrung his hands over "an external threat to the main engine." So did Obama, who told a friend, "I'm really running against the economy, Iran, and energy prices."

The Obamans could see why Romney wanted to wage an all-economy-all-the-time campaign. But they believed that both the candidate and his operation were flawed. Boston was certainly good at killing, Plouffe pointed out—and that was hardly unimportant. He and Obama were impressed by how the Romneyites had played the super-PAC game; if not for Restore Our Future, they were convinced, Santorum would have prevailed. But Boston was all tactics and no strategy, Axelrod argued, which explained the campaign's rightward lunges to survive each battle, with no regard for the war to come.

That war, to be sure, would largely be fought on the economy. But by staking his entire claim to the presidency on his superiority in that sphere, Romney had endowed the Obamans with a dead-simple strategic imperative: to disqualify him as an economic steward. And thanks to Bain, the Ryan budget, and Mitt's job-creation record in Massachusetts, the president's team believed they had ample material to work with.

Then there were questions of character. The Obamans had been polling and focus-grouping on Romney for months. What they had discovered was that, while voters liked him on paper—successful businessman, governor, family man, close to his church—the more three-dimensional exposure they had to him, the less favorable their impressions were. The Bain and income tax controversies, along with his Richie Rich gaffes, had fed perceptions of him as an alien to the middle class at best and a Wall Street greedhead at worst. According to Joel Benenson's research, 90 percent of voters had opinions about Mitt; his ratings on the "cares about people like me" scale were abysmal. A surprising number of focus group participants even brought up the Seamus story as a sign of his callousness. (Plouffe was almost as fixated on trying to figure out how to exploit the car-roof-riding canine as he was on keeping the Strait of Hormuz open.)

"You live in Pittsburgh and you've got dirt under your fingernails, who do you want to have a beer with?" a senior strategist for the reelect observed to a reporter. "It ain't Mitt Romney. You're like, 'Shit, I'd rather have a beer with the black guy than him.'"

The disembowelment the Obamans had in mind would be savage—and a stark deviation from the animating spirit of 2008. Although they had hit McCain hard four years earlier, running more negative ads than any campaign in history, the balance between hope-and-change and search-and-destroy had still tilted to the sunnier side. Tearing Mitt to pieces posed risks to Obama, whose likability was among his main political assets. And it ran contrary to his self-image as a herald of an elevated brand of politics. But Obama was resigned to running a nastier, grittier campaign this time. I'm an incumbent, he told his team. This goes with the territory. The country can't afford for us to lose.

Yet one aspect of 2008 would be not only revived but also amplified in 2012: the expansion of the electorate and the appeal to what Messina called the "Obama base." With the nation evenly divided, the GOP nominee all but guaranteed 47 or 48 percent at the polls, and Obama's standing less than robust with independent voters, the reelect would have to rely on turnout among the ascendant coalition that had fueled his landslide four years back: minorities (especially Latinos), socially liberal college-educated whites (especially women), and young voters.

For Obama, this would mean employing the powers of incumbency to jazz up those voting blocs. But it would also entail another angle on the disqualification of Romney. Over the past months, Chicago had staged incursions into the Republican arena, with ads and media hits aimed at Romney's seeming lack of core convictions—to give him fits with the right and elongate his season in the barrel. Now the campaign shifted gears. "He's the most conservative nominee that they've had going back to Goldwater," Plouffe told *The New York Times*.

When it came to the Obama coalition, the president's team saw it as critical to keep Romney from shimmying to the center—even as they continued to stoke his image as spineless. Plouffe believed there was precedent for merging the two threads into a single yarn: Bush 43's indictment of Kerry as both a flip-flopping phony and a liberal extremist.

"When Romney tries to Etch A Sketch, we're not just gonna say, 'Oh, there goes old Mitt Romney again! Who knows where he stands?'" Plouffe explained. "We're gonna say, 'He is once again showing he'll say anything— he has no core.' But we're also gonna say, 'Don't be fooled, we know where he stands. Potentially abortion will be criminalized. Women will be denied contraceptive services. He's far right on immigration issues. He supports efforts to amend the Constitution to ban gay marriage.'"

But the Obamans intended to go beyond painting Romney as excessively conservative. "He's the fifties, he is retro, he is backward, and we are forward—that's the basic construct," one Chicagoan said. "If you're a woman, you're Hispanic, you're young, or you've gotten left out, you look at Romney and say, 'This fucking guy is gonna take us back to the way it always was, and guess what? I've never been part of that.'"

EVERY WEDNESDAY NIGHT, the members of the Obama high command convened at One Prudential Plaza. On April 11, they were in Messina's office when someone walked in and reported that Hilary Rosen, a Democratic strategist and CNN pundit, had just said something stupid on TV. Appearing on *Anderson Cooper 360,* Rosen was talking about Romney's approach to gender issues. "[He is] running around the country saying, 'Well, you know, my wife tells me that what women really care about are economic issues, and when I listen to my wife, that's what I'm hearing,'" she said. "Guess what? His wife has actually never worked a day in her life."

Rosen had just slammed a stay-at-home mother of five and breast cancer survivor with MS; Twitter was blowing up over her comments. The reaction in Chicago was instantaneous and unanimous: We have to denounce her—so who's going to send the first tweet?

Messina did: "I could not disagree with Hilary Rosen any more strongly. Her comments were wrong and family should be off limits. She should apologize." Followed by Axelrod. "Also disappointed in Hilary Rosen's comments about Ann Romney. They were inappropriate and offensive." Followed by Cutter: "Families must be off limits on campaigns, and I personally believe stay at home moms work harder than most of us do."

Rosen was putting her own kids to bed in Washington when she heard a cacophony of chirping from incoming tweets on her desktop computer. That thousands were condemning her from the right came as no surprise, but Chicago's piling on seemed inexplicable—until she received an e-mail from Cutter a few minutes later. We have to protect Michelle, it said.

The urgency in Obamaworld about shielding the first lady was high. She remained by far the most popular figure in the administration. In a role reversal from 2008, she was less polarizing than her husband; she was a crossover figure who energized volunteers while appealing to the middle.

The campaign feared that if she became a lightning rod again, she would retreat. And the best way of keeping her from being attacked was to declare spouses and families a no-go area, as Cutter had been doing since the last campaign, when she served as Michelle's chief of staff.

No one was more adamant about that prohibition than the president himself. A month earlier, he'd been furious when Santorum brought up Malia in an interview with Glenn Beck, questioning her taking a spring break trip to Mexico despite State Department travel warnings. (Messina phoned Santo's strategist Brabender and warned, "If he talks again about the girls, we're going to have a problem.")

Obama barely knew who Rosen was. Does she work for the campaign? he asked Plouffe in the Oval Office the morning after the foofaraw flared up. No, she doesn't, Plouffe replied. Doesn't matter, Obama said. We need to be unambiguous. Families are off-limits, period. This isn't how we play.

A few hours later, a message went out from Michelle's official Twitter account: "Every mother works hard, and every woman deserves to be respected." Next it was her husband's turn. "There's no tougher job than being a mom," he told an Iowa TV anchor in an interview in the Diplomatic Room. "When I think about what Michelle's had to do . . . that's work. Anybody who would argue otherwise, I think, probably needs to rethink their statement."

The Romneys were both chagrined about Rosen's comments, but quickly clocked the potential upside. "She said *what?*" Ann exclaimed to Katie Packer Gage over the phone. Well, that's offensive to me, Mrs. Romney went on. And, boy, it's stupid politically. We can really go after them on that.

And Boston promptly did, signing Ann up for Twitter and having her send her maiden missive: "I made a choice to stay home and raise five boys. Believe me, it was hard work." Within twenty-four hours, the campaign was selling bumper stickers that read MOMS DRIVE THE ECONOMY, the RNC was hawking coffee mugs (MOMS DO WORK: VOTE GOP), and Beth Myers blasted out a fund-raising e-mail with the subject line "War on Moms" that read, "If you're a stay-at-home mom, the Democrats have a message for you: you've never worked a day in your life."

That Rosen had said nothing of the sort was irrelevant in Romneyland. Since the start of the contretemps over contraception, Democrats had been pummeling Republicans for waging a "war on women," to no small effect. Romney was on the wrong side of a yawning gender gap: nineteen points, 57–38, according to a mid-April ABC News/*Washington Post* poll. Anything that might begin to close that margin and reverse the overarching dynamic was worth trying. And the sight of the White House and Chicago tossing Rosen under the bus (and then rolling back and forth over her on the pavement) encouraged the Romneyites to keep flogging the flap.

The Obamans were dubious that *l'affaire* Rosen would budge a single vote, so deeply burned in were Romney's problems with the fairer sex. A year earlier, in April 2011, with his rivals on the right all having pledged to end federal funding for Planned Parenthood, Romney joined them. A year later, at a March campaign event in Missouri, he shorthanded his position thus: "Planned Parenthood, we're going to get rid of that."

The degree to which that quote stuck to Romney startled the reelect's research director, David Simas. In focus group after focus group, undecided female voters voiced hostility toward Mitt for his supposed desire to abolish Planned Parenthood; they saw him as paternalistic and controlling. (One member of Mitt's ad team described the quote to colleagues as the "Let Detroit Go Bankrupt" of social issues.) By contrast, even at the height of the Rosen ruction, not a soul in the focus groups brought her comment up.

The picture was hazier with two other components of the coalition of the ascendant: Latinos and the young. Obama's leads with them were even greater than with women: a jaw-dropping forty-seven points, 69–22, among Hispanics, and twenty-six points, 60–34, among voters aged eighteen to thirty-four. The problem with both was a lack of enthusiasm.

Obama's relationship with the Latino community had been rocky. There was disappointment about his failure to achieve comprehensive immigration reform. There was dismay about the 2010 defeat of the DREAM Act, which promised a path to citizenship for those who arrived in the country illegally as children. There was disquiet over the administration's having carried out a record number of deportations. As for young folks, they had been brutalized by the awful job market and deflated by the paucity of progress on issues they cared about, especially climate change.

Romney's self-inflicted wounds with Hispanics were severe. Beyond the toxic rhetoric of "self-deportation," Mitt had vowed to veto the DREAM Act if it were passed and proudly welcomed the support of some of the political figures most despised by Latinos for their harsh restrictionist stances on immigration—from former California governor Pete Wilson to Kansas secretary of state Kris Kobach. But the Obamans feared that Boston and the conservative super PACs would wage a viciously negative ad assault designed to suppress Latino turnout. And they worried that the kids would do what they usually did on Election Day: shrug and stay home.

The Obamans had a little more than six months to eradicate these cases of electoral ennui. On April 14, in an interview with Univision, the president promised to pursue immigration reform in 2013 if he were reelected. A week later, he devoted his Saturday radio address to his support for forestalling a hike in interest rates on federally subsidized student loans, and then set off on a barnstorming tour of colleges in Colorado, Iowa, and North Carolina.

Behind the curtain, more moves were afoot, in particular the possibility of implementing a modified version of the DREAM Act through executive action. Obama's political team was divided over the proposal. Plouffe worried it might be seen as amnesty by fiat, raising the hackles of white working- and middle-class voters in states such as Ohio and Virginia, while others argued that it would jolt Hispanics out of their tepidness toward Obama. The president was leaning toward doing it, persuaded by the merits of the policy and willing to roll the dice on the politics.

The most furtive scurrying, though, revolved around an even more freighted proposition: Obama at last revealing himself as in favor of gay marriage. Since the September 2011 meeting in the Roosevelt Room when he told his people he was ready to go public, they had deliberated over the execution and timing ad infinitum and ad nauseam—but now a rough plan was in place. On Saturday, May 5, Obama would formally kick off his campaign with rallies in Ohio and Virginia. The next week, Chicago would flood the airwaves with a sixty-second positive ad, backed by a $25 million buy, in nine battleground states. Shortly thereafter, Obama would cast off the cloak of obfuscation and make civil rights history.

The plan was solid. The plan was sound. The plan was exciting, even. But there was one small problem with the plan: someone forgot to tell Uncle Joe.

B IDEN HAD NEVER GIVEN much thought to same-sex matrimony. He was all good with the gays, no doubt about that; Joe had no patience for discrimination of any kind toward anyone. He remembered that, when he was a boy, his father spoke out when people made anti-gay cracks. In the Senate and the White House, Biden had gay staffers—though he wasn't sure who or how many. (His gaydar was nonfunctional.) His wife, Jill, was for gay marriage, as were his children. But his church was against it, and that meant something to Joe, as the contraception hoo-ha demonstrated all too clearly.

Biden's epiphany came at the end of April, when he was out in L.A. on a fund-raising trip. At an LGBT round table at the home of a gay couple, he spent some time in the kitchen with them and their two young kids, who gave him flowers; the warm family scene moved him. The first questioner at the event asked, What do you really think about us—gay people?

I think it's all about love, Biden said, and then it dawned on him: *It's time.*

The L.A. sojourn was part of a busy and satisfying spring for the VP. After the uneasiness between him and the Davids in the fall, his role in the campaign had been carved out cleanly. Chicago told his chief of staff, Bruce Reed, that Biden would be the "sharp tip of the spear"—stepping out early, ahead of Obama, and framing the argument against the Republicans and Romney. In a series of big policy speeches on topics from manufacturing to tax reform to foreign policy, he'd done the job with gusto.

Returning from the West Coast, Biden started preparing for an upcoming appearance on *Meet the Press.* In his nearly forty years in Washington, he had been on the show some forty times. (Only Bob Dole and John McCain had made more appearances.) Joe loved the format. He loved the set. He felt right at home. None of which deterred his staff from prepping him to the gills. One of Biden's challenges in transitioning from the Senate to the vice presidency had been getting used to the fact that he was no longer a free agent; that whenever he opened his mouth, he was representing the administration. His people always worried when he went on *Meet* that his comfort level would lull him into behaving like a senator again—into speaking just for himself.

So Bidenworld approached his murder-boarding with diligence and care. The West Wing was involved, too; Plouffe and Carney sat in. Over several days, they devoted upwards of twelve hours to drilling Biden. They covered domestic policy, economics, foreign affairs, the campaign, the works. The only notable thing they somehow left out was gay marriage.

It was Friday, May 4, when Biden sat down with David Gregory to pre-tape their chat for that Sunday's show. When Gregory posed the question, Biden didn't think twice—and made a beeline for the kind of place his advisers feared. "I am vice president of the United States of America; the president sets the policy," he said. "I am absolutely comfortable with the fact that men marrying men, women marrying women, and heterosexual men and women marrying one another are entitled to the same exact rights, all the civil rights, all the civil liberties."

Biden went home after the taping thinking that he hadn't made news and had done nothing wrong. That he'd been clear he wasn't enunciating new policy, just stating a personal opinion. He knew that Obama was planning to voice his support for same-sex marriage at some point this year, but he had no inkling that anything had been settled. Late that afternoon, his staffers sent a transcript of the interview over to their West Wing colleagues, highlighting the portion on gay marriage. Bidenworld assured the VP that no heads were exploding in the vicinity of the Oval.

Plouffe's head was still firmly attached to his neck, but he wanted Biden's on a platter. *WHAT THE FUCK?* was his reaction when he took a look at the transcript. *We were going to do this! In the next two weeks! As a fucking surprise! HOW CAN THIS HAVE HAPPENED?!*

Plouffe had been planning the coming-out party since early in the year. When Obama returned from the Christmas holidays in Hawaii, he raised again with Plouffe and Pfeiffer the readiness he expressed in the fall: to let the world know that his evolution on gay marriage was complete. We can't stall out the clock through the election with me not telling voters I'm for gay marriage and then turn around after Election Day and say, "Oh, by the way . . . ," Obama said. So the next time I'm asked, I'm just going to say it.

Plouffe and Pfeiffer implored Obama to reconsider. This is gonna be a big civil rights moment in American history, said Pfeiffer. Let's not do it because Jake Tapper asks you at a press conference. Let's do this in the time and moment of your choosing.

"Find the time and moment soon rather than later," Obama replied.

For the next four months, an inner circle within the president's inner circle explored options and weighed political implications. Benenson polled on the subject; subtle questions were thrown into the campaign's focus groups. The potential benefits were clear: rousing young voters and raking in dollars from gay donors. As were the potential costs: turning off culturally conservative Democrats and independents in critical states such as Iowa, Ohio, North Carolina, and Virginia. There was also a broader risk: that undecided voters across the board would say, Why in the world is Obama focusing on *this* when the economy is still so shaky?

Plouffe was a rigorous, data-driven, nothing-to-chance operative, sometimes wrong but rarely in doubt. But on gay marriage, his mental spreadsheet spit out pure uncertainty. *Could help, could hurt, could make winning harder, could make winning easier—it's a crapshoot,* he thought. Messina was even more nervous. Axelrod and Pfeiffer both believed that Obama would be a better candidate if he were being authentic, but they saw the dangers, too. Only Michelle and Jarrett seemed immune to the heebie-jeebies; they counseled the president to do what was in his heart, politics be damned.

The queasiness in Chicago and the White House led to the kind of slow walking and stutter stepping that produces four-hour miles. Endless meetings were held. Plans were made and scrapped. There were always excuses for delay—the payroll-tax extension, the contraception dustup, the anniversary of bin Laden's death.

Obama, meanwhile, was increasingly antsy. He understood the political hazards in play but took comfort in a conversation he'd had a year earlier with Ken Mehlman. In addition to his Bush and RNC pedigrees, Mehlman was a Harvard Law School classmate of Obama's who made headlines when he strode out of the closet in 2010. Mehlman argued that, as a political attribute, strong leadership transcended issues. In 1984, he told the president, one out of four Ted Kennedy backers in the Democratic nomination contest voted in the general election for Ronald Reagan. "This can be a political winner for you," Mehlman said. "It will show you're a guy who stands up for what he believes."

Obama was sick and tired of not being that guy on this issue. He had long considered his gay marriage answer weak; now it was becoming embarrassing. He assumed the question would come up in his debates with Romney, and he dreaded answering it lamely. More immediately, there was the Democratic platform at the party's convention in Charlotte, North Carolina, in which party members and activists wanted to include an unequivocal endorsement of marriage equality. I am not going to have a convention where I am taking a different position on this than my party, Obama told Plouffe. It's not sustainable.

Charlotte was scheduled to start on September 4. Plouffe and the rest of the inner-inner circle wanted a decent interval between Obama's coming out and the party jamboree. They settled on the second half of May. Obama was booked to appear on *The View* on May 14, when he would be in New York for an LGBT fund-raiser. Maybe they would do it there. Or maybe in a more decorous interview setting. (Mehlman advised Plouffe to use a solitary female interviewer and soft lights.) No final decision on timing or venue had been made, but Obama knew it would be soon. To Plouffe, it was essential that there be no impression his hand was being forced by the convention.

All of which explained Plouffe's fury at Biden. As convoluted as the VP's comments on *Meet* had been, it was obvious that the press was going to cast them as an endorsement of gay marriage—and thus make it seem that Obama's hand indeed had been forced, but by Delaware's favorite son instead of the North Carolina convention.

The West Wing labored mightily that weekend to refill the toothpaste tube, with attempted walk-backs, tweets, and a flurry of phone calls to reporters. But by late Monday afternoon, May 7, the White House was caked in Crest. On *Morning Joe,* Education Secretary Arne Duncan was asked if he supported gay marriage and replied flatly, "Yes, I do." At his press briefing, Carney was peppered with more than two dozen questions on the subject ("He opposes bans on gay marriage, but he doesn't yet support gay marriage?" "Why can't you from this podium say whether or not the president supports or opposes same-sex marriage?") and some outright catcalls ("You're trying to have it both ways before an election").

The next morning, Plouffe and Pfeiffer met with Obama in the Oval, told him they thought the situation was untenable, and advised that he do an interview the next day with ABC's Robin Roberts.

Having caught the highlights of Carney's briefing, Obama was inclined to agree. "I've got to put Jay out of his misery," he said, and signed on with the plan.

Obama's attitude toward Biden was his usual mixture of protectiveness, amused detachment, and eye-rolling exasperation. He wasn't angry. He wasn't worked up. He left all that to Plouffe. But on Tuesday he began to express annoyance, not at what Biden had done but about the fact that he hadn't heard a peep from Joe since he unleashed the shitstorm. It was redolent of an incident in 2008, when a Biden gaffe in October—a prediction on the stump that if Barack were elected, "an international crisis" would erupt within six months to test his mettle—provoked anger in Obama but induced no immediate apology from Joe. The silence had bothered the candidate then; it was bothering the president now.

Biden was on the road that Monday and Tuesday. Also simmering. Ever since *Meet*, various West Wing and Chicago persons had been dumping all over him (anonymously) in the press—casting aspersions on his motives, claiming he had privately opposed the idea of Obama coming out and then publicly front-ran the president to further his 2016 ambitions. Joe was shocked and hurt by the treatment, found it incomprehensible. "I don't understand why everyone's so mad at me," he told a confidant. I was asked a question. I answered it honestly. I said something I know the president agrees with and was going to say anyway. What's the harm? Is the president upset? Or just his staff?

Biden's communications director, Shailagh Murray, informed Biden that Obama *was* upset—and why. Oh, Joe said. On Wednesday morning, hours before the Robin Roberts interview and right after the president's daily intelligence briefing, Biden hung back and apologized to Obama for the fuss he'd caused. I'm sorry I put you in a tough spot, the VP said. But he also raised the issue of the West Wing pile-driving him in the press. Are you telling these people to do this? Tell them to stop! What's the deal?

The act of contrition was all the president needed to hear to put him back on Biden's side.

Don't worry about what you said, Obama told him. Don't worry about the staff sniping. Don't worry about the media. The most important thing, Joe, is that you and I don't let other people divide us. Whatever comes down the road, we're in this thing together, and that can never go astray.

At a certain point, I've just concluded that, for me personally, it is important for me to go ahead and affirm that I think same-sex couples should be able to get married," the president said, a touch awkwardly, on camera with Roberts in the Cabinet Room. The statement meant nothing in terms of policy. The politics were up for grabs. But when Obama walked back into the Oval Office, it was as if a crushing weight had been lifted from his shoulders. "I feel so good about that," he said to Plouffe.

Out in Oklahoma City, where he was campaigning, Romney felt less swell. Having declined to answer a reporter's rope-line question about gay marriage earlier in the day, he held a brief afternoon news conference to address Obama's move. His tone was far from strident. "This is a very tender and sensitive topic, as are many social issues, but I have the same views I've had since running for office." Invited to skewer the president for the sin he himself had so often been charged with—flip-flopping—Mitt again trod lightly. "I believe that based upon the interview that he gave today, he had changed his view, but you're a better judge of that than I."

Romney and his people saw Obama's decision as a naked effort to appeal to his base—pure and simple constituency politics. But they saw no advantage in trying to play the game in reverse. With few exceptions, Mitt's senior advisers were personally moderate or liberal on most social issues; they had no lust for a contentious debate on gay marriage. Their core calculus heading into the general election was that any day spent talking about topics besides the economy was a day out the window. The trouble was that this left the candidate betwixt and between: holding positions on paper that the Obamans could use to rile up their supporters, but failing to capitalize on their appeal to social conservatives with a full-throated articulation.

In the White House, Plouffe greeted Romney's reaction to the news with guarded but growing optimism. With gay marriage, the president and his people had done something for which Mitt and his team had so far demonstrated no appetite: taking a considerable, if calculated, risk. And while it was far too early to render a verdict on its impact, the early signs were encouraging to the Obamans. When the administration repealed "don't ask, don't tell" and ceased defending the Defense of Marriage Act in court, the president's people had put on their flak jackets, but the public outcry was close to nil. Now the same muted reaction greeted the president's statement on same-sex unions. And despite all the worries that Biden had stolen his boss's thunder, Obama was showered with press coverage that was salutary and often glowing—his new posture interpreted not as cravenly expedient but as coming clean.

In the days ahead, Obama would reap some unexpected political benefits from endorsing gay marriage. Just as Bush 43's courtship of African American voters played well with white suburbanites in 2000, the president's stance proved resonant with college-educated women. Some in Chicago had worried about alienating churchgoing black voters, but the campaign's research saw not the slightest evidence of that. Instead, Obama's imprimatur had the effect of dramatically increasing support for gay marriage among African Americans—an outcome in which the president took enormous pride.

And then there were the anticipated dividends. The night after the Roberts interview, May 10, Obama attended a fund-raising dinner at the Hollywood home of George Clooney. The organizer of the supper was Jeffrey Katzenberg, the CEO of DreamWorks Animation and a near billionaire, who led his introduction of the president with a hosanna—"Yesterday, he did the right thing yet again"—that drew loud applause and cheers from the star-studded crowd. But the evening yielded more than praise: an extraordinary $15 million haul.

For much of the past year, Obama had been determined to keep his mind on his job and push off the preoccupations of the campaign. Yet the one worry he could never banish from his brain was money. As low as his opinion of Romney was, the main reason Obama believed he could still be beaten was that he might be outspent, not by Boston per se but by Mitt's operation in combination with the Republican super PACs. The conserva-

tive millionaires and billionaires conspiring against Obama had always unsettled him and still did. The question was what kind of defenses his
campaign might deploy against them. What Obama didn't know was that
his arsenal had been enhanced earlier that day—with the anonymous delivery of a mysterious envelope, like something out of John le Carré.

15

FAILURES TO LAUNCH

THE MYSTERY BRUNETTE WALKED into the lobby of the Bank One Building, in Evanston, Illinois, and took the elevator to the seventeenth floor. Reaching the office that was her destination, she asked to see Pete Giangreco, but was told he had stepped out. "He doesn't know me," the brunette said. "It's probably good that he's not here—just give him this." And handed over an unmarked manila envelope.

Giangreco was a Democratic direct-mail maven and Obaman in good standing, a veteran of the 2008 campaign and consultant to the current one. When he returned to his office and opened up the envelope, Giangreco found a bound, fifty-four-page booklet that made his eyes get as big as saucers. The first page bore the title THE DEFEAT OF BARACK HUSSEIN OBAMA and that day's date, May 10. The next fifty-three laid out a $10 million plan to trash the president and disrupt the Democratic convention: TV spots, outdoor ads, aerial banners over Charlotte, all designed to revive the 2008 furor over Obama's incendiary former pastor. "The world is about to see Jeremiah Wright and understand his influence on Barack Obama for the first time in a big, attention-arresting way," the document said. "The metrosexual black Abe Lincoln has emerged as a hyper-partisan, hyper-liberal, elitist politician" who has "brought our country to its knees."

I can't believe someone put this in writing, Giangreco thought at first. *Am I being set up?* But the level of detail and names in the document made him suspect otherwise. Behind the plan were a bevy of brand-name Republican operators, including former Huntsman ad maker Fred Davis. And its ostensible financial backer was Joe Ricketts, the seventy-year-old founder of TD Ameritrade and patriarch of the family that owned the Chicago Cubs.

The Obamans were always on a hair trigger in matters of race. A scheme fusing race with major dollars put Giangreco in full Defcon mode. Grabbing the phone, he called Messina and said, "I need to come see you."

Um, okay, Messina replied. When?

"Right the fuck now," Giangreco replied.

The genesis of what the document called "The Ricketts Plan" was a parable of the post–*Citizens United* era. The man who commissioned it was another billionaire with the bit between his teeth. A native Nebraskan based in Wyoming, Ricketts presided over a politically divided clan. His eldest son, Pete, was the Republican national committeeman in the Cornhusker State. His three other kids lived in the Windy City and ran the Cubs: Todd was conservative, Tom was apolitical, and Laura was an Obama bundler and lesbian activist. Their father had been a Democrat, then a Republican, and was now an independent. But his driving cause was fiscal restraint, and his distaste for Obama intense.

Ricketts had long dabbled in politics, but after the Court's 2010 ruling, he stepped up his game. That year, he started an advocacy group (Taxpayers Against Earmarks) and a super PAC (the Ending Spending Action Fund), both of which had some success. He was keen to play in the presidential and ready to dole out $10 million to defeat Obama.

Ricketts wasn't interested in just dashing off a check to Crossroads, though. He was a solo act, an entrepreneur; he wanted his own deal. But in a presidential contest in which total spending might top $2 billion, a mere $10 million was a pittance. So Ricketts was in the market to maximize the bang for his buck—which was what led him inexorably to the door of Dr. Demon Sheep.

After the collapse of the test-tube candidacy, Davis was on the hunt for some new deep pockets into which he could dip his paw. He pitched Ricketts's political fixer, a youngish Washington climber named Brian Baker, for the business. An edgy West Coast avant-gardist like Davis and a doughy midwestern septuagenarian like Ricketts weren't a natural fit. But the potential combination was a sign of the times, and just the kind of thing that was causing jitters in Obamaworld. Whether the match turned out to be made in heaven or in hell, it was all but certain to produce mischief.

In January, Ricketts, his sons Pete and Todd, and Baker flew out and met Davis in his sleek aerie high in the Hollywood Hills. The adman regaled them with war stories and showed some of his work. With Ricketts on his feet, apparently ready to leave, Davis put on a spot he cut for McCain that included Reverend Wright, which the candidate had refused to air. Over images of McCain recovering from his Vietnam wounds, the narrator praised him for "honor[ing] his fellow soldiers by refusing to walk out of a prisoner-of-war camp," and hit Obama for not "walk[ing] out of a church where a pastor was spewing hatred." The screen filled with a clip of Wright fulminating: "Not God Bless America! God *Damn* America!" Followed by the tagline "Character matters, especially when no one's looking."

Ricketts was overwhelmed. "If the nation had seen that ad," he declared, "they'd never have elected Barack Obama."

Two months later, the same cast of characters plus two of Davis's associates met at Ricketts's palatial apartment on the seventy-seventh floor of the Time Warner Center, in Manhattan. The failure of McCain to use Wright against Obama came up again, along with a broader discussion of an article of faith on the right: that the mainstream press had failed utterly to vet Obama in 2008. After two hours, Davis and his team left the meeting with the assignment to put together a $10 million proposal. They also left with a reading list from Ricketts, which included Dinesh D'Souza's latest bestseller, *The Roots of Obama's Rage.*

Davis and his team spent the next six weeks drafting the proposal. Conservative though they were, the consultants weren't pursuing an ideological agenda; they were chasing a fat paycheck. The plan was designed to pander to what they believed were Ricketts's predispositions. Davis's colleague Bill Kenyon penned the "metrosexual" line. Davis winced but left it in, because he thought Joe would like it. The decision to build their proposal around Wright was based on Ricketts's admiration for the Davis ad: "Our plan is to do exactly what John McCain wouldn't let us do," they wrote. Starting in

Charlotte, they imagined rolling out a national TV and print campaign, including newspaper ads based on Wright's infamous post-9/11 sermon about how "America's chickens are coming home to roost." One proposed ad had the copy "Not God Bless America . . ." superimposed over a picture of the pastor. Another featured a close-up of an angry-looking rooster.

The group convened again on the morning of May 10, at Todd Ricketts's home in Wilmette, on Chicago's North Shore. Joe Ricketts didn't attend but had deputized his sons to handle the meeting. The consultants ran through the proposal and heard no objections from Todd or Pete; it seemed to Davis and Kenyon that both brothers were enthused. The only naysayer in the room was Baker, who thought the singular focus on Wright was a big mistake. Tom Ricketts, the chairman of the Cubs, was negotiating with City Hall for financial help in rebuilding Wrigley Field. "This will cause a massive problem for your brother, and for the team," Baker said. "This will *not* go over well in Chicago."

When the meeting ended, just after noon, Baker drove Davis to his next appointment: an Evanston lunch with Bruce Rauner, a Republican private equity multimillionaire considering a run for Illinois governor in 2013. In the car, Baker told Davis he was nervous about what the Romney camp would think of a Wright-centric super-PAC effort. *They're going to hate it,* Baker thought. *This thing is a shit show.* "What's Plan B?" he asked Davis.

The adman had brought ten copies of the proposal with him to Wilmette. Some remained with the Rickettses, some with Baker, and some with Davis and his team. Within two hours, however, one of the originals was in the hands of the Mystery Brunette—and soon after on the desk of Giangreco, just one block away from the restaurant where Baker had dropped Davis off for his lunch with Rauner.

GIANGRECO DELIVERED THE DOCUMENT to One Prudential Plaza late that afternoon. Flipping through its pages, Messina muttered, "Jesus Christ. Can you believe this? Can you *believe* it?"

The question was what to do next. Once Messina was convinced that the proposal was legit and not some elaborate ruse, he convened an Obamaworld conference call to strategize. Giangreco told the story of how the manila envelope had come over the transom. (He looked at security video from the lobby of his building to see if he recognized the Mystery Brunette; he did not.) Giangreco knew Tom Ricketts slightly; their kids played hockey together. But given the situation with the Cubs and the city, it made no sense to Giangreco that anyone in the Ricketts family would want to make the proposal public.

Messina, Plouffe, and Axelrod didn't care where the document came from. They wanted to slip it to the press tout de suite. Four years earlier, when Wright posed an existential threat to Obama, the idea of injecting the reverend voluntarily into the media bloodstream would have seemed nuts. Now it seemed obvious. Exposing the Ricketts proposal would kill it in the crib, and that was no small thing; the plan could have wreaked havoc in Charlotte. A gale of negative publicity might also take Wright off the table for other super PACs. It would send a message to conservative mega-donors and Republican operatives that if they crossed the line when it came to race, there would be a price to pay. And it would stir up indignation in Obama's base, especially among African Americans.

The Obamans didn't want their fingerprints on the disclosure, so they used a third-party cutout to funnel the Ricketts document to *The New York Times*. To preserve deniability, Obama wasn't told about the scheme. Plouffe only informed him that a story about a super PAC planning to smear him with Wright would be appearing soon in the *Times*.

"That's probably going to make some people . . . uncomfortable," the president said.

Davis's team was more than discomfited when reporters from the *Times* got in touch on May 16. "Ohfuckohfuckohfuckohfuckohfuckohfuckohfuck-ohfuck—oh, *fuck*!" Kenyon yelped.

Rickettsworld was no more pleased. A frantic round of speculation and investigation broke out as to how the document had leaked—one that continued for months thereafter. Fingers from the Davis side pointed at Baker, on the theory that he feared his objections to the plan would be overridden and was somehow trying to curry favor with Boston by killing it, albeit messily. Others pointed at Todd Ricketts's wife, who was in the Wilmette house during the presentation, or his domestic help. Another theory involved Davis's lunch with Rauner, who was close to Mayor Emanuel. But no culprit was ever definitively identified.

The *Times* played the story on page one the next day and splashed it all over the Web—posting the proposal, storyboards it contained for a Wright ad, and graphic multimedia spreads on the players behind the plan and the Ricketts family.

As the Obamans hoped it would, all hell summarily broke loose. From the left, there were calls to boycott TD Ameritrade and other Ricketts businesses. In Chicago, Emanuel put out word through an aide that he was "livid" and cut off communication with the family: "The Rickettses have tried to contact the mayor, but he's said that he does not want to talk with them today, tomorrow, or anytime soon," the aide said. Laura and Tom Ricketts quickly issued statements distancing themselves from the plan. That afternoon, Joe Ricketts did the same; the proposal was dead, Baker told the *Times*. Davis was cast as a scurrilous race-baiter and began receiving death threats.

The Obamans were determined that Ricketts-related splatter would get all over Romney, too. Chicago's rapid-response queen, Lis Smith, discovered that in February Mitt had invoked Wright in a radio interview with Sean Hannity. In reaction to a truncated clip of Obama saying, "We are no longer a Christian nation"—without the next bit, in which the president rattled off a litany of other religions in the American mosaic of faith—Romney told Hannity, "I'm not sure which is worse: him listening to Reverend Wright or him saying that we . . . must be a less Christian nation."

First thing in the morning on May 17, Smith fed the quote to reporters traveling with Romney in Florida, while Axelrod got on Twitter to wonder whether the Republican would disavow the Ricketts plan "or allow the purveyors of slime to operate on his behalf?" On a flight out of Miami, Mitt was asked about the *Times*'s story and claimed he hadn't read the papers yet. In the afternoon, the campaign hastily arranged a press availability at the River City Brewing Company, in Jacksonville, at which Romney repudiated the proposal—but then was hit with the planted question about what he had said on *Hannity*.

"Do you stand by that?" a print reporter asked. "And do you believe that

President Obama's worldview was shaped by Reverend Wright, and if so do you see evidence of that in his policies?"

Mitt's face radiated radical discombobulation, and his words comically followed suit.

"I'm not familiar, precisely, with exactly what I said, but I stand by what I said, whatever it was," he sputtered—carrying his commitment to avoid flip-flopping to its reductio ad absurdum extreme.

Even before Romney twisted himself into that pretzel, he was already bent out of shape. After his flight, he had marched through a four-part fund-raising event. He had given a series of local interviews, one of which had to be redone because the reporter accidently failed to record the session. He had held a round table on debt and spending, followed by a speech—during which the clouds opened up and soaked the crowd. But Romney still had more miles to go before he slept, and more torments as well. From Jacksonville, he would fly to Palm Beach for another set of money-raising gigs.

The ceaseless dash for cash was the greatest agony of Mitt's existence, and one of the largest ironies. A fantastically rich man, he spent an inordinate amount of time begging other rich people for moola. Pitted against Obama's fund-raising prowess, and with his own campaign's coffers in urgent need of refilling for the general election, Mitt believed he had no choice. His buck-raising schedule was physically punishing: he was tired all the time. It was psychically irritating: he hated being lectured on electoral strategy by know-nothing donors. (His staff referred to rope lines at fund-raising events as "advice lines.") And it was politically dangerous. Like many politicians, Romney had a weakness for talking like a cable TV yakker instead of a candidate. "Don't be a pundit," Rhoades nagged him, but that was easier said than done—especially with donors, who incessantly asked pundit-type questions.

The sense of financial desperation also placed Romney in dodgy venues, as was the case with his last event of that night: a fund-raising soiree for thirty at the Boca Raton home of Marc Leder.

Romney had known Leder for years, but he was a dubious character. A private equity hotshot with a net worth in the neighborhood of $600 million, he had run a firm, Sun Capital, whose portfolio was replete with investments in companies that had gone belly-up. The *New York Post* delighted in writing about the debauched bacchanals Leder threw at his home in Southampton. (NUDE FROLIC IN TYCOON'S POOL was one headline.) Under any normal standard of political discretion, Romney would never have been allowed in the same zip code with a Leder-hosted function. But Zwick's shop, in its fund-raising freneticism, had on this occasion lowered the campaign's vetting bar for event hosts to ankle level.

The scene at Leder's house when Romney arrived at around 8:00 p.m. was fit for Tom Wolfean lampoonery: a bonfire of the gaucheries. The massive Italianate house was decorated in the style of an opulent Olive Garden. The guests came in pairs—the men older, finely suited, and stentorian, the women young, nipped and tucked, tight-dressed, and dutifully silent. There were rhinestone-encrusted Romney 2012 pins as party favors for the ladies. Leder's date was a towering Russian with pulled-back platinum hair and a name like Tatiana.

Romney wanted no part of any of it. He was as exhausted as anyone had ever seen him, his hair disheveled, bags under his eyes. His body guy, Garrett Jackson, thought his boss could use a catnap—just fifteen minutes would help. With the guests still arriving, he found a quiet room, Leder's home office, with a comfy chair and deposited Romney in it. "Rest," Jackson said.

Out in the dining area, Jackson and trip director Charlie Pearce swept the room for cameras. In April, there had been a kerfuffle when someone posted a video of Mitt speaking at a donor event in Kentucky, and another when he and his wife were overheard by the press at a Florida fund-raiser. (Ann was caught describing Hilary Rosen's comments as an "early birthday present.") To guests brandishing cell phones, Jackson and Pearce whispered, Pictures are fine, just please no recording.

Romney emerged from his nap time little more refreshed than before. Seated at the head of a U-shaped table next to Leder, he started taking questions from the dinner guests at close to 9:00 p.m. Some were on foreign policy (Iran, Israel). Some were more exhortations than queries ("Why don't you stick up for yourself?"). A great many invited punditry, causing Romney to lapse into Brit Hume mode. Then, well along in the back-and-forth, one attendee asked him this: "For the last three years, all everybody's been told is 'Don't worry, we'll take care of you.' How are you going to do it, in two months before the elections, to convince everybody you've got to take care of yourself?"

"There are 47 percent of the people who will vote for the president no matter what," Romney said. "All right, there are 47 percent who are with him, who are dependent upon government, who believe that they are victims, who believe that government has a responsibility to care for them, who believe that they are entitled to health care, to food, to housing, to you name it . . . These are people who pay no income tax; 47 percent of Americans pay no income tax. So our message of low taxes doesn't connect. And he'll be out there talking about tax cuts for the rich. I mean, that's what they sell every four years. And so my job is not to worry about those people. I'll never convince them that they should take personal responsibility and care for their lives. What I have to do is convince the 5 to 10 percent in the center that are independents, that are thoughtful, that look at voting one way or the other depending upon in some cases emotion, whether they like the guy or not, what it looks like."

Several Romney aides, including Stevens, were within earshot but not really paying attention. They had no reason to think anything Romney said would leave the room, no idea that a camera had, in fact, been running.

When the dinner ended, Mitt was pleased that May 17 was over. The day had been long and brutal, although not as bad for him as it was for Ricketts and Davis. Unlike them, Romney wasn't writhing in agony on the floor—not yet. It would be several months before his own chickens came home to roost.

THE BANG AND CLATTER of the Ricketts ruckus obscured a story that caught the notice of Obama and his people. That same day, the Romney campaign announced that, with the help of the RNC, its fund-raising total for April was $40 million, less than $4 million shy of what the Democratic side had registered for the month. Romney's fanatical buck-raking appeared to be working—even as the money situation in Chicago was causing the Obamans palpitations.

The most visible source of concern was the steep fund-raising drop-off that had occurred from March to April: $53 million to $43.6 million. While

Obama's shift to a more populist, partisan stance might have helped him politically, it had done him no favors with the donor class. Wall Street and much of the *Fortune* 500 were shut off to him now. And while Hollywood, Silicon Valley, and the gay community (fully one in six of Obama's bundlers fell into the last category) were keeping the campaign afloat, its vaunted Web fund-raising machine was sluggish. Small-dollar givers were withholding their largesse, thinking that the president faced little peril from Romney. Plouffe was bullish that the money would eventually turn around. But Messina was so panicked that he quietly instituted a one-month hiring freeze.

Obama remained as detached from his fund-raising efforts as ever. Even as he attended more donor events than any presidential incumbent in history, he was airily oblivious to the people ginning up millions of dollars on his behalf. One day, the president asked Messina, "Who's Franklin Haney?"

Messina explained that Haney, a real estate baron, was one of Obama's top ten bundlers.

"Jim, I couldn't tell you who the top five are—I just have no idea," Obama said, then noted that he did know at least two bundlers: *Vogue* high priestess Anna Wintour and his national finance chair, Matthew Barzun.

Messina didn't mind the president's nonchalance. What he minded was the increasingly likely possibility that the campaign would be financially outmatched. Messina and Plouffe's initial estimate had been that conservative super PACs might raise and spend, at most, $200 million against Obama. Now Rove was boasting publicly that Crossroads on its own would meet or exceed that figure.

Messina and Plouffe were kicking themselves over the miscalculation, for it had led them to badly botch the job of setting up a pro-Obama super PAC. From the start, the White House had been tied in knots over the topic. Given the president's opposition to *Citizens United* and his railing against outside money in the midterms, his advisers believed there was no way he could place his imprimatur on such a group. But with Messina convinced that a super PAC would be needed on their side, there were discussions in late 2010 about dispatching a trusted Obaman to run one. Robert Gibbs, Larry Grisolano, and even Plouffe were all names floated but shot down.

The question was ultimately decided by default, when two young aides on their way out of the White House in early 2011 volunteered for the assignment. Bill Burton, the deputy White House press secretary, had just been passed over for Gibbs's job; Sean Sweeney, Emanuel's chief of staff, had just lost his boss to Chicago. That they had no experience in fund-raising didn't bother the Obama brain trust. Messina and Plouffe's expectations were minimal: a super PAC to take up the slack and be a nuisance for the Republicans. *Who do we trust enough to put outside to not fuck this up?* was the only question in Messina's mind. Besides, he thought, *Jeffrey will always make it right.*

Jeffrey was Jeffrey Katzenberg, who had rustled up a wad of cash for Obama in 2008 and intended to do the same in 2012. But he was also itching to insert himself into the super-PAC game. He had thought about doing so during the midterms but decided to defer because he sensed that the president would disapprove. But the sight of Rove, the Kochs, and their ilk outspending the Democratic side by $100 million in 2010 made him toss aside his qualms. "We're not sitting the next one out," Katzenberg said to his political attaché, Andy Spahn.

Katzenberg was fine with Burton and Sweeney running Obama's outside group, so long as they brought in a front man. Someone facile, fierce, and good on TV, he said. "Someone who can answer Rove." Spahn met the boys in Washington and suggested Paul Begala, James Carville's tangy Texan partner from the Clinton years. The boys agreed, securing $2 million in seed capital from Katzenberg.

In April 2011, Burton and Sweeney announced the formation of Priorities USA Action, with a goal of raising $100 million by Election Day—and then stormed into a brick wall. Everywhere they went, Democratic millionaires told them thanks but no thanks. There were those who objected on the grounds that super PACs were corrupt, corrupting, and terrible for the country. Those who had no stomach for funding negative ads. Those who held back because they had no clue who Burton and Sweeney were. And those who balked because they believed that Romney could never win.

Increasingly desperate, the boys tried another tack. Whenever a fund-raising event appeared on Obama's schedule, they would fly there and position themselves nearby, grabbing his donors and making their plea. But rather than lighting up his contributors, Obama was bumming them out. "I just gave him $70,000 and four hours of my life," one of the richest men in the country told Begala. "I'm much less happy with him now than I was before."

By the end of the year, Priorities had raised only $6 million, including the initial DreamWorks deuce; in January, the group brought in a negligible $58,000. Katzenberg and Spahn were pounding Messina and Plouffe to convince the president to drop his holier-than-thou-ism and endorse the group. Watching Priorities stagger and Crossroads et al. soar, the advisers agreed that the price of principle had grown too high. At a Sunday meeting in the Roosevelt Room, Messina presented Obama with the Priorities numbers and a revised figure for what the Republican super PACs were likely to raise: $660 million.

"How sure are you?" Obama asked, slightly staggered.

"Very sure," said Messina. "I think we need to switch our position" on Priorities. They're sinking without us. Until people understand that it's important to you, they're not going to give. The Clinton donors don't care enough, and our people have never been million-dollar check writers. You gotta give it your seal of approval or it's not gonna work.

Obama detested looking like a hypocrite almost as much as being one. But he hated the idea of losing even more. In early February, it was announced that Obama was officially backing Priorities. Although he, Michelle, and Biden would do nothing actively for the group, his staff and cabinet members would be allowed to attend Priorities fund-raising events.

Obama's reversal was met with multiple yawns: from the press, his grassroots supporters, and donors. Come May, three months later, Priorities still hadn't crossed the $10 million threshold.

For Burton, Sweeney, and Begala, the scarcity of funds imposed strict discipline in terms of mission. They needed to pick a narrow lane and make as much noise with their ads as possible. From the outset, Begala was adamant about three things: that the GOP nominee would be Romney, that he would run on his business credentials, and that Priorities should therefore focus on destroying his economic credibility with the middle class. In his 1994 Senate race against Mitt, Ted Kennedy had run a storied series of ads with laid-off workers from companies controlled by Bain. Seizing on a tried and tested formula, Priorities would do the same.

Priorities' first Bain ad debuted on May 15, two days before the Ricketts story broke. It was called "Heads or Tails" and featured a former worker for GST Steel, a Kansas City mill that went under in 2001 after being bought by Bain. "[Romney] promised us the same things he's promising the United States," the worker said. "He'll give you the same thing he gave us: nothing. He'll take it all."

"Heads or Tails" went up almost simultaneously with the Obama campaign's first Bain ad, a spot called "Steel" that also highlighted workers from GST. "We view Mitt Romney as a job destroyer," said one. Another referred to Romney's former firm as a "vampire."

Priorities was hoping to crank up the reverb in the free-media echo chamber, and its spot in tandem with "Steel" achieved that. The problem was much of the uproar was negative—and voiced by Democrats. Former Obama administration car czar and private equity pooh-bah Steve Rattner disparaged the attacks on Bain as "unfair," saying that the firm had done nothing "they need to be embarrassed about." Former Tennessee Democratic congressman Harold Ford Jr. proclaimed, "Private equity is not a bad thing. Matter of fact, private equity is a good thing in many, many instances." Former Pennsylvania governor Ed Rendell deemed the ads "very disappointing."

And then there was Cory Booker, the African American mayor of Newark, New Jersey, who also happened to be an Obama campaign surrogate. "If you look at the totality of Bain Capital's record, it ain't—they've done a lot to support businesses, to grow businesses. And this, to me, I'm very uncomfortable with," Booker said on *Meet the Press* that Sunday, May 20. High on his horse, Booker went on and on with little prompting from David Gregory, finally tying up Bain and Ricketts in a bow. "This kind of stuff is nauseating to me on both sides. It's nauseating to the American public. Enough is enough. Stop attacking private equity. Stop attacking Jeremiah Wright. This stuff has got to stop."

THE THOUSAND-POUND SHITHAMMER landed on Booker about thirty minutes later. When the call came from Patrick Gaspard, the mayor didn't realize what was about to hit him. I got a little outside the lines, Booker said sheepishly. No, Gaspard replied. You used the word "nauseating" about us. You got more than a little outside the lines.

Campaign aides to both Bill Clinton and George W. Bush were notoriously aggressive about corralling allies who strayed from the farm. The Obamans handled such wanderers with electric-tipped cattle prods. Rendell would receive a zap from Messina, Rattner a poke from his friend Larry Summers. But bringing Booker—a media-savvy rising star seen by some in the party and the press as the next Obama—to heel required a higher-megawatt jolt. Already the RNC was blasting out e-mails touting what Booker had said; surely the Romney campaign would be next. His apostasy could not stand.

Booker and Gaspard went round and round that Sunday afternoon. Booker made the mistake of saying that he wasn't the only Democrat who felt the way he did—and then named some of his many backers in the financial sector. "Cory, we're making a point about the thing Mitt Romney uses as his chief qualifier to be president," Gaspard said. "You gotta fix this."

Let me figure it out, Booker said. Maybe do another interview. Maybe send out a tweet.

"You don't fucking get it!" Gaspard screamed. "You gotta fix this now!"

The Obamans wanted Booker to put out a simple, declarative statement walking his comments back. Instead, on his own, he filmed a three-minute-and-forty-eight-second, straight-to-camera video that he tweeted out. Under fluorescent lights, his laptop open beside him, face pallid with distress, Booker looked like a well-fed captive. Instead of retracting what he'd said, he restated the same points he made on *Meet*, but less colorfully.

Obamaworld was apoplectic. Messina told colleagues that he was "off the Cory Booker train forever." Obama himself was vocally annoyed. He's grandstanding and sucking up to his donors, the president told his aides—at our expense.

The pounding of Booker by the Obamans continued unabated for the next twenty-four hours. On Monday night, after announcing he would not do interviews, Booker appeared on MSNBC's *The Rachel Maddow Show* and heaped praise on the president and his political team. "They have never pressured me to do anything," he said, and then tweeted, "Let me be clear, #IStandWithObama."

At a NATO summit in Chicago that day, Obama was asked at a news conference about his ally's critique. After praising Booker perfunctorily as "an outstanding mayor," Obama took issue with his use of the word "distraction" regarding Bain. "The reason this is relevant to the campaign is because my opponent, Governor Romney, his main calling card for why he thinks he should be president is his business experience," he said. "When you're president, as opposed to the head of a private equity firm, then your job is not simply to maximize profits. Your job is to figure out how everybody in the country has a fair shot . . . This is what this campaign is going to be about."

The Obamans expected pushback from some Democrats when they began their Bain battery. Until then, they had restricted themselves to subtler and less visible forms of tweaking Mitt as an out-of-touch plutocrat. In March, Chicago had fed research to Politico on the extensive renovations that the Romneys mapped out for their La Jolla house, including the plans for a hydraulic auto lift—which the story called a "car elevator," just as the campaign intended. Not even the most delicate Democratic flower would have accused them of playing class warfare over something like that.

Attacking Bain struck at the heart of the Democratic donor class—and the politicians who relied on it for funds. Yet it was seen by Chicago as indispensable to winning. The Obamans had been doing research on Bain since mid-2011, and marrying it up with Benenson's polling on attitudes about the economy. What they found was that many middle-class voters associated the thirty-year decline in living standards with phenomena such as offshoring, outsourcing, downsizing, and the enrichment of the 1 percent— all things that Bain could be made to symbolize. Going after Romney on private equity wasn't merely about making him look rapacious. It was about instilling a sense of distrust in his ability to rebuild a middle class that people like him had done much to undermine.

Far from putting the brakes on their Bain attacks, the Obamans planned to ram the accelerator to the floorboard. For weeks, Axelrod, Grisolano, Messina, and Plouffe had been mulling a plan to shift millions of dollars from the campaign's budget from the fall into the summer—much of it to be spent on negative ads against Romney. Their opponent was still depleted from the nomination fight. He remained a hazy figure in the minds of undecided voters, and thus vulnerable to being defined by the Obamans. By hitting him early and mercilessly on his record in Massachusetts, his tax returns, and especially his time running Bain, they might send him into his convention so hobbled that he would find it impossible to recover.

There was another argument for striking preemptively. All along, the Obamans had feared that Crossroads would come in early in the year and drop a boulder on the president's head. Grisolano, who commanded Chicago's ad budget, had set millions of dollars aside to respond to Rove's attacks. But Crossroads had decided to husband its resources, thinking the money would be better spent in defense of the GOP nominee once he was chosen, and especially after Labor Day. The Obamans were relieved but perplexed by the choice. Axelrod and Grisolano were convinced that the airwaves would be oversaturated in the fall, and voters so disgusted with political ads that they would tune out.

All of this argued for a splurge-now strategy, but there was a huge risk involved. The Obamans were talking about moving roughly half the cash budgeted for September and October into June, July, and August. If Chicago didn't hit its fund-raising projections, the campaign would be dramatically outspent in the fall.

The high command sat down with Obama in the Roosevelt Room on the balmy, lazy afternoon of Saturday, May 26, to present him with their gambit. The president liked the aggressiveness, liked the strategy; but, as with any sane gambler, he had concerns about betting on the come. Though Obama usually left the nitty-gritty of campaign strategy to his team, he had a lot of questions now. If we raise less than we're supposed to in September and October, what are we looking at? What if the other side raises a lot more than we expect? Are we locked in here? If our money's going worse, can we pare down in June? If we fall short, what do we do then?

Messina told Obama there were no guarantees about fund-raising, not with the recent trends. Plouffe told him he should assume that they would have only bare air cover in the fall. Axelrod told him he thought that even the worst-case scenario would be survivable—probably. All of them told him they believed this was the way to go. But they were nervous. They needed the president to sign on with his eyes wide open. *We're staring into the abyss here,* thought Plouffe. *He needs to stare into it, too.*

Okay, Obama said. If you guys say so, go for it. I just hope we don't end up naked at the end.

When the meeting broke up, the president asked to see Messina privately. They went out to the Rose Garden patio and had lunch in the warm sunshine.

"Are you sure?" Obama asked. "What if the money doesn't come?"

"I'm sure," Messina said, but he wasn't going to lie. "There's a real chance we are destroyed on TV at the end."

ONE OF THE OBAMANS was destroyed on TV five days later, when Axelrod made an ill-fated foray to Boston. Chicago's plan was to spend the month of June assailing Romney for his Bay State record. Axelrod was slated to kick things off by leading a rally on the statehouse steps. The decision to send him was odd on its face, but the campaign's communications shop knew that national reporters would be sure to flock to Axe. Basically, he was bait.

The campaign intended for the rally to be a surprise, but a local reporter tweeted out the word the night before. Romney advance man Will Ritter sprung instantly into action, and by the time Axelrod mounted the podium, Ritter had turned the site into a circus of the surreal—complete with air horns, a bubble machine, a heckler-amplifying speaker system, Ritter's dog, bikes, placards, and an army of Romney interns chanting, "Axel-fraud! Axel-fraud! Axel-fraud!"

Axelrod put on a brave face and tried to muddle through, declaring the spectacle "the pageant of democracy" and quipping, "You can shout down speakers, my friends, but it's hard to Etch A Sketch the truth away."

Obama caught the coverage on cable—CNN carried the rally live—and at first seemed to find it amusing. Outside the Oval, he remarked to Pfeiffer, "Seems like Axelrod had a tough day today." But then he sounded perturbed. Why would we have an event with Axe on the statehouse steps, right near Romney headquarters? Obama asked, and walked away.

That night on CNN, Bill Clinton appeared on CNN's *Piers Morgan Tonight,* guest-hosted that evening by his friend the film producer Harvey Weinstein. Weinstein asked Clinton about Romney's Bain experience and its relevance to promoting economic growth. "I don't think that we ought to get into the position where we say this is bad work—this is good work," the former president said of private equity, and then added that Mitt's "sterling business career crosses the qualification threshold."

The collective reaction in Obamaworld was instantaneous, splenetic, and reflexively paranoid. What the fuuuck? Is this intentional? Is he trying to screw us? Such were the themes of the e-mail chain that rocketed around the campaign's upper rantes.

The next morning, the Obamans confronted Clinton through his aide Doug Band. At first, 42 insisted that he'd done nothing wrong: that he made clear Romney was inferior to Obama on policy, on what he would do as president. Within a few hours, Clinton relented, clarifying what he meant— that Romney "crosses the qualification threshold" but "he shouldn't be elected"—and flaying the press for taking him out of context. But the damage had been done. *He handed Romney an ad on a platter,* thought Plouffe.

Obama wasn't any more pleased to see Clinton jumping on the Booker bandwagon. But more troubling were the monthly employment numbers handed to him by Gene Sperling the next day, June 1. Only 69,000 new jobs had been created in May. The unemployment rate had ticked up to 8.2 percent, the first increase since June 2011.

At his regular Sunday strategy meeting in the Roosevelt Room two days later, Obama vented. In the month since the campaign officially took flight, his team hadn't been firing on all cylinders. The president pointed to his two-stop announcement tour; in Columbus, Ohio, there had been tons of empty seats. (Noting the desultory atmosphere, *The New York Times* wrote that Obama's maiden general election rally "had the feeling of a concert by an aging rock star.") Between Clinton, Booker, and what the Obamans derisively referred to as the "*Morning Joe* Democrats," the Bain rollout hadn't gone smoothly. Then there was Axel-fraud, which seemed to annoy Obama most of all. It was amateurish, tactical, and lame.

"Look, we just all need to tighten our games," Obama said sternly. "And that includes me."

The tightening commenced immediately in Obamaworld as Plouffe and Messina rejiggered responsibilities between Chicago and the West Wing. But Obama failed to heed his own directive quite so quickly. On June 8, facing reporters in the White House briefing room, the president was asked, "What about the Republicans saying that you're blaming the Europeans for the failures of your own policies?" To which Obama replied: "We created 4.3 million jobs over the last twenty-seven months, over 800,000 just this year alone. The private sector is doing fine. Where we're seeing weaknesses in our economy have to do with state and local government."

Pfeiffer marched into the Oval Office to inform Obama that he'd gaffed. Anything that could be construed (or purposely misconstrued) as suggesting that he was content with the performance of the private sector was a problem. Obama was defensive at first. Everyone knows I don't think the economy is fine, he protested, because I say so every day. But a few hours later, during a White House photo op, Obama grudgingly revised his comments.

Coming on top of the other hiccups, the flub alarmed Plouffe. It wasn't just the private-sector part, with its implication of out-of-touchness, that he thought was problematic. The second half, which could be interpreted as the president believing that public-sector employment was the remedy for what ailed the economy, was also bad. *Talking like a macroeconomics professor,* Plouffe thought, *always leads to trouble.* Which in this case meant handing Boston a gift-wrapped Big Bertha with which to tee off on Obama.

The Romneyites had been gleefully knocking the ball down the fairway since the *Morning Joe* Democrat backlash had begun. Stitching together the Booker, Ford, Rattner, and Rendell rebukes, Boston compiled a video titled "Big Bain Backfire." On CNBC, Romney crowed, "I think Bain Capital has a good and solid record. I was happy to see President Clinton made a similar statement . . . and called my record superb." Now the campaign went on the air with an ad called "Doing Fine?" It was a frame-by-frame imitation of a devastating 2008 Obama spot that had maced McCain for saying—the day after Lehman Brothers collapsed, triggering a global financial crisis—"The fundamentals of our economy are strong," with the president's "private sector" gaffe a literal and figurative echo.

After months of wallowing in gloom-shrouded dismay, Republicans saw a ray of hope. For the past four years, Obama and the Obamans had been swaddled in a mythos about their command of the dark arts and sweet science of electioneering. Even on the right, there was a grudging admiration that went along with overarching contempt for the president. Obama had proven ill-equipped for governing, sure, but nobody doubted that he and his people knew how to run a campaign.

For Republicans, however, the past month had punctured that perception as Chicago seemed to have suffered an epic failure to launch. Meanwhile, Team Romney had just released its latest fund-raising numbers: a staggering $77 million for May, fully $17 million ahead of what Team Obama had managed. This figure alone would have been enough to set conservative hearts aflutter, but there was more. Romney's positive ratings were rising. The gender gap was narrowing. The Gallup daily tracking poll had Mitt two points ahead of Obama. Suddenly, Republicans were seized with a thought at once heretical and thrilling: maybe their guy wasn't irretrievably doom-struck after all.

★ 16 ★

BAIN PAIN

AN ARMADA OF GLEAMING white private jets descended on Russ Mc-Donald Field, twenty minutes outside Park City, Utah, where their passengers were met and whisked away by a fleet of black cars. It was June 22, a sun-splashed day in the Wasatch Mountains, and nine hundred donors were arriving for the start of what Boston had billed as the First National Romney Victory Leadership Retreat, a reward for the campaign's most generous contributors and bundlers. In the lobby of the Chateaux at Silver Lake, the nabobs were handed canvas tote bags with BELIEVE IN AMERICA stitched on the side. For the next three days, they would revel in a veritable Mittapalooza.

The retreat was a Spencer Zwick production, brimming with star power. The scene sometimes seemed like a ski-lodge simulacrum of a Republican convention. There were party leaders such as Jeb Bush and McCain, statesmen including James Baker III. There were rising stars and potential VP nominees: Tim Pawlenty, Paul Ryan, Virginia governor Bob McDonnell, Ohio senator Rob Portman. There were conservative media eminences: Fred Barnes, Mary Matalin, Bill Kristol. There were business titans: Ken Langone, Meg Whitman. There was Charlie Spies, from Restore Our Future, hitting up donors, and there was Karl Rove, doing much the same for Crossroads.

There was Condoleezza Rice, stealing the show with an impassioned speech that brought the attendees to their feet. There was the Boston brain trust, patiently answering question after question about polling, strategy, and the electoral map.

Mitt and Ann seemed to be everywhere at once, giving talks at private dinners for top-dollar bundlers (him) and at a Women for Romney Victory Tea with figure skater Dorothy Hamill (her). On Friday night, both Romneys spoke at a cookout in Olympic Park, at the base of a training mountain surrounded by ski jumps. Ann was funny and personal, playfully roasting her sons, four of whom were in attendance, and offering a warm tribute to her husband. Mitt delivered his stump speech with greater fire and fluency than usual. *You know what?* thought Langone. *I was wrong—this guy can connect!*

For Romney, the retreat was something close to nirvana. He had lived in Park City for three years when he was heading the 2002 Olympics, so the event was a sort of homecoming, and Zwick made sure it ran like clockwork. Surrounded by his family and by individuals of means who needed no persuasion about the virtues of capitalist achievement, Romney was in his element. The donors were loving him and loving the retreat, and he loved that.

But Romney's joy derived as much from a different embrace: that of the party's panjandrums. Never before had the Republican establishment fully accepted him. Never had there been a laying on of hands. In Park City, his back was emblazoned with the palm prints of the great and the good.

On the Friday night before his speech, he was introduced by Jim Baker, the former secretary of state, secretary of the treasury, and White House chief of staff. Nicknamed the Velvet Hammer, Baker was for Republicans of a certain age the gold standard of probity, wisdom, streetwise caginess, and streetfighter moxie. His words about Romney were glowing, all about how Mitt was uniquely suited to occupying the Oval Office at this moment in history.

Talking to reporters afterwards, Baker reminisced about a similar event in Vail in 1976, when Gerald Ford had asked Baker to run his general election campaign. "That's what I see going on here," the Velvet Hammer said. "We are going to have a different result. This year we are going to win."

Romney had no doubt that the race ahead would be tough and close, but he was optimistic. He had brought on board a well-regarded outsider, former Bush 43 counselor and RNC chair Ed Gillespie, as a senior adviser. He had assigned Beth Myers to manage his vice-presidential selection process, and Mike Leavitt to handle his presidential transition planning. With the horrors of the nomination fight well and truly behind him, Romney rolled out of Park City firmly focused on the future—and blissfully unaware of how viciously his past was about to bite him in the ass.

WASHINGTON AWOKE TO SWELTERING heat and high expectations on June 28. For weeks, the political world had been awaiting the Supreme Court's ruling in *National Federation of Independent Business et al. v. Sebelius, Secretary of Health and Human Services, et al.*—the case to decide the constitutionality of Obamacare. This was the last day before the Court's summer recess. The clock was down to zero.

Since March, when oral arguments in the case were seen as having unfolded abominably for the administration, a consensus had formed on all sides about the likely outcome: in part or in toto, the Affordable Care Act would be overturned. The White House and Chicago were braced for that eventuality, but Obama was serene. His private prediction was that the law would be upheld, 5–4, with Justice Anthony Kennedy siding with the Court's liberal bloc.

Obama was watching CNN in a room just off the Oval when the network errantly reported that the individual mandate had been struck down. Five interminable minutes passed before White House counsel Kathy Ruemmler burst in with a smile and two thumbs up. Obama had been proven both right and wrong: the Court vindicated the mandate as constitutional, but with Kennedy dissenting and Chief Justice John Roberts in the majority—on the argument that the penalty contained in the ACA for failing to obtain insurance was not an illegitimate regulation of commerce but instead a legitimate tax.

The Obama administration disagreed with that reasoning, but who cared? All that mattered was the verdict. Speaking in the East Room, Obama was at pains not to gloat. "Whatever the politics," he said, "today's decision was a victory for people all over this country whose lives will be more secure because of this law." But among his people there were tears of joy and cheers of exultation. On Twitter, Gaspard blurted, "It's constitutional. Bitches."

Despite all the controversy around the ACA, Obama's team had come to view it as an electoral winner. Anyone who had turned against 44 because of the law was already lost; undecided voters had factored it into their thinking and remained on the fence. But across the coalition of the ascendant, Chicago's research found that the ACA was a plus. For months the campaign had been developing direct mail and ads aimed at women and young voters that homed in on health care reform's specific benefits for them. Guaranteed coverage was popular with African Americans and Hispanics, whose rates of uninsurance were high. Chicago was already on the air with Spanish-language spots touting the ACA. Now Grisolano would crank the volume of that advertising up to eleven.

Romney was in Washington when the Court issued its ruling. Before the cameras on a balcony across the street from the Capitol in the scorching sun, Romney said, "What the Court did not do on its last day in session, I *will* do on my first day if elected president of the United States. And that is, I will act to repeal Obamacare."

For Romney, the Court's decision was the worst of all worlds. Boston had been praying for the ACA to be struck down, allowing Mitt to spend the fall attacking Obama for wasting a year, in the midst of an economic crisis, pushing an unconstitutional law—a position that might have held broad attraction in the middle of the electorate, which repeal did not. On the right, the only solace in Roberts's decision was that it deemed the individual mandate a tax. But for Boston, that caused further squeamishness, as it raised questions about whether the mandate in Romneycare was one, too. Confronted on the topic a few days later on MSNBC, Fehrnstrom said that Mitt believed the mandate was not a tax at either the state or federal level, thus agreeing with the administration and infuriating conservatives.

The depth of the muddle was depressing to Mitt. *Maybe Santorum was right about me and Obamacare,* he thought. *Rick could just scream, "The mandate! The mandate!" But I can't.*

From Washington, Romney flew up to New York for a meeting arranged by Langone at the Union League Club, off Park Avenue. The attendees were the same sort of machers—Rupert Murdoch, Lloyd Blankfein, Stanley Druckenmiller, and about thirty others—that the Home Depot founder had put together to lure Christie into the race. Only this time the purpose was to give Mitt advice about how to beat Obama.

Romney showed up and dove right into the discussion. Langone jostled him to make more noise about Simpson-Bowles. The Court's health care ruling was raised. Education was broached. But the most heated topic on the table was immigration.

Obama had thrust the issue into the news two weeks earlier, when he announced that he would use executive authority to enact a modified DREAM Act. Frustrated by the months of internal debate, the president had brought the issue to a head with Jack Lew and Ruemmler. Don't make my political decision for me, he said. Don't tell me it's going to hurt me or will be seen as overreaching. I just want to know if I have the legal authority or not. With Ruemmler maintaining that he did, Obama was all in, unveiling what he called "a temporary stopgap measure" that would "lift the shadow of deportation" from 800,000 young illegal immigrants who had entered the country under age sixteen.

The Obamans knew that the move put Romney in a bind, given his DREAM Act veto pledge. But Plouffe and Messina assumed that Mitt would swiftly side with the president to avoid worsening his dismal numbers with Hispanics.

Romney felt trapped. On the one hand, he was still worried about upsetting the right, from which he needed energy and big turnout in November; he also feared that shifting his position would leave him open to charges of expediency. On the other, he understood that he couldn't risk further alienating Latinos.

So he attempted to split the difference. In one halting swoop, Romney praised Marco Rubio, who was working on his own DREAM Act alternative; criticized Obama for making it "more difficult to reach a long-term solution" by taking his action outside the context of comprehensive immigration reform; but indicated that, even so, he would not repeal the order if he were elected.

Messina was flabbergasted. "They couldn't have fucked this up any worse," he said in a staff meeting the next morning. "Their people are pissed, Latinos are pissed, and he looks like an asshole."

Obama was perplexed, too. "I'm surprised," the president said, pondering Romney's behavior. He seems to have latitude with his party now, or he wouldn't have taken the opportunity to try and heal himself a little bit. But apparently he doesn't believe he has enough latitude to go the whole nine yards. It was weird, Obama thought.

In truth, everything about Hispanics was vexed in Romneyland. Mitt had been talking since December about releasing a comprehensive immigration plan. Chen and the rest of his policy team agreed that doing so might help with Latinos, but they couldn't figure out what to put on paper that wouldn't enrage the GOP's anti-amnesty ranters. Rhoades had no thirst for any issue that would distract from the economy or inflame the right. Stevens believed that Romney could never escape the positions he'd taken during the nomination fight, as well as four years earlier. The president will pull out what you said in 2008, Stevens said. No matter what you say now, that stuff is gonna be there.

Ed Gillespie shook his head when he heard the conversations. From his experience with Bush, who garnered upwards of 40 percent of the Latino vote in 2004, Gillespie knew it was possible for a Republican to compete for that demographic. And that unless Romney did, he was doomed in Florida, a state he had to win. But here was Stevens, resisting running Spanish-language ads because he considered them a low priority for a cash-strapped campaign. And here was Romney, arguing that it was better to stick to lethal positions than be charged with inconsistency—talking as if this were a fundamental test of character.

The Langone gang at the Union League Club agreed with Gillespie, starting with Univision CEO Randy Falco. As I'm sure you know, our network has extraordinary reach in the Latino community, Falco said to Romney. The president has been on our air a dozen times. You've been on once. Consider this an open invitation; you can contact me directly.

"You're allowing other people to paint you as the anti-immigrant candidate," Falco went on. Whether you think Hispanics will agree with you or not, they deserve to hear your point of view. "Even if you don't agree with what I just said, if you don't start paying attention to our community, there won't be a Republican Party in ten to fifteen years," Falco added forcefully.

Before Romney could respond, Murdoch slammed his hand on the table and said, "He's right!"

The News Corp chief had only grown more vociferous and cantankerous in his disdain for Mitt in the course of the nomination battle; a few days before the Iowa caucuses, he tweeted that Santorum was the "only candidate with genuine big vision for [the] country." Now he laid into Romney on immigration.

I don't know if it's you or your advisers, but you've put yourself in a very bad way on this issue, Murdoch said. Talking about self-deportation—it's ridiculous. You're going to need to soften your rhetoric and come up with a more humane policy. If you can't figure out a way to appeal to Hispanics, there's no way for you to win.

Taken aback, Romney turned defensive. Obviously, I understand the significance of the Hispanic vote, Mitt said weakly. Latino outreach is important. (He noted that one of his sons spoke Spanish.) I know I took some positions in the primary that are difficult to deal with in the general election, Romney went on. But my positions are my positions. I don't have the option of changing them.

"I am not going to be seen as a flip-flopper," Romney said.

Murdoch left the meeting unimpressed, and wasn't shy about letting the world know. "When is Romney going to look like a challenger?" he tweeted later that afternoon. "Seems to play everything safe, make no news except burn off Hispanics."

Langone understood Romney's aversion to being cast as a flip-flopper. But he also thought that if Mitt didn't fix his Latino problem, he was done for. A week after swooning in Park City, Langone was having doubts again.

And he was not alone—though the source of the misgivings among others at the Union League Club was different. After a respite, the Obamans were starting to open up again on Romney with both barrels over Bain. One of the machers suggested that Mitt do more to defend his record in private equity. Romney waved off the suggestion and spouted boilerplate about class warfare.

Murdoch's lieutenant, Joel Klein, could barely believe the candidate's insouciance. Klein had worked in the Clinton White House. He knew a thing or two about negative campaigning.

Obama is about to make Bain a synonym for organized crime, Klein thought. *And this poor schmuck doesn't even see it coming.*

BOB WHITE SAW IT as clearly as Cassandra previsioned the fall of Troy. At fifty-six, White had been at Romney's side for most of his adult life. After growing up working class in Woburn, Massachusetts, he went to work for Mitt at Bain and Company in 1981 and was Bain Capital's first hire three years later. From the Olympics through the statehouse and into the presidential arena, White was Mitt's alter ego, aide-de-camp, in-house historian, personnel vetter, and gut-checker, all on a volunteer basis. (A part owner of the Boston Celtics, he was as rich as Romney.) Mitt called him "my wingman" or TQ—short for The Quail, a nickname based on the family of birds that includes the bobwhite. White called himself "Friend of Candidate." His devotion to Mitt was matched by and bound up in his devotion to Bain. Now he was laboring to save both of his four-letter loves from being left in ruins.

White recalled all too well the way Ted Kennedy had used Bain against Romney in 1994: to knock down his claims to being a job creator and cast him as a job destroyer. White viewed those famous laid-off-worker ads as impugning not only Mitt's business acumen but his (and Bain's) integrity. White considered the claims infuriating, unjust, despicable. He expected even worse in 2012.

Mitt's friend was bound and determined that Boston be ready. In April 2011, before Romney entered the race, White stood at a whiteboard, drawing charts and matrices, trying to elucidate the intricacies of private equity for Mitt's political schlubs. White believed there was a positive story to tell about Bain: the successful ventures, the charitable endeavors. But he was more concerned with Bain investments that presented political vulnerabilities: deals where the firm got fat but the portfolio companies failed; companies that laid off workers, engaged in offshoring, or were guilty of malfeasance. We need deep dives on all of these, White said. We need to be set up for rapid response when the attacks come.

For the better part of the next year, White immersed himself in research-ing the problem investments. By April 2012, he had timelines, fact sheets, and contact lists for them all. On a parallel track, he identified workers and executives at thriving companies to provide on-camera testimonials. That month, he established a three-person SWAT team, as he called it, dedicated solely to Bain.

White took little comfort from the Booker/Clinton backlash in late May. After its initial steelworker spot, Priorities rolled out another, then another, and then another in its Kennedy-style campaign. The ads didn't have much money behind them, but they lit up cable and the Web, especially one called "Stage," released in late June. It featured a former employee of an Indiana paper company bought by Bain, who told the story of coming in to work and being instructed to build a thirty-foot dais—from which it was announced that he and his co-workers were fired. "Turns out that when we built that stage," the hard hat said, "it was like building my own coffin."

The Obamans tested hundreds of spots in 2012; none was as effective as "Stage," which quickly racked up three million hits on YouTube. But even more problematic for Boston was a June 21 story in *The Washington Post* alleging that when "Romney was actively involved in running Bain . . . it owned companies that were pioneers in the practice of shipping work from the United States to overseas call centers and factories making computer components" in "low-wage countries like China and India."

Chicago knew the story was coming a week in advance, even before the reporter called Boston for comment. The Obamans had learned from the first Bain flare-up how combustible the issue was; a single spark could ignite a blaze. Their plan had been to wait until July to torch Romney on Bain and his income taxes. The *Post* piece caused them to grab their flame-throwers ten days early, queuing up a series of ads citing the paper's report that would unfurl over the next few weeks.

On the stump, Obama seized on the story with gusto and perfect pitch. "It was reported in *The Washington Post* that the companies [Romney's] firm owned were 'pioneers' in the outsourcing of American jobs to places like China and India," Obama said. After pausing pregnantly for three long beats, he exclaimed, in a tone that mixed incredulity and disgust, "Pio-neers!" Another beat. "We don't need an outsourcing pioneer in the Oval

Office. We need a president who will fight for American jobs and fight for American manufacturing."

Up in Boston, the *Post* story set White's hair on fire and his SWAT team into action. The piece was full of inaccuracies, White believed, but the errors weren't easy to prove. There were a lot of firms involved, more facts to gather, executives to contact. Six days later, ducks in a row, the campaign sent a delegation to the *Post* to demand a retraction, which was not forthcoming, then released a detailed rebuttal of the story to the press. The document was comprehensive, and White was proud of that. But in the era of Twitter and the freak show, the six-day turnaround scarcely qualified as rapid response.

Hobbling White's ability to move more swiftly was a factor hidden from the outside world: the staunch refusal of Bain to assist Boston on defense. A decade removed from the firm, Romney was a distant memory to all but a few executives; the institutional loyalty to Mitt was minimal, and the desire to wade into partisan politics nil. Bain's upper management and employees were split among Republicans and Democrats. There were even some Obama bundlers, who pleaded with Messina and Axelrod not to drag the firm into the campaign—extracting only a concession that Chicago would refrain from using an infamous photo of a young Mitt and some Bain associates clutching greenbacks.

The Bain brigade found the attacks on the firm upsetting, but hurt feelings were less important than protecting the franchise. The best way to do that, the firm's leadership decided, was to keep their heads down and avoid anything that resembled taking sides—publicly or privately. The only point of contact between Bain and Romneyland was managing director Sean Doherty, who spoke exclusively to White. Far from colluding with The Quail, Doherty more often gave him the stiff arm. In the spring, White had asked if Bain might provide an official breakdown of Romney's tenure: deals, revenues, and so on. Doherty politely refused. When the *Post* story broke, Doherty saw factual problems with it, too. But his attitude was: *Problem for the campaign, not a problem for Bain.*

Rationally, White was sympathetic to the firm's point of view. "Bain isn't in the campaign business," he would tell his colleagues on Commer-

cial Street. But White wasn't unemotional when it came to Bain. He and
Mitt were Bain men through and through. Bain had shaped them, Bain had
made them, Bain was their fountainhead; their reverence for the firm was so
encompassing that it left them with a massive Bain blind spot. But now
Romney was being "Bain-boated," as White put it, and Bain would do little
to help. For TQ, the situation was agonizing, torturous.

The intransigence of Bain was just one of the hurdles White was facing.
In meeting after meeting at campaign headquarters, he argued, sometimes
heatedly, that the time had come to man the barricades. To fight back against
the falsehoods and stand up for Romney's work in private equity. To air ads
featuring the pro-Bain testimonials they had collected. What White wanted
was a robust defense coupled with a muscular offense. What he found was
that Boston didn't have the inclination to do either—and that even if the will
had been present, the wallet, astonishingly, was not.

M YERS, RHOADES, AND STEVENS drove from Boston to Wolfeboro on July
3 to see Romney, who had slipped off the trail for a holiday break with
his family. The day was picture-perfect, cloudless and calm. Sitting down
with Mitt and Ann on the back deck of the house overlooking Lake Winnipesaukee, the trio took no pleasure in introducing dark clouds into such a
postcard setting. But they really had no choice. The cupboard was bare, and
unpleasant measures were required to refill it.

That Boston found itself impoverished was dumbfounding on its face.
The campaign was about to release its combined fund-raising number with
the RNC for June: a record $100 million–plus total. From casual observers
to sophisticated students of the interplay between politics and money, everyone and his mother assumed that Commercial Street was swimming in
simoleons.

Yet the money that Zwick's team was collecting now was mostly for the
general election, which meant it couldn't be spent until after Mitt officially
became the nominee in Tampa. Boston had always known that this inter-
regnal period would be tough. But the nomination fight had gone on longer
and been costlier than expected, and the campaign's wealthy contributors

had already written checks for the maximum allowable donations—leaving Romneyland with scant resources until the convention. Now, with the Obamans having robbed their autumn budget to saturate the summer airwaves, Romney was being outspent three or four to one in many markets.

Messina was keeping close tabs on Boston's finances. Just a month after the pivotal White House spending meeting, he was startled to discover what Boston knew all too well. On the basis of Federal Election Commission filings, he sketched out an estimate of what Romneyland's summer budget might look like and showed it to Obama.

"They have no small donors," Messina said. "They're gonna run out of money."

Obama studied the papers and said, "I bet he writes a check."

Given Romney's wealth and history of check writing, much of the world assumed the same. Yet from the outset in Boston, that option had been off the table. Whenever the subject was raised, Myers would say curtly, "Not gonna happen." After doling out $45 million in 2008, Romney felt he had reached his personal lifetime dollar limit in the pursuit of the presidency. Stevens and Rhoades, moreover, believed self-funding would exacerbate Mitt's image problems. *Here's the rich guy trying to buy the race,* thought Rhoades. *Not good.*

The unwillingness of the rich guy to take advantage of being a rich guy for fear of looking like a rich guy was a chain of logic too Ouroborosian to ponder for too long. The Boston brain trust had come up with a potential alternative: using forthcoming general election funds as collateral for a $20 million line of credit. But there were campaign finance hoops to jump through to borrow the money, and in the worst-case scenario, Romney might have to personally guarantee the loan.

Perched next to Mitt at the picnic table on the deck, Rhoades laid out the direness of Boston's straits. Guv, we're getting crushed on the air, he said, and ran through the numbers for his boss.

What about the super PACs? asked Romney. What about Restore?

The super PACs are doing what they're doing, Rhoades replied. They're spending money, but we don't see it having much impact. We think this line of credit is the only way to go.

Romney said he wanted time to talk it over with Ann. In 2008, self-funding had been a necessary evil. In 2012, his reluctance derived in part from not wanting donors to think, *If he's going to write a check, why should I?* But a line of credit was different. In all likelihood, Boston would be able to secure the loan without Romney putting himself on the hook. And even if it came to that, the optics would hardly be as damaging as if he simply whipped out his checkbook. The next day, Romney informed Rhoades that he was in.

Stevens was relieved that Boston's coffers would soon be replenished. The $20 million infusion would provide air cover until Tampa—but only bare cover. Which made the question of how to spend it all the more pressing. The scarcity of dollars was one reason Stevens had no interest in running pro-Bain ads, but his aversion was driven by more than economics.

Unlike White, Stevens had been skeptical that Chicago would fixate on Bain. There were many things Mitt could be hit for: his Bushist policies, his Massachusetts record, social issues, flip-flopping, whatever. That Bain happened to be front and center did little to alter Stuart's uncluttered strategic view: Boston had to attack more than defend, prosecuting Obama on the economy and not letting Chicago put Romney on trial over Bain. *How many people in 2008 thought Obama was a Muslim?* Stevens mused. *How many in 1992 thought Bill Clinton was a womanizer who had problems telling the truth?* The Obama and Clinton campaigns prevailed by not letting themselves be embroiled in those matters day after day. They ran on what they wanted to run on. The Romneyites had to do the same.

Stevens's desire not to litigate Bain put him at loggerheads with White. Stuart respected TQ but thought his feelings for the firm clouded his judgment; when Bob spoke of Bain, it sounded as if he were cooing over one of his children. (This is why you shouldn't referee your own kids' soccer games, Stevens would joke.) The testimonials touting the firm struck him as beside the point. He reminded White that, just as Bain wasn't in the campaign business, the campaign wasn't in the Bain business. Mitt's problem wasn't that he worked in private equity. His problem was that private equity made him so rich that many voters believed he couldn't relate to them. *We can convince people Mitt's not a bad person because he was involved with Bain,* Stevens thought. *But that won't get him elected president.*

Romney wished there were a silver bullet that would accomplish both objectives. Bain had been his bane since the 1994 Senate campaign, and no one had come up with a way of neutralizing the issue. The campaign produced and focus-grouped a number of TV commercials, but none did the trick.

The outsourcing charges against him were weak on the merits, Mitt believed. The bad stuff had happened after he left Bain. He took great satisfaction in the number of newspaper fact-checkers who ruled against the *Washington Post*. But Romney assumed that Chicago knew there were Bain deals in which he'd been involved that were more damning, including a health care company that committed Medicare fraud, on whose board he had served. His suspicion was that the Obamans were trying to lure him into the briar patch. *As soon as I respond to one Bain attack with an ad, they'll hit me with the next one, then the next one, then the next one,* Romney thought. *Pretty soon, the whole campaign will be about Bain.* Close as he was to White, Romney not only deferred to Stevens on politics but agreed with him about one basic principle: "If you're explaining in politics, you're losing."

WHEN HALEY BARBOUR HEARD that line out of Boston, he laughed and thought of another adage, one that he considered more apt: "An attack unanswered is an attack admitted."

Boston's quietude on the air regarding Bain was mystifying to Barbour, who was raising money for Crossroads, and to the other Republican super-PAC guys. Although they underestimated the extent of the financial crisis in Romneyland, they had known all along that the campaign would be far from flush over the summer—and it was their job to fill the void. Restore's Larry McCarthy kept waiting for a smoke signal from Boston that it wanted help on Bain. Rove was sending up white puffs of his own. He pushed Crossroads to do a Bain response ad to alert Team Romney that the group was willing to lend a hand. *Give us a message,* Rove thought, *and we'll follow you.*

Chicago viewed Boston's unwillingness to engage with puzzlement but a certain admiration. *My God, they're disciplined,* thought Messina. *They've got a theory and they're sticking to it.*

The Obamans were determined to unstick them. To the extent that Romney had tried to rebut the Bain attacks, he claimed that the outsourcing, offshoring, plant closings, and layoffs at the companies in question had occurred after he left the firm in 1999 to run the Salt Lake City Games. But on July 12, the *Boston Globe* ran a story saying Romney had signed Securities and Exchange Commission documents listing him as the "sole stockholder, chairman of the board, chief executive officer, and president" of Bain from 1999 to 2002.

The Obamans had been aware of the documents for some time. They were ready to pounce. On a conference call with reporters that afternoon, Cutter let fly: "Either Mitt Romney, through his own work and his own signature, was misrepresenting his position at Bain to the SEC, which is a felony, or he was misrepresenting his position at Bain to the American people to avoid responsibility for some of the consequences of his investments."

The fundamental laws of freak-show physics dictated the shorthanding of the Cutter comment in the media coverage: she had accused Romney of being a felon.

In all the internal debate in Boston over Bain, Romney had never exerted decisive control over how to respond. But he did now. Both outraged by the supposed insinuation of criminality and vaguely gleeful at the opportunity for umbrage, he instructed his staff to arrange a round-robin of interviews the next day with all five TV news networks. Romney's staff often tried to hold Mitt back from the media. There was some hesitation now. But Romney was insistent.

"I want to go out there on this," he said. "Full-bore."

The Romney round-robin took place in Wolfeboro and offered a reminder of how much—for all the emphasis on strategy and strategists, polling and pollsters, media and message—basic candidate skills matter at the presidential level. And of the Grand Canyon–size gap that existed in that regard between Romney and 44. Halting, abstruse, and unconvincing, Mitt managed to create only a greater muddle with his attempt at clarity.

"How should we be thinking about this?" asked Jan Crawford of CBS News. "What was your role? You were the sole owner until 2002?"

"I was the owner of the general partnership, but there were investors, which included pension funds and various entities of all kinds that owned, if you will, the investments of the firm," Romney replied. "I was the owner of an entity which was a management entity. That entity was one which I had ownership of until the time the retirement program was put in place. But I had no responsibility whatsoever after February of 1999 for the management or ownership—management, rather—of Bain Capital."

Obama hadn't been happy about Cutter's insertion of the word "felony" into the conversation. It put the focus on her—and, by extension, him—rather than keeping it on Romney, where he wanted it. But Mitt's round-robin returned the pink to the presidential cheek.

"I guess he doesn't have an answer on this yet," Obama said wryly to Plouffe.

Just as heartening was Romney's response regarding his income tax returns, another story that the Obamans had been pushing frantically alongside Bain for the past two weeks. Feeding oppo to the AP had yielded a story about a Bermuda-based holding company that had never appeared in Romney's financial disclosures. In a speech to the National Council of La Raza, Biden had hit him: "Romney wants you to show your papers, but he won't show us his." Yet Mitt refused to budge. "People always want to get more," he told CNN. "Two years [is all] that people are going to have."

That night, Chicago released a new TV spot titled "Firms." A few days earlier, on a conference call with the campaign's advertising team, someone had thrown out the idea of creating an ad that tied up all of Romney's financial pathogens in one package: the tax havens, the outsourcing, the works. Harking back to the Republican nomination contest, Axelrod observed, It's ironic that a guy who goes around singing "America the Beautiful" has all these foreign problems—and the ad guys were off and running.

The resulting spot used as its soundtrack Romney's off-key rendition of the song at the Villages on the eve of the Florida primary. As Mitt warbled, empty factories and offices appeared on-screen, along with newspaper headlines about Bain shipping jobs to Mexico, China, and India, followed by more about Romney's Swiss bank account, Bermuda, and the Caymans. "Mitt Romney's not the solution," read the final slate. "He's the problem."

After "Stage," "Firms" was the ad that tested best of all the spots run in 2012. The Obamans ran it more than thirteen thousand times around the country, one of the heaviest buys of the cycle.

For Romney, "Firms" was the final body blow of a punishing six weeks. For Bob White, it was worse. The Quail, after all, was the one who had convinced Romney to sing "America the Beautiful" that night in Florida. Now his whimsy had been subverted—its results transformed into a weapon by Mitt's enemies, and a soundtrack for a summer of pain.

I N LATE JULY, Romney set off on a seven-day foreign trip to England, Israel, and Poland. The idea of an overseas expedition had been kicked around Boston for months, and had an obvious precedent. Four summers earlier, the Obamans had staged a sojourn for their candidate so ambitious it would have tested the mettle of a sitting president and his team: eight countries in ten days, including two war zones (Afghanistan and Iraq). Their execution was flawless, the images beamed back home priceless.

The Romneyites had more modest aims and approached their man's trip less exactingly. The lynchpin was the London leg, about which Mitt was ada- mant. As a former president of an Olympic organizing committee, he always attended the Games, and with Ann's dressage horse, Rafalca, in competition this year, there was no way he wouldn't be there. The next two stops were chosen haphazardly, after other options in the Middle East, Latin America, Europe, and Canada were discarded. While Romney's foreign policy advis- ers were in favor of the trip to burnish his global credentials, the rest of his team saw little upside. No one was really in charge of the thing. No senior political or communications advisers would be along for the ride. The itin- erary was a jam-packed jumble of photo ops, interviews, and fund-raisers, with no coherent message strategy.

A small handful of Mitt's people were nervous about the lack of prepara- tion. One of them was Kevin Madden, Romney's 2008 spokesman and a shrewd operative who had just rejoined the team. This kind of junket is a high-stakes high-wire act, Madden kept telling the Boston brain trust. "There's a big difference," he said, "between building a schedule and plan- ning a trip."

And Romney wasn't even thrilled with the schedule. After spending sev- eral days on an exhausting West Coast fund-raising swing, he woke up in Santa Monica around 5:00 a.m. on July 24, and flew to Reno, Nevada, to give a speech on foreign policy; it was the last time he would feel free to criticize Obama before his stint abroad. He then boarded his jet for the two-flight, eleven-hour schlep to London, with a stop in Boston to pick up Ann. Settling into his seat and getting his first gander at his calendar for the next week, Romney moaned, "You guys are killing me."

The Gulfstream 5 ferrying him and Ann across the pond touched down at Heathrow early the next morning. When the flight attendant jostled him awake, he looked like death warmed over: barely able to open his eyes, his usually perfect hair sticking every which way. (Ann applied some water to try to tame the multitude of cowlicks.) Arriving at the IOC Hilton, he had four hours of downtime before sitting for an interview with NBC News's Brian Williams. To the extent that there was a strategy for the London piece of the trip, it was for Romney to strut his Olympic credentials and bask in the glow of the Games in sessions with Williams, *Today*'s Matt Lauer, and CNN's Piers Morgan.

In a drawing room at the Tower of London, Williams asked about dressage; Mitt professed ignorance. ("This is Ann's sport," he said.) Then the anchor tendered an innocuous question about the Games: "In the short time you've been here in London, do they look ready to your experienced eye?"

"You know, it's hard to know just how well it will turn out," Romney said, and referenced press reports about various challenges the Games were facing. "There are a few things that were disconcerting, the stories about the private security firm not having enough people, the supposed strike of the immigration and customs officials, that obviously is not something which is encouraging . . . [Then there are] the people of the country. Do they come together and celebrate the Olympic moment? And that's something which we only find out once the Games actually begin."

The Olympic comments were not included in the package that Williams aired that night. But in Chicago, a young Obaman on the digital rapid-response team named Matthew McGregor noticed them in the NBC News transcript. British-born, a former Labour Party and union operative, McGregor shipped the transcript to some pals in the British press, flagging the potentially rankling bits. *The Times* of London turned a piece around fast, splashing the story on its website the next morning, under the headline MITT ROMNEY CASTS DOUBT ON LONDON 2012 PREPARATIONS.

The Obamans had been trying to throw a spanner in Romney's works

for days: deriding the trip as an exercise in expatriate buck-raking, critiquing his management of the 2002 Games for their reliance on taxpayer
subsidies. But McGregor's intercession turned the frame into Romney-as-
not-ready-for-prime-time-player—and one-man special-relationship wreck-
ing crew.

In London, Prime Minister David Cameron aimed an obligue shot at
Romney's achievement in Salt Lake: "We are holding an Olympic Games in
one of the busiest, most active, bustling cities anywhere in the world. Of
course it's easier if you hold an Olympic Games in the middle of nowhere."
The city's mayor, Boris Johnson, took a contemptuous jab—"There's a guy
called Mitt Romney who wants to know whether we are ready!"—eliciting
anti-Mitt booing from a crowd of sixty thousand in Hyde Park. The story
led local, national, and international newscasts, and set the Web ablaze. Before the day was out, Mitt had committed two more gaffes, apparently for-
getting Labour leader Ed Miliband's name when they met and blurting out
that he'd sat down with the head of Britain's secret intelligence service,
MI6—when such sessions were normally kept on the down-low. By midday,
Mitt had earned his own Twitter hashtag: #Romneyshambles.

On Commercial Street, panic set in—not just about what was unfolding
in Britain but about the rest of the trip. In a tizzy, Stevens packed a
bag, bought an airline ticket, and flew to London. When he arrived, the
Murdoch-owned *Sun* was carrying a blaring banner headline that read
MITT THE TWIT.

Romney's private reaction was annoyance with the entire brouhaha: he
had answered truthfully, as a former Olympic organizer, referring to problems that were well known. In public, he furiously, slavishly backpedaled.
"I'm *absolutely* convinced that the people here are ready for the Games," he
told Lauer that day, before attending the opening ceremonies.

Romney called Rhoades to see how badly the coverage of trip was playing back home.

"I'm not going to lie to you," Rhoades said dejectedly. "It's not very
good."

The mood in the White House was decidedly more jovial. National
security aide Ben Rhodes recounted in detail the Boris Johnson rally for

Obama. The president cracked up. It's a good rule, when you go to a country, not to insult the people who live there, Obama said. And then, if you're gonna do it, don't do it more than once.

As Romney flew off to Israel, he knew that the whole trip was already ruined; after London, nothing else would break through or matter. He was wrong and right. In both the Holy Land and Polonia, Mitt delivered decent speeches that were ignored. But both legs of the trip produced more bad headlines—largely as a result of what had become an openly hostile atmosphere between Mitt, Ann, and the Romney staff and the press on the plane. When reporters in Warsaw shouted questions at Mitt, a young press aide, Rick Gorka, snapped, "Kiss my ass." The Romneys were not displeased.

On his way back to Boston on July 31, Mitt sent an e-mail summarizing the foreign trip to a handful of his aides: "A+ work by the team . . . Operations was extraordinary—smooth as a Swiss watch, no offense to non-Swiss peoples. I can only imagine what the media looks like at home. And I don't think I want to find out."

For Democrats and Republicans alike, Mitt's adventure abroad capped a period that called into question the basic competence of the candidate and his campaign. In the space of just six weeks, Romney had traveled from the triumphalism of Park City to the humiliation of Piccadilly Circus. Mitt was beat up and bummed out; he knew he needed to turn the page. But he took comfort in the fact that a huge chance was close at hand.

The morning after his return stateside, Romney tramped into Commercial Street for a hastily arranged meeting. He wanted to hear, one last time, the views of his brain trust about who his running mate should be. After months of cogitation, Mitt had nearly arrived at his vice-presidential destination—though the road that had delivered him there had been neither straight nor smooth.

17

PROJECT GOLDFISH

IN CONVENTIONAL POLITICAL TERMS, Romney's challenge in picking a VP presented a complex puzzle. With Tampa less than a month away, he was running four to six points behind the incumbent in the national polls. He was hurting with women, hurting with Hispanics, hurting with blue-collar whites. His standing in the industrial Midwest and the West was shaky. The Republican base remained unenthused by him and the middle of the electorate unimpressed. The quandary was which of these maladies he should try to heal with his running mate. For many members of the Republican smarty-pants set, one thing was increasingly clear: Romney needed a game changer.

Romney didn't see it that way, at least not at the start. When he tapped Beth Myers to lead the search for his VP, Mitt put forth two criteria and a precept. The criteria applied to the candidates: that they be qualified, and immediately *perceived* as qualified, to be commander in chief; and that there be nothing in their backgrounds that could become a distraction for the campaign. The precept applied to Myers and her assignment. When decision time came, Romney said, he wanted to have a choice—not be informed, with the clock ticking, that there was really only one viable option.

What Mitt was looking for was an orderly process and a no-drama pick. For his veepstakes to be, in other words, as un-Palinesque as possible.

The Palin precedent hovered over Myers. The story of how McCain arrived at his selection—and in particular the hasty, half-assed pseudo-vetting she received—had attained wide infamy. And that, in turn, dramatically brightened the spotlight shining on Myers as she took up her task; she was stunned when the announcement of her appointment generated scads of headlines. The attention and scrutiny that came with it made Myers nervous, but also hypervigilant. She took extravagant precautions to minimize the likelihood of chaos, surprises, or leaks.

Myers set up her operation in a third-floor office on Commercial Street that became known as "the clean room." There was a locking PIN pad on the door, library carrels inside, and a number of fireproof, waterproof safes in which materials on the candidates were stored. Myers kept the keys to the safes in a tea tin in her desk; anyone needing access had to go through her. The vetting team consisted of five people: a savvy political researcher, Ted Newton; his assistant, Chris Oman; and three lawyers brought on board from outside the campaign, Tim Flanigan, Chris Landau, and Mark Nielsen. Because Boston's servers were under continual assault by Chinese hackers, the computers in the clean room were not connected to the Internet. Myers insisted that the team be extremely cautious about what they put in e-mail. Newton and Oman concluded it was best to communicate in code. Based on their junk-food-saturated vetting diet, they called their undertaking Project Goldfish (after the crackers)—ultimately giving each of the VP finalists an aquatic code name.

In keeping with the secretive nature of Project Goldfish, there would be no polling of potential running mates. (Neil Newhouse was disappointed; he had a questionnaire ready to go.) Romney conferred with grandees such as Jim Baker and Dick Cheney but refrained from showing his cards. Even among his senior advisers, there were only a handful with whom he had discreet ex-parte discussions during his early deliberations, including Stevens, Leavitt, and Zwick, the last of whom he consulted about which contenders would provide the most fund-raising pop. Beyond that, the conversation boiled down to Mitt and Beth.

Myers's plan was to have Project Goldfish completed by Memorial Day. In April, she presented Romney with a list of two dozen names, which he whittled down to eleven: New Hampshire senator Kelly Ayotte, Texas senator John Cornyn, Chris Christie, Mitch Daniels, Bill Frist, Mike Huckabee, Bob McDonnell, Tim Pawlenty, Rob Portman, Marco Rubio, and Paul Ryan. Within a month, the vetters had assembled preliminary research books on the eleven, which Romney perused and then rendered his short list: Christie, Pawlenty, Portman, Rubio, and Ryan.

In Mitt's eyes, the candidate dubbed Fishconsin by the vetters held a special place among the final five. During the nomination fight, Romney had come to like Ryan a great deal. Their initial contact occurred in November, when Mitt sought the House budget chief's counsel on entitlement reform. Soon Ryan was peppering Romney with e-mails offering policy and political advice. The time the two spent campaigning together in Wisconsin around the primary lit Romney up. In his daily call with Rhoades, he rabbited on about how super-duper Ryan was. *The Guv sounds like one of my buddies with a crush on a new honey,* thought Rhoades.

Romney provoked no equivalent swoon from Ryan. In 2011, Fishconsin had considered diving into the presidential pond himself, in no small part because of his skepticism about Mitt. Like Christie, Ryan was beseeched to enter the fray by members of the billionaires' club, and especially those associated with the Koch brothers. But Paul's wife, Janna, wasn't keen on him running; she thought Romney was good enough. And the rigors of a presidential bid didn't thrill Paul, either. At a meeting one day in his office on Capitol Hill with one of the Kochs' political advisers, Ryan remarked, "Wouldn't it be easier just to be picked as vice president? Because then it's only, like, two months."

Ryan's misgivings about Romney were mainly ideological. Although Mitt was a conservative, his familiarity with and commitment to *movement* conservatism was tenuous, Ryan thought. He was faintly appalled by Romney's attachment to Stevens, whom Ryan saw as clueless and indifferent when it came to the movement. In his e-mails and conversations with Romney, Ryan took on the role of tutor, trying to bring Mitt up to speed and help him overcome the wariness of the party's purists and warriors. At the peak of the Gingrich bubble, Ryan told Romney over the phone, "Mitt, there's not a vast right-wing conspiracy, but there is a small right-wing conspiracy—and you're not doing well with them."

When Ryan learned he had made Romney's short list, he was alternately excited and dubious. The positions Ryan had advanced on entitlements, tax reform, and the budget were highly detailed and exceedingly controversial. "There's a lot of sharp knives in my drawer" was a phrase he used with friends to sum up the problem. And he saw no indication that Romney was eager to grab hold of such a serrated running mate.

Fishconsin wasn't alone among the final five in doubting he'd wind up being picked. Pawlenty believed he wouldn't because he was from Minnesota, which was destined to end up in the Democratic column in November. Rubio believed he wouldn't because he barely knew Romney; they had been on the trail together only once, and who in their right mind would saddle himself with a stranger as his understudy? Christie believed he wouldn't because it made no sense to have a ticket featuring a pair of northeastern governors; he also thought Mitt would shy away from anyone who might overshadow him—and Christie, being Christie, felt that was a certainty.

Submitting to being vetted by Myers's team was a serious commitment. The procedure amounted to a political body-cavity search. There was an intrusive, seventy-plus-part questionnaire to answer, income taxes and health records to turn over, and more. Yet despite their assessments that they were unlikely to be chosen, Ryan, Rubio, Pawlenty, and Christie had all agreed by mid-May to open up their kimonos—leaving only the fifth man fully clothed. Unlike the others, Portman believed he might well be picked. But the prospect of being tapped filled him with no small degree of anguish.

PORTMAN'S VEEPISH VIRTUES were easy to see. A former congressman, U.S. trade representative, and head of OMB, he had as firm a grasp of fiscal issues as anyone in Washington. He was solid, stolid, and whip smart. He had won election to the Senate in 2010 in arguably the most important battleground state on the map—snagging 57 percent of the vote and carrying eighty-two of Ohio's eighty-eight counties. Portman was no firecracker, but his staid dependability and managerial affect would reinforce Romney's argument that he was capable of fixing what ailed the capital and the economy. Portman's blandness might even be an asset, making Romney look comparatively dashing.

There were, however, two things about which Boston and the rest of the political world were not aware regarding Portman: that his son Will, a junior at Yale, was gay; and that Portman was planning at some point soon to publicly abandon his opposition to same-sex marriage.

When Romney called with the short-list news, Portman put him off, saying that he wanted to consult his family—his wife, his two other children, and Will. Although Will was out of the closet at Yale, he wasn't ready to be out on the national stage, and Portman wasn't prepared to announce his newfound support for gay marriage. Father and son had been talking about going public together for a while, but they wanted to do it on their own timetable. If Portman were picked, that plan would be out the window.

A week later, Portman called Romney and declined to go forward, without explaining about Will. Portman hoped that would be the end of the story—but it wasn't. Instead, speculation was rampant in the press about whether his name was on the short list. Reporters inquired constantly if he was being vetted. Portman didn't want to lie, and hated being coy. In late May, he asked Myers if she had any objection to his putting out a statement saying that he had chosen not to be considered.

"Oh, no, don't do that!" Myers exclaimed. That wouldn't be smart, and it would be harmful to us. You need to talk to Stuart.

Portman was a Stevens client; more, the two were friends. Soon, Stuart was on the line explaining the source of Boston's distress. On May 21 on Fox News, Mitch Daniels had given Romney a kick in the shins when he told an interviewer "Of course not" when asked if he was being vetted. "If I thought that call was coming," Daniels added, "I would disconnect the phone."

Stevens pleaded with Portman not to add injury to insult. If you put out a statement saying you turned us down, Democrats will jump all over it: Nobody wants to be with Romney! What does that tell you about the guy? Et cetera. Why don't you just put your name in the mix and see what happens?

Portman sympathized with Boston's plight, had no desire to do anything to hurt Romney. But he also didn't want to continue living this lie, he told Stevens—and decided to come clean with him and Myers about Will. Both of the Romneyites assured Portman that his son's sexual orientation was irrelevant. Doesn't help us, doesn't hurt us, Stevens said. Portman made clear that if he were picked, he would also announce that he was changing his position on gay marriage. That might cause the campaign heartburn, he said. No, it's fine, Myers and Stevens replied. There's no reason for any of this to preclude you from being on the short list.

Portman's circumstances were mighty strange—not just living a lie but living it in no-man's-land. What he cared about most was his family, and especially protecting Will. But between the freak show and the press corps's obsession with the veepstakes, removing himself from the short list would raise more questions than it answered. Reporters would furiously try to figure out why he was standing down, possibly beating a path to New Haven.

Portman went back to his family and told them about his talks with Boston. I haven't been very successful in convincing the media that I'm not on the list, he said. If I continue to stay off it, the press is gonna get to the bottom of this soon and maybe start saying, "It's because your son is gay."

Portman's wife and kids were in favor of whatever he was in favor of.

If this is something you want, Dad, I'm ready to go, Will said cheerfully.

With that, the fifth man joined the short list in mid-June—even as one of the other four was behaving as if he wanted to be scratched off it. Although Christie had agreed to be considered more than a month earlier, the vetters were having a hard time extracting information from Trenton. Christie's material was coming in late, and what came in was incomplete.

Myers's irritation was palpable and acute. Project Goldfish had already missed its Memorial Day deadline; a new one was set for July 1. Myers planned to deliver final vetting dossiers to Romney on the same visit to New Hampshire in which they would discuss the campaign loan. As the end of the month drew near, four of the files were in fine shape: those of Rubio (Pescado), Pawlenty (Lakefish), Portman (Filet-O-Fish), and Fishconsin. But the one belonging to the candidate that the vetters dubbed Pufferfish was still an awful mess.

M YERS AND ROMNEY MET in Wolfeboro to go over the quartet of completed final dossiers and the ragged Pufferfish file. Four of the candidates were less than ideal in various dimensions. Rubio was fresh-faced but inexperienced, falling short in the ready-to-be-president department. Pawlenty packed little political punch. For all of Portman's attractive qualities, his downsides were abundant, too. His executive-branch experience came under Bush 43, from whose legacy Mitt wanted distance, not further association; and Portman, though not nearly as rich as Romney, was a multimillionaire.

Then there was Christie. The initial research on the New Jersey governor set off warning bells for Romney. Among other items, there were stories about an investment scandal involving Christie's brother, Todd. Russ Schriefer tried to ease Mitt's mind regarding the assorted contretemps, saying, Oh, all that stuff was vetted in the governor's race. Romney scoffed. *Nothing is vetted in a governor's race!* he thought. *A presidential race is a whole different ball game!*

Now, as he looked over the Christie vetting file, the conclusion was inescapable: the Pufferfish option was kaput, making Fishconsin seem like the best catch in the aquarium.

The likelihood that Romney would wind up with Ryan was met with unhappiness by Stevens. Stuart didn't see Ryan as the only answer—or any answer at all. Stevens liked Paul personally, but he was wary about being forced to take ownership of his budget and Medicare plans; he feared that Mitt would be sliced and diced by the blades in Ryan's drawer. Stevens had little idea what was going on with the vetting. Myers kept him out of that loop. Right around the time that Mitt was giving up on Christie, Stevens began strenuously pushing for him.

The irony here was thick, given Stevens's strident opinions about Christie's behavior during the Hamlet of Drumthwacket period. But Chicago's financial superiority and the pounding that Romney was taking from its negative ads had convinced Stevens that Boston would have to rely on earned media to compete. It was here that Christie was golden. The press scorned Mittens, but loved Big Boy. His voice was like an air horn, cutting through the clutter. There was no one better at making the referendum case against Obama, at nailing the president to the wall with ferocity and caustic humor. Christie's temperament was ideally suited to the unfolding tenor of the race.

"We're in a street fight, and he's a street fighter," Stevens told Romney. "He's the *best* street fighter—and he's comfortable saying things that you're not comfortable saying."

A few days later, Stevens happened to catch Christie on C-SPAN giving a speech in Washington at the Brookings Institution. It was bighearted brawlerism at its best: direct, no-nonsense, confident, and self-congratulatory, unflinchingly conservative but comfortably nudging up against centrism, with nods to bipartisan cooperation. At the end, Christie unfurled an anecdote about visiting his cancer-stricken mother in the hospital in her dying days. "She reached over, and she grabbed my hand, and she said, 'Go to work, it's where you belong,'" Christie said. "'There's nothing left unsaid between us.'"

Stevens e-mailed a video link of the speech to Romney. Take a look at this, he wrote. A little while later, Stevens's cell phone rang. It was Romney, having just watched the speech. "Wow," he said.

In the nine months since Christie's endorsement of Romney, Boston had formed a mixed view of Big Boy. He was a fund-raising dynamo, but he and his staff were overbearing and hard to work with, demanding in ways that would have been unthinkable from any other surrogate. Trenton insisted on private jets, lavish spreads of food, space for a massive entourage. Romney ally Wayne Berman looked at the bubble around Christie and thought, *He's not the president of the United States, you know?*

Chronically behind schedule, Christie made a habit of showing up late to Romney fund-raising events. In May, he was so tardy to a donor reception at the Grand Hyatt New York that Mitt wound up taking the stage to speak before Christie arrived. When the Jersey governor finally made his grand entrance, it was as if Mitt had been his warm-up act.

Punctuality mattered to Romney. Christie's lateness bugged him. Mitt also cared about fitness, and was prone to poke fun at those who didn't. ("Oh, there's your date for tonight," he would say to male members of his traveling crew when they spied a chunky lady on the street.) Romney marveled at Christie's girth, his difficulties in making his way down the narrow aisle of the campaign bus. Watching a video of Christie without his suit jacket on, Romney cackled to his aides, "Guys! Look at *that!*"

But Mitt was grateful for Christie's endorsement and everything else he'd done. He appreciated Chris's persona, his shtick, his forcefulness, his intuitive connection with voters. That night at the Grand Hyatt, at a high-dollar dinner after the main event, Christie's argument for Mitt was more compelling than anything the nominee could manage. Romney was aware of how jaundiced Stevens was about Christie—which made Stuart's advocacy for choosing the guy as VP all the more suasive.

On July 8, the vetting of Pufferfish restarted. A list of questions arising out of the public record and Christie's incomplete file from June was drafted. Mark Nielsen, who had been Romney's general counsel as governor, was put on the case. What commenced was an eleven-day crash operation, filled with eighteen-hour deskbound stints for the vetters. The scenario wasn't precisely Palinesque; her vet had consumed less than a week. But in some ways, it was worse. With Romney about to set off on his West Coast fundraising swing and then on to the foreign trip, Project Goldfish was up against the clock—and running headlong into more intransigence from Trenton.

The sole interface between Commercial Street and Christieworld was Myers and Palatucci. The calls were not infrequent. Trenton's view of the vet was unusual, but par for the course when it came to Christie: We'll help you, but on our terms and timing, and if that's not sufficient, go pound sand.

Palatucci thought Myers was erratic and hysterical; Christie agreed. Myers had questions not only for Palatucci but *about* him. Aware of a series of stories in *The New York Times* about a shady chain of New Jersey halfway houses owned by a company at which Palatucci was an executive, she instructed her team to start vetting the aide. Calling around to politically plugged-in friends, Myers asked, What's the deal with Palatucci? Does he have baggage? Is there a cloud over him in the tri-state area?

The list of questions about Christie to which the vetters wanted answers was extensive and troubling. More than once, Myers reported back that Palatucci's response was, in effect, Why do we need to give you that piece of information? Myers told her team, We have to assume if they're not answering, it's because the answer is bad.

For the past two and a half years, Christie had received skin-blanching exposure from the klieg lights of the national media. But the vetters were stunned by the garish controversies lurking in the shadows of his record. There was a 2010 Department of Justice Inspector General's investigation of Christie's spending patterns in his job prior to the governorship, which criticized him for being "the U.S. attorney who most often exceeded the government [travel expense] rate without adequate justification" and for offering "insufficient, inaccurate, or no justification" for stays at swank hotels such as the Four Seasons. (Beyond the expense abuse, the report raised questions for the vetters about Christie's relationship with a top female deputy who accompanied him on many of the trips.) There was the fact that Christie worked as a lobbyist on behalf of the Securities Industry Association at a time when Bernie Madoff was a senior SIA official—and sought an exemption from New Jersey's Consumer Fraud Act. There was Christie's decision to steer hefty government contracts to donors and political allies such as former attorney general John Ashcroft, which sparked a congressional hearing. There was a defamation lawsuit brought against Christie, arising out of his successful 1994 run to oust an incumbent in a local Garden State race. Then there was Todd Christie, who in 2008 agreed to a settlement of civil charges by the Securities and Exchange Commission in which he acknowledged making "hundreds of trades in which customers had been systematically overcharged." (Todd also oversaw a family foundation whose activities and purpose raised eyebrows among the vetters.) And all of that was on top of a litany of glaring matters that sparked concern on Myers's team: Christie's other lobbying clients; his investments overseas; the You-Tube clips that helped make him a star but might call into doubt his presidential temperament; and the status of his health.

Some of these were probably nothingburgers—though the vetters still needed answers. Some were inarguably disturbing, such as the IG report. (Lanhee Chen, who normally lent a hand on the vetting on policy matters, thought the Justice Department report was troubling enough to take it up directly with Romney.) But, added together, they were a potential political nightmare.

Ted Newton, managing Project Goldfish under Myers, had come into the vet liking Christie for his brashness and straight talk. Now, surveying the sum and substance of what the team was finding, Newton told his colleagues, If Christie had been in the nomination fight against us, we would have destroyed him—he wouldn't be able to run for governor again. When you look below the surface, Newton said, it's not pretty.

EARLY SUNDAY MORNING, JULY 15, Romney got on a conference call with the Boston brain trust to talk about the veepstakes. For the first time, he revealed to his senior team who was on his short list and asked for their opinions, without tipping his own hand.

The overwhelming consensus was for Ryan. Rhoades, Newhouse, Gillespie, and Peter Flaherty were all in Camp Fishconsin. The arguments in Ryan's favor were many. He was young, telegenic, Irish Catholic, with blue-collar appeal, and might put his state in play. He would rouse the base and sharpen the policy contrast with Obama. While the Ryan budget and Medicare plan were political cons, Romney was half pregnant with them anyway—so why not marry their most articulate defender? Mike Leavitt and Bob White argued that Mitt should pick the best governing partner; privately, both expressed support for Ryan. Look, Mitt, you've never worked in Washington, Leavitt said. Having someone who can swing a bat for you on the Hill and knows the budget inside out makes a lot of sense.

But Stevens remained unconvinced about Ryan, and adamantly in favor of Christie. Shielded from the crash vet and what it was turning up, Romney's chief strategist was making a purely political argument—one that contradicted the considered judgment of virtually everyone else on whom Mitt relied for advice. Such was the potency of the Romney–Stevens bond that Mitt kept Christie in the pack.

Romney was somewhat shielded from the Pufferfish vet, too, but knew it wasn't going smoothly. Myers informed him that a significant problem had not been solved: the strictures of the same pay-to-play regulations that kept Christie from tapping Wall Street cash in New Jersey.

Romney's lawyers were still looking into the matter. It was complicated. One possibility was that, if Christie were picked as VP, Romney would no longer be able to raise money from many financial institutions for the rest of the campaign. Not great, but manageable, maybe. Another possibility was that Boston would have to return the cash it had already raised on the Street—unacceptable. The attorneys had been exploring workarounds; none was watertight. Myers had pressed Palatucci for help figuring it out; none was forthcoming.

The easiest solution would be for Christie to resign as governor if he got the nod. A few hours after the conference call, Romney phoned him to float that notion. "Are there any circumstances in which you'd consider resigning to become the nominee?" Mitt asked.

Christie asked for time to think it over.

Romney said that his lawyers were still working on the pay-to-play conundrum.

"Why don't you talk to your counsel and see what happens?" Christie said.

Romney hung up the phone convinced by Christie's reaction that resignation was not in the cards. (He was correct.) "Look, let's find out if we can get an answer" on pay-to-play, he told Myers. But let's keep pushing on the vet—and pushing on Trenton.

Four nights later, on July 19, Myers's team put the finishing touches on the Pufferfish vetting dossier. Included was a DVD with some of Christie's most outlandish or unnerving YouTube hits: his castigating a pro-gay-marriage New Jersey assemblyman as "numb nuts," his angrily berating a constituent while chasing him down the Seaside Heights boardwalk, brandishing an ice cream cone. But the main event was the thirty-five-page written report titled "Chris Christie memo 71912 FINAL."

After eleven days of teeth-gnashing labor, several of the issues that the vetters had unearthed around Christie were still unresolved. Though the New Jersey governor believed that he and Palatucci had been fully cooperative, Myers and her team viewed Trenton as recalcitrant. Newton and Nielsen were sticklers. They were uncomfortable producing a final report they considered incomplete. Nielsen, who drafted the document, made a point of being meticulous about framing and flagging the problems, including a refrain in bold applied to a number of items.

On Todd Christie's securities-fraud settlement: "[Governor] Christie has been asked to disclose whether Todd Christie incurred any monetary or other penalty as a result of the SEC/NYSE action. **If Christie's possible selection is to move forward, this item should be obtained.**" On Christie's defamation lawsuit: "Christie has been asked to provide the terms of the settlement of this matter. **If Christie's possible selection is to move forward, this item should be obtained.**" On Christie's household help: "Christie has been asked to provide the names and documented status of all domestic employees. This material has not been received. **If Christie's possible selection is to move forward, these items should be obtained.**" On Christie's lobbying clients: "Christie has provided only one of the twelve or so [public disclosure] filings made [in the time he was a lobbyist] . . . **If Christie's possible selection is to move forward, these items should be obtained.**"

Then there was this: "In response to the questionnaire, Governor Christie indicates that he has no health issues that would hinder him from serving as the vice-presidential nominee. Published reports indicate that Christie suffers from asthma and was briefly hospitalized last year after he suffered an asthma attack. He is also obese and has indicated that he struggles with his weight. 'The weight exacerbates everything,' he is quoted as saying. Christie has been asked to provide a detailed medical report. Christie has been asked to provide a copy of all medical records from his most recent physical examination. **If Christie's possible selection is to move forward, this item should be obtained.**"

Romney reviewed Christie's vetting materials the next day. At the outset of his VP search, Mitt had wanted an orderly process. The frantic, late Pufferfish crash vet had blown that desire sky-high. But Romney still hewed to the criteria he'd set out, one of which was to avoid a running mate who might become a distraction. Despite the language in the report indicating that Christie had not been sufficiently forthcoming with his medical records, Romney and Myers agreed that what he had provided put their minds at ease about his health. But the dossier on the Garden State governor's background was littered with potential landmines. Between that and the pay-to-play snag, there was no point in thinking about Christie further. With the clock running out, Romney pulled the plug again, this time for good.

During the foreign trip, Mitt meditated on the choice that now seemed inevitable: Ryan. Beyond all the political pros and cons, Romney felt comfortable with Paul. He reminded Mitt of junior partners he used to work with at Bain: eager, earnest, solicitous, smart, and not at all threatening. White had a phrase for these buttoned-down go-getters, which he applied to Ryan: "client-ready."

On the flight home from Poland, Romney inhaled a long profile of Ryan in *The New Yorker*, which traced the congressman's ascendancy to the position of de facto intellectual and ideological leader of the GOP. Impressed by what he read, he gave the piece to Stevens, who paged through it on the plane, too. What do you think now? Romney asked.

"I can't tell you who to fall in love with," Stevens said with a shrug.

The impromptu meeting in Myers's office the day after Romney returned home took up about forty-five minutes. With Christie out of the picture, Stevens switched to making the case for Portman. Romney remained mum about which way he was leaning.

When the meeting was over, he stayed behind with Myers. In five days, she noted, a so-called protective pool of reporters would start accompanying him at all times, making it difficult to orchestrate the kind of secret maneuvers that a vice-presidential unveiling entailed. Unless we want to get real cloak-and-dagger, you should probably make up your mind pretty soon, Myers said.

"Oh, okay," Romney said. "Then I've made my choice—I'll pick Paul Ryan."

Romney called Ryan and asked him to come to Boston for a sit-down.

Ryan hung up the phone, stunned. Are we ready? he asked his wife, Janna. I think this is it.

Ten days later, it was.

OBAMA WAS EN ROUTE from the White House to Chicago when the Romney-Ryan ticket debuted on the deck of the USS *Wisconsin* in Norfolk, Virginia, on Saturday, August 11. The president was headed to the Windy City for a belated fifty-first birthday party cum fund-raiser at his Kenwood home and a meeting at One Prudential Plaza. He was surprised by the Ryan pick, couldn't fathom the political calculation that led Mitt to choose the front man for a set of policies that were so broadly unpopular.

I don't get it, Obama said to Plouffe and Pfeiffer. Why is he doubling down?

When the president arrived at Chicago HQ, he greeted the troops and settled in for a presentation from Messina. The campaign manager addressed the Ryan pick and, more broadly, the state of the race on the eve of the conventions. Back in May, when the campaign made its decision to front-load its spending, money had been a huge worry. No longer. Chicago's fund-raising was starting to crank, as enthusiasm rose in the Democratic base and small donors began coming back to the fold.

In that same springtime discussion in the Roosevelt Room, Messina had walked Obama through a variety of plausible pathways to 270 electoral votes. Three months later, all of them were still operative. The only thing that had changed was that, by Chicago's calculations, the dynamics of the electoral map had shifted: whereas in May the most crucial state had been Colorado, now it was Ohio. If we can block him there, Messina said, there's almost no way he can win the election—and Ohio was looking better for Obama every day. The attacks on Romney over Bain, outsourcing, and taxes were turning the industrial Midwest into a "killing field" for Mitt, Messina said.

Romney's weakness with working-class voters was one reason why many of the Obamans assumed he would pick Pawlenty as his running mate. Obama had predicted T-Paw, too. Though Boston had forsworn doing running-mate research, Chicago had not. The Obamans polled and focus-grouped extensively on Romney's options in order to be ready to respond. Their research showed that Pawlenty's "pro-beer, pro-hockey" persona might have helped ameliorate the nominee's case of affluenza. The second-best pick was Portman, who would have given Romney a small but significant bump in Ohio.

Putting Ryan on the ticket, by contrast, did nothing good for Romney, in Chicago's view. Not only did his presence highlight Medicare and the budget, where the Obamans believed that they were playing the winning hand, but it would let them twin up Romney with the terminally unpopular congressional wing of the GOP. It also seemed to represent a bedrock strategic surrender. For more than a year, Boston had doggedly pursued Stevens's vision of the race as a referendum, trying to keep the focus on Obama's economic mismanagement, high unemployment, and moribund GDP growth. The elevation of Ryan seemed to signal a sharp U-turn, highlighting the issues of deficits, entitlements, and taxes—and, in so doing, accepting Chicago's framing of the election as a choice.

The mainstream media interpreted Romney's move precisely that way: as a bracing attempt to change the game. "The selection of Mr. Ryan . . . was an effort to reset the race with President Obama after a withering assault on Mr. Romney by Democrats" was the take of the *New York Times*'s story on the VP pick. "The decision instantly made the campaign seem bigger and more consequential, with the size and role of the federal government squarely at the center of the debate."

Yet the month of August made a mockery of stipulations of largeness or significance. Day by day, the freak show looked like more of a freak circus as cable and the Web were consumed with wild-eyed eruptions on the left and right: over a Priorities ad suggesting that Romney was responsible for killing the wife of a man who lost his health care coverage after a Bain takeover of his employer; over a comment on the stump by Biden, before a largely black audience, that the Romney-Ryan plan to "unshackle Wall Street" would "put ya'll back in chains"; over a TV interview by the Republican Senate candidate in Missouri, Todd Akin, in which he employed the phrase "legitimate rape" (after which, Akin said, "the female body has ways to try to shut" down any resulting pregnancy); and over charges by Senate majority leader Harry Reid regarding Romney's income taxes.

Reid's dislike for his fellow Mormon stretched back years, but his feelings had come to a boil during the nomination contest, when Romney spoke of self-deportation. Determined to take Mitt down, Reid had spent much of July harping on his taxes. In an interview with the Huffington Post, the Nevadan brazenly claimed he had spoken to a Bain investor who informed him that Romney "didn't pay any taxes for ten years." Two days later, Reid took to the Senate floor to repeat the accusation.

The resulting brouhaha was a sight to see. Boston accused Reid of

McCarthyism; RNC chair Reince Priebus called him a "dirty liar"; South Carolina senator Lindsey Graham seconded the motion. Reid's office fired back, calling Priebus and Graham "cowards" and "henchmen for Romney." Reid refused to back down an inch, believing he had a gold-plated source. The conversation he cited in the Huffington Post had been with another member of his and Romney's church: Jon Huntsman Sr. As the story persisted, fingers were pointed at Huntsman in the press. Huntsman denied being the source for Reid. The Nevadan didn't care; he remembered the conversation well. More important, Reid was accomplishing his goal: flooding the media zone and forcing Romney to play defense.

Reid shared with the Obamans that his source was Huntsman Sr. Plouffe and Messina were over the moon about the stunt; their boss expressed no disapproval of it, either. Obama's affection for Reid was warm and long-standing; the majority leader had been among the first and most influential Democrats to urge him to seek the White House back in 2007. Watching Reid's antics now, the president chuckled. "Harry's just like a dog with a bone," Obama said. "He's not going to let go of this."

That Reid was getting under the Romneys' skin was all too apparent. On August 16, Mitt held a brief press availability in South Carolina, where he tersely claimed that he had never paid an effective tax rate of less than 13 percent in the past ten years. That night, in a taped interview with NBC's *Rock Center,* Ann expressed the couple's emotions more nakedly. Asked why they had refused to be "more transparent" and release more tax returns, she visibly tensed up and snapped, "Have you seen how we're attacked? Have you *seen* what's happened?"

Boston was seeing more than the attacks. Romney's pollsters were weighing the effects of the air assault by the Obamans and Reid's dominance of free media. In the campaign's focus groups, the tax returns came up all the time—and in the form of questions about Romney's character. When Newhouse studied transcripts of the sessions, one phrase jumped out again and again: "What's he hiding?"

For countless voters, Romney's finances weren't the only thing that was obscured. In the course of a cruel and bloody summer, the Obamans had succeeded in blotting out any redeeming elements of Mitt's biography and character: his business acumen, his devotion to his faith, his love of family. What was left was the image, as Haley Barbour put it, of Romney as "a quintessential plutocrat married to a known equestrian."

For Boston, the next chance to repaint the picture would come at the Tampa convention. The goals of the show they intended to put on were straightforward: to reintroduce America to Romney, to render him softer, sympathetic, likable—human. Vast amounts of planning had been devoted to the effort. Then two hurricanes and a Hollywood star swept into Florida and blew those plans to bits.

18

THE GOOD, THE BAD, AND THE UGLY

THE DOPPLER RADAR IMAGES started looking dodgy a week out, around the time the first tempest swept by the southern coast of Guadeloupe and into the Caribbean Sea. That was when the weather authorities upgraded the swirling mass of wind and rain to Tropical Storm Isaac. By Saturday, August 25, two days before the Republican convention was slated to begin, Isaac had developed an eye and was passing over Haiti—and Rhoades was on the ground in Tampa, acting like a FEMA director.

Although the programming of the convention was Russ Schriefer's responsibility, the decision about whether to cancel the first day came down to the campaign manager. The pressure not to abort was intense. The RNC apparatchiks reminded Rhoades of the mayor of Amity Island in *Jaws*: There is no shark! But with Isaac barreling straight toward Tampa Bay, Rhoades gritted his teeth and pulled the plug on Monday. A scrambling Schriefer was left to cram four nights of activities into three, including pushing Ann Romney's speech to Tuesday, when Chris Christie would deliver the keynote address.

Heavy weather was becoming a tradition at Republican conventions. Four years earlier, almost to the day, McCain's team had shut down the first night of their shindig in St. Paul as Hurricane Gustav pounded the Gulf

Coast—to avoid discussion of the Bush administration's failure to handle Katrina. For the McCainiacs, though, Gustav was a blessing in disguise. It allowed them to dispense with a speech by Dick Cheney and relegate 43 to a short talk by video hookup from the White House.

Boston had been luckier in terms of awkward guests. Neither Dubya nor his dad was interested in addressing the delegates in Tampa; both would be out of the country. Cheney made it clear well in advance that he would not attend. While the Romneyites felt compelled to invite Sarah Palin, they were jittery about slotting her into the 10:00 p.m. broadcast network TV hour, as they assumed she would demand. Happily, Palin declined to appear at all before such negotiations became necessary.

That left only Donald Trump to contend with. Since his endorsement of Romney in February, Trump had been a regular presence in Romneyland. He had done robocalls *(Phenomenal robocalls!)* slamming Santorum in Michigan, Ohio, and Illinois. He had hosted a fund-raiser for Romney in Vegas on the night in May when Mitt locked up the nomination. But Trump had turned out to be less Clooneyesque as a fund-raising magnet than Boston had hoped. And some of those with Romney's ear suggested that the billionaire was ripe for Sister Souljahing. Mike Murphy e-mailed Mitt, You've got the best sound bite in the world: "Trump, you're fired." I'm hoping to hear that.

Romney wanted to keep the Donald inside the tent pissing out. To sate Trump's desire to be a presence at the convention without letting him give a speech, Boston had settled on having him introduce a brief video onstage on Monday night. (It featured the Donald sacking an Obama impersonator.) Still, Rhoades and others worried about Trump ranging freely amid the press scrum in Tampa. They decided to take an unorthodox step: to dispatch a communications professional to give Trump media training.

Boston first asked former Bush press secretary Ari Fleischer to conduct a session with Trump, to tamp down his birther talk at the convention. But there was no way Fleischer would take on that assignment without hazard pay. So one of Rhoades's loyalists, Brian Jones, was called into duty. Jones flew to New York, handed the Donald a stack of documents with precise talking points, and then walked him through his training, playing to Trump's sense of persecution by the liberal press.

You know how reporters are, Jones said. They're going to try to get you off-message. Don't let 'em. Just stay focused on the economy and Governor Romney's unique qualifications and credentials.

Yeah, yeah, I get it, Trump said.

No one knew if he really did, though, or if he would stay on script. The Washington lobbyist and longtime McCain hand Charlie Black, who had served as Trump's Beltway fixer for a dozen years, warned Schriefer, "Look, if he's out there, you just wasted a night's news, because no matter what else happens, *he's* the news."

The cancellation of the convention's first night untied the Trumpian knot, as the Donald was otherwise engaged for the rest of the week. Boston heaved a heavy sigh of relief, and an even deeper one when Isaac veered away from the southwest Florida coast. By Monday, the meteorological storm had passed without incident—just as the second tempest, the human typhoon, rolled into Tampa.

BIG BOY HAD BEEN LOOKING forward to his big night in the Big Guava. Christie's Tuesday keynote would be his first speech to a national audience, a chance to launch himself into orbit in the same way that Obama had at the 2004 Democratic convention in Boston. Christie been working on the text for weeks, editing and revising, churning out umpteen drafts. He was fired up and ready to go. But what greeted him on Monday morning in the *New York Post* enflamed him in a different way.

FAT CHANCE read the blaring banner on the front page, beneath a photo of him pointing a finger, mouth agape. The accompanying story bore the headline CHRISTIE CHOSE NJ OVER MITT'S VP ROLE DUE TO FEARS THAT THEY'D LOSE. Citing "sources" including an unnamed "Romney source," the piece reported that Boston had "demanded" Christie step down from the governorship if he wanted to be Mitt's running mate; and that Christie refused because he was "certain Romney was doomed."

Christie was flabbergasted. However unhelpful Trenton had been during the VP vetting, Christie thought the process was sacrosanct. He blamed the story on Boston—which in turn blamed it on Christieworld, with its self-promoting ways. Schriefer, headed to an interview on *Fox and*

Friends, called his New Jersey client to ask if he or his people were the "sources" for the *Post.*

"Are you out of your fucking mind?" Christie barked. "You think *I* had something to do with this? This came from *you* guys! Not from me! What the hell is my incentive to get involved in this? I'm about to give the keynote—I'm on a run here. I'm gonna get involved in that? For what reason?"

"I didn't think so, Chris, but I had to ask," Schriefer said meekly. "I've been told to ask."

"Well, yes, and that's the answer," Christie said. "You knew the answer before you even asked."

In addition to managing the convention, Schriefer had been playing point with Christieworld on the governor's keynote, with which Boston was satisfied in almost every way. There was only one hang-up: a conflict between a theme in Ann Romney's remarks ("Tonight, I want to talk to you about love") and a line in Christie's ("Tonight, we choose respect over love"). But after going back and forth with Palatucci over the matter in multiple phone calls and making little headway, Schriefer finally relented—proving once again that Big Boy could be both an unstoppable force and an immovable object.

There was a whole lotta love in Ann's speech that night at the Tampa Bay Times Forum: love for children, grandchildren, the country, and her fellow females. ("I love you, *women!*" she shouted.) But mostly her speech was about "the deep and abiding love I have for a man I met at a dance many years ago." Besides Mitt himself, no one was in a better position than Ann to humanize her husband. She praised him as a "warm and loving and patient" man who is "there when late-night calls of panic come from a member of our church whose child has been taken to the hospital." The crowd ate it up. Watching from a box in the hall, Mitt thought, *She knocked it out of the park.*

Christie came armed with a three-minute video that he insisted be played before he spoke. It was an ode to himself and to New Jersey, as was much of his speech. Lumbering out onstage, clapping his hands, Christie talked for twenty-four minutes—the first sixteen devoted to his mother and father, his biography, his achievements in his state. He mentioned the nominee just seven times, speaking of Mitt purely in the abstract. Christie's only criticism of Obama was implicit: "It's time to end this era of absentee leadership in the Oval Office and send real leaders to the White House." He never uttered the incumbent's name. There was little humor and no spark.

Many of the reviews of Christie's speech were pans. From the left, Rachel Maddow called it "one of the most remarkable acts of political selfishness I have ever seen." From the right, *Washington Examiner* Byron York wrote that the speech "failed to convey the spirit—the essential Christie-ness—that millions have seen in YouTube videos of the New Jersey governor in action." On Fox News, Chris Wallace gibed, "For a moment, I forgot who was the nominee of the party." But the appraisal that got the most attention was from Politico, which declared it "a prime-time belly-flop."

For the past three years, Christie had been on an uninterrupted roll. The keynote was supposed to be his shining moment. Instead it was his first significant national failure.

Much as Christie attempted to ignore the chorus of criticism, he couldn't put the Politico story out of his mind. The piece included a sentence—"Several political figures close to Mitt Romney made acerbic comments to reporters, making clear they thought Christie laid an egg"—that convinced him the whole thing was a Boston-fueled hatchet job. Christie believed he had laid himself on the line for Mitt, done everything the campaign had asked. Now, between Politico and the *New York Post,* he had been shat on twice in forty-eight hours by people he was trying to help. The treatment was galling, infuriating. More than that, it was hurtful.

Rhoades's assessment was that the *Post* story had poisoned the well for Christie's speech, much as Romney's Brian Williams interview wrecked his foreign trip right out of the gate. On Wednesday morning, he called Christie to apologize for any Boston involvement in the Politico story.

"You guys had this speech for a week before it was given," Christie told Rhoades. "You did not ask me to make one change in the speech. Now you fucking guys are cutting my nuts off. You know what, Matt? I'm tired of it. I've worked hard for Governor Romney. I like him. And I see that you guys, for whatever reason, are playing this game."

Christie simmered and brooded for much of Wednesday. On the phone with Schriefer, he sounded irked and defensive. "You wanted me to mention Romney sooner?" he said. "You wanted me to do something else? You wanted me to attack Obama? You should have told me."

That evening, Christie arrived later than usual to a high-end donor dinner at the Hyatt Regency hosted by Dan Loeb and Paul Singer. Expecting the typical Christie bravado, the two hundred donors in the room were slack-jawed at what they got instead. Midway through his speech, Christie drifted into a point-by-point rebuttal of the Politico piece and the punditry on that day's *Morning Joe*—a riposte that consumed half of his time onstage. Never before had anyone seen Christie evince insecurity, but it was oozing out of him now.

When the dinner was done, Christie hustled to the convention hall, where he had interviews to do with Hannity and Piers Morgan. He ran into Ron Kaufman, Mitt's pal and Washington smart guy.

"Guvanah," Kaufman said in his thick Boston accent, "I want you to know that this stuff did not come from the campaign."

Christie had been endeavoring to swallow his anger all day long. He assumed that Stevens was behind the Politico story. ("Your fucking partner did this," he told Schriefer. "I know it and you know it.") His opinion of Boston in toto was scarcely better, though. In the preceding months, he had become convinced that Romney's operation was a gaggle of clowns who couldn't organize a one-ring circus. Now here was Kaufman claiming that the guys in greasepaint weren't trying to feed Christie to the lions—no! They loved him, they respected him, they wanted to buy him a bushel of cotton candy.

It was just too much.

Standing on a public concourse, in front of the Churchill Lounge cigar bar, with delegates streaming by, the governor of New Jersey started bellowing at the top of his lungs, putting the perfect punctuation mark on his day, his time in Tampa, and his feelings about Boston:

"Don't bullshit me, Ron!"

And: "You're a fucking liar!!"

And: "I'm tired of you people!!!"

And: "Leave me the fuck alone!!!!"

And then—with Kaufman chasing after him, crying, "Guvanah! Guvanah! Guvanah!"—Christie stalked off down the concourse to go be on TV.

R OMNEY REASSURED CHRISTIE that he thought the speech was boffo. Rhoades told Mitt that the television reaction shots of his face suggested otherwise: that he looked angry during the keynote. Romney had known the cameras were on him, of course. *I was trying to look interested and supportive!* he fretted. His team suggested he stay out of the hall until his own speech Thursday night. Mitt grudgingly agreed. The most important address of his life, an oration that would be watched by thirty million people, was twenty-four hours away, but Romney had yet to practice it once. Because it wasn't finished.

The Romney speechwriting operation was still the same mess it always had been—only worse. Following the CPAC and Detroit Economic Club fiascos, repeated attempts had been made to bring order to the chaos spawned by the Mitt-and-Stuart system of mutual dependency. Rhoades authorized the hiring of a veteran GOP speechwriting duo: Matthew Scully and John McConnell, who had worked with 43 and Cheney. Wary of Stevens's reaction, Rhoades arranged to put them on contract secretly. Myers and Flaherty were maddened by Stuart's grip on speechwriting, but powerless to break it. After taking a few stabs at easing Stevens away from his compositional monopoly, Gillespie gave up. *It's like sticking your hand into a wood chipper,* he thought.

The convention address represented the culmination of this dysfunction. By the time Romney arrived in Tampa on Tuesday, he had rejected four or five drafts by the outside writer brought on board to pen the speech, former Bush 43 adviser Pete Wehner. He had rejected a draft by Scully and McConnell. Another draft, by Hayes's team, was floating around, unread. Romney and Stevens, commencing seventy-two hours earlier, had cobbled together still another clump of words, which was now the operative draft—and which much of the Boston brain trust considered mediocre.

That afternoon, they gathered in Romney's eighteenth-floor suite in the Marriott across the street from the hall. Unhappiness suffused the room.

The Wehner draft had been imperfect, they all agreed. But there was no reason to have scrapped it and started over from scratch. Everyone had seen this movie before, but the stakes this time were incomparably higher. Romney had a huge amount of political damage to repair. The eyes of the world would be upon him as never before. Yet here they were, endeavoring to bind up a wound that was entirely self-inflicted, with no doubt in the room about who was to blame.

Crammed around the dining room table in the suite, the brain trust paged through the working draft, saying little that was complimentary. Fehrnstrom had a fair number of notes; Gillespie had even more. As the cacophony of suggestions swelled, Stevens became increasingly agitated.

I have a bunch of edits and a bunch of questions, Gillespie said, placing a piece of paper on the table.

Picking up a pen, holding it like a knife, Stevens silently stabbed at the paper, scrawling an X through Gillespie's offerings.

Through it all, Mitt remained unaccountably calm. He, too, had seen this movie before, and it didn't faze him—even though it was apparently shaping up to be a box-office bomb.

As the meeting broke up, Romney sat at the table, studying the Scully-McConnell draft on his iPad. Coming upon a section about his father and mother, who were married for sixty-four years, he began to read aloud: "If you wonder what their secret was, you could have asked the local florist. Because every day Dad gave Mom a flower. That's how she found out what happened on the day my father died—she went looking for him, because, that morning, there was no flower."

Choking up, Romney said softly, "That's beautiful—that's absolutely beautiful." It would be nice to find a way to work it in, he added. Maybe that's the conclusion.

Yeah, sure, maybe, we'll figure it out, Stevens said dismissively.

Romney's chief strategist had a heaping amount on his plate already—but he just kept piling on more and more, like John Belushi at the buffet in *Animal House.* In addition to Romney's speech, Stuart had pulled an all-nighter to write Ann's. And now he was sticking his nose into the drafting of Ryan's.

The seventeen days since his selection had been a whirlwind for Fishconsin. In terms of policy expertise and media savvy, Ryan was infinitely better equipped than Palin to handle the sudden glare. But in terms of electrifying the right, his selection was similar to hers. And because he hadn't expected to be picked, the upending of his life was nearly as disorienting. Returning to his home in Janesville, he was thunderstruck by the motorcade that ferried him to his house. Seeing his neighborhood turned into a Badger State Green Zone by the Secret Service, he wondered, *What did they tell my neighbors?* To his lead adviser, Dan Senor, he kept saying, "This is an out-of-body experience."

Just like Palin in 2008, Ryan was determined not to disappoint the man who had elevated him to new heights. He was desperate to hit a home run in Tampa and kick butt in his debate with Biden. With his convention speech, Ryan planned to push big conservative ideas and take a cudgel to Obama. By that Tuesday, not only was the speech locked, but Ryan had memorized it. When Stevens attempted to stick his oar in—plumping for more plaudits for Mitt, passages about how he played with his grandkids on the campaign bus—Senor and the rest of the Ryan camp shut him down. This isn't how Paul operates, they said. If we start making changes now, it'll mess with his performance.

Fabulous, Stevens said. So what we're gonna get is a great delivery of a crappy speech.

Ryan tried to calm his nerves on Wednesday by watching movies with his wife in his hotel—but the gambit had the opposite effect. By sheer coincidence, they happened to catch an airing of the HBO film *Game Change,* about Palin's travails. Ryan was riveted, but soon regretted it. What the hell was I doing watching *that*? he asked Senor later.

In his speech that night, Ryan didn't prove to be the magnetic performer that Palin was. But the hall embraced him anyway. Both in the building and in the broader precincts of Right Nation, Ryan's anti-Barack bon mots—including a pointed barb about dispirited college graduates "staring up at fading Obama posters," wondering when they would find a job—were gobbled up like bonbons. The problem for Boston was that Ryan's speech, like Christie's, did little to present Romney in a new light. That task would basically be reserved for (or relegated to) the convention's final evening.

The reintroduction began a little after 8:30 p.m. on Thursday night, and was so compelling that many wondered why it hadn't started weeks or months earlier. Ann and Tagg had pushed for the inclusion of personal testimonials, helping Schriefer and his team identify people who could attest to Mitt's character. Leading the way were the Oparowskis, Ted and Pat, an elderly couple who told the story of their leukemia-stricken son, David, and how Romney, whom they knew through church, visited the dying fourteen-year-old, helped him write a will, and gave the eulogy at his funeral. Pam Finlayson told the story of her daughter, born prematurely with brain damage. Romney, Finlayson's clergyman, visited the girl in the ICU, where he "didn't just see a tangle of plastic and tubes—he saw our beautiful little girl, and was clearly overcome with compassion for her."

The Oparowskis and Finlayson brought many in the hall to tears. They were followed by Bob White, at last allowed to shine a light on the nobility of Bain. The work of White and his SWAT team was featured in two videos, which made the case that Mitt was a job creator, not a ruthless corporate raider. Tom Stemberg, the boss of Staples, proclaimed that Romney "knew the value of a dollar." Ray Fernandez, the Hispanic CEO of Vida Pharmacy, declared, "My life today is better because of Bain Capital." Jane Edmonds, an African American liberal Democrat who served under Romney in the Bay State, extolled his virtues. Three Olympians did the same. They were followed by a ten-minute biographical video that even the Obamans conceded was a thing of beauty.

Altogether, the humanization of Romney consumed close to two hours. By any standard, it was a supremely effective stretch of political stagecraft. The only trouble was that none of it appeared in the prime-time broadcast hour, so it was seen only by the comparatively tiny cable TV audience.

In terms of time, Schriefer's flexibility was limited. Almost the entirety of the 10:00 p.m. hour would be swallowed up by the night's marquee speeches: Marco Rubio and Romney. That left about seven minutes to work with. He had considered filling them with the bio video, but network producers told him they would not run it, using the airtime for commentary instead. Under other circumstances, Schriefer might have been willing to gamble that they would change their minds. But not when he had an ace up his sleeve: a guest star so glamorous and iconic that the cameras would find it impossible to turn away.

CLINT EASTWOOD'S PRESENCE in Tampa was supposed to be a surprise, but in the late afternoon, the convention orchestra started practicing the theme to *The Good, the Bad, and the Ugly*—and the jig was up. Eastwood's appearance had come together in less than a month. Boston's desire to have him onstage was driven by many impulses: the quest for ratings, the yen for excitement, and a degree of political logic. Yet the idea would never have been on the table at all had Romney not been starstruck.

Mitt first met the eighty-two-year-old star in late July in Carmel, California, the seaside town near Monterey Bay where Dirty Harry had once been the mayor. A Romney donor, former Sun Microsystems CEO Scott McNealy, arranged a dinner for Mitt and Ann with Eastwood, his wife, Dina, McNealy, and McNealy's wife, Susan, at Eastwood's Tehama Golf Club. The club was closed, but Clint brought in a chef, and the six of them had a ball. Romney was struck by how much Eastwood-in-the-flesh was like the celluloid version. *He looks like Clint Eastwood, he sounds like Clint Eastwood—hey, it's Clint Eastwood!* Mitt thought. *And that Dina—what a hoot! This is just so . . . cool!*

It had already occurred to Romney how terrific it would be to lure the actor to Tampa. Earlier in the year, Eastwood had appeared in a Super Bowl ad for Chrysler called "Halftime in America," which many conservatives viewed as a tacit endorsement of Obama and the auto bailout. Having Eastwood at the convention would be a chance to recapture the flag. Without asking directly, Romney started to bait the hook. Look, I'd love your help, he told Clint. I'd like to stay in touch.

On August 3, Eastwood turned up in a battered Jeep Wagoneer at a Romney fund-raiser in Sun Valley. Mitt called him up onstage. "I was doing a picture in the early 2000s called *Mystic River* in his home state," Eastwood said of Romney. "I said, God, this guy is too handsome to be governor, but he does look like he could be president. As the years have gone by, I'm beginning to think even more so that. He's going to restore a decent tax system that we need badly so that there is a fairness and people are not pitted against one another of who's paying taxes and who isn't. Also, we don't want anybody taking away the Olympic medals, taxwise, from the Olympic athletes. The government is talking about getting a couple of nickels. It's now more important than ever that we need Governor Romney, and I'm going to be voting for him, as I know most of you will be. We've got to just spread the word and get the whole country behind this, because it's going to be an exciting election."

Taking back the microphone, Romney said excitedly, "He just made my day—what a guy!"

Romney instructed his team to try to make the convention thing happen. "Clint doesn't say a lot, but he says it well, and he's a big presence," Mitt explained. It would make a difference in places like Michigan and Ohio. We don't have many Hollywooders on our team. It would be great to have *him*.

Schriefer planned to have Eastwood speak on Wednesday, but the compression of the schedule pushed the star's appearance to Thursday. That morning, Eastwood and the McNealys boarded a private jet in San Jose and headed to Tampa. The Romneyites had conveyed that they wanted Clint to speak for five to seven minutes and say something similar to what he'd said in Sun Valley. Eastwood, however, was playing it loose; McNealy, even looser. The tech executive was an ardent libertarian and Obama scold. He had made a top-ten list of Clint's movies with politically incorrect subtitles that skewered the president, and showed it to Eastwood on the plane. Clint got a kick out of that.

On the ground in Tampa, the traveling party made its way to the Marriott in a black SUV. At the security checkpoints and in the hotel, cops and Secret Service agents greeted Eastwood like a hero: Hey! Clint! *In the Line of Fire*!

"Would you take a bullet?" Eastwood growled back, quoting one of the movie's signature lines.

Schriefer, Stevens, and Zwick paid a call on the star in his hotel suite late in the afternoon. Eastwood's turn onstage was a few hours away, and Schriefer still wasn't sure they were on the same page regarding content. Eastwood had brought a DVD with him and played it for the Romney people. It featured a clip from *The Outlaw Josey Wales,* in which the Native American character Ten Bears says, "It's sad that governments are chiefed by the double-tongues."

You can use that for my introduction if you want, Eastwood said.

Um, thanks for that, Schriefer said, but we're all set on your intro. Let's talk about what you're going to say. He reminded Eastwood of the Idaho fund-raiser, suggesting that he use the *Mystic River* line again, as well as throwing out a few others. ("Last time you heard from me, it was halftime in America. Now we're at the two-minute warning. We need Mitt Romney.") Eastwood nodded and said little. Schriefer also reminded him of the tight time constraints, and asked if he wanted to use notes or the teleprompter. Eastwood said nope to both.

Schriefer reassured himself that it would be fine: *He does award shows all the time, knows his way around a camera—he's Clint Eastwood, for heaven's sake.*

Two of Schriefer's colleagues didn't share his sanguineness. Gillespie thought it was madness to put anyone—*anyone*—onstage in the most important hour of the convention without a script. It's a big risk, he told Schriefer, and I wouldn't do it, but it's not my call. Kevin Madden had been at the Sun Valley event and couldn't understand why anyone would want a repeat. Eastwood's remarks had been rambling, his offstage behavior erratic. (Romney's traveling aides were convinced that Clint had had a few pops and flirted with a female finance-team staffer.) When Madden was consulted about which morning shows Eastwood should be booked on for Friday, his answer was blunt: none of them.

Up in his suite at the Marriott, Eastwood was still noodling over his remarks. He turned on the radio, tuned in an oldies station, and heard Neil Diamond singing "I Am . . . I Said." Clint liked Neil, but the lyrics pulled him up short: "I am, I said, to no one there. And no one heard at all, not even the chair." *What a dumb line,* Eastwood thought. *Talking to an inanimate object!*

Eastwood arrived at the hall ninety minutes before he was supposed to go on, and was stashed away in a private holding room backstage. Schriefer popped in and checked with him again, running down the key directives one more time: five minutes, Sun Valley redux, etc.

Eastwood said, "Yep." But the truth of it was, he was having other ideas.

Watching the onstage proceedings on a monitor, taking in the humanization of Romney, Clint thought, *Everybody's just saying, "We love Mitt." I don't want to be the tenth guy up there saying the same thing. It's obvious I like Mitt, or I wouldn't be here. I want to say something . . . different.* When a staffer asked if he wanted some powder for his face, Eastwood said no. "I want to *shine.*"

Standing in the wings a few minutes before his entrance, "I Am . . . I Said" reentered Eastwood's mind. *Hey, you know, there's something there,* he thought.

Eastwood asked a stagehand, Hey, do you have a stool?

Sure, the stagehand said, and quickly presented Clint with two options: one with a back and one without.

"I like that one," Eastwood said, pointing to the model with a back. Could you put it on onstage before I go out? Just to the left of the podium? Thanks.

The roar in the hall was deafening when he strode out there, with a Josey Wales silhouette on the massive screens behind him. Two minutes later, Eastwood motioned to the chair and said, "I've got Mr. Obama sitting here; I was going to ask him a couple of questions." And then launched into an imaginary colloquy with the president. At times borderline profane ("What do you want me to tell Romney? I can't tell him to do that. He can't do that to himself"), at times meandering, it was partly an homage to Bob Newhart and 100 percent Dada dinner theater. And it was just getting going when Eastwood passed the five-minute mark.

Romney and Stevens were watching Eastwood together backstage. The candidate seemed to think it was funny—at least at first. "Did you guys practice this?" he asked Stevens.

"No," Stevens said. "I have no idea what he's doing."

Stevens's head was exploding at the sight of the disaster occurring on-stage. (*He's gone insane!*) Not wanting to upset Mitt, Stevens excused himself, went into another room, and vomited.

Schriefer was on the convention floor. When he first saw the stagehand bring out the chair, he thought, *That's odd.* Now he was in a state of panic. Rushing backstage to the control room to try to give Eastwood the hook, he ran into Stevens—who started screaming, This is terrible! It's a car crash!

Schriefer attempted to calm Stevens down. Stevens would not be calmed. As Eastwood kept going—past seven minutes, eight minutes, nine minutes, ten minutes—Stevens lost all control. He was throwing things, howling, cursing, and weeping, until he dropped his head into his hands.

The reaction of the Romneyites out in the hall was only mildly less operatic. Their in-boxes were flooded with e-mails from reporters. Twitter was exploding with shock, bafflement, and ridicule.

"What the fuck *is* this?" Fehrnstrom exclaimed to Rhoades.

"I don't know!" Rhoades replied, and called Schriefer. Dude, dude, dude—get him off!

Eastwood finally exited the stage after twelve excruciating minutes, which he concluded with the only pre-approved line that he delivered: "Make my day." Though the audience in the hall laughed at some of his jokes, the tone of the reception had shifted as Eastwood went on and on. No longer enraptured, the crowd seemed nervous for him—as if they were rooting for a doddering uncle as he struggled through a wedding toast, and were relieved when he yielded back the mic.

Twenty minutes later, an earnest Rubio come and gone, Romney paraded through the hall and mounted the rostrum with a new challenge before him: not just to give a knockout speech, but to obliterate the memory of Eastwood. It was a tall order. The speechwriting chaos had continued right up through Thursday, with Romney still making last-minute edits late that afternoon. (*This may not be put to bed until* after *it's delivered,* Romney thought.) His aides weren't sure whether Mitt had done a single run-through with the final text.

In a blue suit, red tie, and white shirt, Romney spoke for thirty-nine minutes. His performance was workmanlike in every detail. He bashed his rival with gusto: "President Obama promised to begin to slow the rise of the oceans and to heal the planet; my promise is to help you and your family." He offered plainspoken language about the economy: "What America needs is jobs—lots of jobs." He made references to his faith and his church. And he invested with feeling the one—and only one—stanza that anyone would remember: the lovely story about his parents and the flower, which was a rose.

Boston feared that the coverage of Romney's speech would be swamped by the Clint imbroglio. They were right to be worried. On TV and the Web, and in newspapers around the country, Mitt's speech was mostly an afterthought, criticized for being substance-free on policy and failing to mention the troops in Afghanistan. But it was Eastwood who got most of the ink. On *Meet the Press,* Tom Brokaw observed, "Four years ago, the Republican convention gave *Saturday Night Live* Sarah Palin. This time we'll be seeing a lot of Clint Eastwood." On *The Daily Show,* Jon Stewart opined, "Amidst the tired rhetoric, empty platitudes, and overwrought attacks, a fistful of awesome emerged in the night, where it spent twelve minutes on the most important night of Mitt Romney's life yelling at a chair."

Boston pointed to an uptick in Romney's favorability ratings to suggest that Tampa had been a success. Schriefer and others clung to the fantasy that Eastwood hadn't been so bad. The Romneys had a different point of view. Ann and Tagg Romney were dismayed by the Thursday-night fiasco: How could this have happened? they kept asking.

Mitt's nose was out of joint, too. The critical hour of the last major event before Election Day that was under the campaign's complete control had been riddled with unforced errors—not just Eastwood but the omission of mention of the troops. And yet, as was the case after the foreign trip, no one was called on the carpet or fired. Denominationally, Romney was a Mormon, but temperamentally he was a stoic WASP from top to toe. Flying out of Tampa to New Orleans to tour the storm damage from Isaac, he swallowed his upset and pushed forward, while Eastwood was winging back to California.

It would be a little while before Clint understood what a kerfuffle he had caused. (McNealy called him an "improvisational genius.") And when he did, it didn't bother him a bit. "If somebody's dumb enough to ask me to say something," Eastwood remarked, "they're gonna have to take what they get."

What the Republicans had gotten was an object lesson in the dangers of celebrity casting. The Democrats were paying close attention. Their convention in Charlotte would commence just five days after Tampa, and it, too, would feature an intergalactic mega-star up onstage. In some ways, the risks for the Obamans would be smaller, because the performer was a politician. But in some ways they would be greater. Because the fellow's role would be no mere cameo—and his last name happened to be Clinton.

19

OFF THE LEASH

THE FORTY-SECOND PRESIDENT had been lazing around the Hamptons during the Republican convention. Yet Bill Clinton's televisual presence in Florida (and the other battleground states) that week was ubiquitous, inescapable. On the eve of the GOP hoedown, Chicago had released an ad that featured Clinton speaking direct-to-camera: touting Obama's "plan to rebuild America from the ground up," arguing that "it only works if there is a strong middle class," observing that "that's what happened when I was president," and concluding that "we need to keep going with his plan." The commercial ran sixteen thousand times, more than all but two other Obama spots in 2012. It was a mere trailer, though, for the role that Clinton would play in Charlotte.

The impending Democratic convention forced a pair of challenges on the Obamans. Having spent the spring and summer turning the tables on Romney—framing the race as a referendum on *him* rather than on the incumbent—they had managed to distract attention from the president's economic record and defer debate about his plans for a second term. But neither issue had disappeared by any means. The one area where Romney consistently led Obama in the polls was the ability to manage the economy, which remained the paramount concern of voters. For all the missed opportunities and miscues in Tampa, the Republicans had done a creditable job of portraying Obama as a well-meaning but ill-equipped CEO, whose performance merited a handshake, a gold watch, and early retirement. In Sunday-show interviews the weekend between the conventions, Axelrod and Plouffe were asked the most basic question: Is the country better off today than four years ago? Both were flummoxed.

The task of providing a compelling answer in Charlotte had been bequeathed to Clinton. While Obama pivoted to the future, Bubba would revisit the past. When it came to distillation, exposition, and validation, Clinton was peerless—if he was on his game, that is, which he sometimes wasn't these days.

The heft of the burden being laid on his shoulders was difficult to overstate. And so was the degree to which the reconciliation between him and Obama remained a work in progress.

In the months since the Obamans made their pilgrimage to visit 42 in Harlem in November 2011, they had been engaged in a full-court Clinton press. In early December, 44 agreed to appear with him at an event in Washington promoting green buildings, a pet cause of Clinton's. Both presidents tossed bouquets to each other, but Obama's were especially fragrant.

"When Bill Clinton was president, we didn't shortchange investment," Obama said. "We lived within our means. We invested in our future. We asked everybody to pay their fair share. And you know what happened? The private sector thrived, jobs were created, the middle class grew—its income grew. Millions rose out of poverty. We ran a surplus. We were actually on track to be able to pay off all of our debt. We were firing on all cylinders. We can be that nation again."

After the event, a reporter called out, "President Clinton, do you have any advice for President Obama about the economy?" A grinning Obama interjected, "Oh, he gives me advice all the time," as Clinton looked on, beaming.

Behind the scenes, however, things were less smiley. Though Clinton had agreed to appear in the Davis Guggenheim Obama documentary and take part in some joint fund-raisers, his participation became ensnarled in a nasty hangover from four years earlier. Hillary Clinton had concluded the 2008 Democratic nomination fight with $20 million of debt. Over time, she had paid down most of it, but a stubborn $263,000 remained. Now, Bill Clinton's gatekeeper, Doug Band, issued an ultimatum to the Obamans: the price of WJC's involvement in the campaign was the retirement of HRC's balance due.

The first reaction of Messina and Plouffe was: *Fuck this*. The second was to wonder whether Bill and Hillary were aware that the extortionate demand was being made, or if Band, whom the Obamans code-named "Douchebag," was acting unilaterally.

Obama volunteered to call the former president to check it out. Messina said no way.

"I'm never going to ask you to talk to Bill Clinton about *this*," Messina said. "That's crazy."

The Obamans contacted Clinton intimate and former DNC chair Terry McAuliffe. You know what? McAuliffe said. I can't tell you for sure—it might just be Doug. But I can tell you that Hillary's debt is important to President Clinton. Maybe you oughta just pay it off.

The Obamans detested being held hostage. It reminded them of everything they hated about Clintonworld. But Obama finance chair Matthew Barzun believed that the money could be scratched together, albeit with great effort. (Obama donors knew that part of the debt was owed to Hillary's chief strategist, Mark Penn, whose harsh anti-Obama posture in 2008 left a bitter aftertaste among Barack's supporters.) Messina and Plouffe decided that it made more sense to switch than fight. They sorely needed Clinton. We don't have a choice, Plouffe said.

The series of Obama-Clinton fund-raisers kicked off in late April at McAuliffe's stone manse in McLean, Virginia. For the first and maybe the last time in history, Clinton was early and Obama late. Watching a golf tournament on TV in a back room, Clinton caught a news report about the federal sex-and-money trial of John Edwards—prompting him to offer an energetic disquisition on the flaws in Edwards's legal strategy, how it was lunacy for the defendant to have admitted this or that about his relationship with his mistress, Rielle Hunter. (One Obaman in the room thought: *Awwwkward*.)

When Obama arrived, the two men hugged, chatted about golf, and wolfed down a fast dinner. It was the first personal time they had spent together since their strained outing on the links seven months earlier. The atmosphere was friendly enough, but the table talk superficial.

Under a big white tent in McAuliffe's backyard, packed with six hundred donors, Clinton took the microphone to introduce Obama, who stood with his arms folded, looking pensive, apprehensive, and uneasy. "I'm going to tell you a couple of things I hope you'll remember and share with others," Clinton began—and then uncorked a detailed and lusty defense of Obama's term. The stimulus? Sliced two points off the jobless rate. The auto bailout? Saved 1.5 million jobs. Obamacare? Consumers and employers were about to get $1.3 billion in refunds from insurance companies. The slowness of the economic recovery? Financial crises after housing collapses take at least ten years to come back from.

"Why do I tell you this?" Clinton said. "Because somebody will say to you, 'Maybe, but I don't feel better.' And you say, 'Look, the man's not Houdini; all he can do is beat the clock.' He's beating the clock."

Obama had never heard Clinton talk about him this way. Heading back to the White House, he was bowled over by his predecessor's forcefulness—and touched by his effusiveness. "That was kind of great," he said marvelingly to Messina. "*He* was pretty great."

The sweetness of Barack and Bill's second date didn't spark a flaming romance, however. Obama found hanging out with Clinton wearing, at times exasperating. In New York for another night of fund-raising a month after the McAuliffe event, Clinton held Obama captive in the presidential limo, curbside at the Waldorf, regaling him with a lengthy anecdote, grabbing his hand when Obama tried to hop out of the car before Clinton finished. (Bill, we have to go, Obama kept saying. Just one more second! Clinton kept insisting.) Upstairs at the hotel, they were supposed to share a one-on-one meal, but Obama couldn't handle any more undiluted Clinton. Casting about for buffers, he invited a gaggle of aides—Band, Gaspard, Jarrett, Lew—to join them, and spent much of the dinner asking the underlings about their kids rather than picking the fellow-presidential brain.

It was Clinton's political indiscipline that rankled Chicago and the West Wing. The obvious example was his comment in May about Romney's "sterling" business career. No one in Obamaworld believed that Clinton was trying to harm the reelection effort. Many did assume, though, that he was currying favor with the private equity kingpins—both for the sake of his philanthropic fund-raising and for his wife if she sought the White House in 2016. (Hillary's private reaction to "sterling" was, in fact, not dissimilar to Chicago's. "Bill can't do that again," she told her aides disapprovingly.)

But the Obamans continued to grin, bear it, and pull Clinton closer. In early June, with 42 in Chicago for a Clinton Global Initiative (CGI) session, Axelrod and Messina met with him for another polling-and-strategy down load. While the state of the race was less forbidding than in November, the contest remained too tight for comfort, and the Obaman desire for Clinto-nian engagement greater than ever. The campaign wanted him in ads, on the stump, on the fund-raising circuit—for as much time as he could spare. Clinton apologized for "sterling" and said again he was game to help.

Axelrod had been thinking about adding another item to the wish list: that Clinton deliver the speech in Charlotte placing Obama's name in nomination—something no ex-president had ever done before. Chicago's research was unequivocal: On the economy, Clinton's credibility with voters was off the charts. There was no one who could vouch for Obama's steward-ship more powerfully, Axelrod believed. And no one who could more deftly rip Mitt and the Republicans a new one. When Axelrod put the idea to Obama, the president instantly saw the logic.

Barack called Bill from Air Force One on July 25 to offer him the mar-quee speaking slot on the convention's penultimate night. Stunned and de-lighted, Clinton accepted on the spot—and then dove headlong into his assignment. For four years, his most acute frustration with Obama had been over 44's inability or unwillingness to make the case for his own achieve-ments, to sell them to the country. Now Clinton saw an opportunity, and even a responsibility, to remedy the shortcoming. All through August, as he brainstormed the speech with his erstwhile White House lieutenants, Clinton repeated a three-word sentence like a mantra: "Explanation is elo-quence."

Yet Clinton also saw another opportunity at hand—to help himself as well as Obama. In 2008, Clinton's outsize role in his wife's campaign had been controversial, at times destructive. In the eyes of countless liberals and

African Americans, that race had left him a diminished figure. Many of Clinton's deficiencies then derived directly from the way he had spent his time after leaving the White House: at a remove from politics, out of the new-media loop, surrounded by sycophants, rich people, and rich sycophants. In other words, Nolan Ryan had lost his fastball.

But in the years since then, largely unnoticed, Clinton had been gradually regaining his form. He had campaigned all over the place for Democrats in the midterms. Stepped up his reading on economics and policy. Studied Romney and the Republicans closely. And although, as "sterling" attested, Clinton was still rusty, he could feel his mechanics coming back, his arm strength building. Charlotte would be his chance to show the world that he could still bring the heater.

Though Axelrod was in communication with Clinton, he was aware that Chicago would have no input in the speech—which made him and his colleagues queasy, especially after Eastwood. Two longtime Clinton adjutants now serving Obama, Bruce Reed and Gene Sperling, had been assigned to mediate between the realms. As convention week dawned in Charlotte, Axelrod asked tentatively, Um, when do you think we might see a draft?

Reed laughed and reminded Axelrod of a home truth: Clintonworld had always run on a just-in-time business model. Why would it be any different now?

THE QUEEN CITY CONVOCATION opened on the stifling Tuesday afternoon of September 4. Unlike their Republican counterparts, the Obamans had proactively shortened their bash to three days well in advance. Though the weather forecast was a cause of some anxiety in Charlotte—with Obama scheduled to deliver his Thursday night speech outdoors at Bank of America Stadium—there was none of the panic prevalent in Tampa. And that was just the first of the contrasts between the two events. With few exceptions, what unfolded in Charlotte over the next seventy-two hours was an object lesson in minute planning, well-orchestrated enthusiasm, and strategic coherence.

The opening session at the Time Warner Cable Arena was, in effect, coalition-of-the-ascendant night. Representing Hispanics were San Antonio mayor and keynoter Julian Castro and congressman Xavier Becerra of California; representing African Americans, Massachusetts governor Deval Patrick, Charlotte mayor Anthony Foxx, and Cory Booker; representing women, HHS secretary Kathleen Sebelius, Illinois congressional candidate Tammy Duckworth, and Lilly Ledbetter. And then there was the main event, Michelle Obama, not only covering those last two constituencies but doing much more besides.

For Michelle, Charlotte was the symbolic terminus of a journey she had started four years earlier in Denver. She had entered that convention a vilified figure and exited it a venerated one. Since then, she had carefully conserved her political capital, resisting the demands of the West Wing during the midterms, wanting to save herself for the moment when she could help Barack the most. In the spring, her husband's advisers had kicked Hilary Rosen to the curb in order to protect Michelle. All those efforts had paid off. With an approval rating of 66 percent, Michelle was more popular than her husband (or any other Democrat save the Clintons) by a mile.

She had started work on her address early—very early. By mid-August her speechwriter, Sarah Hurwitz, had a solid draft. When Michael Sheehan, the veteran Democratic speech and debate specialist, started doing runthroughs with Michelle more than a week before the convention, she had taken full ownership of her text. Sheehan noted a passage that alluded to voter suppression, a growing cause of concern in the campaign, as a number of states had passed voter identification laws that seemed designed to depress minority participation. "That's a pretty good section," he remarked.

"Yes, I want that in there," Michelle said firmly.

POTUS generally made a point of staying out of FLOTUS's way when she was preparing oratory. He didn't try to coach her, didn't offer tips, didn't review her remarks in advance. But when Axelrod and Favreau started raving about Michelle's speech as it was coming together, Obama made an exception and took a look at the text—and was struck by how personal it was, how much it referred to the girls.

"This one's going to be tough for me to watch," he told Favreau, "because I'm going to cry."

When she walked out onstage in a bright-pink silk dress, sleeveless to show off her guns, the ovation that greeted her was earsplitting. For all of

Michelle's popularity and visibility, her stage presence and theatricality still came as a shock. She was warm and natural, charming and convincing, passionate and pitch-perfect. In the stories she told of her humble roots and of her and Barack's salad days ("We were so young, so in love, and so in debt"), she presented a counterpoint to the privilege of the Romneys. In her devotion to her kids ("My most important title is still mom in chief"), she rooted herself in centrist, even conservative, values. With the powerful anecdotes she unfurled—about how, when she was a girl, her MS-stricken father would "wake up with a smile, grab his walker, prop himself up against the bathroom sink, and slowly shave and button his uniform"—she went beyond telling to showing. In the testaments to her husband's character, she both vouched for and humanized him. "Today, after so many struggles and triumphs and moments that have tested my husband in ways I never could have imagined, I have seen firsthand that being president doesn't change who you are," she said. "No, it reveals who you are."

The verdict of the talking heads was unanimous. Fox News's Brit Hume: "Extremely impressive woman." CNN's Wolf Blitzer: "The first lady hitting not a home run, but probably a grand slam." CNN's Donna Brazile: "Love is in the air."

The Twittersphere heartily agreed. "I think the president is the second-best speaker in the household," tweeted one wag. And while that may have been an exaggeration, Michelle had certainly raised the bar—not just for her husband but for the Big Dog, whose speech still wasn't written.

H E WAS UP IN his suite at the Hilton, two blocks away, while Michelle was raising the roof of the hall. He had arrived in Charlotte the night before with his aide, Justin Cooper, and nothing resembling a draft; just a pile of notes, a clump of facts and figures, and a headful of scattered strophes. But by the time Clinton and Cooper hit the hay at around 3:00 a.m. on Wednesday, they had a bunch of words on the page. Later that morning, Clinton summoned an assortment of his oldest and most trusted aides—Reed, Sperling, Paul Begala, former White House chief of staff John Podesta, national security adviser Sandy Berger, and press secretary Joe Lockhart—to help him land the plane.

For everyone in the suite, the scene was at once intoxicatingly and ach-ingly familiar. All had worked on innumerable high-stakes Clinton speeches in years past, from convention addresses to States of the Union to election-night celebrations, and it had always been just like this: a bunch of guys around a table playing verbal pepper with the boss; Clinton armed with his yellow legal pad and a Sharpie, scratching out stanzas in his nearly illegible lefty scrawl, handing them to an aide to be typed up and printed out, then furiously crossing out what he'd written and scribbling something new. The sense of camaraderie was high. *Man, it's great to have the band back together,* thought Begala.

That morning at a campaign event in Iowa, Paul Ryan had offered a prediction about Clinton's speech: "My guess is we will get a great rendition of how good things were in the nineties, but we're not going to hear much about how things have been the last four years." Begala, being mischievous but not without purpose, took out his iPad and showed Clinton a news story with Ryan's quote.

"Well," Clinton said, chuckling, "I guess he's gonna be surprised."

Clinton had a lot of a specific business he wanted to get done in the speech, much of it related to Ryan. At the Republican convention, Romney's running mate had launched an attack on Obama on Medicare, claiming that the president was raiding the program to the tune of $716 billion in order to fund Obamacare. *Ridiculous,* Clinton thought. The Romney-Ryan plan to turn the other big federal health care program, Medicaid, into a block grant and cut it by a third over the next ten years made Clinton see red. Then there was the matter of welfare reform.

Starting earlier in the summer, Boston had taken an unusual tack by putting footage of Hillary into a negative ad aimed at Obama. (It featured her famous scolding of him from 2008: "Shame on you, Barack Obama!") In mid-August, the Romneyites played the Clinton card again, this time using Bill. A new ad praised him for signing welfare reform into law in the nine-ties and claimed that Obama—whose administration had announced it would allow states to apply for waivers from the law's work requirements—was "gutting" one of Clinton's most cherished achievements.

Bill was loaded for bear on that topic. But above all he was focused on the elemental question that Axelrod and Plouffe had muffed over the weekend: Is the country better off today than four years ago? According to Clinton's former pollster, Stan Greenberg, Chicago was right to be wary about claiming that the economy had improved, since it flew in the face of the experience of voters. In the suite, Begala repeated the point: Stan says that if you tell people things are looking up, they get angry, so you shouldn't. But Clinton was determined to hurl himself straight into the teeth of that maw.

"I can do this," he said. "I'm the only one who can."

To Clinton's way of thinking, it was demonstrably true that circumstances had improved. And in making the argument, he could go even further, providing context about the scale of the economic calamity Obama had inherited. One line in the speech was written with that objective: "No president could have repaired all of the damage that he found in just four years."

For more than an hour in the early afternoon, Clinton compulsively wordsmithed that sentence, coming back to it again and again. Finally he settled on a crucial edit, changing the line to invoke his own legacy: "No president—*not me, not any of my predecessors, no one*—could have repaired all of the damage that he found in just four years." Some of the eminences of Old Clintonia at the table were less than keen on 42 making that key insertion. But Bill was adamant.

That one line is the heart of this deal, he thought. *The whole ball game.*

By then the speech was in decent shape, but thousands of words too long. The Obamans had scheduled Clinton to take the stage at 10:25 p.m. and speak for twenty-five minutes. No one in the campaign or in the suite was addled enough to think he would not run over. Still, in an effort to show the Obamans a draft not quite as long as *Infinite Jest,* 42 and his team spent the rest of the afternoon cutting and cutting.

Clinton was hyperconscious that the speech would be flyspecked by the press. Any line that could conceivably be misconstrued as him throwing an elbow at—or demonstrating anything less than total zeal for—Obama was excised. Any line that was too cute or cheap: ditto. A shot at Eastwood was discarded, and so was a joke of Begala's: "Every time I hear Mitt Romney and Paul Ryan say they're gonna fix Medicare, it reminds me of what the veterinarian said about my old dog Buddy. That was not a fix. It was a cut.

And there's a difference."

With dusk settling in and Axelrod about to jump out of his skin at having not seen the text, the speech still had a small defect: no ending.

"You know, I could just riff," Clinton said, and everyone cracked up.

At around 7:00 p.m., the speech was finally dispatched to Axelrod, who looked it over with Plouffe and Favreau. All three were shocked by its brevity, and unsurprised by its quality. They had only a few edits, which Clinton uncomplainingly accepted. Around 9:15, he wandered down the hall of his hotel to a room where a prompter was set up for a run-through. As Clinton rehearsed, Obama called to tell him the speech was great. Clinton said thanks and finished his rehearsal. The speech clocked in at twenty-eight minutes.

Clinton ambled out onto the blue-carpeted platform at 10:40, languidly clapping his hands to the strains of "Don't Stop," by Fleetwood Mac—his theme song. The speech he proceeded to unfurl bore a passing resemblance, but no more, to the one he had practiced. The text as prepared for delivery was 3,279 words; as delivered, it was 5,888. Much of what had been cut in the suite, he reinserted on the fly, and simply ad-libbed still more. In full effect was Clinton's capacity to perform like an aw-shucks country lawyer armed with a public policy Ph.D., boiling down complex arguments to their bare (and highly memorable) minima.

On the divergence in core values between Democrats and Republicans: "We believe that 'We're all in this together' is a far better philosophy than 'You're on your own.'"

On the GOP's case against Obama: "In Tampa, [it] was actually pretty simple, pretty snappy. It went something like this: 'We left him a total mess. He hasn't cleaned it up fast enough, so fire him and put us back in.'"

On Medicare: "When Congressman Ryan looked into that TV camera and attacked President Obama's Medicare savings as, quote, 'the biggest, coldest power play,' I didn't know whether to laugh or cry. Because that $716 billion is exactly, to the dollar, the same amount of Medicare savings that he has in his own budget! You've got to give him one thing: it takes some *brass* to attack a guy for doing what you did!"

On welfare: "The claim that President Obama weakened welfare reform's work requirement is just not true. But they keep on running ads claiming it. You want to know why? Their campaign pollster said, 'We are not going to let our campaign be dictated by fact-checkers.'" A long pause. "Now, finally I can say: that *is* true."

Clinton strayed far into the weeds. He cited reams of facts and figures. He merrily carved up today's Republicans while singing odes to Eisenhower, Reagan, Bush 41, and Bush 43—purposely leaving out a litany of Democratic presidents, in order to cloak himself in bipartisanship. Bumper sticker after bumper sticker rolled off his tongue: "We simply cannot afford to give the reins of government to someone who will double down on trickle-down."

Between his wanderings off script and the nonstop punctuations of applause, Clinton not only blew past his allotted time, he nearly doubled it. The only question was whether, well past 11:00 p.m., the networks would cut away. But the images of Clinton mid–tour de force were irresistible to any producer with a pulse. Looking on agog, the Obamans began to wonder if he would go on all night, while up on stage, Clinton radiated as much palpable pleasure as he ever had in public. A few hundred feet in front of the podium, delegates could almost feel the breeze from his tail wagging.

For all of the joshing in the suite about Clinton free-forming his conclusion, that was exactly what he did. "I love our country so much," he said. "I know we're coming back. For more than two hundred years, through every crisis, we've always come back. People have predicted our demise ever since George Washington was criticized for being a mediocre surveyor with a bad set of wooden false teeth. And so far, every single person that's bet against America has lost money, because we always come back. We come through every fire a little stronger and a little better."

Seconds later, Obama emerged from the wings and joined Clinton on the dais. Turning to meet him, Clinton enacted a deep bow. The two men shook hands and shared a long clinch—both smiling broadly, Obama patting and rubbing Clinton's back. The crowd lost its mind.

The Obamans departed the arena in a state of delight: two nights, one grand slam and one no-hitter. Clinton's old hands were even more ecstatic. Through the years, they had seen the boss deliver many speeches, including addresses at every convention since 1988. They had seen him more poetic, more dramatic, more emotional—but never more effective. "When you add in his age and that he's been retired from office for twelve years," one said, flipping the metaphor from pitcher to slugger, "it's like Ted Williams flirting with .400 at the age of thirty-nine." Late that night, well past midnight, Clinton summoned them back to his suite, where he was holding court. Picking at a plate of vegan bean dip, Clinton told story after story about conventions past, barely mentioning his speech or the election at hand. But then someone asked about Obama—if they'd talked backstage, how their conversation had gone, what advice Clinton had given 44.

I told him that when I was in the hospital with my heart condition, I got flowers and poems, which was nice, Clinton said. But what made me feel better was an explanation from the cardiologist: This is what we're gonna do, this is how it's gonna work, here's your prognosis, here's why you're going to be all right. I told Obama the same thing I've been telling you all: explanation is eloquence.

A S CLINTON REVELED AND reminisced, Joe Biden was huddled in a tiny room beneath the stage at the convention hall, staring into a teleprompter, fussing with the presentation of his speech. Joe hated the prompter. Always had. He was a stutterer as a kid, and stutterers have trouble reading aloud. So there he was with Sheehan—another stutterer, by chance—at 2:30 a.m., reformatting his speech for Thursday night, underlining certain words and phrases, trying to get the text . . . just so. Clinton, he knew, had raised the bar again, but Biden was certain he could clear it. He told people all the time: Hey, man, as a speaker, I'm every bit as good as Bill!

Traditionally, Biden would have had a night to himself during the convention, like he did back in 2008. But then they shortened the event to three days—and wanted to give Wednesday to Clinton. When Axelrod first brought up the idea to Obama, the president had only one hesitation: "What's Joe going to say?" he asked.

Biden said he wanted to think it over. His team did some historical research on convention TV ratings and concluded that speaking on the final night, just before Obama, might put Joe in front of a bigger audience. Let's do it, Biden said.

By Thursday, the plan for Biden and Obama to speak outdoors at the stadium had been washed out by fear of rain. (Wednesday saw buckets of it.) That night in the hall, Biden strode onstage and pointed to his wife and Mrs. Obama in the front row; Michelle flashed a thumbs-up back. His speech was replete with crowd-pleasing lines: "Osama bin Laden is dead, and General Motors is alive." It was filled with pellets fired at Mitt: "Romney said that as president, he would take a jobs tour. Well, with his support for outsourcing, it's going to have to be a foreign trip." The next day, it received scant media coverage, but that was okay with Joe—especially when he learned that his TV ratings were right up there with Clinton's.

Obama and his team were braced for a lukewarm reception for his speech. In a sense, he would be competing against his wife, his predecessor, and his own history and reputation. At the previous two Democratic conventions, his turns at the rostrum had been historic: the first launching him into outer space, the second accepting the first major-party nomination bestowed on an African American. That magic would be impossible to rekindle even with a speech that shot for the stars.

Obama's advisers had been insistent that his speech pursue more earthbound objectives in any case. Their goal was to have him put forth an agenda for the future without going much beyond what he had laid out in January's State of the Union. Obama was forever pushing for bigger and bolder policy ideas. But his people saw no point in taking needless risks when they were playing a winning hand. They wanted Obama to look forward—not loftily, not lyrically, not audaciously, but in a subdued tone and plainspoken language that might appeal to wavering independents.

In a blue suit, blue tie, and white shirt that night in the arena, Obama enacted those instructions. The first two-thirds of the speech combined the laundry-list quality of a SOTU with a sledgehammer-like repetition of the theme that the election was a choice. (He used that word or a variant of it twenty times.) There was a conspicuous nod to humility that cited Lincoln. The broadsides at Romney were fairly flaccid. ("You might not be ready for diplomacy with Beijing if you can't visit the Olympics without insulting our closest ally.") There were no memorable lines. The only part of the speech he appeared to relish was the final bit, in which he returned to a leitmotif from 2008. "The election four years ago wasn't about me," he said. "It was about you. My fellow citizens—you were the change."

The reviews, as expected, were not kind. When Favreau complained that the speech was being treated unfairly, Obama shrugged. You know how it goes, he said. The media's gonna take their shots.

Obama was skillful at concealing his frustrations from his aides, but frustrated he was. In the press and among political professionals, the verdict on Charlotte was that the convention had been a triumph—to a large extent because of Clinton, not Obama. The current president was grateful for what the former had done for him. But the gushing accolades for Bill's speech reminded Obama of the political constraints that kept him from being as wonky, backward-looking, or defensive as he instinctively wanted to be. That's the kind of speech I'd like to give, he said to his aides. Even though I know that I shouldn't.

It would take some time for the tangible effects of Clinton's stem-winder to sink in fully. But in Boston, the early signs were startling. Before Charlotte, Neil Newhouse was certain that no convention could have an appreciable impact on voters' perceptions of whether the country was on the right or the wrong track. Those perceptions, overwhelmingly pessimistic, had been locked in place since the start of the campaign, boding ill for Obama. But within seventy-two hours of Charlotte's finale, the right-track/wrong-track numbers had begun to move—dramatically—in favor of the Democrats. Romney's pollster was dumbfounded. When his colleagues asked him to explain the phenomenon, Newhouse shrugged and offered one word: Clinton.

Mitt's Bill problem was going to be much bigger than a single speech, however—for the Maximum Canine, having first shed his muzzle, was now straining at his leash. Provoked by Boston, empowered by Charlotte, Clinton was eager to hit the trail. He called Messina and started plotting a schedule that would turn him into Obama's general-election supersurrogate: a tireless ally with a massive megaphone and the capacity to talk the owls down from the trees.

His first foray took place five days after the convention closed, on

September 11, when Clinton headlined a grassroots rally at Florida International University in Miami. Though political hostilities were customarily halted in observance of national unity on the anniversary of the terrorist attacks on America, Clinton demonstrated only a modicum of restraint. In for a dime and a dollar, he opened fire on the GOP ticket over Medicare, providing the first nasty shot in a day that would have many—and would wind up haunting Romney right through to November.

20

THE WAR COUNCIL

MITT'S CELL PHONE BUZZED AT around 9:30 p.m. on September 11. He was on the runway in Jacksonville, having just landed after a flight from Reno. On the line was Lanhee Chen, calling from Boston with a clamant matter to discuss: the campaign's response to fires blazing in the Middle East.

Taking off from Nevada in the afternoon, Romney had been dimly aware of the tumult in the region. That morning, in an effort to quell a burgeoning fundamentalist street protest in Cairo over a crude anti-Islam video originating in the United States and circulating on YouTube, the American embassy in Egypt had released a statement saying it "condemn[ed] the continuing efforts by misguided individuals to hurt the religious feelings of Muslims—as we condemn efforts to offend believers of all religions." But the protest only escalated, with rioters breaching the Cairo embassy's walls, tearing down the American flag, and hoisting up a black banner bearing a Muslim declaration of faith.

While Romney was airborne, a more serious upheaval flared in Libya. Armed with rocket-propelled grenades and antiaircraft weaponry, Islamist militants stormed and torched a lightly defended U.S. diplomatic mission in Benghazi. There were news reports that a U.S. citizen had been killed. Scuttlebutt on the Hill was that the dead American was a State Department officer.

A conference call was thrown together on Commercial Street, with Chen, Rhoades, Stevens, and Gillespie taking part. In the conservative blogosphere, the Cairo embassy's statement (reaffirmed via Twitter after the breach of its perimeter) was being cast as an apology for free speech and an expression of sympathy for the demonstrators. Requests for comment on the breaking Mideast news were pouring into Boston. In Egypt and Libya, circumstances on the ground were chaotic; in the States, facts were scant and hazy. The initial consensus on the call was to wait until morning, see where things stood. But one Romneyite, Rich Williamson, had a different posture.

Williamson was a longtime Republican foreign policy hand and an outside adviser to the campaign. His résumé included stints in the Reagan and both Bush administrations; under 43, he had held two UN ambassadorial posts. He had also been a U.S. Senate candidate in Illinois and chairman of the state's Republican Party. He viewed Obama through a Fox News prism with a Windy City overlay: as a feckless Hyde Park peacenik. The zotzing of bin Laden and Obama's drone policy meant nothing to Williamson—he saw them as fig leaves. The Cairo embassy's statement struck him as an outrage and an expression of the president's proclivity for appeasement. The notion that some anti-Islam Internet video had anything to do with anything was pure bullshit. What was happening in Egypt, Libya, and elsewhere in the region was obvious: Obama's Middle East policy was unraveling.

Williamson made that argument on the call, and vehemently. The governor needs to speak out on this, the ambassador rumbled. Williamson considered Romney brilliant but unmotivated by ideas, and regarded Boston as defensive and amateurish. Winning the White House meant whipping out a switchblade, he believed: *Axelrod gets in a knife fight every morning to work up an appetite for breakfast.* To Williamson, Egypt and Libya offered a chance to start a scrap. If Romney got cut up, that was okay—voters would see that he cared enough to bleed.

By the end of the call, Williamson had stampeded the Boston brain trust into a pristine state of groupthink. Everyone now saw it as essential for Romney to weigh in—a slam-dunk show of strength. The language they drafted was not as provocative as Williamson would have liked, but it was still plenty spicy. The campaign planned to blast a press release to reporters, embargoing it until midnight, when 9/11 would be over. All that remained was for Chen to secure Romney's sign-off.

On the phone with the candidate, Chen quickly ran through the day's Mideast chronology, then read Romney the statement that would be going out in his name: "I'm outraged by the attacks on American diplomatic missions in Libya and Egypt and by the death of an American consulate worker in Benghazi. It's disgraceful that the Obama administration's first response was not to condemn attacks on our diplomatic missions, but to sympathize with those who waged the attacks."

"Do *you* like the statement?" Romney asked. "Is this the group's consensus?"

Chen said that he did and that it was.

"Okay, this sounds right to me," Mitt said. "Let's do it."

Romney got off the plane and headed to his hotel to meet Ann, who was awaiting him. Even with his campaign's all-economy-all-the-time focus, he had long hoped that the pungent critique of the administration's foreign policy in *No Apology* would gain some traction—and been frustrated that he had not dented Obama's rock-solid commander-in-chief ratings. Now, suddenly, the turmoil in the Middle East and the administration's cravenness had presented him with a mile-wide opening. *Apology in the face of an attack on America and an American—unimaginable!* he thought.

In his suite, Mitt found Ann sacked out. He was exhausted, too. But as he lay there in bed, his excitement and agitation kept him tossing and turning, unable to fall asleep. Not wanting to wake his wife, he slipped out from under the blanket, settled in on the couch, and popped an Ambien—thinking all the while, *Boy, Obama is going to be in a world of hurt tomorrow.*

THE MORNING LIGHT SHONE HARSHLY on Romney's fitful reverie. Just before eight o'clock, he jumped on a conference call with his team and listened as Chen ran down what had taken place overnight, as September 11 ticked into September 12.

At a little past 10:00 p.m., as Boston was delivering its statement to the press, the White House had disavowed the communication from the Cairo embassy as "not cleared by Washington" or "reflect[ing] the views of the United States government." The Romneyites took this as a cue to break their embargo a full ninety minutes before midnight, thus mugging Obama on 9/11 and making their tactical injection of campaign gamesmanship into a multifaceted international crisis all the more incendiary. Chicago duly expressed outrage: "We are shocked that, at a time when the United States of America is confronting the tragic death of one of our diplomatic officers in Libya, Governor Romney would choose to launch a political attack," said campaign spokesman Ben LaBolt.

That the situation in Egypt had been eclipsed by Benghazi became clearer early that morning: not one but four American consular personnel were dead, including Ambassador Christopher Stevens. On the question of the Cairo embassy statement, the press was poking holes in Romney's criticism that it had been "the administration's first response" to the attacks—when in fact the statement had preceded the incursion and it now appeared that the embassy had been acting on its own. The cable pundits were flaying Boston for making a "rush to judgment," for behaving in a "patently political" fashion, for desperately chasing the news cycle.

Listening to Chen, Romney tensed up as he realized that he'd jumped the gun by leaping into a rapidly shifting situation with piecemeal information. Leaning back in his chair and gripping both armrests, he raised his voice to cut off the conversation on the call.

"Guys, we screwed up," Romney said. "This was a mistake."

The question was what to do now. The press was asking whether Romney was standing by his statement. His team was unequivocal: to give any quarter would only deepen the hole he was in; he would look weak, vacillating, flip-floppy. Romney was scheduled to visit his local headquarters that morning for a rally, which could be converted into a press conference. You have to step up and fight through this, Gillespie said. Paul Ryan agreed: "Mitt, we can't back off." So did Williamson: "We have no reason to be apologetic."

Romney was right there with them. The man who had written *No Apology* wasn't about to apologize, especially when he still believed that his rival had committed that sin on America's behalf. Although Romney acknowledged that he had reacted too soon, he thought he was correct on the merits: the Cairo embassy had reaffirmed its statement after its walls had been breached; the embassy was part of the administration; the president, therefore, was ultimately responsible for the misguided attempts to placate the agitators.

The press conference was held two hours later at Romney's Jacksonville campaign digs, a small space one door down from an exotic reptile shop in a scruffy strip mall. After Romney read a prepared statement that expanded on the previous night's press release, he opened the floor to questions—and felt as though the room had been invaded by pygmy rattlesnakes and frilled dragons from next door. With each tough question, Mitt's rhetoric became more inflammatory. Invoking the word that was on his mind but not in his written remarks, Romney said, "The statement that came from the administration was . . . akin to apology and, I think, was a severe miscalculation."

Romney had confidence in his ability to explain himself when he felt he was on solid ground. When his footing was shaky, as it often was on foreign policy, he tended to get hot—too hot. In the space of a few minutes, he hurled some variant of the word "apology" at the administration seven times. Watching from Boston, Rhoades saw another political nightmare blossoming on the screen, picked up his phone, and called Madden in Jacksonville. "Let's end this—now," he said urgently.

A few minutes later, Obama appeared in a setting more august than a storefront next to Blazin' Reptiles. From the presidential podium in the Rose Garden, he spoke about the loss of Ambassador Stevens and the three other Americans in Libya with a mixture of solemnity and resoluteness. "No acts of terror will ever shake the resolve of this great nation, alter that character, or eclipse the light of the values that we stand for," Obama said. "Today we mourn four more Americans who represent the very best of the United States of America. We will not waver in our commitment to see that justice is done for this terrible act. And make no mistake: justice will be done."

Joe Biden had caught Romney's press conference live on TV that morning. The VP's reaction was brief and to the point: "He's a horse's ass."

Obama had been too busy preparing his Rose Garden remarks to pay much attention to Mitt. But afterwards, standing in the Outer Oval Office with Carney, Pfeiffer, and Ben Rhodes, the president noticed clips of Romney in Jacksonville being shown on cable.

So what did he say? Obama asked his aides.

"You're not going to believe it, but he's doubling down," Carney said.

Obama was astounded. In the past twenty-four hours, protests had erupted at U.S. diplomatic missions in a dozen countries. Chris Stevens was the first serving American ambassador killed in hostilities since 1979. The corpses in Benghazi were still warm. And here was Romney, the Republicans' choice to be commander in chief, trying to score cheap political points.

"It's practically disqualifying," Obama said.

Obama's disgust was still evident a few hours later, when he was asked about Romney's gambit in an interview with Steve Kroft of *60 Minutes*. After noting that the Cairo embassy statement "came from folks on the ground who are potentially in danger," Obama added acidly, "My tendency is to cut folks a little bit of slack when they're in that circumstance rather than try to question their judgment from the comfort of a campaign office." And then he stuck the boot in once more: "Governor Romney seems to have a tendency to shoot first and aim later."

The heaping of scorn on Romney by the White House and other Democrats came as little surprise. But the GOP was almost as unforgiving. Within hours of Mitt's press conference, former advisers to McCain, Bush 43, and Reagan had torn into the nominee on the record. "It almost feels like Sarah Palin is his foreign policy adviser," Dubya's 2004 chief strategist, Matthew Dowd, sneered. Speaking on background, Republican critics were even more blistering: "This was a deliberate and premeditated move, and it totally revealed Romney's character . . . as completely craven and his candidacy as serving no higher purpose than his ambition," said one. On Capitol Hill, party leaders declined to echo Romney's criticism or rise to his defense; when reporters asked Mitch McConnell about Mitt's comments, he turned and walked away.

By the end of the day, Romney recognized that he had erred again. The conclusion he drew from the episode was stark: on national security, the media narrative was tilted so lopsidedly in Obama's favor that prosecuting the topic was a fool's errand. *Lesson learned,* Mitt thought.

That deduction would have unforeseen consequences for Romney down the line. It also elided the nature and scale of the screwup. In truth, the Benghazi tragedy was a horrendous failure on the part of the administration; the unrest unspooling across the Middle East was just the kind of externality that had worried the president's team for a year. But by inserting himself in the story—not once but twice—and deliberately repeating a mistake that had been roundly criticized, Romney had distracted attention and scrutiny away from the White House. A potentially brutal blow to the president had been deflected by the man who hoped to replace him.

From the London fiasco to Tampa to Benghazi, self-sabotage was becoming a leading leitmotif of the Romney enterprise—and was costing him dearly. Twelve days into September, with Election Day less than eight weeks away, Obama's narrow edge in the battleground states had widened to three or four points. Across the ideological spectrum, a storyline was setting in: Romney was losing, knew he was losing, and was starting to panic.

In fact, Mitt was unnaturally calm. Up against an incumbent president who had badly outspent him over the summer, he was running inside the margin of error, with plenty of time and three debates ahead. All Romney needed was to catch a break, just a little luck, to spring him from his rut and into a stretch of sunlight. What he got instead was an icy blast from the past.

ROMNEY HOPPED INTO HIS Suburban outside the FBI building on Wilshire Boulevard, in L.A. It was the afternoon of Monday, September 17. He had just received his first national security briefing from the intelligence community and was on his way to an evening of fund-raising in Orange County. Mitt was in a chipper mood, wearing a coy I've-got-a-secret look after his classified download from the spooks—when he heard Garrett Jackson behind him, saying, "Guv, we've got a problem."

Back in May at the Marc Leder fund-raiser in Boca Raton, Romney had lit a fuse with his unvarnished disquisition about the 47 percent of voters he believed were beyond his reach. Now the bomb had detonated on the website of *Mother Jones,* which had posted surreptitiously recorded video of Mitt's after-dinner Q&A. The source of the footage was unknown. (It would turn out to be a disgruntled bartender.) The video was grainy, but the audio was clear. The story was rapidly mushrooming into a monster.

Romney spent the next hour in the car, headed to Costa Mesa, on a conference call with Boston. By turns contrite and combative, he argued that his words were being wrenched from their proper context. All he had done was talk about the electorate, about the 47 percent that constituted Obama's base, about how he was focused on the middle, on persuadable voters. I've probably said something like this a hundred times, Romney said. This time it just came out badly.

The Romneyites knew they were dealing with more than an ordinary flap, knew they had to respond. Precisely how wasn't obvious, though. Stevens insisted that Romney needed to say something on camera that night so the TV coverage wouldn't feature only the offending video. The question, then, was whether Mitt should offer a full-throated mea culpa. But the sand traps with that option were many. *Mother Jones* had posted only a few clips from the Leder fund-raiser, not the full video. Boston had no clue what might be coming next, or whether footage from other events with Mitt saying roughly the same thing might be floating around. There was also the *No Apology* conundrum, yet again—and the fact that, even if the book had not been thusly titled, Romney didn't believe he had anything to apologize for.

A press conference was arranged for Romney between events at the Segerstrom Center for the Arts. Just after 7:00 p.m. local time, the candidate read a brief statement and took three questions. The closest he came to expressing regret was to say that his remarks about the 47 percent were "off the cuff" and "not elegantly stated." He noted that he had been playing pundit, "talking about the political process of drawing people into my campaign." He offered analysis of his analysis: he could have "state[d] it more clearly in a more effective way." As to the substance of his comments, Romney said, "It's a message which I'm going to carry and continue to carry." Then he added, "Of course I want to help all Americans—all Americans—have a bright and prosperous future." His affect was detached and his tone impersonal throughout.

Obama was in Ohio for a pair of campaign events when the 47 percent story broke. In the presidential limo, Plouffe showed him the video on an iPhone. It's gonna be hard for Romney to say he misspoke, Obama said. That's a genuine sentiment he expressed, not some slip of the tongue.

"Yeah," Plouffe said. "This is going to be a thing."

Plouffe thought back to Obama's experience in 2008, when he was secretly audiotaped at a San Francisco fund-raiser talking about small-town people who "get bitter" and "cling to guns or religion." Bad as that was politically, Plouffe knew that if the gaffe had been captured on video, it would have been far worse. He fully expected Romney to try to kill the story with an apology. When Mitt didn't, Plouffe thought, *We're off to the races here!*

Obama and his people instantly twigged to the most damaging part of Romney's remarks: that he had said of half the country, "My job is not to worry about those people. I'll never convince them that they should take personal responsibility and care for their lives." The president considered it cynical in the extreme, but not unexpected. This shows who the real Mitt Romney is, Obama told his aides.

The next night, Obama was scheduled to be a guest on the *Late Show with David Letterman.* Letterman was sure to raise the 47 percent topic, giving the president his first chance to comment publicly on the controversy. Plouffe and Pfeiffer saw the appearance as a big moment; they carefully rehearsed an answer with Obama that would dovetail with the theme of the negative TV ads being ginned up in Chicago. To Letterman's question, Obama replied devastatingly but without rancor.

"When I won in 2008, 47 percent of the American people voted for John McCain," he said. "They didn't vote for me. And what I said on election night was, even though you didn't vote for me, I hear your voices and I'm going to work as hard as I can to be your president."

Around the same time Obama was taping his chat with Dave, Romney was on Fox News's *Your World with Neil Cavuto.* Not giving an inch, he more or less repeated what he had said at Leder's house: "Those that are dependent upon government and those that think government's job is to redistribute, I'm not going to get." By the next night, Mitt's tune had changed, albeit only slightly. In Miami at a televised Univision forum, he addressed the 47 percent issue implicitly. "My campaign is about the 100 percent of

America," he said, "and I'm concerned about them." The following day, in an interview with *60 Minutes,* he repeated that formulation. His tone remained static, remote, and abrupt, even as the story, with its "secret video" irresistibility, continued to reverberate on every TV channel, in every corner of the Internet, and on every inky op-ed page across the country.

In private, Romney was engaged in an orgy of rationalization and self-censure. Reviewing the now available transcript, he fixated on the query that had prompted his infamous reply: "How are you going to do it, in two months before the elections, to convince everybody you've got to take care of yourself?" *What an idiotic question,* Romney thought. He told himself that the part of his answer about not worrying about the moochers applied only to those two months; he couldn't persuade them to change their lives *before* Election Day. He cursed himself for answering at all; he was only trying to be polite. (*Stupid, stupid, stupid.*) Lying awake at 4:00 a.m., brooding on another self-administered gut punch, he remembered something Mike Leavitt once told him: In politics, for good or ill, we're defined by things we never would have imagined would define us. For Leavitt, it was the 2002 Salt Lake City Olympics; for Jimmy Carter, Desert One. Mitt wondered if 47 percent would define him—a painful possibility. *The only reason I'm in this race is to help people who are hurting,* he thought. *The rich will do fine with or without me; it's the rest who need my experience and economic direction.*

Yet for all of Romney's personal angst, in the days after the 47 percent story broke, he took no decisive steps to ameliorate the fallout. Unlike Obama in 2008 after the Jeremiah Wright eruption, Romney didn't push to give a major speech to set the record straight and slay the dragon. He didn't insist on doing an op-ed or a sit-down interview devoted to the topic. He didn't call his team together for an all-hands-on-deck brainstorm. He simply stewed.

Romney's passivity baffled many members of the Boston brain trust. They believed the video conveyed a misimpression of the man they knew. They also saw it as politically ruinous—reinforcing the plutocratic image that the Obamans had spent millions to burn into the minds of voters. Stevens, meanwhile, was unconvinced that Romney needed to do more to heal himself. "I can't tell you we're gonna win," Stuart said to Mitt. "But I don't think we're gonna lose because of this."

The campaign's paralysis brought forth venom from a GOP establishment that had always distrusted Romney's operation. On the eve of the 47 percent video's surfacing, Politico had published a lengthy exposé on Romneyland's managerial dysfunction, zeroing in on its chief strategist as the main culprit. All around Washington, fellow consultants were sniping at Stevens, incredulous at the wide influence Romney granted him. "You never let the artist run the art gallery," one of Haley Barbour's confidants quipped. "If you sent Stuart to the 7-Eleven and said, 'Get a loaf of bread and a quart of milk,' he might not show up for a week and a half."

The establishment's dismay was made manifest by a string of top-shelf conservative pundits. Bill Kristol deemed Romney's 47 percent remarks "stupid" and "arrogant," adding that Mitt had "little substance to say about the future of our country." David Brooks compared him to Thurston Howell III. Peggy Noonan captured the Republican disenchantment with Boston most comprehensively. "It's time to admit the Romney campaign is an incompetent one," Noonan wrote. "It's not big, it's not brave, it's not thoughtfully tackling great issues. All the activists, party supporters and big donors should be pushing for change."

At the highest levels of Romneyland, some were agitating for a transformation from within—notably Fishconsin. When Ryan was chosen for the ticket, he had assumed (like the rest of the political world) that his selection signaled a full-on acceptance of framing the election as a choice. Instead, his month on the ticket had been marked by strategic muddle, with Stevens continuing to shape the campaign as a referendum. As for the sharp knives in Ryan's drawer, such as his Medicare plan, Romney had handled them wearing hazmat gloves.

The 47 percent crisis crystallized Ryan's discontent. Unless the campaign affirmed the choice paradigm, the election would boil down to dueling referenda—and Romney-Ryan was likely to lose. On Sunday, September 23, Mitt and much of his brain trust gathered for a post-47-percent strategy meeting in L.A., where the nominee was back on the fund-raising hamster wheel. Ryan, holed up at home to prep for his debate against Biden, videoconferenced in from Wisconsin. With ardor, the running mate made his case, articulating the perils of a pure referendum, pressing for big ideas, opining that they had a duty to give the American people a clear choice.

Stevens sat sulkily, arms folded, deaf to Ryan's premise, saying little. By the end, Ryan had prevailed.

The next morning, a public memo went out from Gillespie consecrating Fishconsin's apparent victory: "The election is a choice," it baldly stated. Both its content and its authorship suggested to many campaign Kremlinologists that Stevens had been sidelined.

But Ryan wasn't the sole force for change in Romney's orbit. By the time of the L.A. meeting, an external faction was taking shape: a group of prominent Republicans, mostly elected officials, who feared Mitt was falling into an outright death spiral and hoped to pull him out. Although the gathering was still in its formative stages, it was slated for the next Sunday, September 30. And though it had no formal name, everyone who knew about the assembly was calling it the War Council.

THE WAR COUNCIL LOOMED on Romney's calendar but was distant from his mind. In periods of chaos, Mitt went into task-management mode. He liked the tangibility and specificity of a mission-critical undertaking. To no small extent, what kept him from obsessing over the 47 percent—perhaps to his detriment—was the presence of just such an activity: preparing for his first debate with Obama in Denver on October 3.

Romney had started debate prep unusually early and sunk a gargantuan amount of time into the endeavor. In June, he had assigned its organization to Myers, alongside her veepstakes duties. On the unexceptional theory that he would enter October trailing or at best neck and neck in the race, Mitt believed that pretty much the whole election could come down to the debates. He told Myers that he wanted to treat prep as "the Manhattan Project of the campaign." His first session had taken place at the Park City donor retreat, in June. Since then, he had logged countless hours on drills, briefing books, and a three-day debate camp in Vermont during the Democratic convention. A week out from Denver, he had already done seven full mock debates; between now and showtime, he would do another three.

The funny thing was, Romney had always detested debate prep. When he ran for governor, Myers, then his sparring partner, whipped him again and again; Mitt became so annoyed one time, he threw his notes on the floor. In 2008, he found the multiplayer mock debate format particularly uncongenial. All the stand-ins had boned up on the questions beforehand; he was hearing them for the first time, stumbling through his answers, his self-esteem plummeting. No more mock debates! Mitt decreed.

But mocks were a nonnegotiable part of preparing to face off against Obama, especially given that Romney had not partaken in a one-on-one debate since 2002. Portraying the president was Rob Portman, who had earned a reputation as the GOP's most skillful doppelganger. Over the years, Portman had enacted the roles of Lamar Alexander against Bob Dole, Al Gore against George W. Bush, Joe Lieberman and John Edwards against Dick Cheney, and Obama against McCain. His imitation of the president in mocks with Mitt was pure Method acting. Every detail—from the phrases and intonations to the monochrome ties—was letter-perfect. His immersion was so complete that, on more than one occasion, Portman fell into character by mistake during stump speeches in Ohio. (*Oh, God, I've become Obama!* he thought.) Rhoades routinely compared Portman to Daniel Day-Lewis; he was Fauxbama.

Portman was no believer in playing soft to build a candidate's confidence. In the early mocks, he pounded Romney into the dirt. Sometimes Fauxbama would throw the kitchen sink at Mitt: a long string of charges related to Bain or his Massachusetts record. Other times, he would mischaracterize Romney's policies or refuse to let him have the last word. Or he would slyly try to provoke Mitt with passing references to Swiss bank accounts, Olympic sweetheart deals, or Mormonism. ("As a man of faith, would you agree . . . ?")

Then there was a charge that drove Romney batty, which Fauxbama deployed in two or three different mocks: Governor Romney, not because you work, but because you're relying on your investments, you make more in one day than the typical American family makes in a year. How can you relate to what's going on out there in Ohio, in Iowa? In each instance, Romney was irritated—and never came up with an answer. "What am I going to say to *that?*" he complained.

Presiding over the process strategically and stylistically was Stevens. Even as his influence in Boston was being diminished by Gillespie, the chief strategist still had the conch when it came to the image Romney would project in front of the cameras. Just as Stevens's adages undergirded the campaign at the start, they hovered over the run-up to Denver. Stuart wanted Romney to be likable, comfortable, to look as if he was enjoying himself (so that voters would think they would enjoy watching him be president). He wanted Mitt to control the stage; he wanted a kinetic debate. "Remember, Custer was *chasing* the Indians," Stevens said, warning Romney not to let Obama bait him. "Let's don't debate this guy; let's dominate this guy."

By the end of September, Romney was engaged in some form of debate prep almost every day. Though he and Portman had been virtual strangers just months before, the Ohio senator was gradually being incorporated into Mitt's innermost circle—no longer serving only as Fauxbama but called upon as a general-purpose adviser. With Portman's help, Romney's mock performances were getting stronger and stronger, and his substantive chops were showing through elsewhere. On Univision and *60 Minutes,* Mitt had been so impressive that the Obamans had taken note, crediting his debate prep for his newfound ease and fluency. In both appearances, the only question on which he whiffed was the 47 percent.

The candidate and his debate team had zero doubt that the subject would come up in Denver, either as part of an attack by Obama or in the form of a question by moderator Jim Lehrer. On Saturday, September 29, in a meeting at Mitt and Ann's townhouse in Belmont, any number of suggested responses were put on the table: variations on "I care about the 100 percent" and "I misspoke." Someone proposed rebutting Obama by saying, Well, Mr. President, I'm sure there are things you've said that you'd like to take back—like your comment about bitter people clinging to firearms and God. But Romney shot the rejoinder down; it would be like trying to kill a pterodactyl with a flyswatter.

Early the following afternoon, Romney and Portman took the stage in John Hancock Hall, in Boston's Back Bay, for their one formal, full-dress pre-Denver mock. After the 47 percent video, Rhoades's paranoia about secret tapes was high; he had the campaign's advance team repeatedly sweep the building for bugs or hidden cameras. Romney turned in a terrific performance; Portman was proud. The only flaw was Mitt's response regarding the 47 percent, which was woefully wishy-washy. Watching in the hall, Mike Leavitt shook his head. "That's not good enough," he said to Myers.

When the team gathered downstairs in a conference room for a post-mortem, no one disagreed—including Romney. With Denver just three days away, he and his people still had not come up with a decent answer to the evening's $64,000 question. It wasn't even as if they had narrowed the options to A and B. They were still trying to cobble together a solution out of options A through F. After listening to Stevens and others toss out more ideas, Romney finally said, "Guys, is this terminal?"

No, it's not, Eric Fehrnstrom said. If Obama goes after you on the 47 percent, you don't need to apologize or soft-pedal. You need to express outrage. You need to be indignant.

Slipping into character as Romney, Fehrnstrom cut loose: It's offensive and insulting, Mr. President, to suggest that I don't care. I served as a missionary. I served ten years as a pastor in my church. I served the Olympics without pay. When I was governor, every child in my state had health care, and we had the best schools in the nation. Under your administration, Mr. President, more people are in poverty, more are on food stamps, the poor are getting crushed. How *dare* you say that I want to write off half of the country? How *dare* you say that I don't care?

Romney was furiously scribbling notes. When Fehrnstrom finished, Mitt was all fired up. In an instant, he took the lines and made them his own—reciting his version with more passion than some in the room had ever seen from him before. When Romney finished, his people burst into applause.

There was more to go over, but they had been in the theater for three hours now. Leavitt and Portman had already left; they had somewhere else to be, and so did Romney. While the mock had been winding down, the War Council was convening on Commercial Street.

We've got to get going, Myers said. Everybody is there.

THE IDEA FOR THE WAR Council emanated from Meg Whitman, the former CEO of eBay and GOP nominee for the California governorship in 2010, who had been friendly with Romney since working for him at Bain and Company in the eighties. Whitman thought Mitt was in serious trouble and needed to hear a sampling of advice from outside his bubble. She proposed the notion to Myers, who handed off its execution to Portman.

Portman worried about rattling Romney, messing with his head so close to Denver. But he, too, believed the campaign was on the brink. One of the oddest things about Mitt, Portman had come to recognize, was that he had so few close friends, particularly in national Republican circles. With much of the establishment flogging the candidate, Portman thought that his new chum could use a hug—along with a bit of tough love on the 47 percent— from some high-level GOP allies.

Portman invited nine people to be war councillors. Three of them (Christie, Pawlenty, Rubio) had scheduling conflicts. The other six were now seated with Portman around the long rectangular table in the third-floor conference room at Romney HQ: Whitman, Leavitt, New Hampshire senator Kelly Ayotte, South Carolina governor Nikki Haley, Virginia governor Bob McDonnell, and former New Hampshire governor John Sununu. The Boston brain trust lined the periphery.

By the time Romney arrived from his Back Bay dress rehearsal, the War Council had heard a presentation by Neil Newhouse on the campaign's internal polling. For several days after the release of the 47 percent video, Newhouse had simply shut down Boston's research and waited for the earth to stop trembling. Nearly two weeks later, it was clear that the damage had been severe. Romney was at least three or four points behind in every battleground state—with Obama at 49 percent nationally. In Ohio, the gap was closer to eight points; in Virginia, what had been a dead heat was now trending dramatically in the president's favor. *I knew things were bad,* McDonnell thought. *But we're in a lot worse shape than I thought.*

Once Mitt was seated at the head of the table, Whitman quickly commanded the floor. Whitman's own gubernatorial campaign had been torn to bits by a 47-percent-like imbroglio, when her former housekeeper of nine years, an undocumented Latina, accused Whitman of "throwing me away like a piece of garbage" after she asked for help with her legal status. Reflecting on that experience, Whitman told Romney bluntly, From where I sit, you have a lot of work to do. The 47 percent is killing you. You haven't dealt with it, and you must. You need to show compassion. You need to connect. You need to apologize—not in the debate or after the debate, but *before* the debate, in a speech, in an interview, somewhere.

Leavitt seconded Whitman's recommendation, with no small degree of emotion. You've got to get this behind you, he told Romney. You have to do it before the debate. This is a moment where people want to hear you say, "Sometimes we choose the wrong words. What I said is not what is in my heart. I feel badly that people found it hurtful." You need to have that conversation with the American people. You have to say you're sorry, and you have to do it *tomorrow.*

McDonnell wasn't sure Romney had to bow and scrape, but his appraisal of the candidate's public image was harsh. "Mitt, let's just be honest," McDonnell said. "You'd be a great president. Your policies are right. I believe deeply in them. But for some reason, people don't like you."

McDonnell had ideas about how to counteract the picture of Romney as an unfeeling, out-of-touch fat cat: Mitt had to be a friendly, optimistic, happy warrior, talking about pocketbook issues in the way that voters did around their kitchen tables. He should start telling intimate and authentic stories, start sharing himself. You and your wife are good people, McDonnell said. You've given back. Folks need to see that. They need to see your heart.

Haley agreed. I've seen you on the campaign trail, she said. I know what kind of person you are. You need to let your guard down and show people the real you. You can turn this around. People want to hear that you understand their struggles. You don't need to be *sharing* their struggles, but they need to know you know that their struggles exist.

Listening to some of the councillors' suggestions, Romney's advisers labored not to roll their eyes. Stevens had had reservations about holding the meeting at all; now he slouched in the corner, eating fruit, saying nothing. (When he finally piped up, Sununu swiveled in his chair and cracked, "Stuart? You're here? I thought you were dead.") That the 47 percent remarks remained an open wound was indisputable. But trying to heal it in the three days before Denver struck the Romneyites as impractical—and the councillors' ideas about how to do so, half-baked. *How do you speak from the heart from a teleprompter?* Rhoades wondered. *Or is Mitt supposed to get up there and do a Jimmy Swaggart?*

At the end of the table, Romney listened intently, taking notes, occasionally pushing back or cutting in. To the councillors he seemed tired, very tired, and also taken aback by their level of candor. Romney had walked into the War Council thinking that it was a supercharged surrogates meeting, not a come-to-Jesus huddle. The bizarreness of the whole affair was lost on no one. Though the councillors wanted Mitt to win, most of their relationships to him were politically and personally remote. Glancing around the table, Leavitt thought, *If you were looking to reach the soul of Mitt Romney, you probably wouldn't pick this group.*

But for Romney, the show of support was touching—and also clarifying. After an hour of back-and-forth around the room, there was no escaping two things: the depth of the crisis Romney was facing and the necessity of a greater degree of self-exposure. There was so much talk about Mitt's myocardium, the room full of politicians sounded like a cardiologists' convention. Romney took the point.

When it came to the 47 percent, Mitt was with his advisers: Denver would be his chance to get past the controversy. In front of a television audience of tens of millions on Wednesday night, he would have the opportunity to create a genuine moment.

All along, Romney had understood that the debates would be critical. But now the stakes were infinitely greater. At the start of the meeting, Rhoades had laid out a five-point plan for the resuscitation of Romney's staggering campaign. The plan's first point was: score a knockout in Denver. If Mitt failed to pull that off, Rhoades admitted, the other four points were moot. The race would basically be over.

The direness of that forecast was an echo of the media consensus: DENVER DEBATE DO-OR-DIE FOR MITT ROMNEY ran a recent Politico headline. Few Republicans in the capital or anywhere else in the land disagreed. For a brief shining moment in Park City, Romney and his party's leaders had seemed bonded in solidarity. But that had proven to be a mirage. The upper spheres of the GOP—from elected officials to donors to the conservative super PACs—were ready to walk away from Romney unless he triumphed in the Mile High City. In 1996, after Bob Dole lost his first debate to Bill Clinton, his campaign had spent the full month before Election Day circling the drain. That same sinkhole now confronted Romney.

The slim reed to which Mitt clung was his readiness for Denver. Earlier in the week, he had called Christie, pleading with him to appear on three network Sunday shows and make the case that Romney wasn't a goner.

Christie happily complied. "I have absolute confidence," he told George Stephanopoulos, "that when we get to Thursday morning, George, all of you are going to be shaking your head, saying it's a brand-new race with thirty-three days to go."

And Romney believed it. He had mastered his material, tapered his attacks, and chiseled his counterattacks. The only question was what kind of game his opponent would bring. As Fauxbama, Portman had shown Romney a variety of looks—the president as aggressor, the president as defender, the president as rope-a-doper. But all were based on one faulty assumption: that the Obama who showed up wouldn't make Clint Eastwood appear prophetic.

21

MILE-HIGH MELTDOWN

THREE HOURS AFTER the War Council ended and nearly three thousand miles away, Obama took the stage under a harvest moon at Desert Pines High School, in Las Vegas. The president had pitched up outside Sin City for three days of debate camp ahead of Denver. In a white dress shirt with the sleeves rolled up and a pale blue tie loosened at the neck, Obama opened his remarks by saying he was looking forward to the forthcoming cage match. "I know folks in the media are speculating already on who's gonna have the best zingers," he noted. "Governor Romney, he's a good debater. I'm just okay."

Obama's self-deprecation made headlines, and was widely seen as spin—part of a systematic effort by Chicago to lower expectations. But, in truth, it was pretty much on the money. Obama had never been an agile debater or much enjoyed debating. His general aversion to political exhibitionism was magnified exponentially when it came to televised forensics. He saw debates as phony through and through: stagy, hokey, superficial, and insubstantial, judged on the basis of clever sound bites (a.k.a. zingers) by political pundits under the misimpression that their job was to act like Siskel and Ebert—and revealing of nothing about the qualities required for a successful presidency.

None of which was to say he hadn't been hankering to kick Romney's ass. Over the summer, Obama surprised his advisers with his zest for going mano a mano with Mitt. More than once he declared to Axelrod, Messina, and Plouffe, If you guys can get me to the first debate in a tie race, I'll put this thing away.

Like his opponent, the president had started prepping early—earlier than in 2008 and earlier than most incumbents. His first meeting with his debate team was in the Roosevelt Room in mid-July. Around the table were familiar faces: Axelrod, Bauer, Benenson, Lew, Plouffe, and Anita Dunn. Karen Dunn (no relation to Anita), a former Hillary Clinton staffer, was on board to help manage the operation and plot strategy.

Captaining the squad was Ron Klain, who had co-led Obama's prep in 2008. At fifty-one, Klain was a brainy, sometimes brusque lawyer who had clerked for Supreme Court justice Byron White and then morphed into a Beltway super-aide. On Capitol Hill, he had worked for Biden and Tom Daschle; in the White House, he had overseen Clinton's judicial nominations and served as vice-presidential chief of staff to both Biden and Al Gore. As Gore's point man in the 2000 hanging-chad battle in Florida, Klain had suffered a heartbreaking defeat. But it had led to his being played by Kevin Spacey in the HBO movie *Recount,* which made him semi-hemi-demi-famous.

Klain delivered a frank warning to Obama in the Roosevelt Room: incumbents almost always lose their first debate. Ford in 1976, Carter in 1980, Reagan in 1984, Bush 41 in 1992, and Bush 43 in 2004 all were clobbered, and the reasons were straightforward. For any challenger, sharing the stage with a sitting president—behind identical podiums, in nearly identical costumes—obliterated the gap in stature between them. Incumbents suffered from high expectations: voters assumed they would be good. But incumbents were invariably rusty: for four years they had been focused on governing, not giving timed answers with an opponent up in their grille. Challengers were in fighting shape after debate-filled nomination contests. Challengers had ample time to prep; incumbents were, well, busy.

Obama was determined to defy those precedents and structural forces. All summer, he lugged around thick briefing books on Romney's policies and record, filling the margins of the documents with questions and dispatching them to his team for answers. (In September alone, he made more than a hundred such requests, many at a level of detail that had Klain thinking, *This is insane.*) The more Obama internalized Romney's agenda, the more he champed at the bit to lay bare its contradictions and outlandishness. "I can't wait to debate this guy," Obama told his team in August.

He conducted three mock debates in Washington before leaving for camp. Like Portman, John Kerry put great effort into inhabiting his role—a process he found distasteful, given his feelings for Mitt. Kerry had been at his pal Ted Kennedy's side during the 1994 Massachusetts Senate race; he recalled Teddy's denunciations of Romney as a grasping fraud. To anyone in earshot and absent the faintest whiff of self-awareness, Kerry unloaded on Mitt: He's an arrogant, stiff, inauthentic, patrician elitist with no common touch at all. As Kerry boned up on Romney's economic proposals, he was galled by their make-believe-ism. *The hardest part about playing this guy,* he thought, *is always having to go to this place of total bullshit.*

Kerry's contempt for Romney was nothing compared with Obama's, however. The president disliked a fair number of Republicans. But even Eric Cantor and Mitch McConnell didn't cause the bile to gurgle in his throat the way Romney did. (*At least Cantor and McConnell have* some *principles,* Obama thought.) Mitt's lurches to the right, his denial of the shared genetic code between Romneycare and Obamacare, and the travesty of trickle-down gimmickry that was his tax and budget plan had convinced Obama that his opponent was a sham. Benghazi and the 47 percent had persuaded him that Romney lacked any character or moral compass. Obama's scorn was so open and searing that Plouffe suggested he tone it down in front of junior White House staffers; it was unseemly.

Obama took the point. I'm gonna have to be careful in the debates, he said. I just can't stand this guy and it's gonna be too obvious.

But in Obama's three Washington mocks, held in the basement of the DNC, the president was unable to disguise his disgust. Questions about Romney's business background reflexively brought out his sarcastic, aloof, condescending side, notorious in his debate history and deeply feared by his team.

When Bain came up, Obama was supposed to say something such as,

Governor Romney had a distinguished career as a businessman, and I have no quarrel with that; but it's different being a businessman than a president. Instead, Obama sneered. Governor, you and I have both made choices, he said to Kerry-as-Romney at one point. We both went to Harvard Law School. I came out and became a community organizer, helping displaced steelworkers. You chose to make money—and that's . . . *okay*.

Nasty Obama wasn't the only Bad Obama who cropped up in the DNC basement. There was also Pedantic Obama, who was almost as problematic. On topic after topic, the president was a font of facts and figures but bereft of a sharp message. Challenged by Kerry, he habitually succumbed to a tendency his team referred to as "chasing rabbits": litigating strenuously and endlessly, answering in pointillist detail, abandoning his broader objective to take a detour into the tall grass. Asked about health care, he didn't tout the benefits of the Affordable Care Act or hit Romney for wanting to voucherize Medicare. Rather, he disgorged a skull-numbing explanation of the ACA's Independent Payment Advisory Board (IPAB), the entity Sarah Palin once decried as a "death panel."

Obama's twin weaknesses were glaring, but the current political context made them seem less threatening. Benenson's polling of the battleground states showed the president with an even wider lead than Newhouse's did: six to eight points. For Obama, unlike Romney, there was nothing do-or-die about Denver; all he needed from the first debate was a near draw. For his team, that meant keeping both Nasty POTUS and Pedantic POTUS out of camera range.

Before Obama boarded Air Force One for Vegas that Sunday, September 30, he was handed a five-page memo, drafted by Anita Dunn and Klain, that laid out the final strategy for Denver. Its implicit premise was the paramount importance of concealing both Bad Obamas. Its explicit goals were to preserve the president's likability advantage over Romney and highlight his economic agenda for a second term—something many undecided voters doubted he actually possessed. Its tactical thrust was that Obama would refrain from attacks, be positive and visionary, hover above the fray. Its essence was summed up by a pithy Axelrod coinage featured in the memo: "The bigger you are, the harder he falls."

THE SITE OF OBAMA's debate camp was the Westin Lake Las Vegas, which wasn't actually in Vegas at all. Seventeen miles east of the Strip, in Henderson, Lake Las Vegas was a 3,600-acre monument to the collapse of the real estate bubble—a palm-fringed sprawl of unfinished lots, half-built homes, and desiccated golf courses. The hotel grounds featured a replica of the Ponte Vecchio, some canals with lonely gondolas, and not a soul in sight. When the presidential motorcade came to a halt outside the lobby, Jay Carney scoped out the scene and thought, *It looks like we're in Venice after the zombies have taken over.*

For the next three days, Obama toiled with his team in this strange stockade. In the mornings and afternoons, they ran through drills on the six topics that the Commission on Presidential Debates had announced would be in play in Denver: the economy and job creation, the deficit, entitlements, health care, the role of government, and dealing with gridlock in Washington. Each evening, Obama and Kerry conducted a ninety-minute mock debate. In between, the president reviewed video, worked with style coach Michael Sheehan, and studied postmortem memos written by Klain.

Obama made no secret that he wasn't having fun with any of it. "This is stupid," he said. "I hate this," he said. "I'm counting down the days until this is over," he said. He wasn't exactly bitching and moaning; often, there was a smile on his face when the words came out of his mouth. But they reflected the underlying antipathy to debates that he had labored for months to suppress.

Obama's dyspepsia was compounded by his hardening views of how Romney would behave onstage. Over the summer, he'd studied a DVD compilation of his opponent's best moments in the GOP debates and concluded that the way Romney won was by bullying his rivals. (I'm not gonna let him bully *me*, Obama told Klain.) Now the president was simply incredulous at the charges that Kerry-as-Mitt hurled at him. "This guy will say *anything*," Obama marveled.

The president's disdain for the process and for Romney was combined with a discomfort with the punch-pulling strategy that his debate team had devised. Obama grasped intellectually the need to preserve his likability, but he strained against the strictures of that imperative. "I really feel like I need to pop him," Obama said. If I can't, there's no way I can score.

Klain reached for a basketball metaphor that would resonate with the hoops-mad Obama. He cited Paul Westphal, the former NBA All-Star guard who had no defensive game but put a ton of points on the board. Look, Klain said, the goal here is for you to go into the debate, talk about your agenda, talk to the American people about your plans to make things better. You're at your podium making jumper after jumper—that's how you score. And even though Romney is at his podium making buckets, too, you're scoring more. You win the game, like, 150–130.

Yeah, fine, Obama said. "But what am I supposed to do when he starts spewing his bullshit?"

The president's team did not advise total disengagement. But with the need to stifle Nasty Obama uppermost in their minds, they counseled pivots and counterpunches. One memo drafted on the fly in Henderson carried a telling title: "Key Romney Attacks, and How You Move Away." Equally revealing was their approach to the 47 percent video, which, dreading ugliness, they advised Obama not to raise on offense. Instead they prepared a counterpunch to deliver if Romney smacked him over food stamps or dependency:

> Now, there are people who game the system at the bottom and at the top, and we shouldn't tolerate either. But when Governor Romney writes off nearly half the country—47%—as victims who will never take responsibility for their lives, let's understand who he's talking about. Most of these Americans are working. They pay plenty of taxes. Most of the rest are senior citizens who've worked a lifetime, and are living on the Medicare and Social Security they've earned. Then there are students and veterans and soldiers who are serving us today. These are folks we should be fighting for—not dismissing.

The president dutifully rehearsed the 47 percent counterpunch along with his other jabs, delivering them decently in the afternoon sessions, only to stumble in the nighttime mocks. Though he managed to keep Nasty

Obama at bay, Pedantic Obama was ever present. He not only returned to the IPAB but did it twice in a single session. When the team showed Obama the video afterwards, the president chuckled. "Yeah, you're right," he said. "That didn't work."

Yet even as he acknowledged the folly of chasing rabbits, Obama kept diving into any hole in sight, then trying to justify his excursions to his team. You guys don't want me to explain anything, he said plaintively. You say when I'm explaining I'm losing. But sometimes explaining can be effective.

What was going on in the president's mind was difficult for his team to discern. But his invocations of the virtues of explanation made it sound as if Bill Clinton had taken up residence there. For four years, Obama's policies and achievements had been trivialized. His own White House had often failed to sell them effectively. Republicans had lied about them shamelessly. In Charlotte, 42 had earned raves for a wonky, backward-looking exculpation of Obama's tenure—while 44 was panned for a forward-gazing, risk-free address driven by the same theory that underlay his debate strategy now. Obama wanted *his* chance to set the record straight.

The push-and-pull between Obama and his team went on for three days. The debate format—which allowed each candidate a two-minute statement on each topic, followed by nine minutes of free-form discussion—played to the president's worst instincts, feeding his sense that he had plenty of time to make multiple, complex points. I just thought I could explain it, Obama kept saying. I thought there'd be a second question. I thought I'd get back to it in the discussion period. I thought . . . I thought . . . I thought.

But digressiveness was only part of the problem with his mocks. He was low-energy, slow-talking, soporific. He was inconsistent, all over the place, never delivering the same lines twice. There were no anecdotes, personal touches, or human texture—just meandering data dumps.

When Obama's team raised concerns with him, he occasionally expressed mild exasperation: "Aren't you guys ever satisfied?" More frequently, he said, "I hear ya—I'll get it next time."

But he did not. In the first mock, on Sunday night, Obama turned in a desultory performance. On Monday, he was mildly better. On Tuesday, he took a step backwards, relapsing to Sunday's level.

In the staff room after the final mock, Plouffe voiced alarm upon reviewing video of cutaway shots that showed Obama's expressions while Kerry-as-Mitt was talking. Sheehan had advised the president to glance down at his notes when he wasn't speaking, but sporadically and briefly. Obama was doing it for interminable stretches without looking up, and he was scowling and grimacing.

"These cutaways are *terrible*," Plouffe said. We have to show him more video, we've got to talk to him. This is *not good*.

For the past forty-eight hours, the debate team's senior members had mulled the question of what to do. Their strategy of papering over Obama's flaws having proved a failure, they considered the idea of confronting the president in a more fundamental, forceful way—but decided against it. Obama was in a rotten mood. Nobody wanted to make it worse. And nobody wanted to dent his confidence so close to Denver. Axelrod repeatedly reminded his colleagues that Obama was the ultimate game-day player. Not once in his political career had he ever suffered a major performance failure; he always found a way to pull his chestnuts out of the fire. After all, he was . . . Barack Obama.

Obama himself had reassured his team in Henderson. You know, this is just practice, he said. "When it's real, I'll dial it up."

The Obamans crossed their fingers and hoped that it was true.

But as they flew out of Vegas for Denver that Wednesday morning, October 3, the doubts among them were pervasive. Klain was especially broody. Back in July, when he'd laid out for Obama the reasons why history would be against him in the first debate, the president had replied with brio, Let's see if we can break the string. But now Obama was throwing Klain's lecture back at him, talking about how his inflated lead over Romney and the media's desire for a comeback story made it all but impossible for him to win. Klain had served on every Democratic presidential debate prep team for the past twenty years. Never had he seen a candidate less revved up to take the stage.

Sitting on the plane next to Carney, Klain turned and sighed.

"His head is in the wrong place," Klain said. "This isn't gonna be a good night."

———

THE RIGHTNESS OF ROMNEY'S head was evident for all to see. Months earlier, when he began his prep, he had said with some agitation to his team, "Guys, guys, I need to know my stuff—I'm going up against the *president of the United States*." But now similar words were coming out of him all gee-whizzy: "I can't believe I'm about to go debate the president of the United States!" Romney joked with Stevens about his wardrobe for the big night. Maybe he would wear a dress shirt buttoned up all the way but no tie. The press would go crazy if he sported "the Ahmadinejad look," Mitt cracked.

Romney had arrived in Denver two days before Obama, giving himself time to get acclimated. His hotel, the Renaissance, turned out to be a nightmare: forty-five minutes from the University of Denver debate site and overlooking railroad tracks. The trains rumbled loudly and around the clock; guests found hotel-provided earplugs in their bathrooms. The first night, Mitt barely caught a wink. But his mood was so upbeat, he offered no complaint. (The next night, on the eve of the most important political event of his life, his shut-eye was dependent on a box fan placed in his room to drown out the noise.)

Obama was staying not far away, at the Doubletree. Arriving in the afternoon, he had minimal downtime before the debate. His dinner came late; he had to eat in a rush. For reasons surpassing understanding, he was unable to find a phone line to connect him to his daughters in Washington. Romney, meanwhile, was backstage at the debate site, surrounded by his kids and grandkids, playing Jenga.

A few minutes before the 7:00 p.m. start time, Romney huddled with Stevens and Myers for a final pregame pep talk. "You control this debate from four corners," Stevens said. "Don't take the rhythm of the debate from him. It all comes to you. You control it. All these people wanted to be here, at this moment. You're here. You're gonna own this."

Romney smiled and said, "I think we'll have fun."

The paradigm for the entire debate was established in the first five minutes. October 3 was, by coincidence, Barack and Michelle's twentieth wedding anniversary. In his opening statement, Obama met the eyes of his wife in the front row. "I just want to wish, sweetie, you happy anniversary and let you know that a year from now we will not be celebrating it in front of forty million people," he said.

Rob Portman had predicted that Obama would do this very thing. In every one of Romney's ten pre-Denver mocks, Fauxbama opened with a shout-out to Michelle. Gillespie had supplied Romney with a funny follow-up, which he delivered in his opening. "Congratulations to you, Mr. President, on your anniversary; I'm sure this was the most romantic place you could imagine—here with me," he quipped. The audience laughed. Even Obama laughed. Mitt was off and running.

For the next ninety minutes, Romney put on a clinic. He was clear, crisp, confident, energetic, fluent on policy, and in complete command of his bullet points. His indictments of Obama were sharp without being shrill. He was tough but likable, aggressive but not off-putting, convincingly presidential but recognizably human. He came across as a pragmatist and a manager, the very sort of Mr. Fix-It that many around him had wanted him to be in 2008 and again in 2012—like the Mitt who ran for office in Massachusetts in 1994 and 2002.

Tonally and substantively, Romney aimed for the middle of the electorate. He touted his record in the Bay State, especially on education, and talked up bipartisanship. He declared that "regulation is essential" and hit Obama from the left on Dodd-Frank, calling it "the biggest kiss that's been given to New York banks I've ever seen." Some of his claims were false, such as the boast that his health-care plan covered folks with preexisting conditions. Others were disputable, notably an assertion that his budget plan did not entail a $5 trillion tax cut tilted toward the wealthy (as many independent analysts maintained). "I know that you and your running mate keep saying that," Romney said to Obama. "Look, I've got five boys. I'm used to people saying something that's not always true but just keep on repeating it and ultimately hoping I'll believe it. But that is not the case."

Through it all, the president was the man who wasn't there—passive and somnolent, enduring the experience rather than embracing it, not an ounce of verve or fight or passion in him. Stylistically, Obama's performance was Henderson redux, only worse. The split-screen shots captured him staring down at his notes even more than in the mock video that had unnerved Plouffe. Though Nasty Obama made no appearances, Peevish Obama did.

When Jim Lehrer tried to cut him off—"Two minutes is up, sir"—the president protested, "No, I had five seconds before you interrupted me."

In the Obama staff room backstage, the president's team wondered if their man was suffering from aphasia. Midway through the debate, Romney tossed a hanging curve into Obama's wheelhouse, remarking, in an exchange about tax policy, "I maybe need to get a new accountant." Axelrod waited for the president to swing: *The last thing you need, Mitt, is better accountants; yours seem to be doing a bang-up job already.* But Obama let the pitch sail by. A little later, the debate team groaned when he mentioned the IPAB. When he did it a second time, they groaned louder. When, astoundingly, he did it a third time, a hush fell on the room. *A triple IPAB?* thought Klain. *This debate is over.*

In the Romney staff room, the excitement was so great that people found it hard to remain in their chairs. At the end of the ninety minutes, when Lehrer signed off with "Thank you, and good night," a whoop went up. Myers shouted, "That was a game changer!"

Romney exited the stage and headed back to his side's holding room, where he found the hall lined with his people as if it were the locker-room runway at Notre Dame. Cheering, screaming, huzzahing at the top of their lungs, they hailed the conquering hero. Mitt and Ann embraced. "Dad, you crushed him!" Tagg exclaimed.

Romney could hardly contain himself. Bewildered by Obama's limp performance, he was most stupefied by the absence of any mention of the 47 percent. "I was ready for it!" Mitt insisted.

Stevens found Romney minutes later. "You were right," Stuart said. "It was fun, wasn't it?"

"Yeah, it *was* fun," Romney said.

Back at the Renaissance, Gillespie came into Mitt's suite and gave him a hug. Garrett Jackson had read Romney some of the Twitter reaction, but Mitt had no idea how the story was being covered otherwise.

"I feel like it went well," he said to Gillespie. "How's it playing?"

"All you have to do is turn on MSNBC to know," Gillespie answered, grinning. "They're in tears."

The consensus that Romney had cleaned Obama's clock wasn't confined to the left, let alone its institutional voice on cable. A CNN instant poll found that 67 percent of viewers gave Mitt the win; a Democracy Corps focus group showed a spike in his favorable ratings on the basis of the debate. From the right, Bill Kristol blogged that Romney had turned in "the best debate performance by a GOP candidate in more than two decades." From the center, Politico's Roger Simon said it looked as if "someone had slipped [the president] an Ambien."

But the caterwauling from Obama devotees was earsplitting indeed. On Twitter, super-blogger Andrew Sullivan spat out a series of harsh judgments: that Obama had shown himself "too arrogant to take a core campaign responsibility seriously," that the debate had been "a disaster" for the president. On MSNBC, as Gillespie indicated, the reaction was something akin to a collective primal scream.

"I don't know what [Obama] was doing out there!!!" Chris Matthews bayed. "I don't know how he let Romney get away with the crap he threw at him tonight! . . . Where was Obama tonight?! . . . What was he doing tonight?! He went in there disarmed!!! . . . What was *Romney* doing? He was *winning*!!!"

Lawrence O'Donnell was more subdued, but no less pointed. "The president clearly came in with what I would call a presidential strategy in the debate," he said. "Team Obama might want to look at that tonight and say, 'We've got to change that.'"

OBAMA BEELINED IT BACK to the Doubletree after the debate for a small anniversary party with his wife, Jarrett, his friend Marty Nesbitt, and a few others. Momentarily unconnected to the mediasphere, he was unaware of the universal perception that he'd bombed. *Romney did fine, but I did fine, too,* Obama thought. *I got my points across.*

Michelle and Valerie had sat next to each other during the debate, as was their wont in 2008, and both were stunned by the strength of Romney's performance. Leaning over and nudging Michelle, Jarrett whispered, "Boy, he's good." Back at the Doubletree, they were slightly shaken by what had occurred; there was no doubt in FLOTUS's mind that her husband had lost.

Once POTUS had a chance to sample the coverage on his iPad, he began to get the picture—but even then, he resisted the world's verdict. When Plouffe arrived at the hotel after a futile half an hour with the press, trying to spin the unspinnable, he met Obama in the hallway outside his suite.

"I didn't think it was that bad," the president said.

"Yeah, it was that bad," Plouffe replied. "We just have to figure out how to fix it."

Klain was on his way to the hotel, too, but became snarled in traffic. Eventually his cell phone rang, with Obama on the line.

"It didn't feel that bad to me, but it seems like it's pretty bad," said 44. "I feel like I executed the strategy."

"I think we had a failure of strategy and execution both," Klain said.

Klain went on to tell Obama that he would have scored the debate 60/40 for Romney, but it was being covered as an 80/20 wipeout. The disparity, Klain said, was due largely to the meltdown of the Democratic base and the novel impact of social media, especially Twitter, which amplified every meme with a fierce instantaneity. (During the ninety minutes of the Denver debate, there were 10.3 million tweets about it.) In the past, presidential debate performances had been judged by their effect on undecided voters. Here, Obama was being pilloried not for failing to move to the middle but for missing opportunities to decapitate Romney.

Obama's high command convened an emergency meeting at the hotel, which ran well into the early hours of the morning. Every presidential campaign starts out with a game plan, but aware that it is provisional, that unexpected events will inevitably arise and compel the coaches and players to go back to the drawing board. Chicago's execution hadn't always been flawless, but it had never once been forced to deviate from its playbook. Now it was reformulating its strategy on the fly and under pressure.

Obama had two rallies scheduled for Thursday: the first in Denver and the second in Madison, Wisconsin. Given the base-driven dynamics the debate had laid bare, his people decided that the first crucial step was for the president to come out strong and fiery—to counteract the perplexity, disappointment, and pissed-offedness of his supporters.

That morning, just before 10:00 a.m., Plouffe rode with Obama in the presidential limo to the event in Sloan's Lake Park. Listen, the body language here is as important as what you say, Plouffe explained. You need to really bring it.

Obama rolled his eyes and said, "I got it, I got it."

I know you're annoyed by this, but it's really important for the news, Plouffe continued. People have to see you picking yourself up, because we're asking them to pick themselves up, too.

The president reminded Plouffe that they had been in similar straits before: in 2008, when Obama's shocking loss in the New Hampshire primary to Hillary threatened to eclipse his victory in Iowa and sink the whole enterprise. The day after, Obama did an event in Boston where he came out swinging, buoying his downcast backers. For the president, that moment had always been a touchstone. *I have to keep my head up,* Obama thought. *I know what I have to do here.*

In Denver, the president met a crowd twelve thousand strong; in Madison that afternoon, the throng was nearly three times as large. In both places, Obama offered no excuses and ripped into Romney, advancing Chicago's agreed-upon line that Mitt had essentially lied his way to victory the previous night. "Governor Romney may dance around his positions," Obama said in Wisconsin. "He may do a tap dance and a two-step. But if you want to be president, then you owe the American people the truth."

For the president's adherents, the rallies and the headlines that they generated might have been heartening. But for Obama, they were something else. On the rope lines in Denver and Madison, his fans called out, We've got your back! Obama knew they were well-intentioned. But their words also forced a painful reckoning with his loss—with the fact that he had let millions of his people down.

Heading back to Washington, he told Jarrett, "I have to fix it."

The question for the Obamans was not just how to repair the damage from Denver but how much there was to repair. After less than twenty-four hours, the impact on voters was impossible to gauge; Benenson's next round of numbers would begin to tell the tale. On a conference call with Chicago's crew of pollsters, Axelrod was already looking toward the second debate, on October 16 at Hofstra University, in New York. There, Obama would have his best chance to clean up the mess he'd created in the Mile High City.

Paul Harstad, who'd been polling for Obama since his 2004 Senate race, conveyed a grim sense of urgency about the task ahead.

The next debate *better* turn things around, Harstad said. Another performance like this one could be fatal to the campaign.

ROMNEY FLEW OUT OF DENVER, landing late that afternoon in Virginia's Shenandoah Valley—where Gillespie noticed the change instantly. The state troopers on the tarmac were standing a little more straight-backed than before. The road to Mitt's rally with Paul Ryan in Fishersville was bumper-to-bumper; the size of the crowd, upwards of ten thousand, was causing tie-ups. Gillespie had experienced this moment before with other Republican nominees, when all at once people started looking at them and seeing a president. Normally, the party convention was what did it; for Romney, it was Denver. On the way to the event, Gillespie said, "Governor, I think something really did happen last night."

Before the rally, Romney and Ryan sat for a satellite interview with Sean Hannity. Toward the end, the host asked Mitt the question inexplicably absent in Denver. "The left seems furious at this tape where you talked about the 47 percent," Hannity said. "Why didn't President Obama bring that up? What would you have said if he did bring it up?"

"Well, clearly, in a campaign with hundreds if not thousands of speeches and question-and-answer sessions, now and then you are going to say something that doesn't come out right," Romney replied. "In this case, I said something that's just completely wrong."

Romney was caught off-guard by Hannity's question. He didn't expect Sean, of all people, to ask about the 47 percent. Mitt was still saving up his indignant answer for the next debate. All he meant to say was that the 47 remark had *come out of his mouth* completely wrong; he wasn't planning on apologizing or making news. But across the media spectrum, his comments were read as the next step in a strategy of center-tacking reinvention that had begun in Denver. Romney couldn't quite believe it. Without trying, he had somehow found the antivenom, at least as far as the press was concerned.

The next twelve days would be the most magical of the Romney campaign. From the moment he walked off the stage in Denver, the money poured in. Every donor Zwick talked to was infused with the sudden certainty that Mitt was going to win. In Washington, Karl Rove's phone was ringing off the hook; the billionaire banker Harold Simmons, who had already contributed more than $10 million to Crossroads, called to say, If you need more, I'll donate more. Even journalists were giving Romney the benefit of the doubt. His press secretary, Andrea Saul, thought, *Now I know what it's like to work for a Democrat!*

Newhouse cranked up his numbers machine on Thursday night. What he saw by Friday morning was a rapid tightening of the race; Romney had gone from three points down in the battleground states to one point up. More powerful to Newhouse's eye was the shift in what pollsters call information flow—the universe of news about the candidates and whether the mentions are positive or negative. By this metric, Romney went from a minus 17 to a plus 5. *You just don't ever see numbers move like that,* Newhouse thought.

Romney arrived in Florida that day, October 5. On the campaign bus, he and Stevens began discussing how to build on the new interest after Denver, the way more people were seeing Mitt for who he actually was rather than Chicago's fat-cat caricature. Stevens suggested that Romney finally open up, start telling personal stories on the stump, maybe weave the Oparowskis, from the convention, into his standard speech. Romney had long been reticent about going there, about exploiting his good deeds for political gain. But Ann and Tagg had been urging him to show his true self. His war councillors had recommended the same.

That night in St. Petersburg, at a downtown water park, Romney told the crowd about a graduate school classmate who had become a quadriplegic and devoted himself to spinal injury research. He told the tale of his relationship with fourteen-year-old David Oparowski, how he'd helped the boy write out his will. "I've seen the character of a young man like David," Romney said. "He had his eyes wide open. There's a saying: 'Clear eyes, full heart, can't lose.' David couldn't lose. I loved that young man." The *Washington Post* wrote up the story of Mitt-as-tearjerker for the next day's paper, in glowing terms.

For Romney, the challenge now was to sustain the incredible roll he was on. Mitt understood the importance of the next debate as clearly as the Obamans did. The format for Hofstra would be a town hall meeting, with questions posed by voters. In Orlando that Saturday, he met with his debate team to start prepping. Brimming with confidence though he was, Romney knew that the second debate would be radically different from Denver—and not just in terms of structure. Obama's going to be tougher to beat next time, he told Portman. We really have to practice.

Obama was taking the day off. He needed time to think. Three days after Denver, advice was pouring in from every Democratic quarter about what he should do. Almost no one on the planet could understand what he was going through or up against. The next day, however, the president was heading out to Beverly Hills, where he would be hanging with someone who did. For perhaps the first time in his life, Barack Obama was genuinely curious to hear what Bill Clinton had to say.

22

INTERVENTION

THE $35 MILLION ESTATE of Jeffrey Katzenberg sat on Loma Vista Drive at the top of Beverly Hills, occupying six acres, with a majestic view of the City of Angels sprawled out below. Obama and Clinton arrived there that Sunday afternoon, October 7, for lunch with Katzenberg and a handful of the rich and famous. Though the White House publicly described the event only as a "thank you" for a "small group of donors," it was, in fact, a Priorities USA function—the sort of shindig that Obama had sworn never to attend.

For Katzenberg, having two presidents in his concert-hall-size living room was a fitting reward; no Democratic buck-raker had raised more dough in 2012. Katzenberg pitched the lunch to invitees as a once-in-a-lifetime experience—what he called "unobtainium." He recommended that they donate $1 million to Priorities, and bagged three checks in that amount just the Friday before. He pledged to keep his guests' presence secret. (To ferry them to a public campaign fund-raiser afterwards, there would be a private shuttle with tinted windows.) In the end, nine tycoons from the worlds of Hollywood and high tech turned up: Reid Hoffman, Irwin and Joan Jacobs, Vinod Khosla, Seth MacFarlane, Sean Parker, Mark Pincus, Eric Schmidt, and Steven Spielberg.

Obama wasted no time in addressing the debacle in Denver—cutting off Katzenberg before he had a chance to offer opening remarks. "I had too many voices in my head," Obama began. The advice I got from my team was good, but in the moment I couldn't sort it all out. I know what I need to do now. It won't happen again.

Clinton, too, offered reassurance to the kingpins arrayed on Katzenberg's couches. I don't think the president did so bad, and I'm sure he'll be better the next time out, Clinton said. Each one of these debates is its own deal. And, listen, no one's ever won the second debate by winning the first debate.

Until Denver, Clinton had watched in wonder as Obama caught break after break. Although the economy wasn't roaring back to life, neither the European banking crisis nor the unrest in the Mideast had caused it to nosedive. Meanwhile, Romney's ineptness staggered Clinton. After the release of the 47 percent video, he remarked to a friend that, while Mitt was a decent man, he was in the wrong line of work. ("He really shouldn't be speaking to people in public.") As for Obama, Clinton trotted out for his pals the same line again and again: "He's luckier than a dog with two dicks."

Though the first debate brought the incumbent's streak of good fortune to a crashing halt, Clinton was insistent that the Obamans not overreact. On the phone to Axelrod, 42 counseled restraint at Hofstra, warning that if 44 was too hot or negative in a town hall debate it would backfire. Now, at the end of the Priorities event, the presidents went off to huddle on one of Casa Katzenberg's two immense porches, where Clinton repeated the advice. Don't try to make up the ground you lost, he said. Just be yourself.

Obama faced a more immediate challenge, which was to arrest the metastasizing panic among his supporters. In 2008, Plouffe had airily dismissed Democrats who lost their minds in the midst of Palinmania as "bedwetters." But now there was a similar drizzle as the public polls sharply narrowed—and worse. On October 8, Pew Research released a survey that put Romney ahead 49 to 45 percent among likely voters. "Did Barack Obama just throw the entire election away?" blared the title of another Andrew Sullivan blog post.

Chicago's internal polling strongly suggested that he had not. After tightening for seventy-two hours post-Denver, the numbers stabilized, with

Obama still holding a 50–47 lead over Romney. The only fallout, by Benenson's reckoning, was that Republican-leaning independent voters who fled Romney's column in the wake of the 47 percent had returned there. What Denver had done was wash away the Democratic gains of September. The race was back to where it had been following the conventions.

Benenson's data made it easier for Obama to do what he had to do: buck up his supporters, his staff, and himself. As the full desultoriness of his Denver performance sank in, the president was consumed by a sense of responsibility for the fallout—and shadowed by fears, for the first time in months, that his reelection was at risk. Outwardly, he took pains to project the opposite. When his staffers asked how he was doing, he replied, extra-emphatically, "I'm GREAT." To Plouffe, who had volunteered to soothe Sullivan, Obama joked, Someone's gotta talk him off the ledge!

Returning from the West Coast to the White House, the president conducted his first post-Denver national television interview, with ABC News on October 10. Faced with an onslaught of debate-related questions from Diane Sawyer—"What *happened*?" "*Why* did it happen?" "Was it the altitude?" "What did Mrs. Obama say?"—he maintained a steadfast composure. In a radio interview with Tom Joyner, he was coolly assertive: "As some of these e-mails that go around with my picture on them say—and I can't quote the entire thing, but—*I got this!*"

That afternoon, Obama met with his debate team in the Roosevelt Room. He opened by saying he had read a memo drafted by Klain a few days earlier about what went wrong in Denver and how to fix it before Hofstra, now six days away. He agreed with most of it but wanted everyone to know that they hadn't failed him; he had failed them. "This is on me," Obama said.

"I'm a naturally polite person," he went on. Part of my problem is "erring on the side of being muted. We have to get me to a place where internally I'm not biting my tongue . . . It's important for me to be fighting."

There's a lot at stake in this election, Obama continued, and I think we're still in good shape. But we need to win these next two debates—and that's what I intend to do. I only wish we didn't have to wait another week. I really want to get back out there.

The debate team was buoyed by Obama's energy and determination.

And they received another boost twenty-four hours later from his second in command, when Biden took on Ryan in the vice-presidential debate in Danville, Kentucky.

The undercard had been elevated from sideshow to marquee event the moment that Romney selected Ryan. But Obama's bellyflop in Denver upped the stakes even more, with Chicago desperately needing a win—and a certain type of win—to calm the party's base. Klain, Axelrod, and others on Obama's debate team parachuted from Denver into Biden's prep sessions in Delaware to urge the VP to be ferocious. "This is the storyline: goal-line defense, and you force a fumble," Michael Sheehan told him.

Biden needed little encouragement. Having been in the spotlight four years earlier—when his televised tangle with Palin drew a larger TV audience than any of Obama's toe-to-toes with McCain—the vice president had been cramming to tackle Ryan on policy. His confidence level was high. Now the Obamans were telling him that, for once, he didn't need to ratchet down his Bidenness—he could just be himself. *Hallelujah,* Biden exulted. *I never thought I'd see this day.*

Ryan, meanwhile, took the stage in Danville feeling nervous—burdened by the sky-high expectations of the right, which was certain that he would massacre the boobish Biden, and by his own persistent worries about letting Romney down. Mitt's been slaving away at this for five years, Ryan told his aides. I don't want to make some gaffe and screw it up for him.

Ryan's measured performance embarrassed neither himself nor the man who picked him. But Danville was Uncle Joe's show. Before the opening bell, Biden was reminded by his advisers to smile. Onstage, he mugged, chortled, cackled, sniggered, guffawed, and threw his hands skyward. Seven minutes in, he accused Ryan of peddling "a bunch of malarkey." A few seconds later, the Obamans, having learned a lesson in social-media insta-spin from Denver, were all over Twitter with #malarkey.

The snap polls made the debate a draw. Boston and much of the conservative media accused Biden of being rude and borderline unhinged. ("It was like the Joker showed up," Romney remarked to Stevens.) Democrats were elated, as was Obama, who caught the debate on TV on Air Force One as he flew back to Washington after a day of campaigning in Florida.

"You did a great job," he told Biden by phone. "And you picked me up."

In thirty-six hours, Obama would set off for another three-day debate camp, in Williamsburg, Virginia. But watching his understudy had already provided him with one helpful insight.

"These are not debates," Obama observed to Plouffe. "These are gladiatorial enterprises."

THE FIRST LADY WORRIED about her Maximus and his return to the Coliseum. In truth, she had fretted over the debates even before Denver. In July, around the time her husband's prep started, she met with Plouffe and expressed firm opinions. That Barack had to speak from the gut, in language that regular folks could understand. Had to avoid treating the debates like policy seminars. Had to keep his head out of the clouds. (Michelle's advisers paraphrased her advice as "It's not about David Brooks; it's about my mother.") FLOTUS loved POTUS like nobody's business, but she knew his faults well.

In the wake of Denver, she was unfailingly encouraging with her husband: Don't worry, you're going to win the next one, just remember who you're talking to, Michelle told him. Before a small group of female bundlers, she pronounced that Barack had lost only because "Romney is a really good liar."

Privately, however, Michelle was unhappy about how her spouse's prep had been handled. The late arrival in Denver. The rushed meal at the crappy hotel. Not being able to reach Sasha and Malia by phone. He seemed overscheduled, overcoached, and underrested. At first, she conveyed her displeasure via Jarrett, who flooded the inboxes of the debate team with pointed e-mails, employing the royal "we." But the day before debate camp in Williamsburg, Michelle delivered marching orders directly to Plouffe: If the president wants our chef there, he should be there; if he wants Marty Nesbitt there, he should be there. Barack's food, downtime, exercise, sleep, lodging— all of it affects his frame of mind. All of it has to be right.

Plouffe saluted sharply and thought, *I guess the first lady understands the stakes here.*

That same Friday, October 12, Obama's debate team gathered again in the Roosevelt Room for a final pre-camp session. The president was presented with a piece of overarching advice and a memo, both of which would have been inconceivable before Denver. The advice was: Be more like Biden, whose combativeness, scripted moments, and bluff calls on Ryan ("Not true!") had all proved effective tactics. The memo was an alliterative flash card to remind Obama of what it called "the Six A's":

Advocate (don't explain)
Audience
Animated
Attacks
Answers with principles and values
Allow yourself to take advantage of openings

Klain had no shame about such contrivances—whatever worked. His relationship with the president was not straightforward or particularly close. In 2010, Klain had wanted to graduate from Biden's chief of staff to become Obama's when Rahm Emanuel departed, but he was rebuffed directly by 44, who told Klain that he was insufficiently no-drama to step in after Emanuel's polarizing reign. Klain, not for the first time, ditched government for private-sector enrichment. But he found the intellectual challenges and sheer buzz of politics impossible to resist. Right after the Denver disaster, he offered to resign from the debate team, but Obama refused to let him. Klain's ego, pride, and future ambitions were all wrapped up in fixing what had gone wrong in the Mile High City.

He turned Obama's prep regime upside down: new strategy, new tactics, new structure. In Williamsburg, there would be an intense concentration on performance, including speeding up Obama's ponderous delivery. There would be less policy Q&A and more rehearsal of set pieces and lines that popped. Less emphasis on programmatic peas and spinach, more on anecdote and empathy. Contrary to Clinton's advice, there would be plenty of punching to go along with the counterpunching. Fixating on likability was out; following instinct was in.

Camp commenced on Saturday at the Kingsmill Resort, on the James River. Lush and green, the site had none of the funky juju of Lake Las Vegas, though there was a touch of weirdness: the hotel was hosting a "Ferraris on the James" event, so the lawn out front was a shimmering sea of souped-up sports cars.

Two levels down from the lobby of the Resort Center, on the precisely built replica of the Hofstra town hall set, the president spent most of Saturday sharpening his answers with Klain and Axelrod. That night, his mock went better than any in Henderson or at the DNC. The debate team wasn't ready to declare victory yet, but they were relieved. Obama's friend Nesbitt was exultant. "That's some good shit!" he told the president, patting him on the back. "That's my man! He's back!"

In the Sunday daytime sessions, Obama showed still more improvement, honing a solid attack on the 47 percent and another on his rival's economic agenda. ("Governor Romney doesn't have a five-point plan; he has a one-point plan, and that's to make sure folks at the top play by a different set of rules.") As the team took time off for dinner before Obama and Kerry went at it again, Klain thought, *Okay, we're getting to a better place.* Plouffe thought, *He's locked in.*

A little before 9:00 p.m., they returned to the Resort Center. Obama and Kerry grabbed their handheld microphones and took their places—and the president proceeded to deliver the Mock from Hell.

Even before Nasty Obama snarled at Kerry-as-Mitt and Anita Dunn as CNN's Candy Crowley at the 39:35 mark, Klain was mortified. The president's emotional flatness from Henderson and Denver was back. He was making no connection with the voter stand-ins asking questions. He was wandering aimlessly, digressing compulsively, not merely chasing rabbits but stalking them to the ends of the earth. His cadences were hesitant and maple-syrupy slow: phrase, pause, phrase, pause, phrase. His answers were verbose and utterly devoid of message.

In Klain's career as a debate maestro, he had been involved in successes (Kerry over Bush three times in a row) and failures (Gore's symphony of sighs in 2000). But he had never seen anything like this. After all the happy talk from Obama and his consistent, if small, steps forward, the president was regressing—with forty-eight hours and only one full day of prep between them and Hofstra.

Obama and Nesbitt went back to the Pettus House, a colonnaded redbrick mansion on the riverbank, where they were bunking. Nesbitt knew the mock had not gone well; Anita Dunn had asked him to talk it over with Obama. He and the president stayed up late playing cards, watching football, hashing out what hadn't worked, how the president was still struggling to find the zone. "You can't get mad" at Romney's distortions, Nesbitt said. "You come off better when you just say, 'Now, that's fucking *ridiculous.*' When you laugh, that shit works, man."

In Obama's hold room at the Resort Center, his staff was moving past puzzlement and panic toward practical considerations. "What are we going to do?" asked Plouffe. The lesson that he had taken from Denver was that you could no longer count on fourth-quarter Obama; what you saw in practice was what you got on the debate stage. If he doesn't have a good mock tomorrow, there's no reason to believe that it'll get fixed when he gets to New York, Plouffe said.

Two schools of thought quickly emerged within the team. The first, pushed by Bob Barnett—who in addition to his super-lawyer status was a longtime debate prepper and was there serving on Kerry's staff—was that Obama needed to be shown video in the morning. "This is what we did with Clinton," Barnett sagely noted. The other, advanced by Favreau, was that Obama should be given transcripts. He's a writer, Favreau argued. Words on the page will make a deeper impression.

The full transcript was in hand within forty-five minutes—and became a source of gallows humor. As the clock ticked well past midnight, Favreau stagily read aloud some of Obama's most dreadful answers. Soon his colleagues joined in, with Axelrod, Benenson, and Plouffe offering recitations and laughing deliriously over the absurdity and horror of the circumstances.

Klain regarded the video-versus-transcripts dickering as beside the point. Every day in Henderson and Williamsburg, the team had put Obama in front of a video monitor. Every day they explained what he needed to do to improve. Every day he said, "I got it." But apart from momentary flashes of adequacy, nothing had changed; the idea that further illustration of his badness would fix things was folly.

Barnett and others believed that Obama's playbook had to be stripped down more dramatically, to a series of simple and crisp bullet points on the most likely topics to come up in the debate. Klain agreed and wanted to go a step further. In 1996, Democratic strategist Mark Penn had devised something called "debate-on-a-page" for Gore in his VP face-off with Jack Kemp. Klain suggested they do the same for Obama: a sheet of paper with a handful of key principles, attacks, and counterattacks.

Axelrod and Plouffe thought something more radical was in order. For the past six years, they had watched Obama struggle with his disdain for the theatricality of politics—not just debates, but even the soaring speeches for which he was renowned. Obama's distrust of emotional string-pulling and resistance to the practical necessities of the sound-bite culture: these were elements of his personality that they accepted, respected, and admired. But they had long harbored foreboding that those proclivities might also be a train wreck in the making. Time and again, Obama had averted the oncoming locomotive. Had embraced showmanship when it was necessary. Had picked his people up and carried them on his back to the promised land. But now, with a crucial debate less than two days away—one that could either put the election in the bag or turn it into a toss-up—Obama was faltering in a way his closest advisers had never witnessed. They needed to figure out what had gone haywire from the inside out. They needed, as someone in the staff room put it, to stage an "intervention."

The next morning, October 15, Klain stumbled from his room to the Resort Center, eyes puffy and nerves jangled. He'd been up all night hammering together and e-mailing around his debate-on-a-page draft. In Obama's hold room, the team gathered and laid out their plan for the day. They would screen video for the boss. They would show him transcripts. They would present him with his cheat sheets. They would devote the day to topic-by-topic drills until he had his answers memorized.

Normally, the whole group would now meet with the president to critique the previous night's mock. Instead, everyone except Axelrod, Klain, and Plouffe cleared the room just before 10:00 a.m. Obama was on his way. The intervention was at hand.

WHERE'S EVERYBODY ELSE?" Obama asked as he ambled in across the speckled green carpet, with Jack Lew at his side. "Where's the rest of the team?"

We met this morning and decided we should have this smaller meeting first, one of the interventionists said.

Obama, in khakis and rolled-up shirtsleeves, looked nonplussed. Between his conversation with Nesbitt the night before and a morning national security briefing with Lew, he was aware that his people were unhappy with the mock—but not fully clued in to the depth of their concern.

The president settled into a cushy black sofa at one end of the room. On settees to his left were Axelrod, Plouffe, and Lew; to his right, in a blue blazer, was Klain, now caffeinated and coherent.

"We're here, Mr. President," Klain began, "because we need to have a serious conversation about why this isn't working and the fundamental transformation we need to achieve today to avoid a very bad result tomorrow night." We're not going to get there by continuing to grind away and marginally improve, Klain went on. This is not about changing the words in your debate book, because the difference between the answers that work and the answers that don't work is just 15 or 20 percent. This is about style, engagement, speed, presentation, attitude. Candidly, we need to figure out why you're not rising to and meeting the challenge—why you're not really *doing* this, why you're doing . . . something else.

Obama didn't flinch. "Guys, I'm struggling," he said somberly. "Last night wasn't good, and I know that. Here's why I think I'm having trouble. I'm having a hard time squaring up what I know I need to do, what you guys are telling me I need to do, with where my mind takes me, which is: I'm a lawyer, and I want to argue things out. I want to peel back layers."

The ensuing presidential soliloquy went on for ten minutes—an eternity in Obama time. His tone was even and unemotional, but searching, introspective, diagnostic, vulnerable. Psychologically, emotionally, and intellectually, he was placing his cards face up on the table.

"When I get a question," he said, "I go right to the logical." You ask me a question about health care. There's a problem and there's a response. Here's what my opponent might say about it, so I'm going to counteract that. Okay, we're gonna talk about immigration. Here's what I'd like to say—but I can't say that. *Think about what that means.* I know what I want to say, I know where my mind takes me, but I have to tell myself, *No, no, don't do that—do this other thing.* It's against my instincts just to perform. It's easy for me to slip back into what I know, which is basically to dissect arguments. I think when I talk. It can be halting. I start slow. It's hard for me to just go into my answer. I'm having to teach my brain to function differently. I'm left-handed; this is like you're asking me to start writing right-handed.

Throughout the campaign, Obama had been criticized for the thin gruel of his second-term agenda. Now he acknowledged that it bothered him, too, and posed a challenge for the debates.

You keep telling me I can't spend too much time defending my record, and that I should talk about my plans, he said. But my plans aren't anything like the plans I ran on in 2008. I had a universal health care plan then. Now I've got . . . what? A manufacturing plan? What am I gonna do on education? What am I gonna do on energy? There's not much there.

"I can't tell you that, Okay, I woke up today, I knew I needed to do better, and I'll do better," Obama said. "I am wired in a different way than this event requires."

Obama paused.

"I just don't know if I can do this," he said.

Obama's advisers sat silently at first, absorbing the extraordinary moment playing out in front of them. In October of an election year, on the eve of a pivotal debate, the president wasn't talking about tactics or strategy, about this line or that zinger. He was talking about personal contradictions and ambivalences, about his discomfort with the campaign he was running, about his unease with the requirements of politics writ large, about matters that were fundamental, even existential. *We are in uncharted territory here,* thought Klain.

More striking was Obama's candor and self-awareness. The most self-contained president in modern history (and, possibly, the most self-possessed human on the planet) was laying himself bare, deconstructing himself before their eyes—and admitting he was at a loss.

All through his career, Obama had played by his own rules. He had won the presidency as an outsider, without the succor of the Democratic establishment. He owed it little, offered less. He had ignored the traditional social niceties of the office, from the White House Christmas party photo lines to the swanky Georgetown soirees. He had largely resisted the media freak show, swatting away its asininities. He had refused to stomp his feet or shed crocodile tears over the BP spill, because neither would plug the pipe spewing oil from the ocean floor. He had eschewed sloganeering to sell his health care plan, although it meant the world to him.

Now he was faced with an event that demanded an astronomical degree of fakery, histrionics, and stagecraft—and while he was ready to capitulate, *trying* to capitulate, he found himself incapable of performing not just to his own exalted standards but to the bare minimum of competence. Acres of evidence and the illusions of his fans to the contrary, Barack Obama, it turned out, was all too human.

Axelrod was more intimate with Obama than anyone in the room. The president's humanity and frailties were no secret to Axe—nor was 44's capacity for self-doubt. Since Denver, Obama had been subjected to a hailstorm of criticism, a flood of panic, and a blizzard of psychoanalysis. Like every president, he claimed he was impervious to it. But Axelrod knew it was a lie. *All this shit is in his head,* the strategist thought.

Look, said Axelrod softly, we know that you find these debates frustrating, that they're more performance than substance. It's why you are a good president. It's why all of us feel so strongly about your winning. But you have to find a way to get over the hump and stop fighting this game—to play this game, wrap your arms around this game.

For the next hour, the three Obamans tried to carry the president across the psychic chasm. Plouffe reminded him of the stakes. "We can't have a repeat of Denver tomorrow night," he warned. "Right now, we're not losing any of our vote, but we're on probation. If we have another performance that causes people to scratch their heads, we're gonna start losing votes. We gotta stop this now."

Over Obama's despair about his lack of an agenda, Plouffe and Axelrod took him on. "You *do* have an agenda, goddammit!" Plouffe said. "This isn't a bunch of BS you're selling. This is an agenda the American people support and believe in. But they're not gonna believe in it if you don't treat it that way, by selling it with great fervor. If you sell your agenda and Romney sells his agenda with equal enthusiasm, we will win.

"Think about this," Plouffe went on. "You have two debates left. So take out Romney, take out moderator questions: you've got basically seventy-five to eighty minutes left of doing this in your entire life. That's less than the length of a movie! You can do this! I know it's uncomfortable. I know it's unnatural. But that's all. That's the finish line, you know?"

Klain abandoned Paul Westphal in favor of a new sports analogy. The Tennessee Titans lost the Super Bowl a couple of years ago because their guy got tackled on the one-yard line, he said—the one-yard line! That's where we are. The hardest thing for any candidate in a debate is to know the substance. You have that down cold. All we need is a little more effort on performance. You need to go in there and talk as fast as you can. You need to add a little schmaltz, talk about stuff the way that people want to hear it. This isn't about starting over, starting from scratch. We've got most of it right. The part we have left to get right is small. But as the Titans proved, small can mean the difference between winning and losing.

Obama's aides couldn't tell if their words were sinking in. "I understand where we are," the president said finally. I'm either going to center myself and get this or I'm not. The debate's tomorrow. There's not much we can do. I just gotta fight my way through it.

As the meeting wound to a close, the Obamans felt relief mixed with trepidation. Oddly, for Klain, the president's lack of confidence about his ability to turn himself around was comforting. After all the blithe I-got-its of Henderson, Obama for the first time was acknowledging that a genuine and serious modification of his mind-set was necessary.

Plouffe felt less reassured. "It's good news/bad news," he told Favreau afterwards. "The good news is, he recognizes the issue. The bad news is, I don't know if we can fix it in time."

The full team reconvened in Obama's hold room. Klain ran through his memo on the previous night and explained to the president the *new* new format for his prep: for the rest of the day until his final mock, they were going to drill him incessantly on the ten or so topics they expected to come up in the debate, compelling him to repeat his bullet points over and over again. Klain also presented Obama with his debate-on-a-page:

MUST REMEMBER
1. (Your) Speed Kills (Romney)
2. Upbeat and Positive in Tone
3. Passion for People and Plans

4. OTR [Off the Record] Mindset—Have Fun
5. Strong Sentences to Start and End
6. Engage the Audience
7. Don't Chase Rabbits

BEST HITS
1. 47%
2. Romney + China Outsourcing
3. Heaven & Earth
4. 9-11 Girl
5. Sketchy Deal
6. Mass Taxes—Cradle to Grave
7. Pre-existing and ER
8. Women's health
9. Borrow from Your Parents

REBUTTAL CHEAT SHEET
1. Jobs—The 1 point plan
2. Deficits—$7 trillion and The Sketchy Deal
3. Energy—Coal plant is a killer
4. Health—Pre-existing fact check and the ER
5. Medicare—He wants to save Medicare . . . by ending it!
6. Bus Taxes—60 Mins in rebuttal (i.e., pivot to personal taxes)
7. Pers Taxes—Tax cuts for outsourcing (i.e., pivot to job creation)
8. Gridlock—Romney brings the lobbyist back
9. Benghazi—Taking offense
10. Education—Borrow from your parents and/or Size Doesn't
    Matter

That the intervention had had some effect on Obama was immediately apparent, though how much was unclear. He brought a new energy and focus to his afternoon drills. When he delivered an imperfect answer, he stopped himself short: "Let's do that again." In Henderson, Obama had been so intent on escaping camp that he took off one day for a visit to the Hoover Dam. Now he refused even brief breaks for a walk by the river. As the afternoon went on, the debate team concocted cutesy catchphrases to cue him at the slightest hint of backsliding.

"Fast and hammy! Fast and hammy!" Klain would say when his delivery was too lugubrious.

"Punch him in the face!" Karen Dunn chipped in when he missed a chance to cream Kerry-as-Mitt.

For Klain, the turning point came that afternoon, during a session in which Obama was fielding questions from junior members of the team who were standing in as voters. Tony Carrk, a researcher, introduced himself as Vito, a barbershop proprietor from Long Island, and asked which tax plan—Obama's or Romney's—would be better for small-business owners like him. Without missing a beat, the president savaged Mitt's plan with verve, precision, and bite, closing with some good-natured joshing about Vito's shop.

The perfect town hall answer, Klain thought.

That night, for the final mock, Kerry was instructed to bring his "A" game. With the team on pins and needles, Obama earned a solid B-plus. The contrast with the previous night was so dramatic, it called to Axelrod's mind the triumphant scenes in *Hoosiers.* When it was over, the team rose in unison and gave Obama a standing ovation.

"All right, all right, all right," the president said, waving them off, smiling abashedly.

The next morning, before setting off for Hofstra, the team gathered once again in Obama's hold room to review the mock. No one was remotely certain they were out of the woods. The past three days had carried them too close to the abyss for firm convictions of any kind. But the president's mood could not have been more buoyant. Running through the team's critique, he reveled in their praise of a particularly strong answer.

"Oh, you guys liked that?" Obama said, grinning broadly. "That was fast and hammy, right?"

As THE PRESIDENT HAD been suffering his dark night of the soul, Romney was basking in the bright sunshine that had been bathing him since Denver. In Virginia on the day that the Pew poll put him ahead in the race, he stopped his motorcade to greet a gaggle of elementary school kids lining the road to wave as he rolled by. Everywhere he went, his crowds were big and boosterish, telling him he was going to win the election—especially after he laid another beat-down on Obama in the next debate.

Romney's Kingsmill was a Marriott in Burlington, just north of Boston, where he prepped with his team on the Sunday and Monday before Hofstra. Mitt was armed with his own debate-on-a-page, though his was even more miniature than Obama's, containing just four bullet points. The second, third, and fourth were concrete and unambiguous: "Meet the attacks from the president head-on"; "Don't just answer the question; speak to the questioner"; "Give specific contrast points on issues." The first was more ineffable but also most essential: "The same Mitt Romney shows up" as the one who did in Denver.

Acclimating Romney to the town hall format was a central component of his prep. More than one presidential candidate had been tripped up by being untethered from a lectern (the grandpa-in-search-of-a-bathroom wanderings of McCain) or the vagaries of interacting with voter-questioners (Bush 41 staring at his watch). And Mitt's awkwardness around actual human beings on the campaign trail had been amply demonstrated. Portman predicted that Obama would try to press his likability advantage by turning the debate into a touchy-feely-fest. In one of the mocks, Portman illustrated the point by answering a question from Myers while moving closer and closer and closer to her—and then plopping into her lap as he finished.

The Romneyites were worried about another element of Hofstra: Candy Crowley. In negotiations between Boston, Chicago, and the debate commission, an agreement had been reached that the town hall moderator was to serve only as a neutral facilitator. But in a number of interviews, Crowley suggested that she intended to play a more active role. "Once the table is kind of set by the town hall questioner, there is then time for me to say, 'Hey, wait a second, what about X, Y, Z?'" she said.

Romney was a stickler for rules of every kind, and had tangled (to no good effect) with debate moderators repeatedly during the Republican nomination fight. With Chicago in concurrence, Boston complained about Crowley's comments to the debate commission to try to head off conflict later. But that did nothing to stanch Romney's trepidation. At one point in

Burlington, with Peter Flaherty playing the moderator in a purposefully aggressive fashion, Romney snapped, "Oh, be quiet, Candy!"

Team Romney assumed that Obama, having left so many bullets in the chamber in Denver, would come out brandishing Uzis in both hands at Hofstra. On the 47 percent, Mitt had his answer down cold; on Bain, he immersed himself in mind-numbingly detailed briefing materials on the firm's investments. Bob White proposed another tactic: pointing out that Obama's own financial portfolio included a fund with a distant connection to the Cayman Islands. That Sunday in Burlington, White showed up bearing research that illustrated the attenuated linkage. Though some of the Romneyites were dubious, Mitt was intrigued.

No topic in Romney's prep for Hofstra was more vexed than Benghazi. In the month since the tragedy, the right had seized on the story in all of its dimensions: the security lapses beforehand; the limited military response the day of the attack; the administration's explanation in the aftermath, especially the suggestion by UN Ambassador Susan Rice that the uprising had been a spontaneous demonstration as opposed to a premeditated terrorist attack. In Obama's Rose Garden remarks on September 12 and two other speeches, the president had used the phrase "acts of terror" in the context of Benghazi. But on three other occasions when he was asked directly whether the attack was the work of terrorists, he had declined to say yes—fueling charges from the right that the administration was seeking to limit the president's political exposure. Fox News was wall-to-wall Benghazi. John McCain was on the warpath and pressing Mitt by phone on the exigency of joining him there. On every rope line, all Paul Ryan heard was Benghazi, Benghazi, Benghazi.

Both despite and because of all the heat that the issue was generating, Boston wanted no part of it. The campaign's research showed (as did Chicago's) that Benghazi meant next to nothing to the small slice of voters who remained undecided. Stevens saw it through his usual prism: as a distraction from the economy. But debate prep forced the issue on Romney. He had to figure out what to say if the subject came up at Hofstra—which was likely, given the amount of news coverage it was generating.

The Burlington deliberations on the matter were interminable and quibbly. Romney feared that advancing any of the right's main lines of attack on

Benghazi would leave him vulnerable to being blindsided by information to which Obama had access but Mitt did not. This isn't a level playing field, he said. I need to be on solid ground.

In the end, Romney settled on soil that was not only solid but ultrasafe: critiquing Obama for traveling to Las Vegas for a political event on September 12, in the aftermath of the attacks. If it had been me, Mitt said, I would have stopped everything, called all hands on deck, managed this thing. That's what I did in Boston when we had the Big Dig tunnel accident.

With conservatives craving raw, red rib eye, Romney was planning to serve up tofu. Yet even the prospect of delivering this wan attack made Mitt slightly queasy. His grapplings with Benghazi had already inflicted too much damage on the campaign.

You know, he told Portman, I'm just not sure this is a winner for us.

BENGHAZI WAS MUCH ON Obama's mind, too. The answers he rehearsed in Williamsburg on the topic were among his best: fiery and full of conviction. The way that the right was piling on Rice made him furious. His national security aide Ben Rhodes was convinced that Romney would assail Obama for having not labeled Benghazi a terrorist attack. Now, a few hours before the debate, as Obama ran through some final prep at a Marriott on Long Island, Rhodes walked him through the transcript of his Rose Garden speech, with its "acts of terror" language. The president rehearsed his answer again, with gusto. *Boy, he nailed that,* Rhodes thought.

For all the progress Obama had made in his Monday night practice session, his team was anything but serene as the witching hour approached. Backstage at Hofstra, Klain was a nervous wreck. *One pretty good mock, one disaster in the past forty-eight hours,* Plouffe thought. *So which Obama shows up?*

Just then, the president emerged from his holding room, a few minutes before heading onstage. He found Klain, Plouffe, Axelrod, and Jim Messina in the hallway.

"Guys, I'm going to be good tonight," Obama said. "I finally figured this out."

When the lights went up at Hofstra, it took all of one answer for the

Obamans to realize that the president wasn't kidding. Replying to the first questioner, a twenty-year-old college student worried about finding work after graduation, Obama locked eyes with the young man and spoke crisply and pointedly. In the space of six sentences, the president plugged higher education and touted his job creation record, his manufacturing agenda, and his rescue of the auto industry—plunging an ice pick into Romney by invoking "Let Detroit Go Bankrupt." When Mitt cited his five-point economic plan in answer to a follow-up from Crowley, Obama let loose with his one-point-plan zinger. He was fast. He was hammy. He was gliding around the stage.

In the staff room, Obama's increasingly giddy team kept track of his progress, using his debate-on-a-page as a scorecard, ticking off the hits one by one as he delivered them. On outsourcing to China ("Pioneers!"), immigration (self-deportation), women's issues (Planned Parenthood), and more, the president was not only proving himself an able student but making Romney pay for every rightward lunge he had taken during the nomination contest.

Romney responded aggressively but with visible annoyance as he found himself forced to keep doubling back to answer attacks from minutes earlier, which made him appear petty and threw him off-rhythm. In Denver, Mitt's propensity for gaffes had vanished as if by magic; at Hofstra, presto-chango, it returned. Boasting of his commitment to gender equity in the Massachusetts statehouse, he referred to the résumés he reviewed for cabinet posts as "binders full of women." (On Twitter, the Obamans were all over it: #bindersfullofwomen.)

About two-thirds of the way through the ninety minutes, Romney tried to roll out Bob White's hit on Obama's financial portfolio. "Mr. President, have you looked at your pension?" Romney asked.

"You know, I don't look at my pension," Obama said without missing a beat and with a mile-wide smile. "It's not as big as yours, so it doesn't take as long."

The debate was now a little more than an hour old. The next question from the audience had to do with Benghazi. Obama explained the steps he had taken in the wake of the killings and then turned his attention to his opponent. "While we were still dealing with our diplomats being threatened, Governor Romney put out a press release trying to make political points," the president said sternly.

Romney got in his jab about the inappropriateness of Obama's political jaunt on September 12. But, as Rhodes predicted, Romney went further. "There were many days that passed before we knew whether this was a spontaneous demonstration or actually whether it was a terrorist attack," he said. "And there was no demonstration involved. It was a terrorist attack, and it took a long time for that to be told to the American people."

Obama summoned his highest dudgeon and responded: "The day after the attack, Governor, I stood in the Rose Garden, and I told the American people and the world that we are going to find out exactly what happened, that this was an act of terror. And I also said that we're going to hunt down those who committed this crime. And then a few days later, I was there greeting the caskets coming into Andrews Air Force Base and grieving with the families. And the suggestion that anybody in my team, whether the secretary of state, our UN ambassador—anybody on my team—would play politics or mislead when we've lost four of our own, Governor, is offensive. That's not what we do. That's not what I do as president. That's not what I do as commander in chief."

Obama returned to his stool and took a sip of water. Romney, incredulous, began to splutter.

"You said in the Rose Garden the day after the attack it was an act of terror? It was not a spontaneous demonstration? Is that what you're saying?"

With an icy stare, Obama set a trap: "Please proceed, Governor."

"I want to make sure we get that for the record, because it took the president fourteen days before he called the attack in Benghazi an act of terror," Romney insisted.

"Get the transcript," Obama said—at which point Candy Crowley interceded just as she had promised (or threatened) she would.

"He did, in fact, sir," Crowley said to Romney. "He did call it an act of terror."

"Can you say that a little louder, Candy?" Obama said, twisting the knife in Romney's back. The crowd burst into laughter and applause.

Romney was incensed with Crowley, so much so that he momentarily seemed to forget about Obama and started quarreling with her. In the Romney staff room backstage, Mitt's people completely lost their cool. The moderator had stepped in as a fact-checker, intervening on the president's side in a dispute that was far from cut-and-dried—and where a case could be made that Crowley was wrong. Ben Ginsberg called the control room and shouted, "What the hell was that?"

Minutes later, the debate was over. The Obamans were ebullient. The president's performance hadn't been perfect, but judged against the standards of Denver (or the Mock from Hell) it was pure genius. As he came off the stage, Obama thought he had done well. But having initially misjudged his performance the last time out, he was slightly tentative. "That was good, right?" he asked his people.

Yes, sir, they said. It was.

Backstage in his holding room, Romney paced the floor in a rage, fulminating about Crowley. Ann was equally livid: How could she do this? How could she make herself part of the debate?

Mitt demanded to see a transcript of Obama's Rose Garden remarks. Astonishingly, in all of his prep on Benghazi for Hofstra, no one on his team had ever bothered to review it with him. Romney wanted to get out of the hall and back to his hotel ASAP. Instead he was told he had to cool his heels and wait for the president's motorcade to leave first—the evening's final indignity.

Six nights later, on October 22, the candidates met again, for the third and final debate, in Boca Raton, Florida, on foreign policy. For Romney at this point, the topic could hardly have been less inviting. Snakebit twice on Benghazi, convinced that the media deck was stacked against him, and dismayed that the left was painting him as a warmonger, Romney agreed with Stevens that there was no mileage in doing anything other than hugging Obama, moving past the debate, and returning to campaigning on the economy.

The president's team suspected that Boston might run this play but assumed that Romney would try to redeem himself on Benghazi—if for no other reason than to placate the increasingly fervid right. The first question of the night, from moderator Bob Schieffer of CBS, placed the issue of Libya directly before Romney. Ducking it completely, he spent two minutes talking instead about Syria, Mali, Egypt, and Iran and congratulating Obama for having eliminated Osama bin Laden.

Just as Hofstra left Romney scalded, it had emboldened Obama. In preparing for Boca, he abandoned any visible signs of resistance to the thespianism and dramaturgical devices that his team urged on him. Klain's instruction shifted from "fast and hammy" to "ham with cheese delivery." Obama laughed at that—and couldn't help cracking up every time the diminutive (and very pregnant) Karen Dunn reminded him to pop Mitt in the kisser.

The most memorable line of the night demonstrated that Obama had taken both pieces of advice to heart. In response to a Romney charge that the president was reducing the military too much and too swiftly, Obama said contemptuously: "You mentioned the Navy, for example, and that we have fewer ships than we did in 1916. Well, Governor, we also have fewer horses and bayonets, because the nature of our military has changed. We have these things called aircraft carriers, where planes land on them. We have these ships that go underwater, nuclear submarines. And so the question is not a game of Battleship, where we're counting ships; it's what are our capabilities."

The pundits and the insta-polls all but unanimously rated the debate a blowout for Obama. In the space of eight days, the president had gone from the Mock from Hell through the crucible of Hofstra to the cakewalk at Boca. The final challenge of the campaign—and his career as a candidate—was behind him. Backstage, he walked over to Klain and put his hand on the debate coach's shoulder. His delight and relief were both evident.

You know, I really *have* finally figured this out, Obama said. Just in time for the last debate I'll ever do.

23

LIKE A HURRICANE

BARACK OBAMA AND MITT ROMNEY exited Boca on October 23 and entered the homestretch: the final, frantic, two-week sprint to Election Day, November 6. While a brand-new NBC News/*Wall Street Journal* poll made the race a dead heat nationally, Chicago's internal numbers showed the president narrowly ahead in almost all of the battleground states. Boston's research painted a more encouraging picture for Mitt. With the Denver debate having already uncorked one October surprise, with 2012 having been a year in which the wackadoodle was de rigueur, and with the bar for crazy always low in the final fortnight of a general election, the Obamans and Romneyites braced for the unexpected.

The next day, as if on cue, the Donald reemerged. On Twitter the previous week, Trump had teased that he would soon be making a "major announcement on President Obama." As with all things Trump, it would be big, big, big. A game changer for sure.

Romney was in a mild panic over what his most volatile supporter might have in the works; the last thing Mitt needed in the election's closing days was to be force-fed a shitburger. Does anyone know what this Trump thing is? Romney kept asking his aides. Shouldn't we find out? *How* do we find out?

The Trump thing turned out to be not an announcement *about* Obama but an offer *to* Obama—a deal that, the Donald said, "I don't believe he can refuse." In a YouTube video, Trump sat hunch-shouldered at his desk, face streaked by shadows and coiffure refulgent under pale gold lights, coming across like a combination of Howard Beale and Ron Popeil. "If Barack Obama opens up and gives his college records and applications . . . and if he gives his passport applications and records, I will give to a charity of his choice . . . a check *immediately* for $5 million," he fulminated.

As the offer was being made, Obama set off on a marathon campaign swing that would take him from Iowa to Colorado, California, Nevada, Florida, Virginia, Illinois, and Ohio in the space of forty-eight hours. In L.A., he stopped by the set of *The Tonight Show with Jay Leno*, where the host inquired about Trump's fixation on Obama. "It's like me and Letterman," Leno quipped. "What has he got against you?"

"This all dates back to when we were growing up together in Kenya," Obama replied, straight-faced at first. "We had constant run-ins on the soccer field." Now the president grinned. "He wasn't very good, and resented it. When we finally moved to America, I thought it would be over, but . . ." Obama trailed off into giggles.

The Obamans had been slyly mocking Trump for months—at Romney's expense. Back in May, photographers had snapped pictures of Mitt coming off of his campaign plane in Las Vegas; looming right behind him was the Donald's own logo-sporting plane. (A logistical snafu had delayed Romney's exit, allowing the cameras to be in position for the shot; the holdup involved a meeting between Mitt and Sheldon Adelson.) At first, Axelrod and Grisolano were hesitant about using the photo in ads, thinking it was a tad gratuitous. Their hesitancy didn't last long. Chicago's research showed that, no matter how briefly the image appeared, voters always noticed and remembered Romney juxtaposed with a private jet branded TRUMP.

Soon the Obamans were wedging the photo into spot after spot, using it as evocative shorthand for Romney's wealth and out-of-touchness. Starting in August, there were seven such commercials, on topics ranging from education to outsourcing to taxes. The final one was released while Obama was in the midst of his coast-to-coast ramble—a brutal 47-percent-themed attack ad, titled "No One Was Looking," that would run sixteen thousand times in the election's final days.

Obama found the whole thing hilarious: the Donald's antics, Romney's inexplicable loyalty to him, Chicago's mischief-making. The president made a point of reviewing and signing off on all his campaign spots. Every time he glimpsed the now iconic jet shot in one of them, he cracked up. Hey, hey, look, Obama would say, pointing at the screen. They got Trump in there again!

R OMNEY WAS BESET BY troubles with his allies in the homestretch. Every time he turned around, someone who ostensibly wanted to help him win was inflicting harm instead. The day after Boca, Indiana Republican Senate candidate Richard Mourdock, to whom Romney had provided a glowing endorsement video, declared that "even when life begins in that horrible situation of rape, that is something that God intended." Later in the week, both Sarah Palin and John Sununu provoked race-related dustups, with Palin attacking Obama on Facebook for his "shuck and jive shtick with these Benghazi lies" and Sununu suggesting that Colin Powell's endorsement of the president, announced on October 25, had been made out of black-brotherly solidarity.

The night the Sununu flap broke, Romney was in Defiance, Ohio, sixty miles southwest of Toledo, while Obama was in Cleveland. Both sides were courting the Buckeye State with all their might. A week earlier, the president had enlisted Bruce Springsteen to the cause, sending him to Parma for a gig with Bill Clinton. Now Romney tried to match the Boss and the Big Dog with a celebrity of his own: Meat Loaf.

What Mr. Loaf lacked in glamour, he made up for with enthusiasm. Cloaked in a tentlike black tunic, he performed a sweaty set and exhorted the crowd, "We need Oooohiiiiiioooo!" Backstage, the Meat pumped up Romney in true *Bat Out of Hell* style. "I hate to say this, but I mean it with all my heart," he told Mitt. "If you don't win this election, we're *fucked*."

For Romney, winning the election more or less came down to carrying Ohio. The analysis that Messina had given Obama in August was now clear to all: every one of Romney's plausible roads to 270 ran through that state. And even under the optimistic readings of Newhouse's polls, Mitt was several points behind there.

Nowhere other than Michigan had Romney been more haunted by the legacy of "Let Detroit Go Bankrupt." The car industry directly touched eighty-two of Ohio's eighty-eight counties. With the state's economy steadily improving, Obama had been relentless in touting the auto bailout as a crucial driver of the turnaround and hammering Romney for his opposition to it. For weeks, Rob Portman had been beseeching Boston to cut an ad that took on the issue directly, both to defend Mitt against Chicago's onslaught and to advance the argument that he would be better for the industry. Many scripts were written. All were nixed. No auto ad had aired yet.

On October 27, that changed—but the attempted cure only served to make the patient sicker. On TV and radio in Ohio, Team Romney went up with ads suggesting that, as a result of the administration's restructuring of the auto industry, GM had started offshoring U.S. jobs to China and Chrysler was planning to shift production of Jeeps from the Buckeye State to the Middle Kingdom.

The ads kicked up a mega-fuss, provoking fierce repudiations from fact-checkers, the national press, the local press, Chicago, and, most significantly, the car companies in question. Chrysler CEO Sergio Marchionne labeled the ads "inaccurate." "We've clearly entered some parallel universe," GM spokesman Greg Martin said, rebuking Boston's gambit as "campaign politics at its cynical worst."

For Romney, the backlash felt like the final chapter in a chronicle of a death foretold. From the moment he had seen the headline of his *New York Times* op-ed four years earlier, he knew it would be trouble. He tried and tried to defuse the problem, to no avail. Now his campaign's desperate, last-ditch effort was backfiring in the most important state on the map, turning him into an object of scorn for the industry his father helped build. On his daily conference call with Boston, Romney vented: Why are we doing this? Why are we fighting in an area where we're vulnerable in the closing days?

"This would be like Obama running an Obamacare ad in the last week of the election," he said.

The political storm raging in Ohio, however, was a charming summer squall compared with the baroscopic beast bearing down on the East Coast: Hurricane Sandy. By nightfall on Sunday, October 28, twenty-four hours before Sandy slammed into New Jersey and New York with unprecedented force, it was clear that the normal order of campaigning would be suspended until further notice. For the next four days, Obama would be America's full-time, omnipresent, can-do chief executive. And Romney would be . . . what?

Mitt's instinct was to figure out a way to be involved, to stay in the story. Stuck in the Midwest, he asked his team if there was any way for him to get to New Jersey. Just find a shelter, where people are hurting, so I can go and show that I care, he said. But the practical impediments were nearly insurmountable and the political risks were high; anything storm-related that Romney did would look small next to Obama's official duties and was likely to be perceived as exploitative. Then there was another problem: the Garden State's governor wasn't exactly rolling out the welcome mat.

In a phone call that Sunday, Christie told Romney that the storm was likely to keep him off the grid all week. Appearing on *Fox and Friends* on Tuesday morning, after a harrowing and sleepless night during which his state's shoreline was ravaged, Big Boy was asked by cohost Steve Doocy, "Is there any possibility that Governor Romney may go to New Jersey to tour some of the damage with you?"

"I have no idea, nor am I the least bit concerned or interested," Christie said. "If you think right now I give a damn about presidential politics, then you don't know me."

Christie went on to heap praise on Obama, as he would repeatedly all week long—calling him "outstanding," "wonderful," "tremendous," and deserving of "great credit." The next day, Christie and Obama surveyed the destruction together. "I cannot thank the president enough for his personal concern and compassion," the governor said at their joint press conference afterwards.

Watching Christie wrap Obama in a bear hug left most of the Romneyites somewhere between annoyed and irate. They understood that Big Boy had to act in the best interests of his battered state, but they found the frequency and extravagance of the encomiums excessive. *That's not a bear hug—it's a French kiss,* Ron Kaufman thought.

Mitt tried not to be irritated. By now Romney had become a student of Christie; he had seen so much over the course of the campaign, he practically had an advanced degree in Big Boy studies. He was sure that Chris wasn't trying to hurt him; the man just lacked self-control. Even so, Romney cringed when he spotted a picture on Drudge of Christie and Obama literally in each other's arms. *Oh, boy,* Romney thought. *This really isn't helping.*

For all the fretting by the Obamans about exogenous events that might fundamentally alter the race, when Sandy huffed and puffed, it was Romney's house that took the hit. Through no fault of his own, Mitt found himself irrelevant, without a role to play. He was dealt the cruelest fate imaginable for a presidential challenger: an effective news blackout in the election's last week. Stevens feared that the storm had halted Romney's momentum, allowing Obama to project both leaderly strength and (with Christie's help) a bipartisan aura. For the first time in two years, Stevens confided to his boss that he thought they could lose. And if we lose, Sandy will be why, Stuart said.

But while Stevens now accepted that Romney could lose, he didn't think he *would* lose. Neither did anyone else in Boston. And neither did Mitt.

Romney wasn't measuring the proverbial drapes for the Oval Office yet, or starting to ponder whether Ann could stable Rafalca in the parking lot of the Old Executive Office Building. In his rational, doubtful management consultant's mind, he believed the race was a toss-up. But Newhouse's polls had him running ahead in Florida, Colorado, and other battlegrounds; in Ohio, he was leading among independent voters, a reliable barometer of impending victory. Then there was the matter of Republican intensity, which Romney was experiencing firsthand—the size of the crowds, the rabid enthusiasm, the way Believe in America voters, for the first time, were really believing in *him*. All of it had Romney's gut screaming that he was going to win.

That instinct was reinforced on Friday night, November 2. In West Chester, Ohio, just north of Cincinnati, the Romney campaign staged a sprawling rally in the Square at Union Centre. Some 25,000 souls turned out on a bitterly cold night to see Mitt, but the backstage scene was what fueled Romney's sense of destiny. Along with almost the entire Boston brain trust, a star-studded cast of Republican heavies was on hand, including many former rivals who once detested him. There were the haters from 2008: McCain and Giuliani. The haters from 2012: Perry and Santorum. The local-boy extreme doubters: Boehner and Kasich. The war councillors: Ayotte, McDonnell, and Portman. Every last one was brimming with optimism. All of them said that Romney was bound for glory, and seemed to believe it. The good vibes were so pervasive that Stevens sidled up to Perry and introduced himself.

"I know who you are," the Texas governor said, smiling. "You're the guy who likes my book."

There was only one character notably missing from the upbeat, *This Is Your Life*-like finale: Christie, who remained pinned down in Jersey. Given the media attention to his mash session with Obama, Boston still hoped to get him in a picture next to Romney before Election Day. On Sunday night, November 4, the campaign would be holding a rally in Bucks County, Pennsylvania—just ten miles from Trenton and thus a golden opportunity.

Christie had no intention of attending the event. He was exhausted, frazzled, still consumed by the aftermath of Sandy. But there was another factor. Shortly before the storm hit, Christie had swung through Ohio to campaign for Romney—and come away convinced that Mitt was going to lose the state and the election. *These are Ohio people,* Big Boy thought, attuning his political radar to the crowds. *They're not voting for Mitt Romney.*

Christie was receiving a lot of incoming about the Bucks County event: Romney donors who knew how badly Boston wanted him there were phoning him, nagging him, hassling him, bugging him. The calls were getting on Mary Pat's nerves, too. The couple assumed that the Romneyites were whispering to the press that Chris might show up. On Saturday night, Mary Pat finally couldn't take it anymore. "This is bullshit," she said to her husband. "You need to call Russ."

Christie picked up the phone and spent the next ten minutes screaming at Schriefer. But the gist of his message required all of one second: Stop fucking with me, Russ.

On Sunday evening, though, when Romney arrived in Morrisville, Pennsylvania, the Christie contretemps was quickly forgotten (if not forgiven). Mitt hadn't held a rally in the Keystone State since the Republican primary. His late-stage incursion was an outward sign of Boston's brio;

thirty-six hours before Election Day, the campaign seemed to be putting a new battleground in play.

What awaited Romney at Shady Brook Farm was another 25,000-strong crowd. People had been massing all day in an enormous open field, listening to the Marshall Tucker Band, amped up and full of holler. As the Romney bus cruised onto the farm grounds, Mitt, Ann, and Mitt's brother, Scott, huddled up front, gazing out the window, waving and gawking at the five-deep lines of supporters on the side of the gravel road.

Mike Leavitt walked up and joined the Romneys. For months, the former governor of Utah had been working diligently on Mitt's transition plan for his entry into the White House. But in the past few weeks, Leavitt's labors had ramped up as victory seemed more and more likely. It was all coming together: the huge throngs, the sunny numbers from Newhouse and so many other Republican pollsters, the growing certainty that after four years of Obama the country was pining for a different kind of change. Leavitt was in awe of how far his friend had come. Two nights from now, Romney would be the president-elect of the United States.

Leavitt leaned in and told Mitt that he wouldn't be staying for his speech.

Oh, too bad, Romney said. Why's that?

"I have to go start the engine and warm it up," Leavitt said.

CHICAGO VIEWED Boston's Pennsylvania play as a sign of desperation or delusion. The public polls, with few exceptions, indicated that Obama was destined for reelection, and the president's team had crossed the threshold from confidence to certainty. Chicago's research showed him ahead in every battleground but North Carolina. Early voting had been going on for weeks in many of those states; in Nevada, Iowa, Ohio, and others, Obama had built up a lead that bordered on insurmountable. To test the proposition, Messina asked his analytics team to run worst-case projections—with GOP turnout through the roof, minority and youth participation in the cellar. That Sunday, the results came back: no matter how the data jockeys twiddled the knobs in Romney's favor, Obama still wound up with more than 270 electoral votes.

The previous week had been a strange one for Obama, all but extracting him from politics entirely. On the eve of the storm, he was in Orlando for a joint event the next morning with Clinton. As Sandy's scale became apparent, the White House decided that Obama had to scurry back to Washington. But before leaving, he was able to sneak in a half-hour meeting with his predecessor.

You go be president, Clinton told Obama. Don't worry about the campaign. I'm here for you. Whatever you need me to do this week, I'll do it.

For the next four days, Obama was off the trail. Instead of giving speeches, working rope lines, or doing media interviews, he was on the telephone with the governors of the storm-affected states, dealing with FEMA, playing disaster-relief quarterback. Unlike in Romney's world, the Sandy-related political angst around Obama was close to nil. The president knew that he was winning. He had a job to do. Not once did anyone hear him express anxiety about his absence from the hustings.

Clinton, meanwhile, was making good on his word, campaigning as if his own name were on the ballot. For the past three general elections, he had been a nonfactor in the homestretch. In 2000 and 2008, Gore and Obama, for different reasons, had kept him on the bench; in 2004, he was in the hospital, recovering from heart surgery. Still basking in the afterglow of Charlotte, he had told Messina following the Boca debate that he would give control over his schedule to Chicago for the final week. The Sandy factor fired him up even more. In the six days after he and 44 parted in Orlando, Clinton headlined a head-snapping twenty-one events in seven states—all the while prodding the campaign, Why don't you add a few more stops? The cost of moving Clinton around the country was enormous: $1 million plus. *It's worth every fucking penny,* Messina thought.

The two presidents were reunited on Saturday, November 3, for a massive jamboree at the Jiffy Lube Live amphitheater, in Bristow, Virginia, forty miles outside Washington. Dressed in a brown leather baby boomer's bomber's jacket, Clinton was hoarse and raspy: "As you can see, I have given my voice in the service of my president," he said as he began his remarks. But soon Clinton was rocking the place, wallowing in the applause, praising Obama to the skies, and eviscerating Romney with lightheartedness and humor.

"Barack Obama decided that America could not afford to let the auto-

mobile industry die, and he saved it," Clinton said. "Mitt Romney opposed
what he did. And now he's tied himself in so many knots over this automo-
bile deal, he could be hired as the chief contortionist for the Cirque du
Soleil."

Backstage, Obama sat glued to a monitor, marveling at the joy and
intensity radiating from the stage. "He's really having fun doing this, isn't
he?" Obama said to one of Clinton's aides.

When 42 finished, 44 jogged out to the podium in a rush. "I was enjoying listening to President Clinton so much, I had to run up to get my cue,"
he said. "I was sitting there, just soaking it all in."

Obama called Clinton "the master" and "a great president" and "a great
friend." At the end of the event, they hugged warmly onstage as the sound
system kicked in with "Don't Stop"—not just a nod to the past, but a subtle
sign of deference that would have been inconceivable four years earlier.

With the finish line in sight, thoughts of 2008 were inescapable for
Obama and his people. The next morning, the current and former presidents, Axelrod, and Plouffe boarded Air Force One and flew to New Hampshire for another joint rally. As Obama's limousine carried them north up
the Everett Turnpike from Manchester to Concord, Clinton gazed out the
window and announced, "Man, I love New Hampshire"—calling to mind
both his own comeback-kid revival there in 1992 and Hillary's in 2008, at
the expense of the Obamans.

Even a few months earlier, before the 42-44 bond had been cemented,
Plouffe might have bitten his tongue. Instead he shot back, "We like it here,
too, but we like Iowa a little bit more."

Everyone laughed.

Iowa was where the Obamans found themselves thirty-six hours later.
They had trekked to Des Moines for the president's final rally of the campaign and of his career as a candidate—an event custom-built for uplift, for
nostalgia, for the bittersweetness that always comes with the end of something.

Obama managed to restrain his feelings for much of the last day. At his
first stop, in Madison, and his second, in Cleveland, he was his usual self.
But on the flight into DSM he began to wax nostalgic, particularly when he

was told about a staff plan that had been foiled. The idea was to fly in Edith Childs—the hat-proud South Carolina councilwoman who had inspired Obama's famous 2008 chant of "Fired up! Ready to go!"—to introduce him that night. But Ms. Childs declined the invitation: North Carolina was still in play, and she planned to be there on Election Day to help get out the vote.

That's too unbelievably good to be true, a tickled Obama said. I'm gonna put that in my speech.

Air Force One and the first lady's plane both touched down at around 9:00 p.m. Obama met his wife on the tarmac, at the foot of the aircraft stairs. When their limo pulled up in Des Moines's East Village, the scene was like something out of a movie. A crowd of twenty thousand stretched for block after block from the podium up East Locust Street. Beyond the crowd, a massive American flag flew in the distance. Beyond the flag were the columns and golden dome of the state's majestic capitol building.

Obama's original campaign headquarters was behind the stage—an unassuming, low-slung brick building that now housed a church. Before his speech, the president walked slowly, pensively, through the space, recalling where certain staffers had sat four years earlier, reminiscing about the frigid New Year's Eve when *The Des Moines Register*'s poll announced to the world what the campaign already believed: that he, Barack Hussein Obama, was going to win the nearly all-Caucasian caucuses.

Michelle Obama held her husband's hand. As she traveled around that fall, the first lady had been in a terrific mood about what she was seeing. Perhaps most gratifying was the lack of a backlash against her husband's change of posture on same-sex unions. Gay marriage was supposed to have been the most scalding of hot-button issues, but it had turned out to be a damp squib—and she found that a cause for overwhelming optimism. *We've come a long way,* the first lady thought.

Close to 10:00 p.m., she took to the rostrum and, clearly moved, put the finest point possible on the moment. "As you know, this is a pretty emotional time for us, because this is the final event of my husband's final campaign," Michelle said. "So this is the last time that he and I will be onstage together at a campaign rally. And that's why we wanted to come here to Iowa tonight. Because truly this is where it all began."

A few minutes later, her husband was up there with her. They shared a kiss, a long embrace, and some whispered words.

"I've come back to Iowa one more time to ask for your vote," Obama began. "I came back to ask you to help us finish what we've started. Because this is where our movement for change began. Right here. Right here. Right behind these bleachers is the building that was home to our Iowa headquarters in 2008. I was just inside, and it brought back a whole lot of memories. This was where some of the first young people who joined our campaign set up shop, willing to work for little pay and less sleep because they believed that people who love their country can change it. This was where so many of you who shared that belief came to help. When the heat didn't work for the first week or so, some of you brought hats and gloves for the staff. These poor kids, they weren't prepared! When the walls inside were bare, one of you painted a mural to lift everybody's spirits. When we had a Steak Fry to march to, when we had a J-J [Jefferson-Jackson] Dinner to fire up, you brought your neighbors and you made homemade signs. When we had calls to make, teachers and nurses showed up after work, already bone-tired but staying anyway, late into the night. And you welcomed me and Michelle into your homes. And you picked us up when we needed a lift. And your faces gave me new hope for this country's future, and your stories filled me with resolve to fight for you every single day I set foot in the Oval Office. You inspired us."

As Obama spoke, he made no effort to conceal the emotions to which his wife referred; the president's heart was festooned on his sleeve. His voice, at once gravelly and trembly, repeatedly cracked. First one tear, then two, and then more streamed down his cheeks.

He punctuated his Iowa rhapsody with a "Yes, we can!"

The crowd let loose a roar.

At great length, he told the story of Edith Childs, adding its new kicker: "She said, I'd love to see you, but I think we can still win North Carolina . . . I've got to knock on some doors. I've got to turn out the vote. I'm still fired up, but I've got work to do. And that shows you what one voice can do. One voice can change a room. And if it can change a room, it can change a city. And if it can change a city, it can change a state. And if it can change a state, it can change a nation. And if it can change a nation, it can change the world."

As Obama built to his crescendo, so did the din around him. Finally, finally, he led the audience in the valedictory call-and-response.

"Are you fired up?"

"READY TO GO!"

"Are you fired up?"

"READY TO GO!"

More than a year earlier, Axelrod had told the president that, in order to win in 2012, he would have to recapture the Barack Obama of 2008— he would have to find his way home. On some days during the campaign, he had come close; on others, the distance seemed too great to span. Now, back in Iowa, on the final night, Obama was all the way there: the circle was complete.

For half an hour after his speech, Obama worked the rope line. The temperature outside was just around freezing. Though he wasn't wearing an overcoat, he seemed unfazed by the chill. Back inside the old headquarters, he signed some books and posters, whatever people put in front of him. He talked about the familiar faces he had glimpsed from the stage. They believed in me when nobody else did, Obama said.

The hour was late. It was time to go. But Obama lingered. Taking a last, long look around, he turned to Plouffe and motioned to the door. His expression was rueful, reflective, and satisfied all at once.

"I guess that's it," Obama said—and then strode out into the cold night air.

EPILOGUE

IT WAS NEARLY 2:00 a.m. on November 7 when Mitt and Ann walked into the campaign-staff suite at the Westin Boston Waterfront Hotel. Not long before, Romney had phoned President Obama to concede the election, then delivered a five-minute elegy in the ballroom downstairs. "I so wish that I had been able to fulfill your hopes to lead the country in a different direction, but the nation chose another leader," Romney said. "So Ann and I join with you to earnestly pray for him and for this great nation."

The size and sweep of Obama's victory staggered the Romneys and their people. Twelve hours earlier, they had been convinced that Mitt would prevail—or, at worst, that the race would be a nail-biter. Instead, the Democratic incumbent was on his way to an emphatic 51–47 percent win, in which he carried all but one of the battleground states (North Carolina), pocketed 332 electoral votes, and outdistanced Romney by five million popular votes out of 129 million cast.

Mitt and Ann sat down with a clutch of advisers: Stevens, White, Myers, Kaufman, Zwick. Ann had been crying; she was jagged, inconsolable. "How did this happen?" she asked over and over, saying she feared for the future of America.

Her husband, by contrast, was downcast but composed. In the frantic final hours on the trail, Mitt had told his aides that he was excited about winning but if he lost, that would be okay, too; he would be perfectly happy returning to his normal life, spending more time with his kids and grandkids. Now Romney looked up and saw a commercial playing on TV. It was former Tennessee senator and failed presidential candidate Fred Thompson, hawking reverse mortgages for a company called AAG. Staring at the screen, Mitt indulged in some dark humor.

That could be *me* next, he said.

The Republican Party royalty was just as stunned as Boston but took the loss with less equanimity than did Mitt. Rupert Murdoch, who had watched the election returns with a four-star general, was dismayed. When Obama claimed victory, the officer presented an apocalyptic vision of the president's second term: an anemic America, on its knees, capitulating to Middle Eastern thugs. Expressing a sentiment common among the high command of the right, Murdoch muttered, "Our nation is ruined."

The finger-pointing commenced the day after the election. The billionaires' club trained its fire on Rove, his Crossroads empire, and the rest of the conservative super PACs, which had spent hundreds of millions of dollars— much of it from the billionaires' bank accounts—to run a jillion ads that yielded squat. *Holy shit, we were duped,* thought Langone. Next time, he and his compadres would be damn sure to demand accountability from the likes of Karl before opening up their wallets again.

With the exit polls showing that 15 percent of voters rated Obama's handling of Sandy as the most important factor in their decision—and 73 percent of that subset backing the president—blame was cast on Christie, too. The imputations prompted an uncharacteristic defensiveness on the part of Big Boy, who worried that any lingering perception of party recreancy might hurt him if he ran in 2016. *I'm a loyal guy!* Christie thought. *No one worked harder or did more for Mitt than me!*

Big Boy's sense of where the real fault lay was crystal clear: with the clowns on Commercial Street. On the phone with Ryan two days after the election, Christie listened while Fishconsin talked about how he, too, had been certain that he and Mitt were headed for the White House. "On election morning," Ryan said, "they told me and my wife we were going to win."

"Well, that just shows how shitty they were," Christie harrumphed.

As the poison darts flew hither and yon, the Romneys were in Boston, saying their farewells to the campaign and still trying to wrap their minds around what had occurred. The morning after the election, they both addressed a major-donor breakfast; later that day, they spoke to the entire staff on Commercial Street. The emotional bifurcation was the same as on election night. Mitt was gracious and comforting, but his upper lip remained stiff. Ann was kind and thankful, but damp-eyed and on the verge of losing it—spouting Manichaean warnings about what Obama's reelection meant.

"It will become more clear to you as the days go on and you see what's going to happen to our country," she said in her speech to the staff. "This was a turning point in the history of the nation."

Little in the campaign had gone as planned for Ann. At the start, Boston had touted her to the press as Mitt's secret weapon. Nearly two years later, she remained a mystery to many voters. In Chicago's focus groups, her name rarely came up. Her convention speech was supposed to have been her breakout moment, but it was forgotten within days. The campaign acknowledged once or twice that she wasn't feeling well; in truth, her MS limited her travel and public appearances more than Boston let on. And there were those occasions when she *did* make an impression, just not the right one: in a series of interviews, her pique surfaced, and she sounded sharp or shrill.

Ann hadn't wanted Mitt to try again after his 2008 washout. But once she reversed her position and decided he had to take on Obama to set things right, her psychic investment in the race was stratospheric. The torments Mitt suffered at the hands of Chicago, the press, and the GOP establishment made her ballistic. "Stop it—this is hard," she complained in one media appearance, after Peggy Noonan and others had heaped censure on her husband over the 47 percent. "You want to try it? Get in the ring." Tartly, she dismissed the swell of criticism as "nonsense and the chattering class." On *Meet the Press*, she griped that Mitt "really has been demonized." During her husband's autumn upswing, Ann thought that people were finally seeing the Mitt she knew and cherished. The election was a crushing blow to that illusion; she couldn't comprehend how her fellow citizens had gotten it so wrong.

Mitt believed that the nation had made a mistake, but he didn't feel deflated. *The voters chose to double down,* he thought. *That's their right.* He was grateful to have had the national platform that his father dreamed of but never achieved. *Who would have ever guessed that a kid with skinny legs from Cranbrook School would get to run for president and speak to the entire country? I got a chance to say the things I wanted to say.*

Obama and his people saw Romney as pure ambition. In truth, Mitt was about as ambivalent as any nominee in modern history. He had left a good life to run, and a good life awaited him back at Fin de la Senda when he was finished. In the course of the campaign, he created endless problems for himself but rarely addressed them with pull-out-all-the-stops urgency or last-dog-dies determination. The one weakness he did try to combat was the perception that he was a flip-flopper; but in refusing to deviate an iota from his 2008 positions, he generated fiercer headaches and harsher headlines. He allowed Chicago to define him as a heartless plutocrat without offering an alternative image. (In the exit polls, Romney led Obama on three out of four key candidate qualities—"strong leader," "shares my values," and "vision for the future"—but was crushed, 81 to 18 percent, on the question of who "cares about people like me.") As that perception took hold during the campaign, his attitude toward it seemed to be, *Oh, well, Mitt happens.*

Even so, Romney's management-consultant instincts took hold in the aftermath of November 6. He wanted to understand why he lost, how he lost.

On the Thursday after the election, he met with his brain trust to come up with answers—for both himself and the press, which was clamoring for enlightenment as to why Boston had misjudged the race so badly in the homestretch. In the familiar third-floor conference room, they all gathered one last time. With the exception of Gillespie, it was the same core group that Romney had started out with. Mitt was proud that they'd come through intact, that there had been so much camaraderie and so little infighting— although at that moment, some in the room, such as Zwick, were seething at Newhouse and Beeson for polling numbers and a ground game that had been, respectively, so wrong and so feeble.

Newhouse ran through the exit poll data, explaining that Chicago had dramatically pulled off its coalition-of-the-ascendant play—turning out an electorate even more diverse than in 2008, not less, as Newhouse assumed would be the case. Nationally, the white vote fell from 74 to 72 percent, while the black proportion held steady at 13. Participation among Hispanics rose from 8 to 10 percent, among women from 53 to 54 percent, and among young voters from 18 to 19 percent. Obama's share of each of those blocs ranged from commanding to overwhelming: 93 percent of African Americans, 71 percent of Latinos, 55 percent of women (and 67 percent of unmarried women), and 60 percent of young voters.

Gillespie argued that Obama had won by advancing a series of "rifle-shot policies" aimed at those electoral slices: free contraceptives for women, the DREAM Act for Latinos, cuts in student-loan interest rates for the kids. Gillespie had been spot-on about Romney's need to heal himself with these groups. Now he said of the Obamans, "They played small ball, but they went small in a big way."

Romney found the logic compelling. Obamacare was another example, he said. A majority of the country was against it, but the president's base loved free health care.

Someone mentioned welfare reform—the federal waivers to state work requirements. The administration announced its new policy the day before Biden gave a speech to the NAACP. The base-stroking going on there was pretty blatant, no?

Let's leave that one off the list, guys, Gillespie interposed. We don't want to turn this into a racial thing.

On a certain level, there was nothing especially controversial about the Gillespie-Romney analysis. Sitting presidents of both parties had used the power of incumbency to sweeten the deal for key constituencies since the dawn of the republic. But in Mitt's clumsy hands, the interpretation was a loaded gun aimed at his own foot.

A few days later, on a November 14 conference call with dozens of top donors, Romney offered his take on how Obama had defeated him: "What the president's campaign did was focus on certain members of his base coalition, give them extraordinary financial gifts from the government, and then work very aggressively to turn them out to vote." Rattling off some examples of the benefits to which he was referring, he kept invoking the word "gift." Listening in on the call, Ron Kaufman thought, *Fuck, this is not good.*

Of course, Mitt believed he was speaking confidentially, in a private call, with contributors. Of course, that was foolish—especially for a man who already had been incinerated by a secret video from a donor dinner. Of course, there were journalists listening in on the call, and "gifts" made headlines within hours.

Even after the election was over, the most gaffe-prone nominee in anyone's memory was still coughing up verbal miscues. In offering an explanation for his failure, he explained more than he knew.

OBAMA LAUGHED WHEN HE heard that Romney had described him as Santa Claus in chief, doling out presents to the freeloaders gathered around the White House Christmas tree. "He must have really meant that 47 percent thing," the president remarked to his aides.

Obama and his people weren't surprised that Boston was still reeling. On election night, when Mitt called the president to concede, he had congratulated Obama for his side's turnout efforts—specifically expressing his own team's astonishment at the numbers in Cleveland and Milwaukee, where African American participation was off the charts. When Obama related Romney's comment to Axelrod, Messina, and Plouffe, they all had the same bemused reaction. What Boston was saying, in effect, was, Holy cow, where did all these mysterious minorities come from?

Heading into the race, the perception among political professionals and the press had been that the rival campaign squadrons were more or less evenly matched. But as the smoke cleared, a consensus quickly emerged that the Democrats had methodically been building an atomic clock while the Republicans were trifling with Tinkertoys. Chicago's mockery of Boston was hushed but withering.

The president himself devoted little time to pawing over the entrails of the election. Four years earlier, the moment his epically antagonistic fight with Hillary Clinton ended, any rancor on Obama's part toward her had fallen away. The same happened with regard to Romney.

On the very day that Mitt offered up his theory of electoral dispensations, Obama held a press conference in the East Room of the White House. In his speech on election night, the president had indicated that he intended to sit down with Romney to "talk about where we can work together to move this country forward." Asked about that proposition now, Obama averred that he was serious and offered praise for the man he and his team had spent the past year dismembering.

"I do think he did a terrific job running the Olympics," Obama said. "That skill set of trying to figure out how do we make something work better applies to the federal government . . . He presented some ideas during the course of the campaign that I actually agree with. And so it'd be interesting to talk to him about something like that. There may be ideas that he has with respect to jobs and growth that can help middle-class families that I want to hear."

For Obama, the 2012 election had been harder and uglier than 2008 but also more gratifying. Four years earlier, he had ignited something in the electorate. But he also had been a mere vessel: an antidote to the eight-year reign of George W. Bush and a symbol of racial progress. In 2008, Obama told his advisers, people were betting on hope. In 2012, they were rendering a judgment on his record and leadership. The substantive stakes of the race were huge; if Obama had lost, much of what he had accomplished, starting with health care reform, would have been reversed by Romney and the GOP Congress. But the personal stakes were equally vast. More than he let on, Obama felt the mantle of history heavy on his shoulders, and he had a writer's understanding of the provisional nature of narrative. Had he fallen short in his quest for reelection, his story would have changed overnight, with his presidency recast from a heroic landmark to a failed, one-term accident. In victory, he secured his legacy as a transformative figure—and won the chance to become a great president.

During the campaign, Obama often argued that, with such a clear philosophical and ideological choice before the voters, reelection would give him a mandate, and the upper hand with the GOP. "My hope is that if the American people send a message to [Republicans]," he told *Rolling Stone,* "there's going to be some self-reflection going on—that it might break the fever. They might say to themselves, 'You know what, we've lost our way here. We need to refocus on trying to get things done for the American people.'"

But the weeks and months after Election Day demonstrated that he had been whistling in the dark. On issue after issue, from the budget to climate change to immigration, Republicans remained as intransigent as ever, and Obama remained . . . Obama. In the cauldron of his debates with Romney, the president had been forced to perform against his nature. But his core predilection to play by his own rules emerged undisturbed. The same flaws and foibles that had bedeviled his first term continued to plague his second—and threatened to haunt him to the end. In terms of Obama's ability to govern, the 2012 election did nothing to change the game.

Among Democrats, however, no one doubted the election's long-range political meaning. In consolidating the coalition of the ascendant, Obama had created a template on which his party might build for years to come. With 2016 already looming, the question was who might inherit the Obama base, the Obama machine, the Obama imprimatur.

One obvious possibility was his vice president, whose flirtation with 2016 grew increasingly overt. On Election Day, Biden was asked whether this would be the last time he voted for himself. "No, I don't think so," he replied. That night and over the next two days, he worked his way down a list of Democrats on the 2012 ballot, placing personal phone calls to them all. He courted prominent party leaders from Iowa and other early states. In media interviews, he touted the tightness of his relationship with Obama. ("We're totally simpatico," he pronounced.) And he reveled in high-profile assignments from the president: managing negotiations with the GOP over the fiscal cliff at year's end and heading up the administration's gun-control task force after the horrific school massacre in Newtown, Connecticut.

Then there was Hillary Clinton. Four years earlier, Obama had defied all expectations—and the advice of his own people—by bringing Clinton onto his team. The alliance seemed tenuous and fraught, but it had worked out better than anyone save Obama himself ever expected; he and his former rival proved effective partners. Now, at the close of 2012, with Hillary ready to depart her perch at the State Department, Obama's relationship with the Clintons had reached a new and unforeseen phase. On election night, the instant that Obama hung up with Romney, he turned to Messina and said, "Get Bill on the phone." Amazingly, The One and the Big Dog had become something like friends.

In the weeks that followed, Obama provided the tea-leaf readers with much to study. A round of golf with 42 at Andrews saw 44 skipping out early on the back nine to maintain a one-stroke lead—that was how Clinton told it, anyway, with a big smile on his face. Next came a joint *60 Minutes* interview with Hillary, in which Obama praised her lavishly, calling her "one of the finest secretary of states we've had." Once upon a time, not all that long ago, the Obamas and the Clintons had been the Montagues and the Capulets. Now, more and more, it seemed as if the four most popular political figures in the country—Barack and Michelle, Hillary and Bill—were part of the same powerful family.

No president in memory had cared less about party succession than Obama. The idea that he would place a thumb on the scale if both Clinton and Biden sought their party's 2016 nomination was inconceivable. Yet for the two likely Democratic front-runners in the campaign to come, 44 would be ever present. They would seek to replicate his team's skills at raising money and moving votes. They would woo his rising coalition. They would pray that he delivered them a robust economy. They would strive to defend his record, which they had helped to forge. Neither Hillary nor Joe was really the gambling type. But for good or ill, if they sought the Oval Office, they would have no choice but to double down on Barack Obama.

AUTHORS' NOTE

This book is a sequel to *Game Change*, our account of the 2008 presidential election, in all the obvious ways, but also in its animating impulses, objectives, and techniques. Once again, the campaign we set out to chronicle had been covered with great intensity across a multiplying array of platforms. Once again, we were convinced that many of the stories behind the headlines had not been told. Once again, we have tried to render the narrative with an unrelenting focus on the candidates and those closest to them—with an eye toward the high human drama behind the curtain, and with accuracy, fairness, and empathy always foremost among our aims.

The vast bulk of the material in the preceding pages was derived from more than five hundred full-length interviews with more than four hundred individuals conducted between the summers of 2010 and 2013. Almost all of the interviews took place in person, in sessions that often stretched over several hours. (Beyond these marathon sittings, there were countless telephone and e-mail conversations to follow up and check facts.) Many sources also provided us with e-mails, memos, notes, journal entries, audio and video recordings, and other forms of documentation. Only a handful of people declined our requests to participate.

All of our interviews for the book—from those with junior staffers to those with the candidates themselves—were done on a "deep background" basis. We took great care with our subjects to be explicit about what this term of art meant for this project: that we were free to use the information they provided (once we had determined its veracity) but that we would not identify them as sources in any way. In an ideal world, granting such anonymity would be unnecessary; in the world we actually inhabit, we believe it is essential to elicit the level of candor on which a book of this sort depends.

Inevitably, we were called on to compare and reconcile differing accounts of the same events. But we were struck by how few fundamental disputes we encountered in our reporting. In almost every scene in the book, we have included only material about which disagreements among the players were either nonexistent or trivial. Regarding the few exceptions, we brought to bear deliberate professional consideration and judgment.

In reconstructing scenes and conveying the perspectives of the participants, we relied exclusively on parties who were directly involved or on those to whom they spoke contemporaneously. Where dialogue is within quotation marks, it comes from the speaker, someone who was present and heard the remark, notes, transcripts, or recordings. The absence of quotation marks around dialogue indicates that it is paraphrased—meaning that our sources were in agreement about the nature, texture, and substance of the statement, but there were minor divergences regarding precise wording. Where thoughts or feelings are placed in italics, they come from the person identified or others to whom she or he expressed her or his state of mind.

The interviews for *Double Down* were all governed by a strict embargo, meaning that we agreed to use the information we obtained only after Election Day and only in the book. In a few instances—including, notably, the episode described in Chapter 3 revolving around Obama's list, in which we were the book authors to whom the items on the list were disclosed, shortly after the president shared the contents with his team—our reporting efforts became part of an unfolding story. But that in no way affected our commitment to the embargo. At the same time, our reporting and writing here was grounded in our daily and weekly coverage of the campaign for our respective magazines; a number of passages in the book are drawn from that work.

—Mark Halperin and John Heilemann
   September 2013

ACKNOWLEDGMENTS

A project of this size and duration leaves its perpetrators feeling a little like a tin-pot Greek bank, its balance sheet littered with more towering debts than could ever be repaid in this life or the next.

Our first and most titanic IOU is to our sources, who spent endless hours with us in person and on the phone. We thank them immensely for their generosity, trust, and patience. Big ups also to their assistants, who facilitated many of the interviews.

We are grateful to our incomparable literary agent, Andrew Wylie, who always knows when to hold 'em and doesn't really comprehend the concept of folding 'em. His team at The Wylie Agency fielded our requests with speed and a smile. In a previous life, Scott Moyers was part of that team. It was kismet and our great good fortune that, just after we signed on at The Penguin Press, Scott became the imprint's (and therefore our) publisher.

Ann Godoff, our editor, has earned a reputation as the best in the business: savvy, eagle-eyed, tough-minded yet nurturing, committed above all and before everything to the quality of the words on the page. And, whaddya know, it's true! We were blessed to have her and all the other tremendously talented Penguiners—including Elisabeth Calamari, Tracy Locke, Will

Palmer, Lindsay Whalen, and Veronica Windholz—on our side from start to finish.

Special thanks as well to Chris Anderson, whose genius with a camera is evident in the book's photo insert; to Jane Rosenthal, for a timely home-stretch maneuver on our behalf; and to Elizabeth Wilner of Kantar Media's Campaign Media Analysis Group.

Many of our journalistic colleagues produced terrific coverage of the campaign and its dramatis personae. We benefited in particular from Dan Balz's book *Collision 2012: Obama vs. Romney and the Future of Elections in America;* Politico's series of election e-books, *The Right Fights Back, Inside the Circus, Obama's Last Stand,* and *The End of the Line;* Jay Root's e-book *Oops!,* on Rick Perry; Bob Woodward's *The Price of Politics,* on the debt-ceiling drama of 2011; Ariel Levy's "The Good Wife," on Newt and Callista Gingrich, from the January 23, 2012, issue of *The New Yorker;* Robert Draper's "Building a Better Mitt Romney-Bot," from the November 30, 2011, issue of *The New York Times Magazine;* and Benjamin Wallace-Wells's "George Romney for President, 1968," from the May 28, 2012, issue of *New York* magazine. More generally, we gleaned much from the reporting and analysis of Mike Allen, Matt Bai, David Chalian, David Corn, John Dickerson, Joshua Green, Maggie Haberman, John Harris, Vanessa Hope, Jason Horowitz, Al Hunt, Gwen Ifill, Jodi Kantor, Joe Klein, David Maraniss, Jonathan Martin, Adam Nagourney, Jim Rutenberg, Roger Simon, Ben Smith, Glenn Thrush, Jim VandeHei, Judy Woodruff, and Jeff Zeleny.

Christian Flynn and Amy Howell, of Harvard's Institute of Politics, were gracious enough to provide us superb summer interns: Mattie Kahn and Sheema Golbaba in 2012 and Alexis Wilkinson in 2013. They pitched in with Gillian Brassil, Rhaina Cohen, Eliot Fearey, and Clint Rainey on an editorial escadrille that tackled all manner of tasks with speed and acuity in the face of demanding deadlines. Particular thanks to *Double Down* project manager Frankie Thomas, who was always there when we needed her (and we needed her a lot).

Farther afield, Colleen Evans and Kate MacInnis, of the Ritz-Carlton empire, treated us like kin (and gave us the key to the library). Dave Bernstein lent us a high-class crash pad in the Windy City and never complained about the mess we left behind. Travel wizard Ralph Spielman kept us on the move even when the gods of commercial transit were against us. In Gotham City and on the road, an assortment of glorified short-order cooks, vino peddlers, and front-of-the-house stalwarts attended magnificently to our corporeal sustenance: Mario Batali, Chris Bianco, April Bloomfield, Danny Bowien, Richard Coraine, David Chang, Wylie Dufresne, Frank Falcinelli, Ken Friedman, Suzanne Goin, Daniel Humm, John Mainieri, Carlo Mirarchi, Danny Meyer, Drew Nieporent, Jen Sgobbo, Nancy Silverton, Justin Smillie, Gabe Stulman, and Michael Toscano. The Pressed Juicery kept us fully hydrated. Seamless delivered. And the late, lamented Kinkead's always (always) gave us Table One—site of more meals (and revelations) than we can count, and forever hallowed ground.

In collaborating since 2008, we have shared an unusually large number of professional associations that extend beyond the confines of either of our books. Not a day passes when we don't thank our lucky stars for the support, friendship, guidance, and all-around awesomeness of some of the best people and organizations in this or any other hemisphere. Massive props to the following:

Joe Scarborough, Mika Brzezinski, Willie Geist, Mike Barnicle, Alex Korson, Louis Burgdorf, Allison Filon, and the whole brilliant *Morning Joe* gang; Phil Griffin, Lauren Skowronski, Chris Matthews, Andrea Mitchell, Lawrence O'Donnell, Alex Wagner, the teams at *Hardball, Andrea Mitchell Reports, The Last Word,* and *NOW,* and the rest of our MSNBC family; Tom Brokaw, David Gregory, Erica Hill, Lester Holt, Matt Lauer, Betsy Fischer Martin, and Brian Williams of NBC News; Richard Plepler, Len Amato, Michael Lombardo, Quentin Schaffer, Nancy Lesser, and everyone at the HBO juggernaut; Gary Goetzman, Tom Hanks, and their peerless peers at Playtone; Jay Roach and Danny Strong, our cinematic dynamic duo; Gary Foster, Matthew Hiltzik, and Ali Zelenko, our own War Council; Harry Rhoads, Barbara Daniel, Klair Watson, and the quantum force that is Washington Speakers Bureau; Chris Duffy of Boies Schiller & Flexner LLP; Peggy Siegal; Jeff Fager, Anderson Cooper, and Bob Anderson of CBS News; and the extraordinary Charlie Rose and Yvette Vega.

A loud shout-out, too, to a panoply of common pals to whom we frequently turn for aid, comfort, or cocktails: Mike Feldman, Gary Ginsberg, Savannah Guthrie, Tammy Haddad, Tom Healy, Fred Hochberg, Jeff Kwatinetz, Chris Licht, Terri McCullough, Jonathan Prince, Jake Siewert, Evan Smith, Jennifer Swanson, and Howard Wolfson.

Our most profound thanks are due to two women who labored with fantastic fortitude and grace under ferocious pressure to improve every page (possibly every line) of the book. Elise O'Shaughnessy, of *Vanity Fair,* who performed miracles with her magic scalpel on *Game Change,* found herself pressed back into service in the late stages of the sequel; we are now doubly in arrears to EOS for her unerring way with words. Karen Avrich ran the entire three-year reporting and editing obstacle course right alongside us. Her grasp of the players, eye for detail, cheerful round-the-clock labor, and elegant advice (macro and micro) improved the book mightily. As Joe Biden might say, *Double Down* would have been *literally* impossible without Karen.

From Mark Halperin:

My editors at *Time,* Rick Stengel, Michael Duffy, and Nancy Gibbs, allowed me to cover the 2012 election alongside the best political team in the business, and then to vanish into an air-conditioned abyss to pound out this book. Along with John Huey, they've been exquisite mentors and role models, who still consider journalism a public trust. Holding my hand (and yanking me back on my feet when necessary) was *Time*'s unparalleled public relations squad, including Daniel Kile and Vidhya Murugesan, as well as all my talented colleagues at *Time* and Time.com.

For counsel, wise, ready, and true: Alan Berger, Jeff Jacobs, and Michael Kives at Creative Artists Agency—good warriors, good sports, good pals all.

For support and friendship through the years: Ina Avrich, Bob Barnett, Katie Couric, Ilana Marcus Drimmer, Kyle Froman, Gil Fuchsberg, Nancy Gabriner, Charlie Gibson, Debbie Halperin, Rob Hanning, Bianca Harris, Dan Harris, Andrew Kirtzman, Ben Kushner, Dee Dee Myers, Zenia Mucha, Thomas Nash, Bill Nichols, Su-Lin Nichols, Ann O'Hanlon, Todd Purdum, Kathleen Smith Vane, Amy Welsh, and Iva Zoric. Thank you for keeping me entertained and enlightened, healthy and happy. To my family, all of whom like a good laugh and take me exactly as seriously as I deserve:

Daniel Halperin, David Halperin, Gary Halperin, Hannah Halperin, Madelyn Halperin, Marcia Halperin, Megan Halperin, Morton Halperin, Sandy Harrell, Carolyn Hartmann, Laura Hartmann, Peter Hartmann, RoseAnne McCabe, Diane Orentlicher, Joel Weinstein, Ina Young, and Joe Young.

As noted above, Karen Avrich lived and worked on *Double Down* every step of the way, juggling turn-of-the-century anarchists and present-day pols without ever missing a beat or the joke. She is a dream-come-true collaborator for the same reasons she is an incredible person: dazzlingly smart, sensitive, kind, and fun. She possesses a keen insight into human nature and a double dose of empathy. *Double Down* wouldn't exist without her, and neither would I.

From John Heilemann:

In twenty-five years in the magazine racket, I have been fortunate enough to work for my share of storied editors—but none better than Adam Moss at *New York*. Infinite thanks to him for providing me a home where the stuff that matters is the stuff that *should* matter; for giving me a gilded platform on the choicest real estate in the business; and for surrounding me with an amazing set of colleagues. Of special note: John Homans, whose yen for politics, editorial sagacity, and mild degeneracy make him an ideal co-conspirator and true friend.

In addition to the phalanx of representatives already thanked above, a hearty huzzah for my agents at WME: Ari Emanuel, Henry Reisch, and Marc Korman, all scary good at what they do and sometimes just plain scary (exhilaratingly so).

I am forever humbled by the love and support of my transoceanic posse: Kurt Andersen and Anne Kreamer; John and Michelle Battelle; Lisa Clements; David Dreyer; Michael Elliott, Emma Oxford, and their daughters, Roxana and Gina; Stephanie Flanders; Katrina Heron; Michael Hirschorn; Kerry Luft; Kenny Miller, Rachel Leventhal, and my goddaughter, Zoe Miller-Leventhal; John and Sara Mitchell; Oliver Morton; Neil, Dylan, and Miles Parker and Kay Moffett; Eric Press; Jeff Pollack; Robert Reich; Michael Schlein and Jordan Tamagni; Will Wade-Gery and Emily Botein; Harry Werksman; and Fred and Joanne Wilson. They all rock.

Finally, I am grateful every day and beyond words for the memory of my mother, which lifts me up (and slaps me around) when I get low or cranky; for the example of my father, who never fails to remind me of the enduring values of high honor, low humor, and good beer; and for the constancy and radiance of my wife, Diana Rhoten, without whom I would be worse than lost—unrecoverable. I promised D it would be easier this time. She saw through that lie in a nanosecond and saw me through to the finish line, providing inspiration, reassurance, and the occasional ass-kicking when I needed one. What's bigger and more bountiful than a Botswana-size bouquet? I dunno, but it's coming your way, babe.

INDEX